W9-ALX-598

AN INTRODUCTION TO THEORIES OF PERSONALITY

AN INTRODUCTION TO THEORIES OF PERSONALITY

B. R. HERGENHAHN
Hamline University

PRENTICE-HALL, INC., ENGLEWOOD CLIFFS, NJ 07632

Library of Congress Cataloging in Publication Data

Hergenhahn, B. R. (date).
An introduction to theories of personality.

Bibliography: p.
Includes index.
1. Personality. I. Title.
BF698.H45 155.2 79-20232
ISBN 0-13-498766-7

10 9 8 7 6 5 4 3 2 1

Editorial supervision and interior design by Marina Harrison
Cover design by Miriam Recio
Manufacturing buyer: Ed Leone

PRENTICE-HALL INTERNATIONAL, INC., *London*
PRENTICE-HALL OF AUSTRALIA PTY. LIMITED, *Sydney*
PRENTICE-HALL OF CANADA, LTD., *Toronto*
PRENTICE-HALL OF INDIA PRIVATE LIMITED, *New Delhi*
PRENTICE-HALL OF JAPAN, INC., *Tokyo*
PRENTICE-HALL OF SOUTHEAST ASIA PTE. LTD., *Singapore*
WHITEHALL BOOKS LIMITED, *Wellington, New Zealand*

Grateful acknowledgment is made to the following sources for permission to reprint:

"Approaching the Unconscious" by Carl G. Jung in *Man and His Symbols* by Carl G. Jung et al., copyright 1964 Aldus Books, London. Reprinted by permission.

The Individual Psychology of Alfred, by R. R. Ansbacher, © 1956 by Basic Books, Inc., New York. Reprinted by permission.

"Client-Centered Therapy," by C. R. Rogers, in the *American Handbook of Psychiatry,* Vol. 3, 1st edition, edited by Silvano Arieti, © 1966 by Basic Books, Inc., Publishers, New York. Reprinted by permission.

A Self-Directing Introduction to Psychological Experimentation (2nd Ed.), by B. R. Hergenhahn. Copyright © 1970, 1974 by Wadsworth, Inc. Published by Brooks/Cole Publishing Company, Monterey, California. Reprinted by permission.

(continued on p. 373)

Dedicated with love to my children:

**Laura Ann, Linda Marie, Karon Lee,
Ross James, Keith Fitzgerald, Maxine Athena and Glenn Apollo**

And to my mother, Maxine.

contents

PART THREE SOCIO-CULTURAL PARADIGM

PART FOUR TRAIT PARADIGM

preface

It is my contention that it is in an Introduction to Theories of Personality course that the student experiences the full richness of psychology. It is in such a course that the student experiences everything from psychology's most rigorous scientists to its most mystical nonscientific thinkers. It is in such a course that the student reviews answers to questions like "What accounts for individual differences among people?" and "Why do people act as they do?" It is in such a course that major philosophical questions are confronted like "How are the mind and the body related?", "How much of what we call personality is inherited and how much results from experience?" and "How much of human behavior is determined and how much of it is a function of free will?" It is in such a course that the major theories of human motivation are reviewed and the major schools, paradigms or "isms" within psychology are sampled, e.g., psychoanalysis, behaviorism, humanism and existentialism. It is in such a course that the student is exposed to the history of psychology from Freud to the modern theorists like Rogers, Kelly and Maslow. It is also in such a course that students encounter information that helps them to make sense out of their own lives and their relationships to other people. What other psychology course covers as much territory? My answer is none and, therefore, it is my belief that if a student were to take only one psychology course beyond the introductory course, it should be an Introduction to Theories of Personality course.

Although this text covers all of the topics mentioned above, its main purpose is to summarize the major ways of viewing personality. The text is built around the belief that it is misleading to search for *the* correct theory of personality. Rather, it is assumed that the best understanding of personality comes from looking at it from a variety of viewpoints. Thus, theories representing the psychoanalytic, socio-cultural, trait, learning and existential-humanistic paradigms are offered as different, yet equally valid, ways of approaching the study of personality.

The text is written so as to be compatible with an individualized course format, often called a personalized system of instruction or PSI. Using this approach, the student is usually allowed to go through the material, chapter by chapter, at his or her own pace. Since each chapter is self-contained, the chapters need not be studied in any particular order. Also, certain chapters can be easily omitted if the instructor chooses to do so.

Unlike any existing personality text, each chapter in the present text is concluded with a set of discussion questions and its own glossary. When students can answer the discussion questions and know each term and/or concept in the glossary, they can be reasonably confident that they are ready to be tested on the contents of that chapter. In this sense, the questions and the glossary can be looked upon as a statement of objectives for the chapter in which they are found.

B. R. Hergenhahn
Hamline University

acknowledgments

As anyone who has attempted to do so realizes, writing a book is a complicated, time-consuming endeavor which requires the assistance of a large number of individuals. I would like to spend a moment here to thank those who were especially helpful to me in preparing this book.

First I would like to thank Neale E. Sweet and John Isley of Prentice-Hall; Neale for having enough faith in this book to offer a contract to write it, and John for continuing to support the project after Neale moved on to greener pastures. Next, I would like to thank the following individuals who reviewed either all or part of the manuscript in various stages of its evolution: Stuart Fischoff, Alan G. Glaros, Sanford Golin, Bernard Gorman, Jerald Greenberg, Robert Hogan, Rosina C. Lao, Norman Maison, Elaine Nocks, Robert F. Massey, Vergie Lee Behrens, John B. Morganti, and John B. P. Shaffer. Reviewers have a difficult job in that they must offer constructive criticism without destroying the author's ego completely. All of the above reviewers did their job well, although at a few points my ego was definitely threatened. Elaine Nocks's reviews were especially appreciated since they were affirmative and yet extremely pleasant; even authors need periodic rewards.

Several Hamline psychology students were also very helpful. Ann Mellgren helped in countless ways such as by tracking down allusive references and xeroxing various parts of the manuscript. Cathy Fyfe read the early drafts of the manuscript and made several recommendations which improved grammar and spelling and made the manuscript more parsimonious. Jan Holtz wrote the first draft of hundreds of test items which were then student tested and now appear in the instructor's manual.

Several people also helped with the

arduous task of proof-reading; they were Carol Lindman, Dana Lindman, Wendy Little and Laura Peterson.

Madelon Cassavant typed the entire manuscript three times (thanks to the input of reviewers). One would need to see the scratchings that were handed to her to fully realize how enormous Madelon's task was. If the reader finds the final product readable and understandable it is to a large extent due to Madelon's translation of what was handed to her into English.

Marina Harrison, who has the title of production editor, coordinated all of the activities that occur when a manuscript enters production. Marina was efficient, effective, pleasant and understanding during this critical stage and I owe her a great debt.

Lastly, I would like to thank the psychology staff at Hamline University for covering for me as my time and energy were being diverted from my other responsibilities as I was writing this book. Jerry Greiner, Matt Olson, Charles LaBounty, and Kim Guenther were completely understanding and supportive during this time. I hope I can do the same for them some day.

B. R. Hergenhahn
Hamline University

PART ONE

INTRODUCTION

chapter 1

what is personality?

What is Personality? Perhaps this is one of the most complex questions in all of psychology and yet, there are many answers to it. Answers to the question "What is personality?" range all the way from the popular notion that personality is that which allows a person to be socially effective, to highly technical definitions using mathematical formulations.

The term personality comes from the Latin word *Persona* which means mask. Those defining personality as a mask look upon personality as one's public self. It is that aspect of ourselves that we select to display to the world. This kind of definition implies that there is something about the person that for some reason remains concealed.

Another class of definitions treats personality as a complex set of responses. According to this viewpoint *you are what you do*. Definitions in this category emphasize overt (observable) behavior and de-emphasize hidden components of the personality. Those accepting this position say that if you want to determine a person's personality characteristics, simply observe how the person behaves in various situations.

Still others look upon personality as an internal mechanism that controls behavior. It is the nature of this internal mechanism that determines a person's personality. "Self theories," and "trait theories" fall into this category. For example, a person is said to possess certain traits, and these traits, in turn, determine how a person will behave in any given situation. It should be obvious that, according to this viewpoint, if one wants to change behavior, one must somehow change the personality traits or the self that a person possesses. Since personality traits and the self are generally considered as cognitive in nature (that is, as part of the mind), those accepting a definition of personality emphasizing them are confronted with *the mind-body problem.* Stated simply, the mind-body problem is determining how something mental can influence something physical. This is an ancient philosophical question and one with which all psychological theories with cognitive or mental components must struggle.

Personality as Consistent Behavior Most, if not all, personality theorists would agree that a person's personality can be *described* in terms of consistent behavior patterns. The tendency we all have to respond consistently in various situations is what gives us our individual identity. It is these consistent behavior patterns that make it possible for our future behavior to be predicted with a certain degree of accuracy. When someone we think we know behaves in a manner inconsistent with his past behavior, we are surprised and say, "That is not like him." When people no longer respond to a situation as they did in the past, we say their personality has changed.

WHAT ARE THE ORIGINS OF CONSISTENT BEHAVIOR PATTERNS?

Although most personality theorists would accept our description of personality as consistent behavior patterns, they would part company when it came time to *explain,* or account for, the origins of this consistent behavior. In this section, we will briefly review several explanations of consistent behavior. We will cover each of these explanations more extensively when they occur later in the text.

Genetics Probably what is the most common "lay" explanation of personality is based on genetics. If asked, people on the street would tend to express the belief that personality characteristics are present for the same reasons that such things as eye color, hair color, or physique are present. To ask why a person is shy is basically the same as asking why she is tall. Both characteristics, according to this point of view, are genetically determined. Common statements such as "He has an Irish temper," "She takes after her father," or "He has his uncle's criminal tendencies," all imply a genetic explanation of personality, since they all have an "It's in the blood" tone to them.

The reader should not be left with the impression that only nonprofessionals look upon personality characteristics as being inherited. A number of prominent personality theorists accept inheritance as being at least partially responsible for consistent behavior. In fact, almost all theories of personality are built on something that is inherited, whether it be physiological needs (for example, Freud, Skinner, Dollard and Miller, Maslow), the tendency toward self-actualization (Jung, Rogers, Maslow), or social interest (Adler). Thus, the question is not whether or not genes influence personality, but rather, to what degree they influence personality and in what manner.

The question of how much personality is influenced by genetics harks back to an ancient philosophical theme that has run through psychology from its very inception. The *nativism-empiricism controversy* can be seen in every major category within the field of psychology, and personality theory is certainly no exception. In general, the nativist claims that an important attribute, such as intelligence, is genetically determined. The nativist would say, for example, that the maximum IQ that an individual can possess is determined at conception, and life's circumstances, at best, can help the individual to realize this genetically determined intellectual potential. The empiricist, on the other hand, believes that an individual's major attributes are created by experience. Intelligence, to the empiricist, is determined by a person's experiences rather than by genetic endowment. To the empiricist, the upper limit of a person's intelligence is found in the environment, not in the genes.

The nativism-empiricism controversy (also called the nature-nurture controversy) manifests itself in many ways in personality theory, and, therefore, we will confront it a number of times in this text.

Sociocultural Determinants According to those stressing cultural determinants, personality is a combination of the many roles we play. If you were asked to start a blank sheet of paper with the words "I am" and then to list all the things you are, you would have a rather extensive list. For example, you may be female, twenty years old, a college student, a Methodist, from the Midwest, 5 ft. 4 in., a member of various organizations, a Democrat, attractive, a Virgo, a psychology major, and so on.

Each entry on your list has a prescribed role associated with it, and for each role, society has defined what is acceptable behavior. In other words, each role has a range of behavior associated with it which is culturally acceptable, and if you deviate from that range, you will confront social pressure of some kind.

Other cultural determinants of personality would include the socioeconomic level of one's family, one's family size, birth order, race, religion, the region of the country in which one was raised, the educational level attained by one's parents, and the like.

According to this point of view, culture strongly influences how people in certain categories will behave. One simply does not have the same experiences in a rich home as one would have in a poor home. These fortuitous circumstances into which a person is born certainly have a major impact on personality. Again, this is something that each personality theorist accepts; it is just a matter of how much they emphasize it.

Also under the category of sociocultural determinants of personality are a person's interpersonal relationships. For example, Adler, Horney, and Erikson all stress the importance of children's early relationships with their parents and other relevant individuals to formulating future adult personality characteristics.

Learning Those accepting a genetic explanation of personality represent the nativism side of the nativism-empiricism controversy. Those emphasizing the learning process in their explanations of personality represent the empiricism side. One example of this point of view is the contention that we are what we have been rewarded for being, and therefore, if our history of reward had been different, our personality would have been different. The difference between a successful person and an unsuccessful one, according to the learning theorist, is to be found in patterns of reward, not in the genes.

In any given home, certain behaviors are rewarded, and others are ignored. Those behaviors that are rewarded tend to persist (that is, they become consistent); those behaviors that are ignored do not persist. Language development provides a model of how all consistent behavior patterns are shaped, according to the learning theorists. Since almost all parents want their children to learn to talk, when a child emits a sound that resembles the sound of an actual word, the parents reward the child. For example, if the child, while standing near a sink says, "Waa, Waa," the parents reward the child with attention, bodily contact, water, or, perhaps, all three. Approximations to other words also are rewarded, and gradually, appropriate language behavior develops. According to the learning theorists, all other personality characteristics have a similar origin.

A powerful implication of this theoretical position is that one can control personality development by controlling the circumstances under which rewards are dispensed or withheld. Theoretically, it is possible to create any kind of personality by systematically manipulating reward. Obviously, those emphasizing the genetic basis of personality would deny that personality is as pliable as the learning theorist suggests that it is. The theories of Skinner (chapter 9) and Dollard and Miller (chapter 10) emphasize the learning process.

Existential-Humanistic Considerations There is a growing number of personality theorists who either minimize the importance of knowing the origins of personality or who ignore origins of personality completely. These *existential-humanistic* theories emphasize "What does it mean to be you?" rather than "Why are you the way you are?" Such theories also explore the general implications of human existence. For example, they ask, "What does it mean to be aware that you will ultimately die?" and "How do the human needs for predictability and security relate to the human needs for adventure and freedom?" The theories of Kelly (chapter 11), Rogers (chapter 12), and Maslow (chapter 13) fall into this category.

Unconscious Mechanisms In many important respects, theories which emphasize unconscious mechanisms are the opposite of existential-humanistic theories. The primary concern of these so-called "depth" theories is to discover the underlying causes of behavior. According to this point of view, because the ultimate causes of behavior are unconscious and have their origins in childhood, the search for them is extremely complicated. Complex tools are needed in the search, tools such as dream and symbol analysis, free association, hypnosis, and the analysis of lapses of memory. According to this point of view, because that which characterizes the unconscious mind can manifest itself in consciousness in any number of ways, one cannot really understand very much about a person by studying that of which he is aware. In order to understand personality, one must somehow get beneath the arbitrary manifestations of the unconscious mind to the unconscious mind itself. Obviously, the last thing a personality theorist holding this position would do is to ask a person why he or she acts in a particular way, since the real causes of the behavior are not known to that person. The theories of Freud (chapter 2) and Jung (chapter 3) clearly fall into this category.

Because there are elements of these explanations in almost every theory of personality, perhaps it is safe to say that personality is a function of all of them, and which explanation is emphasized will depend on which specific theory of personality is being utilized. Assuming that, the situation can be summarized as follows:

Genetics Learning Culture-society Self-awareness Traits Unconscious mechanisms	} Personality

ISSUES CONFRONTING THE PERSONALITY THEORIST

Personality theorists are in the unique position in psychology of treating the entire person. Most other psychologists are concerned with only one aspect of humans and study it in depth. Thus, psychologists study such different things as child development, old age, perception, intelligence, learning, motivation, or creativity. It is only the personality theorist who tries to paint a complete picture of the human being. The personality theorist attempts to isolate the many influences on a person and then to explain how these influences combine to create a unique individual.

The task is monumental and is obviously related to developments in all other aspects of psychology. In a sense, the personality theorists, all in their own ways, attempt to synthesize the best possible information from diverse portions of psychology into a coherent, holistic configuration. As personality theorists have attempted this synthesis through the years, they have tended to address a number of questions related to human nature. These are questions for which there are extremely different answers, but no matter what the answer, each personality theory says something directly or indirectly about each of the following issues.

Purpose To what extent is human behavior pulled by the future rather than pushed by the past? Purposive behavior, also called *teleological behavior,* is said to be goal-directed or future-oriented. Is at least part of human behavior determined by future events or by our anticipation of them?

Hedonism To what extent can human behavior be explained in terms of hedonism, or the tendency to seek pleasure and avoid pain? A personality theory that emphasizes hedonism sees human behavior as governed by more or less the same principles that govern the behavior of nonhuman organisms.

How Important Are Unconscious Mechanisms? Of course, the depth theories, such as those of Freud and Jung, treat the unconscious mind as being very important. Theories that emphasize unconscious mechanisms confront questions such as: What is the relationship between the conscious mind and the unconscious mind? How can the unconscious be investigated? Can individuals ever become aware of their own motives and if so, how?

How Important Are Early Experiences? The main question here is how childhood experiences are related to adult personality characteristics. Related questions are: Are there critical, irreversible stages of development? Can the effects of early experiences be completely undone? Freud, for example, said that personality was essentially developed by the end of the fifth year of life. Jung, on the other hand, said that important personality development could not occur until one was about forty years of age.

To What Extent Is Human Behavior Determined? If all the influences acting upon an individual at any given time were known, would it be possible to predict that person's behavior with complete accuracy? If your answer is yes, you are a determinist. If your answer is no, you hold out for at least a little free will. Notice that this question assumes that we could know all the factors influencing a person's behavior, and that, of course, is impossible. For this reason, even strict determinists realize their predictions about behavior must be probabilistic.

What Can Be Learned by Asking People about Themselves? Examining oneself is called *introspection,* so this question concerns the extent to which introspective reports can be trusted. Answers to this question range all the way from the existentialists who claim introspection is the most valuable tool available for studying personality, to the learning theorists who claim it is not only invalid but unnecessary.

Uniqueness versus Lawfulness It is true that each individual is unique, since no cluster of genes or environmental experiences will be the same for two individuals. It also is true that all human beings have a great deal in common. The fact that we share sensory apparatus and a culture with other humans means that we respond as others do to many situations. To a large extent, what we find aesthetically pleasing, what we laugh at, and what causes us to be sad is culturally determined. Also, it has been found that certain behavioral principles apply to all humans. Thus, it is possible to emphasize either the fact that each human being is unique, or the fact that human behavior is governed by general laws. The intense study of the individual is called *idiographic* research, and the study of groups of individuals is called *nomothetic* research. Theorists like Allport (chapter 7) and Skinner (chapter 9) use the idiographic approach, because they emphasize the uniqueness of each individual. Theorists like Cattell (chapter 8) emphasize the nomothetic approach, because they stress traits that many individuals have in common.

HOW DO WE FIND THE ANSWERS?

Epistemology Epistemology is the study of knowledge. It tries to answer such questions as "What does it mean to know?" and "What are the limits of knowledge?" Because science, at least in part, is a method of gaining knowledge, it can be considered an epistemological pursuit.

Science combines two ancient philosophical positions on the origins of knowledge. One of these positions, called *rationalism*, contends that one gains knowledge by exercising the mind; in other words, by thinking, reasoning, and using logic. According to the rationalist, information must be sorted out by the mind before reasonable conclusions can be drawn. The other philosophical position, called *empiricism,* contends that sensory experience is the basis of all knowledge. In its extreme form, *empiricism* states that we know only what we experience. On the one hand, we have the rationalist emphasizing mental operations, and on the other hand, we have the empiricist equating knowledge with experience. It was science that combined the two positions, thereby creating an extremely effective epistemological tool.

Scientific Theory The place where rationalism and empiricism meet in the realm of science is within scientific theory. This marriage of philosophical schools is seen clearly in the following quotation by S. S. Stevens: "Science seeks to generate confirmable propositions by fitting a formal system of symbols (language, mathematics, logic) to empirical observations." (1951, p. 22)

First, there is something that cannot be studied directly, such as gravity, learning, or personality. Then, observations are made which are believed to be related to the phenomenon in question. Since these observations are direct, they are called empirical observations. Next, one attempts to make sense out of these observations; to think about them, to group them, and to synthesize them. This attempt at making observations more constructive by thinking about them in a variety of ways is clearly a rational endeavor.

Thus, in science, observations are made (empiricism) and then they are organized in some meaningful way (rationalism). Next, the scientist has to check to see if the groupings are, in fact, meaningful. If they are, they should indicate where to look for additional information. In other words, if the concepts used to organize the original observations are to be truly useful, they must do two things: (1) synthesize observations and (2) generate new research. This process can be represented schematically as follows:

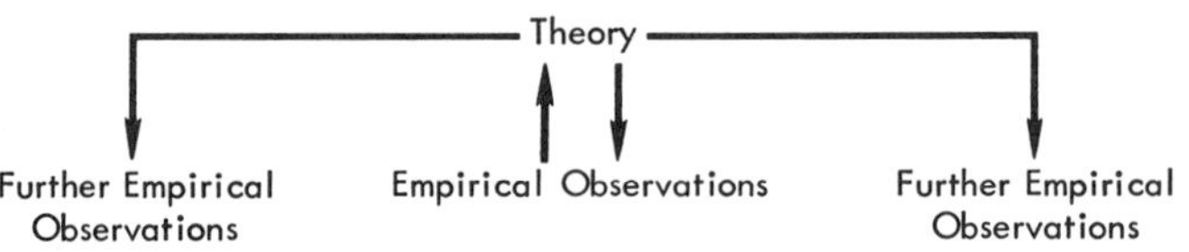

We see that a scientific theory comes into existence in order to explain a number of observations (its synthesizing function) and when it exists, it must be able to suggest other places where the researcher could look for additional information. A theory's ability to generate new research is called its *heuristic* function.

An example of the foregoing would be as follows: Let us say young Freud is talking with a friend when it is discovered that he (the friend) had missed an appointment at the dentist. This observation registers in Freud's sensitive mind. Later, Freud observes other lapses of memory and notes that they all have something in common. They all seem to involve painful or anxiety-related experiences. Freud speculates that all disturbing thoughts are repressed, that is, held in the unconscious mind, thereby preventing the discomfort that would be caused by their conscious recognition.

The theoretical notion of the repression of disturbing thoughts does two things. It helps to make sense out of previously disjointed observations, and it aids in discovering other truths For example, if disturbing thoughts are repressed, the unconscious mind will be a veritable storehouse of such thoughts, which could be released under the appropriate circumstances. In other words, if one could tap the contents of the unconscious mind with such devices as hypnotism, dream analysis, and/or free associations, one should find an abundance of repressed memories. Thus, we have the rudiments of one of history's great theoretical developments.

Science and Personality Theory Scientific theories differ in their rigor. In such sciences as physics or chemistry, theories are highly developed. The terms used in them are precisely defined, and there is a high correspondence among the words, signs, and symbols in the theory and the empirical events it purports to explain. The use of complex mathematics is quite common in such theories.

In psychology, there are theories in almost all evolutionary stages. In areas such as psychophysics and learning theory, psychology has theories that rival those in the physical sciences in terms of rigor. However, many theories in psychology are in their infant stages, containing terms that are not precisely defined, and the relationship between their terms and empirical events is not a tight one. Most personality theories are in the latter category. In fact, some theories of personality make no claim to being scientific in the sense that they can be tested under highly controlled conditions. Such theories claim that their verification comes either from everyday experience or from clinical practice.

To say that most personality theories lack rigor is not to apologize for them, nor is it to conclude that they are not useful. Clearly, this is not the case. Each personality theory can be seen as a way of viewing personality; therefore, each theory gives us a different viewpoint. In the final analysis, we probably learn more about something by viewing it from a variety of angles than we would by burrowing in deeply from one angle.

PARADIGMS AND PERSONALITY

Imagine yourself in a dark room in which you know there is a complex object that you cannot touch directly. As long as the room remains dark, you will know nothing about the object, except that it is there. Now suppose that a faint light illuminates part of the object, thus allowing you to make out part of it. You now know more about the object than you did before, but much remains unknown. Now another beam of light falls on the object, then another and another. You walk around the object, noting what has been illuminated by the various beams of light. Since the beams are coming from different directions, the more beams there are, the more you learn about the object. Some beams are narrow and bright, concentrating on a small area but exposing greater detail. Other beams are broader but dimmer, allowing you to learn about a larger area but in less detail. And, of course, some beams may overlap others. All the beams are useful. In fact, the more beams there are, and the greater the number of angles from which they come, the more information you will have, since each beam illuminates a part of the object of interest that previously was dark.

This analogy is a rough description of what occurs during scientific investigation, only with slight changes in terminology. For example, Thomas Kuhn (1973) indicates that most scientists accept a "point of view" concerning their subject matter as they carry out their research. This point of view guides their research activities and to a large extent determines what is studied and how it is studied. Kuhn calls a point of view shared by a large number of scientists a *paradigm*. For example, years ago most physicists accepted a Newtonian viewpoint in doing their work, but now most follow an Einsteinian point of view. We can say that the dominant paradigm in physics shifted from Newton's theory to Einstein's theory.

In psychology, there has never been one paradigm that permeated all psychological research. Rather, several paradigms have always existed simultaneously. In addition, the term paradigm, as it applies to psychology, corresponds to groups of interrelated theories commonly called a "school of thought" or an "ism" instead of to a single theory, as in the case in physics. In either case, a paradigm can be considered a way of looking at and investigating a certain subject. Therefore, different scientists exploring the same subject matter will go about their work differently, depending upon which paradigm is guiding their research activities. For example, in the realm of learning theory, the researcher following a behavioristic paradigm approaches the study of the learning process much differently than the researcher following a cognitive paradigm, and yet, both researchers are studying the same thing, the learning process.

The most important point to be made here regarding paradigms is that it is not necessary to consider one correct and the others incorrect; they all simply generate different research methodologies. This brings us back to our beam of light analogy. Paradigms can be thought of as beams of light; some paradigms are highly developed and concentrate on a small area, providing great detail but within a limited domain, while other paradigms cover an extremely large domain but do so at the expense of detail. As with our beams of light, both kinds of paradigms are useful in that they furnish information that would otherwise remain obscure.

So how does all this affect personality theory? Personality is a complex topic, and there are many approaches to its study. In fact, these approaches are paradigms and everything that was said above applies to them. In the remainder of this text, we will sample five paradigms that guide research in the area of personality. These five paradigms are listed along with the theories that have been chosen to represent them.

Psychoanalytic Paradigm
Sigmund Freud
Carl Jung

Sociocultural Paradigm
Alfred Adler
Karen Horney
Erik Erikson

Trait Paradigm
Gordon Allport
Raymond B. Cattell

Learning Paradigm
B. F. Skinner
John Dollard and Neal Miller

Existential-Humanistic Paradigm
George Kelly
Carl Rogers
Abraham Maslow

Notice that each paradigm is named for its central theme; that is, the psychoanalytic paradigm focuses on the analysis of the psyche; the sociocultural paradigm focuses on the study of the societal-cultural factors influencing personality; the existential-humanistic paradigm focuses on the problems of human existence; and the learning paradigm focuses on the study of the learning process as it relates to personality development.

Again, the reader need not bother to attempt to find the paradigm which is most correct. It is better to look upon all the paradigms as providing useful information about personality; it is just that the information generated by one paradigm is *different* from that generated by others. To attempt to build a house with only one tool such as a hammer, or a saw, or a screw driver, would be ineffective. Likewise, attempting to understand personality using only one theoretical orientation would leave huge gaps in one's understanding. This text will provide a variety of theories which collectively will provide a much greater understanding of personality than any one of them taken alone could do.

Discussion Questions

1. Describe the mind-body problem.
2. What is the nativism-empiricism controversy? Choose a personality attribute other than intelligence, and explain it from the point of view of both a nativist and an empiricist.
3. Explain what is meant by the statement: "It is theoretically possible to create any kind of personality by systematically manipulating reward."
4. Compare the existential view of personality with the "depth" point of view.
5. Once personality has been described, its origins need to be explained. List as many general approaches to explaining the origins of personality as you can.
6. List and describe as many issues confronting the personality theorist as you can. For example, to what extent is behavior "pulled" by the future as opposed to being "pushed" by the past?
7. What does the personality theorist do that no other psychologist attempts to do?
8. Explain what is meant by the statement: "Science combines rationalism and empiricism."
9. What are the two major functions of a good scientific theory?
10. Discuss Kuhn's concept of paradigm as it applies to the study of personality.
11. Does it make sense to search for *the* correct theory of personality? Explain your position on the matter.

Glossary

Determinism. The belief that all behavior is caused and is therefore not free. According to the determinist, the accuracy with which behavior can be predicted is directly proportional to the knowledge of the causes of that behavior. That is, if all the causes were known (an impossible situation), behavior could be predicted with complete accuracy.

Empiricism. The contention that an attribute is determined by experience rather than by genetics. Within epistemology, it is the belief that knowledge is derived from sensory experience.

Epistemology. The study of the nature of knowledge.

Hedonism. The contention that the major motive in life is to seek pleasure and avoid pain.

Heuristic Function of a Theory. A theory's ability to generate new information.

Idiographic Research. The intense study of a single individual.

Introspection. Self-examination. The directing of one's thoughts inward to discover truths about one's self.

Mind-Body Problem. The problem of specifying how something mental (cognitive) can influence something physical, such as behavior. This question is as old as psychology itself.

Nativism. The contention that an attribute is determined by genetics rather than by experience. opposite of empiricism

Nativism-Empiricism Controversy. (also called the Nature-Nurture Controversy). The argument over the extent to which an attribute, such as intelligence, is influenced by inheritance as opposed to experience.

Nomothetic Research. The study of groups of individuals in order to determine what they have in common.

Paradigm. A term used by Kuhn to describe a theoretical point of view shared by a number of researchers.

Persona. A Latin word meaning mask.

Rationalism. The belief that knowledge can be gained only by exercising the mind; for example, by thinking, deducing, or inferring.

Scientific Theory. Has two major functions: (1) It synthesizes a large number of observations, and (2) it generates new information. – heuristic function

Teleology. Purpose. Teleological behavior is behavior that is being motivated by the future rather than by the past. Teleological behavior is said to be goal-directed.

PART TWO

PSYCHOANALYTIC PARADIGM

chapter 2

sigmund freud

It has been said that humans have had three major blows to their self-esteem. The first came from Copernicus, who demonstrated that the earth was not the center of the universe as humans had so egotistically believed. In fact, Copernicus showed that the earth was not even the center of our solar system, a fact that was not easily digested.

The second blow came from the work of Charles Darwin, who demonstrated that humans were not the product of "special creation" but were descended from and continuous with the so-called "lower animals."

As the dust caused by Darwin's thinking was settling, our self-esteem was salvaged by the belief that humans were *rational* animals. Although we descended from lower animals, somewhere in the process of evolution we became qualitatively different from them by becoming dependent on our intellect. Animals were driven by instinct; only human behavior was rationally determined.

It was Freud who dealt the third blow to human self-esteem by demonstrating that human behavior is primarily instinctive and motivated mainly by unconscious mechanisms. In other words, according to Freud, humans are anything but rational animals. Whether one agrees with Freud's theory or not, it is clear that Freudian concepts have completely revised the way we look at human nature. In fact, it is probably accurate to say that no single individual has so revolutionalized the way we view ourselves as Freud did.

Sigmund Freud was born on May 6, 1856 in Friberg, Austria (now Pribor, Czechoslovakia). When Freud was four years old, he and his family moved to Vienna, where he continued to live for nearly eighty years. His father (Jakob) was a not-too-successful wool merchant and a strict authoritarian as a father. At the time of Freud's birth, his father was forty years old and his mother, who was his father's second wife, was a youthful twenty. Freud was the first of six children born to his mother, Amalie Nathanson Freud. Jakob had two sons by his first wife and was a grandfather when Sigmund was born. It is interesting to note that Jakob Freud's second son by his first marriage was about the same age as Sigmund's mother. It is also interesting to note that Sigmund and his mother had a strong, powerful relationship, the effects of which Freud felt throughout his life.

Freud was always an outstanding student and graduated at the head of his high school class. At home, his brothers and sisters were not allowed to study musical instruments because doing so may have disturbed Sigmund's studies. He entered medical school at the University of Vienna when he was seventeen, but it took him almost eight years to finish a four-year medical course, mainly because he pursued many interests outside of medicine. Freud went to medical school because medicine was one of the few careers open to a Jew in Austria at that time. He was never really interested in becoming a medical doctor but saw the study of medicine as a way of engaging in scientific research.

Cocaine was associated with a major incident in Freud's life. Convinced that cocaine was mainly a tranquilizer, he took it himself and recommended it to his friends, including his fiancée, Martha Bernays. Cocaine addiction became increasingly widespread in Europe, and Freud eventually became the focal point of an international scandal. In spite of all this, Freud was one of the first to discover the analgesic properties of cocaine and just missed becoming the first physician to utilize it in

Sigmund Freud. Courtesy Austrian Information Service, New York.

Freud and his fellow students watching Jean Charcot's demonstration of hypnotism. Culver Pictures, Inc.

eye operations. This missed opportunity for fame was very disturbing to Freud.

Freud hoped to become a professor of anatomy and published a number of highly regarded papers on the topic. He soon discovered, however, that advancement within the academic ranks would be extremely slow for a Jew, and this realization, along with the fact that he needed money, prompted him to enter private practice as a clinical neurologist in 1881.

In 1886, he was finally able to marry Martha Bernays, to whom he had been engaged since 1882. During their five-year engagement, Freud wrote over four hundred letters to his fiancée. They remained married until Freud's death. There were six children, three daughters, and three sons. One daughter, Anna, became a famous child psychiatrist in London.

In about 1880, Freud began working with Josef Breuer (1842–1925), who gave Freud advice, friendship, and loaned him money. Breuer, who was a highly successful medical practitioner, had been having success with a new method of treating hysteria. Hysteria is a term used to describe a wide variety of symptoms such as paralysis, loss of sensation, and disturbances of sight and speech. Originally, it was assumed that hysteria was exclusively a female disorder (*hysteria* is the Greek word for uterus). Breuer found that when his patient, a twenty-one year old female, anonymously referred to as Fraulein Anna O., was encouraged to express her feelings and emotions, some of her symptoms would disappear either temporarily or permanently. The release of tension that came from this "talking cure" was called *catharsis* (not to be confused with cathexis, which we will discuss later in this chapter). Aristotle had originally used the term "catharsis" to describe the emotional release and feeling of purification that an audience experienced while viewing a tragic drama. Breuer's patient herself referred to his technique as the "talking cure" or "chimney sweeping."

Several important facts were learned from Breuer's treatment of Anna O. Clearly, the most important was that her condition improved somewhat when she openly expressed her feelings. This observation interested Breuer to the point at which he saw Anna O. several hours a day for more than a year. During this time, Anna O. began to transfer the feelings that she had toward her father to Breuer. This phenomenon, in which a patient responds to the analyst as if he or she were an important person in the patient's life, is called *transference*. Likewise, Breuer was becoming emotionally involved with Anna O. The phenomenon of an analyst forming an emotional attachment to a patient is called *countertransference*. Because of the time Breuer was spending with Anna O. and the deep feelings they were developing toward one another, Breuer's marriage began to suffer and, as a result, he decided to stop seeing his patient. Anna O. was so disturbed by this that she was thrust into hysterical (imaginary) childbirth. Things became so bad that Breuer and his wife finally escaped by taking a second honeymoon in Venice, where, incidentally, his wife became pregnant.

Breuer's treatment of Anna O. must have been at least partially successful, since it was later revealed that Anna O. (whose real name was Bertha Pappenheim) became Germany's first social worker and also founded a periodical and several student-training institutions.

In 1885, Freud received a small grant that allowed him to study with the famous French psychiatrist Jean Charcot, who was using hypnosis in the treatment of hysteria. This visit was important to Freud for at least two reasons. First, Freud learned from Charcot that it was possible to treat hysteria as a psychological disorder rather than as an organic one. In his practice, Freud had been using electrotherapy. This consisted of applying a painful electric shock directly to the organ in which there was a difficulty, such as a paralyzed arm. Second, Freud heard Charcot, at a reception one evening, assert enthusiastically that one of his patient's problems had a sexual basis. Freud overheard Charcot say "But in this sort of case it's always a question of the genitals —always, always, always" (Freud 1914/1957, p. 14). Freud considered this to be an illuminating experience and thereafter was alerted to the possibility of sexual problems in his patients.

After spending less than six months studying with Charcot in Paris, he returned to Vienna and his association with Breuer. Freud tried hypnosis for a while but was not impressed with the results. Freud eventually gave up hypnosis, because he found that not all his patients could be hypnotized. One of his patients, Frau Emmy Von N., became furious with him over his constant interruptions while trying to hypnotize her. She expressed the desire simply to be allowed to speak her mind without being interrupted.

Next, Freud tried hand pressure instead of hypnosis. He would place his hand on his patients' foreheads and instruct them to begin talking when he released the pressure. Although this technique was successful, he eventually abandoned it and settled on *free association* which he called "the fundamental rule of psychoanalysis."

All of Freud's experiences with hypnosis and hand pressure and his recollection of an essay by Ludwig Borne, which had been given to him when he was fourteen, gradually evolved into the technique of free association. The following quotation from Borne's essay, entitled "The Art of Becoming an Original Writer in Three Days," clearly contains the seeds of what was later to become the technique of free association.

> Take a few sheets of paper and for three days on end write down, without fabrication or hypocrisy, everything that comes into your head. Write down what you think of yourself, of your wife, of the Turkish War, of Goethe, of Fonk's trial, of the Last Judgement, of your superiors—and when three days have passed you will be quite out of your senses with astonishment at the new and unheard-of thoughts you have had. (Freud 1920b/1955, p. 265)

Breuer and Freud worked together on several cases of hysteria and in 1895 published the book *Studies in Hysteria* which is usually considered the beginning of the psychoanalytic movement. Although their book is now regarded as having monumental significance, it then was met with negative reviews, and it took thirteen years to sell 626 copies. Breuer and Freud, who had been extremely close friends, soon parted company because of Freud's insistence that sexual conflicts were the cause of hysteria. This was also the primary reason why Freud was dismissed from the Vienna Medical Society in 1896.

Freud began his highly influential self-analysis in 1897. He began this self-analysis for both theoretical and personal reasons; for example, he had an unhealthy fear of railroad travel. The main vehicle in his self-analysis was the interpretation of his own dreams. This analysis finally resulted in what many consider Freud's greatest work, his book *The Interpretation of Dreams* published in 1900. As with his earlier book written with Breuer, this one also met with considerable criticism, and it took eight years before 600 copies were sold, for which Freud received the equivalent of $209. Eventually, however, the importance of the book was realized, and it was circulated throughout the world.

It was after the publication of *The Interpretation of Dreams* that the psychoanalytic movement began to gain momentum. International recognition finally came when Freud and a few of his close followers were invited by G. Stanley Hall to give a series of lectures in America at Clark University in 1909. Although Freud did not care much for America and never returned, he looked upon his visit to Clark University as highly significant to the development of the psychoanalytic movement.

In 1923, it was discovered that Freud had cancer of the mouth, which has been linked to his habit of smoking twenty cigars a day, a habit that he did not abandon even after his cancer was detected. From 1923 to his death in 1939, he underwent thirty-three operations. Although in constant pain because of his refusal to accept pain-reducing drugs, his mind remained alert, and he worked until the end of his life.

When the Nazis came to power in 1933, they publicly burned Freud's books in Berlin as a Nazi spokesman shouted, "Against the soul-destroying overestimation of the sex life—and on behalf of the nobility of the human soul—I offer to the flames the writings of one Sigmund Freud" (Shur 1972, p. 446). Freud resisted leaving Vienna even after it was invaded in 1938. Finally, after his daughter Anna had been arrested and her house repeatedly overrun by gangs of Nazis, he agreed to go to London. Four of his sisters were later killed by the Nazis in Austria. Freud died in London on September 23, 1939.

For more details of Freud's life, the reader is urged to read one of the most outstanding biographies ever written, *The Life and Work of Sigmund Freud* by Ernest Jones (1953, 1955, 1957).

THE INSTINCTS AND THEIR CHARACTERISTICS

For Freud, all aspects of the human personality are derived from biological instincts. This point cannot be stressed too much. No matter how lofty the thought or the accomplishment, it ultimately relates to the satisfaction of a physiological need. Freud's theory is a hedonistic one in that it assumes that humans, like other animals, continually seek pleasure and avoid pain. When all the bodily needs are satisfied, one experiences pleasure; when one or more needs are not satisfied, one experiences discomfort. The main motive for humans then is to obtain the steady-state that one experiences when all of one's biological needs are satisfied.

An instinct has four characteristics: (1) *a source*, which is a bodily deficiency of some kind; (2) *an aim*, which is to remove the bodily deficiency thereby reestablishing an internal balance; (3) *an object*, which is those experiences or objects that reduce or remove the bodily deficiency; and (4) *an impetus*, which is determined by the magnitude of the bodily deficiency. For example, a person experiencing the hunger instinct will need food (source), will want to eliminate the need for food (aim), seek and ingest food (object), and the intensity with which these activities occur will depend on how long the person has gone without food (impetus).

Life and Death Instincts All the instincts associated with the preservation of life are called the life instincts, and the psychic energy associated with them collectively is called the *libido.* In Freud's earlier writings, he equated libido with sexual energy, but in light of increased evidence to the contrary and because of severe criticism from even his closest colleagues, he expanded the notion to include the energy associated with all of the life instincts, including sex, hunger, and thirst. Freud's final position was that libidinal energy is expended to prolong life. Freud also referred to the life instincts as *eros.*

The death instincts, collectively named *thanatos,* stimulate a person to return to the inorganic state that preceded life. Death is the ultimate steady-state, since there is no longer the struggle to satisfy biological needs. Quoting Schopenhauer, Freud claimed that "the aim of all life is death" (1920a/1955, p. 38). The most important derivative of the death instinct, or the death wish as it is sometimes called, is aggression, which, according to Freud, is the need for self-destruction turned outward to objects other than the self. Cruelty, suicide, murder, as well as aggression, were thought by Freud to derive from the death instinct. Even though Freud never developed thanatos as fully as eros, it was nonetheless an important part of his theory.

DIVISIONS OF THE MIND

The mature adult mind has three divisions: an *id,* an *ego,* and a *superego.* At birth, however, the entire mind consists of only the id. The id consists of pure, unadulterated, instinctual energy and exists completely on the unconscious level. The id cannot tolerate the tension associated with a bodily need and therefore demands the immediate removal of that tension. In other words, the id demands immediate gratification of bodily needs and is said to be governed by the *pleasure principle.*

The id has two means of satisfying bodily needs, *reflex action* and *wish-fulfillment.* Reflex action is responding automatically to a source of irritation. For example, an infant may sneeze in response to an irritant in the nose or reflexively move a confined limb, thereby freeing it. In both cases, reflex action is effective in reducing tension. Coughing and blinking also would be examples of reflex action.

Wish-fulfillment is more complicated. In addition to the characteristics of instincts described earlier, *instincts can be considered cognitive representations of physiological needs.* It is within the id and via the concept of instinct that Freud comes to grips with the mind-body question. The mind-body question asks how physiological events and psychological events are related to each other. It is a question to which every theory with a cognitive component eventually must address itself.

Freud's answer to the mind-body question was as follows: A biological deficiency (a need) triggers in the id an attempt to reduce the tension associated with that need by imagining an object or event that will satisfy the need. For example, the need for food will automatically trigger in the id a food-related image which has the effect of temporarily reducing the tension associated with the need for food; this is called wish-fulfillment. At this point, Freud appears to become quite mystical. Since the id always was and always will be entirely unconscious, what images does it conjure up in response to the various needs? Certainly, it cannot conjure up a hamburger in response to the hunger drive, since it never experienced a hamburger or anything else that is directly related to the reduction of the hunger drive. The alternative seems to be that the id has available to it the inherited residuals of experience from preceding generations. Thus, it has available to it the images of things that consistently satisfied needs of humans through many past generations. It is the latter view that Freud seems to accept and in so doing comes very close to Jung's concept of the collective unconscious, which will be discussed in the next chapter. Hall describes it as follows:

> Freud speaks of the id as being the true psychic reality. By this he means the id is the primary subjective reality, the inner world that exists before the individual has had experience of the external world. Not only are the instincts and reflexes inborn, but the images that are produced by tension states may also be innate. This means that a hungry baby can have an image of food without having to learn to associate food with hunger. Freud believed that experiences that are repeated with great frequency and intensity in many individuals of successive generations become permanent deposits in the id. (1954, pp. 26–27)

In any case, wish-fulfillment can never really satisfy a bodily need except on a very temporary basis. Another component of the personality must develop in order to make real satisfaction possible, and that component is the ego. As we have seen, the id attempts to reduce needs through hallucinations (mental pictures of objects that could satisfy a need). This is called the *primary process*, but the primary process of the id is ineffective in ultimately alleviating the need. The id cannot distinguish between its images and external reality. In fact, for the id, its images are the only reality.

Eventually, the ego develops and attempts to match the images of the id with objects and events in the real world. This matching process was called *identification* by Freud. The ego is governed by the *reality principle* and operates in the service of the id. In other words, the ego comes into existence in order to bring the person into contact with experiences that will truly satisfy his or her needs. When the person is hungry, the ego finds food; when the person is sexually aroused, the ego finds appropriate sex objects; and when the person is thirsty, the ego finds liquid. The ego goes through the process of *reality testing* to find appropriate objects. Since the ego is aware of both the images of the id and external reality, it operates on both the conscious and unconscious level. The realistic efforts of the ego that bring about true biological satisfaction are called *secondary processes,* which are contrasted with the ineffective primary processes of the id. The relationship between the id and the ego is summarized in the following diagram:

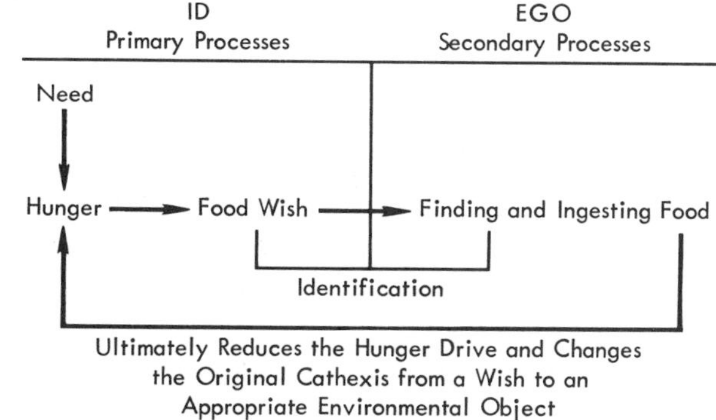

If the only two components of the personality were the id and the ego, we would have a hedonistic, animalistic person who, when in a need-state, would seek immediate gratification of needs (id) from appropriate environmental objects (ego). There is a third component of the personality, however, that makes things much more complicated. The third component of the personality is the superego. The superego is the moral arm of the personality. It develops from the internalized patterns of reward and punishment that the young child experiences. That is, depending on the values of the parents, certain things the child does or says are rewarded and thereby encouraged, and other things the child does or says will be punished and thereby discouraged. Those experiences that bring reward and punishment are gradually internalized, and the superego is said to be fully developed when self-control replaces environmental or parental control.

The fully developed superego has two subdivisions. The *conscience* is the internalized experiences for which the child had been punished. Engaging in these behaviors now, or even thinking about engaging in them, makes the child feel guilty or "naughty." The second subdivision of the superego is the *ego-ideal,* which is the internalized experiences for which the child had been rewarded. Engaging in these behaviors now, or even thinking about engaging in them, makes the child feel successful and proud.

The superego constantly strives for perfection and is, therefore, as unrealistic as the id. Any experience outside the realm of the internalized values of the child is not tolerated by the superego. So now, the job of the ego becomes more complicated. Not only must the ego find objects and events which satisfy the needs of the id, but it also must find objects and events that do not violate the values of the superego. If, for example, the need to urinate arises while one is on a city bus, the id would demand immediate gratification through urination. The ego would allow this to happen by causing, in the case of a boy, the pants to be unzipped, and so on. However, urinating on a city bus would in all likelihood violate an internalized value of the superego, and considerable guilt or anxiety would be experienced as the result of this behavior. The ego, aware of both the needs of the id and of the superego, would probably, in this case, cause the person to get off the bus at the next stop and enter a service station washroom in which urination would satisfy all the components of the personality. It is no wonder the ego is called the executive of the personality.

Cathexis and Anticathexis Cathexis refers to a relationship or a connection between a need and an object that will satisfy the need. The only cathexes that exist originally are those between the biological needs and the images conjured up by the id to satisfy those needs. As we have seen, these wishes are ineffective in satisfying needs, and eventually the ego must find appropriate environmental objects. In this way, the original cathexes between needs and wishes are *displaced* and become connections between appropriate environmental objects. Freud felt that the connections between needs and satisfiers could be displaced easily and were constantly changing as conditions changed.

Anticathexis refers to the inhibition of an impulse by either the ego or the superego. For example, if the need for sex arises in the id, it demands immediate gratification of that need. In most cases, the superego would expend energy to keep this need from being satisfied. The ego's anticathexis would be more of a delaying tactic until an activity that would appease both the id and superego could be found. Cathexis, anticathexis and displacement can be schematized as follows:

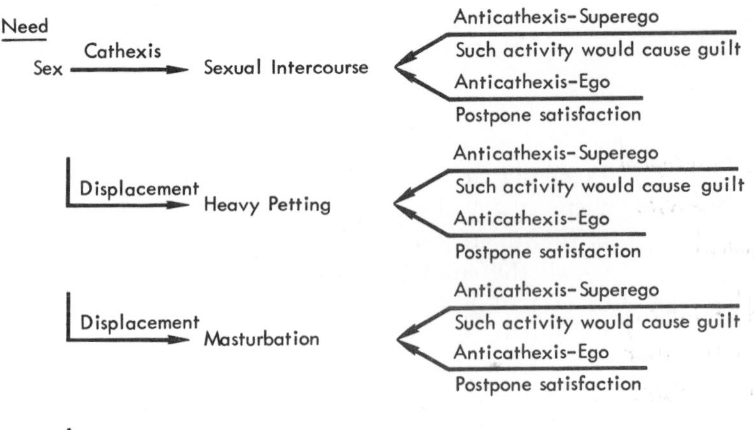

Notice that through the series of displacements, the source, aim, and impetus of the instinct remained the same, only the object changed.

Anxiety According to Freud, the most overwhelming experience of anxiety humans have is when we are separated from our mother at birth. Freud called this experience the birth trauma since we suddenly go from an environment of complete security and satisfaction to one in which the satisfaction of our needs is far less predictable. The feeling of separation that came from birth is, according to Freud, the basis of all subsequent feelings of anxiety.

The function of anxiety is to warn us that if we continue thinking or behaving in a certain way, we will be in danger. Since anxiety is not pleasant, we will do what is necessary to reduce it. That is, we will tend to terminate those thoughts or actions that cause anxiety. Freud distinguished three kinds of anxiety: *reality anxiety*, which is caused by real, objective sources of danger in the environment and is the easiest kind of anxiety to reduce, since doing so solves problems objectively, such as leaving a building that is on fire. *Neurotic anxiety* is the fear that the impulses of the id will overwhelm the ego and cause the person to do something for which he or she will be punished. Perhaps rape would be an example. Generally, this is the fear of becoming animal-like. *Moral anxiety* is fear that the person will do something contrary to the superego and thus experience guilt. For example, if one has learned that being successful was good, then being unsuccessful would cause moral anxiety. Thus, anxiety controls our behavior by causing us to avoid threatening experiences in the environment, to inhibit the impulses of the id, and to act in accordance with our internalized values.

Clearly one of the biggest jobs the ego has is to avoid or reduce anxiety. In addition to anticathexis, the ego has several other processes available to it for use in its battle against anxiety; these processes are referred to collectively as the ego-defense mechanisms.

EGO DEFENSE MECHANISMS

If normal, rational approaches of the ego to the reduction or removal of anxiety are ineffective, the ego may revert to irrational methods called ego defense mechanisms. All ego defense mechanisms have two things in common: (1) They are unconscious; that is, the person is always unaware that he or she is using them, and (2) they falsify or distort reality. Freud's daughter Anna (1936) was mainly responsible for elaborating the ego's mechanisms of defense, and we will consider several of them.

Repression This is the most basic defense mechanism because for any of the other defense mechanisms to occur, repression must occur first. Repression is the mechanism by which the ego prevents anxiety-provoking thoughts from being entertained on the conscious level. These thoughts can be either those innately part of the id, in which case their repression is referred to as *primal repression*, or they can be memories of painful experiences from one's lifetime, in which case their repression is referred to as *repression proper*. In either case, the ego keeps the potentially anxiety-producing thought in the unconscious, with an anticathexis whenever it threatens to reach consciousness.

For Freud, the mechanism of repression was of vital importance, since repressed thoughts do not stop having an influence on our personality; they simply are not readily available in consciousness. The whole purpose of procedures such as dream analysis, free association, hypnosis, and the analysis of such things as slips of the tongue or memory lapses (which we will discuss later) is to attempt to discover repressed thoughts so that their effects on one's personality can come to be understood.

Displacement As we have seen above, displacement is the substitution of one cathexis for another. For example, the ego may substitute an available object for one that is not available, or it may substitute a non-anxiety-provoking object or activity for one that does cause anxiety, as in the chart in which dancing was finally substituted for other sexual activities. With displacement, a person's true desire is repressed and is replaced by a safer desire.

In his book *Civilization and Its Discontents* (1930), Freud indicated that civilization itself depends upon the displacement of libidinal energy from one object to another. When a displacement results in something advantageous to civilization, it is called *sublimation*, such as when sexual impulses are displaced into such activities as painting, writing, building, or just plain hard work. "The sublimation of instinct," wrote Sigmund Freud, "is an especially conspicuous feature of cultural evolution; this it is that makes it possible for the higher mental operations, scientific, artistic, and ideological activities to play so important a part in civilized life" (1930/1961, p. 63).

All impulses can be displaced, even those associated with the death instincts. For example, the impulse toward self-destruction can be displaced to the destruction of others, and an aggressive impulse directed toward a threatening person like a boss or a parent can be displaced to less threatening objects such as other cars on the street while driving home, children, household pets, or, quite commonly, to athletic teams opposing the home town team. These are examples of *displaced aggression,* one of Freud's most popular concepts.

Identification Freud used the term identification in two ways. The one that we have already covered is the process by which the ego attempts to match objects and events in the environment to the subjective wishes of the id. The term identification is also used to describe the tendency to increase personal feelings of worth by taking on characteristics of someone viewed as successful. A statement like "our team won" would be an example. Other examples would include a young woman having her hair styled in a way similar to a respected national leader, or a young man acting suspiciously like Robert Redford after just seeing a movie in which Mr. Redford made love to a number of beautiful women.

The child also identifies with his or her parents (accepts their values), thereby eliminating the punishment that comes from having contrary values. This is how the superego develops.

Projection This is the mechanism by which something that is true of the person and would cause anxiety if it were recognized is repressed and is seen in someone else instead. For example, the statement "I want to go to bed with him" may be true, but because it causes anxiety, it is converted into "He wants to go to bed with me." Also, the statement "I failed the test because I'm stupid," although perhaps true, is converted into statements such as "Our textbook is terrible," "She's the worst teacher I've ever had," or "The test had a number of trick items."

In general, projection is repressing anxiety-provoking truths about oneself and seeing them in others instead.

Reaction Formation This is the mechanism by which objectionable thoughts are repressed by expressing their opposites. For example, the person who is most attracted to sexual materials may become the town censor, or the mother who really does not care much for her child may become overprotective. Freud felt the clue in determining the difference between a reaction formation and true feelings is the degree to which the feelings are emphasized. People displaying a reaction formation tend to be more intense and extravagant in their emotions, as when a boyfriend insists, "I love you, I love you, I love you more than anything in the world," or when someone says "You should meet my mother. She is absolutely wonderful beyond belief." In Shakespeare's *Hamlet,* "The lady doth protest too much," and in so doing reveals her guilt.

The following is a letter written to Masserman, a famous psychologist who was doing work on alcoholism in cats. The letter was written by an antivivisectionist who claimed to be terribly concerned with what Masserman was doing to his research animals. See if you can find evidence in the letter that its author was basically a violent person and his or her affiliation with the antivisectionists was, therefore, a reaction formation:

> I read [a magazine article . . . on your work on alcoholism]. . . . I am surprised that anyone who is as well educated as you must be to hold the position that you do would stoop to such a depth as to torture helpless little cats in the pursuit of a cure for alcoholics. . . . A drunkard does not want to be cured—a drunkard is just a weak minded idiot who belongs in the gutter and should be left there. Instead of torturing helpless little cats why not torture drunks or better still exert your would-be noble effort toward getting a bill passed to *exterminate* the drunks. They are

not any good to anyone or themselves and are just a drain on the public, having to pull them off the street, jail them, then they have to be fed while there and it's against the law to feed them arsenic so there they are. . . . If people are such weaklings the world is better off without them. . . .

. . . My greatest wish is that you have brought home to you a torture that will be a thousand fold greater than what you have, and are doing to the little animals. . . . If you are an example of what a noted psychiatrist should be I'm glad I am just an ordinary human being without letters after my name. I'd rather be myself with a clear conscience, *knowing that I have not hurt any living creature,* and can sleep without seeing frightened, terrified dying cats—because I know they must die after you have finished with them. No punishment is too great for you and I hope I live to read about your mangled body and long suffering before you finally die—and I'll laugh long and loud. (Masserman 1961, p. 35)

6 ***Rationalization*** Through this mechanism, the person rationally justifies behavior or thoughts that may otherwise be anxiety provoking. The ego excuses through logic (although faulty) outcomes that would be disturbing if they were not explained in some way. The "sour grapes" rationalization is quite common. Aesop in 500 B.C. told of a fox who saw clusters of grapes hanging from a trellised vine. It tried everything in his power to reach them but nothing worked. Finally, it turned away saying "The grapes were probably sour anyhow." Minimizing something to which one has aspired but failed to obtain is a common form of rationalization. Likewise, something that at first was not overly attractive may be glorified after it is obtained. This has been called a "sweet lemon" rationalization. Other examples of rationalization include:

I was late because my alarm didn't go off.

I smoked marijuana because everyone is doing it.

I'm glad I wasn't accepted into graduate school; I'm sick of school anyhow (sour grapes).

I guess it's just not my fate to be a scholar.

You can't win 'em all.

If you came from my background, you wouldn't be able to pass an English test either.

I read too much into each alternative on a multiple-choice test item; that's why I do so poorly.

With all the poverty and injustice in the world, how can anyone be expected to study for a test?

7 ***Regression*** With this mechanism, the person returns to an earlier stage of development when he or she experiences stress. For example, a child may revert back to bed wetting or thumb sucking when a new sibling is born. We will have more to say about regression in our discussion of the psychosexual stages of development, to which we turn next.

Freud believed that every child goes through a sequence of develo mental stages and that the child's experiences during these stages dete mine adult personality characteristics. In fact, Freud believed that fo all practical purposes, the adult personality is formed by the end o the fifth year of life.

Each stage has an *erogenous zone* associated with it, which is the greatest source of stimulation and pleasure during that particular stage of development.

In order to make a smooth transition from one psychosexual stage to the next, the child must be neither undergratified nor overgratified, both of which cause the child to be *fixated* at that stage. Fixation and regression go hand in hand since, when a person regresses, he or she tends to go back to the stage at which that person had been fixated.

Oral Stage The oral stage occurs during the first year of life and the erogenous zone during this stage is the mouth. During the early oral stage (less than eight months old) pleasure comes mainly from the mouth, lips, and tongue through the activities of sucking and swallowing. According to Freud, an adult who is fixated at the early oral stage will engage in an abundance of oral activities such as eating, drinking, smoking, and kissing. This person also will engage in activities that are symbolically equivalent to those oral activities such as collecting things, being a good listener (taking in knowledge), or being what is labeled as a gullible person, i.e., a person who "swallows" anything he or she hears. Such a person is called an *oral-incorporative character*.

In the later oral stage (from eight months to about a year), experience is concentrated on the teeth, gums, and jaws, and pleasure comes from activities such as biting and devouring. An adult fixated at the late oral stage could be a fingernail biter and also would like eating. This person also would engage in activities symbolically equivalent to biting such as sarcasm, cynicism, and ridicule. Such a person is called an *oral-sadistic character*.

Anal Stage The anal stage occurs during the second year of life, and the erogenous zone is the anus-buttocks region. It is during this stage that the child must learn to control his or her physiological processes so that they function in accordance with the demands of society. That is, the child must be toilet-trained.

In the first part of the anal stage, pleasure derives from feces expulsion. Fixation at this level could result in an adult having physical problems such as lack of sphincter control, or enuresis. Symbolically, the person would be overly generous, wanting to give away everything he or she owns. Such an individual is called an *anal-expulsive character*.

anal retentive

In the later anal stage, pleasure comes from feces possession. Fixation here could manifest itself physically in a problem with constipation or symbolically in stinginess, parsimony, orderliness, and a tendency toward perfectionism. Such an individual is called an *anal-retentive character.*

Phallic Stage This stage occurs from about the third year of life to about the fifth year, and the erogenous zone is the genital area. This is one of the most complicated and controversial of Freud's stages. It is during this stage when our subsequent adjustments to members of the opposite sex are determined. The phallic stage is the scene of the Oedipus and Electra conflicts, the resolutions of which have profound influences on adult life.

The male child experiences the *Oedipus complex,* which is named after an ancient play by Sophocles entitled *Oedipus Tyrannus,* in which King Oedipus killed his father and married his mother. According to Freud, both male and female children develop strong positive feelings toward the mother because she satisfies their needs. Likewise, both male and female children resent the father, because he is regarded as a rival for the mother's attention and affection. These feelings persist in the boy but change in the girl.

identification with father for vicarious satisfaction of sexual impulses with mother

The boy begins to fear the father as the dominant rival, and this fear becomes *castration anxiety*. That is, the boy develops the fear of losing his sex organs, since they are assumed to be responsible for the conflict between him and his father. The anxiety causes a repression of the sexual desire for the mother and hostility toward the father. Next, the boy identifies with his father, thereby gaining vicarious satisfaction of his sexual impulses toward the mother. In a sense, the boy becomes the father and thereby shares the mother. This describes what was for Freud the healthy resolution of the Oedipus complex. Presumably, the boy grows up seeking a woman with a number of his mother's characteristics, perhaps while singing "I want a girl just like the girl who married dear old Dad."

For the female child, the situation is more complex and more pessimistic. The female counterpart of the Oedipus complex is the *Electra complex,* named after another play by Sophocles entitled *Electra,* in which Electra causes her brother to kill her mother who had killed Electra's father.

Female child rejects mother because she doesn't have a penis

As we have seen, female children also start life with a very strong attraction to the mother. This attraction is reduced, however, when the girl discovers that she does not possess a penis. The female child holds the mother responsible for purposely depriving her of this valued organ. The rejection of the mother is coupled with an attraction to the father, whom she knows possesses the valued organ which she wants to share with him. However, her positive feelings toward the father are mixed with envy since he has something that she does not. She is said to have

penis envy. Freud leaves the female suspended between the mother and father with positive and negative feelings toward both. She is said to be sexually ambivalent. The female child leaves the phallic stage with a double approach–avoidance conflict which can be diagrammed as follows:

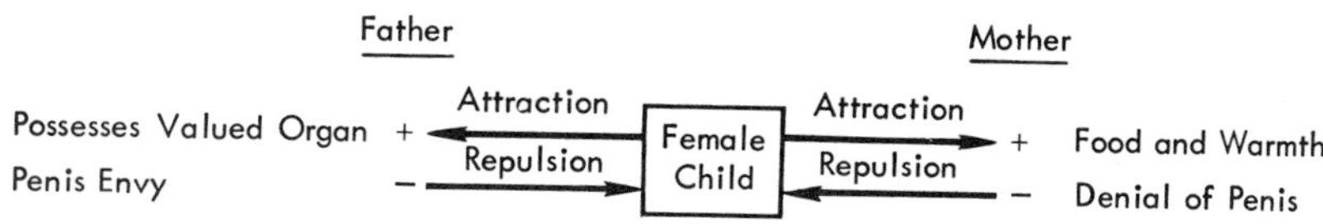

According to Freud, the only hope for the female child is eventually to have a boy baby, thereby finally obtaining a penis, although only symbolically.

Homosexuality is thought to occur if the normal identifications are reversed; for example, if the male child identifies strongly with the mother, or if the female child forms a strong attraction to the father.

Regression to the phallic stage for the male would include displaying many of the father's characteristics and also typically, brashness and an overconcern with masculinity and virility. Regression to the phallic stage for the female would exemplify penis envy-related activities. These activities could include seeking to share a penis; for example, promiscuity or seductiveness, or activities that symbolically castrate men such as embarrassing, deceiving, or hurting them.

The first three psychosexual stages, called the pregenital stages, are by far the most important to personality development. As we mentioned earlier, Freud felt that the basic ingredients of the adult personality are formulated by the end of the phallic stage.

Latency Stage The latency stage lasts from about the sixth year to about the twelfth year. This is a time when sexual interests are displaced to substitute activities such as learning, athletics, and peer group activities.

Genital Stage This is the final stage of development and occurs following puberty. It is the time at which the person emerges from the pregenital stages as the adult he or she is destined to become. Hopefully, the child has now been transformed from a selfish, pleasure-seeking child to a realistic socialized adult with heterosexual interests leading to marriage and perhaps child rearing. If, however, the experiences during the pregenital stages cause fixations, they will manifest themselves throughout one's adult life. Only psychoanalysis could hope to dredge up the remnants of these early experiences, which otherwise would remain repressed into the unconscious, and cause the individual to face them, thereby reducing their influence on one's life.

In fact, the process of psychoanalysis can be viewed as a means of discovering repressed thoughts that are having a negative influence on one's life. The question is, how does one gain access to thoughts that have been actively held in the unconscious all one's life? It is to this question that we turn next.

TAPPING THE UNCONSCIOUS MIND

If repressed anxiety-provoking thoughts are effectively anticathexed by the ego or superego, how then can we come to know what they are? To say the least, it is not easy, but it is the business of psychoanalysts to attempt to do so. Freud employed several methods of determining the contents of the unconscious mind, and we will examine a few of them.

Free Association Earlier in this chapter we showed how the technique of free association gradually evolved. To stimulate free association (the "Fundamental Rule of Psychoanalysis"), Freud instructed his patients as follows:

> You will notice that as you relate things various thoughts will occur to you which you would like to put aside on the ground of certain criticisms and objections. You will be tempted to say to yourself that this or that is irrelevant here, or is quite unimportant, or nonsensical, so that there is no need to say it. You must never give in to these criticisms, but must say it in spite of them—indeed, you must say it precisely *because* you feel an aversion to doing so. . . . Finally, never forget that you have promised to be absolutely honest, and never leave anything out because, for some reason or other, it is unpleasant to tell it. (1913/1958, pp. 134–135)

The idea was that even in conscious expressions, there are hints as to the contents of the unconscious mind that the trained observer could detect. Of course, what is *not* said is as important, if not more important, than what is said. Topics to which patients offer strong resistance provide the analyst with useful hints to problem areas in the unconscious mind.

Dream Analysis We saw earlier that Freud used his own dreams as his primary source of information in his own analysis. Indeed, he saw the interpretation of dreams as "the Royal Road to knowledge of the unconscious" (1900/1953, Vol. 5, p. 608). It was in dreams that the contents of the unconscious were most available, still hidden or distorted, but available.

When we recall a dream, we describe its *manifest content* or about what it appeared to be. More important is the dream's *latent content*, which is the underlying repressed thoughts that caused the dream. Repressed thoughts cannot reach consciousness undisguised even during sleep; they must be at least partially camouflaged. Freud referred to the various mechanisms which distort the true contents of a dream collectively as *dream work.*

One form of dream distortion is *condensation* in which a part of something can symbolize the whole thing, such as when an article of clothing symbolizes a person, one street symbolizes a city, or a lamp symbolizes a house in which the dreamer once lived. *Synthesis* occurs when an idea contained in the manifest content of a dream may actually be a combination of many ideas in the latent content, such as when a childhood pet represents an entire family. *Dislocation* is a displacement of an unacceptable idea to something that is symbolically equivalent and acceptable, such as when penises become objects such as baseball bats or flagpoles, breasts become mountains, balloons, or cantaloupes, and sexual intercourse becomes dancing or horseback riding, to give but a few examples.

Other processes also act upon a dream to make its content more acceptable, but still the latent meaning is always there for the trained observer to discover. But since dreams almost always contain at least some threatening material, the patient and therapist must work quickly before their contents are repressed again. The nature of dreams and the process of repression explain why the memory of dreams is so short-lived.

Everyday Life In 1901, Freud wrote a book entitled *The Psychopathology of Everyday Life* in which he gives numerous examples of how repressed thoughts manifest themselves in the course of everyday living. Being a determinist, Freud believed that all human behavior had a cause, that nothing happened simply by chance—not even accidents. Freud believed that little mistakes such as temporary lapses of memory provided information about the unconscious mind. For example, one may forget a potentially painful visit to the dentist or psychoanalyst. One may forget a date altogether or show up on Saturday instead of on Friday when the date actually was. One may stop at a green light on the way to his or her mother-in-law's house.

Slips-of-the-tongue, which have come to be known as "Freudian slips," are also thought to reveal unconscious motives. Legend has it that once Freud was introduced as Dr. Sigmund Fraud. A professor may reveal something about himself with the statement "She's the breast student I've had for years," or "I'd like to go but I've got to stay home and grade firm papers." Zimbardo and Ruch (1977, p. 416) report that a radio announcer who was reading a commercial for Barbara Ann Bread instead of saying "Barbara Ann for the best bread" read "Barbara Ann for the breast in bed."

Even actual accidents were thought by Freud to have meaning. After all, an automobile accident is a socially acceptable way of not getting somewhere. The main point here is that just because a thought is repressed does not mean that it goes away; it is always there striving for expression, and these manifestations in everyday life are another way of getting a glimpse into the unconscious.

Humor According to Freud, humor allows the expression of repressed thoughts in a socially approved manner. In his book *Jokes and Their Relation to the Unconscious* (1905), Freud indicates that through humor a person can express his or her aggressiveness ("practical jokes") or sexual desires without the fear of retaliation by either the ego or the superego. When a joke is being told, because the energy usually required for anti-cathexis is not needed, it is released in laughter. Jokes, like dreams, are usually forgotten quickly, for they too deal with "dangerous" material. In fact, in order for a joke to be "funny," it *must* contain anxiety-provoking material. According to Freud, we laugh only at things that bother us. An examination of American humor shows sex, elimination, and death to be favorite topics, and this would indicate to a Freudian that they contain an abundance of repressed thoughts. In fact, say the Freudians, if you want to know what has been repressed in a person's unconscious mind, examine what he or she finds humorous.

FREUD'S VIEW OF HUMAN NATURE

To Freud, humans were mainly biological organisms whose master motive was the satisfaction of bodily needs. Cultural achievements in the sciences, arts, and religion were regarded as mainly displacements away from the more direct (and natural) ways of satisfying our biological needs in general, and our sexual needs in particular. Freud looked at humans as hedonistic creatures driven by the same impulses that drive "lower" animals. Things like religion and civilization developed either because of our fear of the unknown or because we needed protection against our own inborn aggressive tendencies. We will have more to say about Freud's views on religion when we discuss Jung in the next chapter.

Freud seemed to grow more pessimistic with age, a fact that many attributed to his worsening cancer of the mouth and throat. In 1930, in his book *Civilization and Its Discontents,* he reacted to the statement "Thou shalt love thy neighbor as thyself," as follows:

> What is the point of a precept enunciated with so much solemnity if its fulfillment cannot be recommended as reasonable? . . . Not merely is this stranger in general unworthy of my love; I must honestly confess that he has more claim to my hostility and even my hatred. He seems not to have the least trace of love for me and shows me not the slightest consideration. If it will do him any good he has no hesitation in injuring me, nor does he ask himself whether the amount of advantage he gains bears any proportion to the extent of the harm he does to me. Indeed, he need not even obtain an advantage; if he can satisfy any sort of desire by it,

> he thinks nothing of jeering at me, insulting me, slandering me and showing his superior power; and the more secure he feels and the more helpless I am, the more certainly I can expect him to behave like this to me . . . Indeed, if this grandiose commandment had run "Love thy neighbour as thy neighbour loves thee," I should not take exception to it. . . .
>
> The element of truth behind all this, which people are so ready to disavow, is that men are not gentle creatures who want to be loved, and who at the most can defend themselves if they are attacked; they are, on the contrary, creatures among whose instinctual endowments is to be reckoned a powerful share of aggressiveness. As a result, their neighbour is for them not only a potential helper or sexual object, but also someone who tempts them to satisfy their aggressiveness on him, to exploit his capacity for work without compensation, to use him sexually without his consent, to seize his possessions, to humiliate him, to cause him pain, to torture and to kill him. *Homo homini lupus* [Man is a wolf to man]. (1930/1961, pp. 110–111)

EVALUATION

If you have found Freud uninteresting, it was my fault, not Freud's. As we pointed out at the beginning of this chapter, few people in history have had the impact on human thought that Freud has had. No major category of human existence has been untouched by his ideas. For example, he has had a profound influence on such areas as religion, philosophy, education, literature, art, and all of the social sciences. It is true that Freud had an exciting style of writing and that sex is an interesting topic about which to write, but there is much more to his popularity than that. Hall and Lindzey summarize the reasons for Freud's influence:

> But a fine literary style and an exciting subject matter are not the main reasons for the great esteem in which Freud is held. Rather it is because his ideas are challenging, because his conception of man is both broad and deep, and because his theory has relevance for our times. Freud may not have been a rigorous scientist nor a first-rate theoretician, but he was a patient, meticulous, penetrating observer and a tenacious, disciplined, courageous, original thinker. Over and above all of the other virtues of his theory stands this one—it tries to envisage a full-bodied individual living partly in a world of reality and partly in a world of make-believe, beset by conflicts and inner contradiction, yet capable of rational thought and action, moved by forces of which he has little knowledge and by aspirations which are beyond his reach, by turn confused and clearheaded, frustrated and satisfied, hopeful and despairing, selfish and altruistic; in short, a complex human being. For many people, this picture of man has an essential validity. (1970, p. 72)

What follows in this text can be understood mainly as a reaction to Freud. Some theories support and extend his thoughts, and others refute them, but it was Freud who was first and that is always the most difficult thing to be.

SUMMARY

Freud shocked the world by demonstrating the importance of unconscious motivation. Though originally intending to become a professor of anatomy, Freud became increasingly interested in mental problems. He learned from Breuer that when a patient openly discusses his or her problems, there is sometimes a release of tension called catharsis. Sometimes a patient responds to a therapist as if he or she were an important person in the patient's life, and this is called transference. Also, the therapist sometimes becomes emotionally involved with the patient, and this is called countertransference. After experimenting with several therapeutic techniques, Freud arrived at free association as a major means of studying the unconscious.

According to Freud, instincts constitute the driving force behind personality. Instincts have a source, an aim, an object, and an impetus. There are life instincts, sometimes called eros, whose energy is collectively referred to as libido or libidinal energy. There are also death instincts, sometimes called thanatos. The death instincts are responsible for aggression, which Freud felt was the tendency toward self-destruction turned outward.

The adult mind is divided into the id, the ego, and the superego. The id is the part of our mind that we share with lower animals and is governed by the pleasure principle. The ego is the executive of the personality and is governed by the reality principle. The superego is the moral component of the personality and is governed by the ego-ideal. When a physiological need arises, the id creates a mental image of an object that will satisfy the need. This is called wish-fulfillment, which is an example of a primary process. Since wishes cannot satisfy needs, the ego must seek out real objects in the environment that will actually satisfy the need. These problem-solving skills of the ego are called secondary processes.

An attachment between a need and an object that will satisfy that need is called a cathexis. If a desired object conflicts with the values of the superego, anxiety will be experienced, the ego will resist forming an attachment to it, and an anticathexis will be said to have occurred. When an anticathexis occurs, the person will typically displace his or her desire to a substitute goal that does not cause anxiety. Freud discussed three kinds of anxiety: reality anxiety, which is the fear of actual dangers in the environment; neurotic anxiety, which is the fear of being overwhelmed by one's id; and moral anxiety, which is experienced when a value internalized into the superego has been violated.

The ego defense mechanisms are unconscious processes that reduce anxiety by distorting or falsifying reality. Repression is the most basic ego defense mechanism, because all the other ego defense mechanisms first employ repression. Repression keeps anxiety-provoking thoughts in the unconscious mind and thus out of a person's awareness. Displacement is substituting a nonanxiety-provoking goal for one that does cause anxiety. If the displacement contributes positively to society, it is called sublimation. If aggression is displaced from its primary goal to a safer one or one that is socially approved, it is called displaced aggression. Identification is affiliating oneself with someone or something that will enhance one's feelings of worth. Projection involves seeing things that are true about oneself but which would cause anxiety if recognized in others instead. Reaction formation is repressing anxiety-provoking impulses by exaggerating opposite impulses. Rationalization is giving "logical" explanations for behavior that would cause anxiety if it were not "explained away." Regression is returning to a more comfortable stage of development when stress is encountered.

Freud believed that each child goes through certain psychosexual stages of development and that the child's experiences during these stages determine what kind of personality he or she will possess as an adult. During each psychosexual stage there is an area of the body that is associated with maximum pleasure called an erogenous zone. If, during any stage there is either too much or too little gratification, fixation results, which means as an adult the person will possess traits characteristic of that stage. The first psychosexual stage is the oral stage. Fixation at the oral stage results in either an oral-incorporative character or an oral-sadistic character. The second psychosexual stage is the anal stage. Fixation at the anal stage results in either an anal-expulsive character or an anal-retentive character. The third psychosexual stage is the phallic stage, which is the scene of the Oedipus and Electra complexes. Typically during this stage, males experience castration anxiety and females experience penis envy. It is the phallic stage, according to the Freudians, that largely determines adult sexual preferences. The fourth psychosexual stage is the latency stage, during which time sexual interests are repressed and displaced to other activities such as learning and peer group activities. The final psychosexual stage is the genital stage from which the individual emerges as the adult he or she is destined to become after various experiences during the preceding psychosexual stages.

Freud's major tools for investigating the unconscious mind were free assocation, dream analysis, everyday life, and humor. While analyzing dreams, he differentiated between a dream's manifest content, or its apparent meaning, and its latent content, or its true meaning. The mechanisms that distort dreams were called collectively dream work and included condensation, synthesis, and dislocation. In everyday life Freud noted that people tended to forget anxiety-provoking experiences, sometimes had "accidents" on purpose, and sometimes exhibited "slips of the tongue" that revealed their true (unconscious) feelings. Freud also noted that humor usually was associated with topics about which individuals were anxious.

Freud was quite pessimistic about human nature. He felt that humans were animals frustrated by civilization. According to Freud, humans are aggressive and selfish by nature. There is no area of human existence that has not been influenced by Freud's ideas. He has had a major influence on art, literature, philosophy, and science. His was the first theory of personality, and all theories of personality since can be considered reactions to Freud's theory.

Discussion Questions

1. Describe three major blows to the self-esteem of humans.
2. Elaborate the importance of the concept of instinct to Freud's theory. In your answer list as many characteristics of instincts that you can.
3. Name the major divisions of the mind and describe their functions.
4. Differentiate between primary and secondary processes.
5. Discuss the relationships among the terms cathexis, anticathexis, and displacement.
6. Elaborate the importance of the concept of anxiety to Freud's theory. Include the different kinds of anxiety in your answer.
7. Discuss the ego defense mechanism of repression, and tell why it is so important to Freud's theory.
8. Discuss the relationship between displacement and civilization.
9. Delineate the two meanings of the term identification in Freud's theory.
10. Define and give an example of the following ego defense mechanisms: projection, reaction formation, and rationalization.
11. Describe the relationship between regression and fixation.
12. Discuss the psychosexual stages of development. Include in your answer the major experiences that occur within each stage and their possible influences on adult behavior.
13. Discuss dreams as a source of information about the unconscious mind.
14. Discuss everyday life situations as a source of information about the unconscious mind.
15. Discuss humor as a source of information about the unconscious mind.
16. Describe the influence Freud has had on various aspects of human existence.
17. How many of the ingredients of Freud's theory do you see operating in your own personality? Give as many examples as you can.
18. Summarize Freud's conception of human nature.

Glossary

Anal-Expulsive Character. A character type which results from a fixation at the early anal stage. Such a person may have trouble controlling his or her bowels and may be overly generous.

Anal-Retentive Character. A character type which results from a fixation at the late anal stage. Such a person may suffer from constipation and may be stingy.

Anal Stage. The second psychosexual stage and the one which occurs during the second year of life during which time the anal area is the primary erogenous zone.

Anticathexis. The inhibition or discouragement of a relationship between a need and a particular object or event that would satisfy that need. For example, although sexual intercourse would satisfy the need for sex, it may cause anxiety, so the relationship is inhibited by both the superego and the ego.

Anxiety. The general feeling of uneasiness that is experienced when one engages in, or thinks of engaging in, activities which violate the internalized values of the superego. Freud distinguished between three kinds of anxiety: reality, neurotic, and moral.

Breuer, Josef. A famous physician who became Freud's close friend and with whom Freud coauthored *Studies in Hysteria* (1895). Breuer was the first to use the "talking cure" while treating hysteria, which later evolved into Freud's technique of free association.

Castration Anxiety. A fear that a male child develops, that he is going to lose his sex organs since they are regarded as the source of difficulty between the boy and his father.

Cathexis. The relationship between a need and an object or event that will satisfy that need.

Charcot, Jean. The famous French psychiatrist who used hypnosis in the treatment of hysteria and who indirectly called Freud's attention to the sexual origins of hysteria.

Condensation. A form of dream distortion in which wholes are symbolized by parts of the whole. For example, a whole house is symbolized by the front door of the house.

Conscience. That part of the superego that results from the internalized experiences for which a child had been punished. This component of the personality is responsible for the experience of guilt.

Countertransference. The phenomenon that sometimes occurs during therapy in which the therapist becomes emotionally involved with a patient.

Dislocation. A form of dream distortion in which an acceptable object is substituted for an unacceptable one. For example, when one dreams of mountains instead of breasts.

Displaced Aggression. Aggression directed toward a person or object less threatening than the one causing the aggressive impulse.

Displacement. The substitution of one cathexis which is anxiety provoking for one that is not. For example, the connection between the need for sex and sexual intercourse is substituted for a connection between the need for sex and dancing.

Dream Work. The various mechanisms that distort a dream's true meaning.

Ego. The executive of the personality whose job it is to satisfy the needs of both the id and the superego by engaging in appropriate environmental activities. The ego is governed by the reality principle.

Ego Defense Mechanisms. Unconscious processes that falsify or distort reality in order to reduce or prevent anxiety.

Ego-Ideal. That part of the superego that results from the internalized experiences for which a child had been rewarded. This component of the personality is responsible for the experience of success and pride.

Electra Complex. The situation that arises during the phallic stage during which a female child is attracted to her father and becomes hostile toward her mother.

Erogenous Zone. An area of the body that is a source of pleasure.

Eros. All the life instincts taken collectively.

Fixation. Arrested development at one of the psychosexual stages because of the undergratification or overgratification of a need. Fixation determines the point at which an adult regresses under stress.

Free Association. Called by Freud "The Fundamental Rule of Psychoanalysis," it entails instructing the patient to say whatever comes to his or her mind no matter how irrelevant, unimportant, or nonsensical it seemed to be.

Freudian Slip. A verbal "accident" that is thought to reveal the speaker's true feelings, such as when Dr. Freud was introduced as Dr. Fraud.

Genital Stage. The final psychosexual stage and the one which follows puberty. It is a time when the full adult personality emerges and when the experiences that occurred during the other psychosexual stages manifest themselves.

Humor. According to Freud, humor is a socially acceptable way of expressing repressed, anxiety-provoking thoughts, for example, thoughts involving sex or aggression.

Hysteria. A general term describing disorders such as paralysis of the arms or legs, loss of senation, disturbances of sight and speech, nausea, and general confusion. Until Freud, hysteria was assumed to be exclusively a female disease. **Hystera** is the Greek word for uterus.

Id. The component of the personality which is completely unconscious and contains all the instincts. It is the animalistic portion of the personality which is governed by the pleasure-principle.

Identification. This term was used in two ways by Freud, (1) the matching of an idinal image with its physical counterpart, and (2) the incorporation of another person's values and/or characteristics either to enhance one's self-esteem or to minimize that person as a threat.

Instinct. For Freud, instincts were the stuff from which personality is shaped. An instinct is the cognitive reflection of a biological deficiency. Instincts have four characteristics: a source, an aim, an object, and an impetus, and can be divided into two categories: life and death instincts.

Latency Stage. The psychosexual stage that lasts from about the sixth year to about the twelfth year of life. It is a time when sexual activity is repressed, and an abundance of substitute activities are engaged in, such as learning and athletics.

Latent Content of a Dream. The dream's *true* meaning, which is usually disguised or distorted by dream work.

Libido. In Freud's earlier writings, libido was the psychic energy associated with the sexual instinct, but later he expanded the concept of libido to include the energy associated with all the life instincts, for instance, hunger and thirst in addition to sex.

Manifest Content of a Dream. What a dream *appears* to be about to the dreamer.

Moral Anxiety. Fear that one will do something contrary to the values of the superego and thus experience guilt.

Neurotic Anxiety. Caused by the fear that the impulses of the id will overwhelm the ego, thereby causing the person to do something for which he or she will be punished.

Oedipus Complex. The situation that arises during the phallic stage in which a male child is attracted to his mother and hostile toward his father.

Oral-Incorporative Character. A character type which results from a fixation at the early oral stage. Such a person spends considerable time engaged in activities such as eating, kissing, smoking, and listening.

Oral-Sadistic Character. A character type which results from a fixation at the late oral stage. Such a person is orally aggressive and may be a fingernail biter and sarcastic.

Oral Stage of Development. The first psychosexual stage and the one which occurs during the first year of life, at which time the mouth is the primary erogenous zone.

Penis Envy. The jealousy the female child experiences because males have a penis and she does not.

Phallic Stage. The third psychosexual stage and the one that occurs from about the third to the fifth year of life, during which time the genitals are the primary erogenous zone.

Primal Repression. Repression of those anxiety-provoking thoughts that are innately part of the id and therefore independent of experience.

Pleasure Principle. The hedonistic principle governing the id that demands the immediate reduction of any tension associated with an unsatisfied biological need.

Primary Processes. The processes available to the id in order to satisfy needs. Those processes are reflex action and wish-fulfillment (hallucinations).

Projection. The ego defense mechanism by which an anxiety-provoking thought is attributed to someone or something else instead of recognizing it as one's own.

Rationalization. Giving a rational, logical excuse for behavior or thoughts that cause anxiety. For example, one concludes that a test on which one performed poorly was ambiguous, rather than concluding that one was not properly prepared or perhaps stupid.

Reaction Formation. The inhibition of an anxiety-provoking thought by exaggerating its opposite. For example, a person inclined toward pornography may become a censor.

Reality Anxiety. Caused by real, objective sources of danger in the environment. It is the easiest kind of anxiety to reduce or prevent.

Reality Principle. The principle governing the ego that causes it to do commerce with the environment in a way that satisfies both the id and the superego.

Reality Testing. The process by which the ego finds environmental experiences capable of satisfying the needs of the id and/or superego.

Reflex Action. The automatic reflexive response aimed at the removal of a source of irritation. Blinking to remove something from the eye would be an example.

Regression. Returning to an earlier stage of development when stress is encountered. For example, a young woman may reactivate a high school relationship when she experiences problems in her marriage.

Repression. The ego defense mechanism by which anxiety-provoking thoughts are held in the unconscious mind, thereby preventing a conscious awareness of them.

Repression Proper. Repression of those anxiety-provoking thoughts that result from painful experiences in one's lifetime.

Secondary Processes. The realistic processes by which the ego operates, in order to bring about true need reduction as opposed to the temporary need reduction which results from the wish-fulfillments of the id.

Sublimation. A displacement which results in a higher cultural achievement, such as when an artistic or scientific activity is substituted for sexual activity.

Superego. The moral component of the personality which has two components: the conscience and the ego-ideal.

Synthesis. A form of dream distortion in which many things are symbolized by one object. For example, an aunt may symbolize all the females in one's family.

Thanatos. All the death instincts taken collectively. The source of aggression which Freud felt was self-destruction turned outward.

Transference. The phenomenon that sometimes occurs during therapy in which a patient begins to respond to the therapist as if he or she were an important person in the patient's life, such as the patient's father.

Wish-Fulfillment. The conjuring up of an image of an object or event that is capable of satisfying a biological need. For example, a hungry person thinks of food-related objects.

chapter 3

carl jung

As we shall see in this chapter, Jung's is a complex theory of personality. In fact, the picture of human nature that he portrays is the most complicated developed by any personality theorist. As might be expected, Jung himself was a complicated person. Many of the details of his life are only recently coming to light, and they often are contradictory. For example, Stern (1976) portrays Jung as a prepsychotic (if not psychotic), opportunistic person with anti-Semitic and pro-Nazi leanings. On the other hand, Hannah (1976), a Jungian herself and a close friend of Jung's, portrays him as a brilliant, sensitive humanitarian who was anything but an anti-Semite or pro-Nazi. The Jung whom Hannah describes is indeed an uncommon, sometimes troubled person with many idiosyncrasies, but these, in her opinion, are attributes of a genius, not of a madman. Jung's own autobiography (1961) does not help much, since it is, Jung confesses, a combination of myth and fact.

It appears that many truths about Jung's personal existence, if they are ever to be known at all, will need to unfold in the future. What follows is a summary of those facts about Jung over which there is little or no disagreement. As far as Jung's theoretical notions are concerned, it is the same for Jung as for any other personality theorist; either his ideas are valid and useful or they are not. The personal experiences that gave rise to those ideas may be interesting in themselves, but they are scientifically irrelevant.

Carl Gustav Jung was born in 1875 in the Swiss village of Kesswyl but grew up in the university town of Basel. Religion was a strong theme running through Jung's early years. There were nine clergymen in his family, including eight uncles and his father, who was a pastor of the Swiss Reformed Church. Jung's father looked upon himself as a failure, and his religion was little comfort to him. Although Jung was close to his father, he considered him to be weak and ineffective. Jung considered his mother to be the dominant member of the family, although he saw her as terribly inconsistent, which caused him to suspect that she was really two persons in one body.

The constant bickering of his parents caused the young Jung to isolate himself from the family in a number of ways. He relied heavily on his dreams, visions, and fantasies, which he interpreted as the revelation of secret knowledge that only a select few individuals were given. The content of dreams and visions remained for Jung throughout his life important sources of information about himself and his future.

When Jung was ten years old, he carved a wooden figure of a man from a ruler and kept it in a little wooden case. Jung dressed the figure in a coat, black boots and a top hat and gave it a little stone of its own.

> This was *his* stone. All this was a great secret. Secretly I took the case to . . . the attic at the top of the house . . . and hid it with great satisfaction on one of the beams under the roof—for no one must ever see it! . . . I felt safe, and the tormenting sense of being at odds with myself was gone. (Jung 1961, p. 21)

This figure became a refuge for Jung, and whenever he was troubled he would visit with his secret friend. It is interesting that Jung dressed

Carl Jung. Courtesy ATP Bilderdienst, Zurich.

his small friend in a way very similar to the way in which the body of a man who was killed by a flood was dressed when Jung, as a child of six, found him.

Another important fantasy that the young Jung had was that he was, like his mother, really two different people. One person he labeled number one (the schoolboy), the other number two (the wise old man). The wise old man was about one hundred years older than the school boy who was apparently the "real" Jung. So strongly did Jung believe in this dual aspect of himself that he would often make a mistake of one hundred years while dating his schoolwork; for example, he would write 1786 instead of 1886. The explanation of fantasies such as this one would later become an important part of Jung's theory.

Jung first wanted to study archaeology, but a dream convinced him to follow in his paternal grandfather's footsteps and become a medical doctor. He received his medical degree from the University of Basel in 1900. Jung's first position was at the psychiatric clinic of the University of Zurich at which he came under the influence of Eugen Bleuler,

Photograph taken during the visit of Freud and Jung to Clark University, 1909. Top row, from left to right: A. A. Brill, Ernest Jones (Freud's biographer), and Sandor Ferenczi. Bottom row, from left to right: Sigmund Freud, G. Stanley Hall (then president of Clark University), and Carl Jung. Courtesy Clark University Archives.

the famous psychiatrist who coined the term "schizophrenia." In 1905, Jung was given a lectureship at the University of Zurich but became increasingly interested in private practice, research, and writing, and in 1913 resigned both his position at the clinic and his lectureship to devote all of his time to these pursuits.

Jung's Relationship with Freud Jung first became interested in Freud after reading *The Interpretation of Dreams.* Jung began to apply Freud's ideas to his own practice and eventually wrote a monograph entitled *The Psychology of Dementia Praecox* (1907), summarizing their effectiveness. In 1906, Jung initiated correspondence with Freud and in the following year, the two met in Freud's home in Vienna. Their first face-to-face meeting was intense and lasted thirteen hours. The two became extremely close friends and when Jung returned to Zurich, a series of letters began which lasted about seven years (see McGuire, 1974).

Jung traveled with Freud to America in 1909 to give a series of lectures at Clark University. It was at about this time that Jung began to express doubts about the emphasis on sexual motivation in Freud's theory. His opposition to Freud was not expressed strongly, however, and the two remained close friends. Jung simply suggested to Freud that his theory might be more palatable to American audiences if he played down the role of sex. Freud looked upon this suggestion as a departure from scientific ethics.

Since Freud wanted a young man who was not a Jew to head the International Psychoanalytic Association, he nominated Jung as the organization's first president. Freud's nomination brought strong opposition from the organization's Viennese members who were mainly Jews and many of whom thought Jung was an anti-Semite. The master prevailed, however, and in 1911 Jung was elected as the organization's first president. It was also about this time that Jung openly expressed doubts about Freud's interpretation of libidinal energy as primarily sexual. Jung's book, *The Psychology of the Unconscious* (1912), and a series of lectures he gave at Fordham University entitled *The Theory of Psychoanalysis* (1913) amplified the differences between Jung's conception of the libido and Freud's. The following exchange of letters exemplifies the early disagreement between Freud and Jung over the nature of the libido. First Jung wrote:

> Is it not conceivable, in view of the limited conception of sexuality that prevails nowadays, that the sexual terminology should be reserved only for the most extreme forms of your "libido," and that a less offensive collective term should be established for *all* the libidinal manifestations? (McGuire 1974, p. 25)

Freud responded to Jung as follows:

> I appreciate your motives in trying to sweeten the sour apple, but I do not think you will be successful. Even if we call the unconscious

"psychoid," it will still be the unconscious, and even if we do not call the driving force in the broadened conception of sexuality "libido," it will still be libido. . . . We cannot avoid resistances, why not face up to them from the start? (McGuire 1974, p. 28)

The relationship between Jung and Freud became so strained that they agreed to stop their personal correspondence in 1912, and in 1914 Jung completely terminated the relationship when he resigned his presidency of the International Psychoanalytic Association and also withdrew as a member. The break was especially disturbing to Jung who was then almost forty years old. The separation from Freud caused Jung to enter what he called the "dark years," a period of three years during which he was unable to read a scientific book. This was also a period of complete withdrawal into himself when he explored in depth his own dreams and fantasies, an activity which brought him, in the opinion of many, to the brink of madness. He emerged, however, with his own theory of personality, a theory which bore only a remote resemblance to that of his mentor, Freud. The results of his long agonizing search of his own psyche is to be found everywhere in his theory.

Jung continued to develop his theory up to the time of his death at the age of eighty-six in 1961 at his tower-home in Bollingen, Switzerland.

LIBIDO, EQUIVALENCE, ENTROPY, AND OPPOSITES

Libido It was over the nature of the libido that Freud and Jung split. Freud saw libido as consisting mainly of sexual and aggressive energy. In other words, Freud, at the time he was associated with Jung, saw as the driving force of personality the energy generated by repressed sexual and aggressive strivings. Jung felt that this view was too narrow and instead defined the libido as general biological life energy that is concentrated on different problems as they arise. For Freud libido was mainly sexual in nature, for Jung it was a creative life force that could be applied to the continuous psychological growth of the person. In the early years of life, according to Jung, libidinal energy is expended mainly on such things as eating, elimination, and sex, but as the person becomes more proficient at satisfying these needs, or as they become less important, libidinal energy is applied to the solution of more philosophical and spiritual needs. Thus for Jung, libido is the driving force behind the *psyche* (Jung's term for personality) which is focused on various needs as they arise, whether those needs are biological or spiritual. Those components of the personality in which considerable libidinal energy is invested are said to be *valued* more than others. Thus, according to Jung, the value of something is determined by how much psychic energy is invested in it.

Principle of Equivalence Jung drew heavily on the physics of his day for his theory of personality. His use of the principles of equivalence, entropy, and opposites demonstrates this clearly. The principle of equivalence is the first law of thermodynamics, which states that the amount of energy in a system is essentially fixed (conservation of energy), and if it is removed from one part of a system, it will show up in another. Applied to the psyche, this means that there is only so much psychic energy (libido) available, and if one component of the psyche is overvalued, it is at the expense of the other components. If, for example, psychic energy is concentrated on conscious activities, then unconscious activities will suffer, and vice versa. We will have more to say about this later.

Principle of Entropy This is the second law of thermodynamics, which states that there is a constant tendency toward the equalization of energy within a system. If, for example, a hot object and a cold object are placed side by side, heat will flow from the hot object to the cold one until their temperatures are equalized. Likewise, according to Jung, there is a tendency for all components of the psyche to have equal energy. For example, the conscious and unconscious aspects of the psyche would have equal energy and thus equal representation in one's life. This psychic balance, however, is extremely hard to achieve and must be actively sought. If the balance is not sought, the person's psychic energy will not be balanced, and thus personality development will be uneven. That is, certain aspects of the psyche will be more highly valued than others. We will have more to say about this when we discuss "self-actualization."

Principle of Opposites This principle is found almost everywhere in Jung's writings. It is very close to Newton's contention that "for every action there is an equal and opposite reaction" or Hegel's statement that "everything carries within itself its own negation." Every concept in Jung's theory had its polar opposite. The unconscious is contrasted with the conscious, the rational with the irrational, feminine with masculine, the animal with the spiritual, causality with teleology, progression with regression, introversion with extroversion, thinking with feeling, and sensing with intuiting. When one aspect of the personality is developed, it is usually at the expense of its polar opposite; for instance, as one becomes more masculine, he necessarily becomes less feminine. For Jung the goal of life, in accordance with the principle of entropy, is to seek a balance between these polar opposites, thereby giving both expression in one's life, a task which is more easily said than done. Such a synthesis is something that is constantly aspired to but seldom accomplished. About the importance of these opposites and the conflicts between them, Jung said:

> The sad truth is that man's real life consists of a complex of inexorable opposites—day and night, birth and death, happiness and misery, good and evil. We are not even sure that one will prevail against the other, that good will overcome evil, or joy defeat pain. Life is a battleground. It always has been, and always will be; and if it were not so, existence would come to an end. (1964, p. 85)

THE COMPONENTS OF THE PERSONALITY

The Ego According to Jung, the ego is everything of which we are conscious. It is concerned with thinking, feeling, remembering, and perceiving. It is responsible for seeing that the functions of everyday life are carried out. It is also responsible for our sense of identity and our sense of continuity in time. There is considerable similarity between Jung's concept of ego and Freud's.

The Personal Unconscious The personal unconscious consists of material that was once conscious but was repressed or forgotten or was not vivid enough to make a conscious impression at first. As in Freud's earlier concept of the preconscious, material in the personal unconscious is readily available to the person, and there is a great deal of interaction between it and the ego.

The personal unconcious contains clusters of emotionally loaded (highly valued) thoughts which Jung called *complexes*. More specifically, a complex is a personally disturbing constellation of ideas connected together by common feeling-tone (Jung 1913b/1973, p. 599). A complex has a disproportionate influence on one's behavior in the sense that the theme around which the complex is organized keeps recurring over and over again in one's life. A person with a mother complex will spend a considerable amount of time on activities that are either directly or symbolically related to the idea of mother. The same would be true of a person with a father complex, a sex complex, a power complex, a money complex, or any other kind of complex.

Jung's early claim to fame was a technique he devised to detect complexes. He took the word-association test developed much earlier by Wilhelm Wundt and redesigned it as a tool to tap the personal unconscious in search of complexes. It was this research on which he lectured at Clark University when he went there with Freud in 1909. Jung's technique consisted of reading to a patient a list of one hundred words one at a time and instructing the patient to respond as quickly as possible with the first word that came to mind. Words such as head, green, water, sing, dead, law, and stranger were used. How long it took the patient to respond to each word was measured with a stopwatch. Breathing rate also was measured, as was the electroconductivity of the patient's skin which was measured with a galvanometer.

The following were used by Jung as "complex indicators," i.e., things that indicated the presence of a complex:

1. longer than average reaction time to a stimulus word
2. repeating the stimulus word back as a response
3. failure to respond at all
4. expressive bodily reactions like laughing, increased breathing rate, or increased conductivity of the skin
5. stammering
6. continuing to respond to a previously used stimulus word
7. meaningless reactions, like made-up words
8. superficial reaction, for example, responding with a word that sounds like the stimulus word (sin-win).
9. responding with more than one word
10. misunderstanding the stimulus word as some other word

Jung used his word-association test in many ways. For example, he found that males tended to respond faster to stimulus words than females did, and that educated people tended to respond faster than uneducated people did. In addition, he found that members of the same family had remarkably similar reactions to stimulus words. The following shows the reaction of a mother and her daughter to several stimulus words (Jung 1909/1973, p. 469):

Stimulus Word	*Mother*	*Daughter*
law	God's commandment	Moses
potato	tuber	tuber
stranger	traveler	travelers
brother	dear to me	dear
to kiss	mother	mother
merry	happy child	little children

For Jung, it was important to discover and deal with complexes, since they require the expenditure of so much psychic energy in disturbing performance and memory, and in inhibiting psychological growth in general.

The Collective Unconscious This was Jung's boldest, most mystical, and most controversial concept. To understand the collective unconscious is to understand the very heart of Jung's theory. The collective unconscious reflects the collective experiences that humans have had in their evolutionary past or, in Jung's own words, it is the "deposit of ancestral experience from untold millions of years, the echo of prehistoric world events to which each century adds an infinitesimally small amount of variation and differentiation" (Jung 1928, p. 162). Not only are fragments of all human history found in the collective unconscious, but traces of our prehuman or animal ancestry are found there as well. Since the collective unconscious results from *common* experiences that all humans have, or have had, the contents of the collective unconscious are essentially the same for all humans. Jung says it is "detached from anything personal and is common to all men, since its contents can be found everywhere" (Jung 1917/1953, p. 66).

These ancestral experiences that are registered in the brain have been called at various times "racial memories," "primordial images," or more commonly, *archetypes*. An archetype can be defined as an inherited predisposition to respond to certain aspects of the world. Just as the eye and the ear have evolved to be maximally responsive to certain aspects of the environment, so has the brain evolved to cause the person to be maximally responsive to certain categories of experience which he or she has encountered over and over again through countless generations. There is an archetype for whatever experiences are universal, those that each member of each generation must experience.

You can generate a list of archetypes yourself by simply answering the question "What must every human experience in his or her lifetime?" One's answer must include such things as birth, death, the sun, darkness, power, women, men, sex, water, magic, mother, heroes, and pain. There is an inherited predisposition to react to instances of these and other categories of experience. Specific responses are not inherited nor are specific ideas; all that is inherited is a tendency to deal with universal experiences *in some way*. *How* the archetypes are responded to depends upon one's life circumstances.

The collective unconscious is by far the most important and influential part of the psyche, and everything in it seeks outward manifestation. When the contents of the collective unconscious are not recognized in consciousness, they are manifested in dreams, fantasies, images, and symbols. Because few people fully recognize the contents of their collective unconscious, most can learn about themselves by studying the contents of their dreams and fantasies. In fact, according to Jung, humans can learn a great deal about their future by studying these things since they symbolize basic human nature, as it someday is hoped to be understood. In that sense, the collective unconscious knows more than any single generation of humans knows. As we shall see later, Jung gathered information about the archetypes from a wide variety of sources, including his own dreams and fantasies, primitive tribes, art, language, and the hallucinations of psychotic patients.

Although Jung recognized the existence of many archetypes, he wrote extensively on only a few. These were the persona, the anima, the animus, the shadow, and the self. We will consider each of these in some detail.

The Persona Persona is the Greek word for mask, and Jung used this term to describe one's public self. The persona archetype develops because of humans' need to play a role in society. This is the part of the psyche by which we are known by other people. Jung points out that some people equate their persona with their entire psyche and that this is a mistake. In a sense, the persona is supposed to deceive other people, since it presents to them only a small part of one's psyche, but if a person believes that he is what he pretends to be, then that person is deceiving himself and that is dangerous. Jung says that "whoever builds up too good a persona for himself naturally has to pay for it with irritability" (Jung 1917/1953, p. 193). Jung describes the situation in which the persona is valued too highly as *inflation of the persona*. As with all components of the psyche, if the persona is valued too highly, it develops at the expense of other components.

The Anima This is the female component of the male psyche. The anima results from the experiences men have had with women through the eons. This archetype does two things. First, it causes males to have feminine traits, and second, it provides a framework within which males interact with females. Because man's relationship with women has included such things as being nurtured (mother), being sexually involved (lover), and just being a friend, all of these are contained in the anima, and elements of each are projected on the women in one's lifetime. Since an archetype can be viewed as an ideal, real women may not correspond to it exactly. In order to make an adequate adjustment, there often must be a compromise between the ideal and the real. If a male insists that a particular woman correspond to his innate images of women, the relationship may be doomed.

The Animus The animus is the masculine component of the female psyche. It furnishes the female with masculine traits and also with a framework that guides her relationship with men. As the anima furnishes men with an ideal of the female, the animus furnishes women with an ideal of the male and the insistence that a particular male live up to that ideal may lead to conflict and disillusionment.

Thus, the male psyche has a strong female component, and the female psyche has a strong male component. The proper adjustment to this situation, according to Jung, is for both sexes to recognize that they possess traits of the opposite sex. Such a realization results in a more well rounded, creative person. Again, a balance should be sought. For a male to deny his female tendencies is to deny an important part of his psyche and, according to Jung, this is unfortunate. On the other hand, for a male to overemphasize his feminine traits is equally unfortunate.

If conscious recognition is not given to any component of the psyche, it will not disappear; it is forced to manifest itself on the unconscious level at which its effect is uncontrolled and irrational. Thus, if a female denies her masculine traits, they will continue to influence her life, but they will do so in indirect ways, such as through dreams and fantasies.

The Shadow This is the darkest, deepest part of the psyche. It is the part of the collective unconscious that we inherit from our prehuman ancestors and contains all of the animal instincts. Because of the shadow, we have a strong tendency to be immoral, aggressive, and passionate.

As with all of the archetypes, the shadow seeks outward manifestation and is projected onto the world symbolically as devils, monsters, or evil spirits. It can even be projected onto a person, as Jung found out when he asked one of his young patients the following question:

> ". . . How do I seem to you when you are not with me?" . . . She said, "Sometimes you seem rather dangerous, sinister, like an evil magician or a demon. I don't know how I ever got such ideas—you are not a bit like that." (1956, p. 91 and 92)

Jung suggested that she was projecting her shadow onto him, and she then replied:

> "What, so I am a man, and a sinister, fascinating man at that, a wicked magician or a demon? . . . I cannot accept that, it's all nonsense. I'd sooner believe this of you!" . . . Her eyes flashed, an evil expression creeps into her face, the gleam of an unknown resistance never seen before. . . . In her glance there lurks something of the beast of prey, something really demoniacal. . . . What have I touched? What new chord is vibrating? Yet it is only a passing moment. The expression on the patient's face clears, and she says, as though relieved, "It is queer, but just now I had a horrible feeling you had touched the point I could never get over . . . it's a horrible feeling, something inhuman, evil, cruel. I simply cannot describe how queer this feeling is." (1956, p. 92)

Not only does the preceding quotation describe the projection of the shadow, it also exemplifies Jung's approach to psychoanalysis. Jung's goal was to introduce his patient to the various components of his or her psyche, and when the components were known, to synthesize them into an interrelated configuration resulting in a deeper, more creative individual. Unlike Freud who thought the unconscious, irrational mind had to be made increasingly conscious and rational if humans were to become truly civilized, Jung believed the shadow should be recognized and then utilized rather than overcome. The animal nature of the shadow is, to Jung, a source of vitality, spontaneity, and creativity. The person who does not utilize his or her shadow, according to Jung, tends to be dull and lifeless.

The Self The self is the component of the psyche that attempts to harmonize all the other components. It represents the human striving for unity, wholeness, and integration of the total personality. When this integration has been achieved, the individual is said to be *self-actualized*. We will have more to say about the self when we consider "life's goal" later in this chapter.

PSYCHOLOGICAL TYPES

Jung felt that there were two general orientations the psyche could take in relating to the world. One was inward toward the subjective world of the individual, and the other was outward toward the external environment. Jung called these orientations *attitudes*, and the former he labeled *introversion* and the latter he labeled *extroversion*. The introvert tends to be quiet, imaginative, and more interested in ideas than in other people. The extrovert tends to be sociable, outgoing, and interested in people and things.

> The first attitude (introversion) is normally characterized by a hesitant, reflective, retiring nature that keeps itself to itself, shrinks from objects, is always slightly on the defensive and prefers to hide behind mistrustful scrutiny. The second (extroversion) is normally characterized by an outgoing, candid, and accommodating nature that adapts easily to a given situation, quickly forms attachments, and, setting aside any possible misgivings, will often venture forth with careless confidence into unknown situations. (1917/1953, p. 44)

The attitudes of introversion and extroversion were first presented by Jung at the International Psychoanalytic Congress at Munich in 1913. They were later elaborated in his book *Psychological Types* (1921). Still later, he used the concepts to explain why different individuals develop different kinds of theories of personality. For example, Freud was an extrovert and thus developed a theory that stressed the external, for example, a sex object. Adler's theory (see the next chapter) stressed the internal "will to power," because Adler was an introvert (Jung, 1917/1953). Jung almost used his own theory instead of Adler's as an example of an introvert's theory but decided not to—however, he easily could have.

In addition to the attitudes or general orientations there are the *functions* of thought. The functions pertain to how a person perceives the world and deals with information and experience. There are four functions:

Sensing	Detects the presence of things. It indicates that something is there but does not indicate what it is.
Thinking	Tells what a thing is. It gives names to things that are sensed.
Feeling	Tells whether a thing is acceptable or unacceptable. It determines what a thing is worth to the individual. Pertains to liking and disliking.

Intuiting Hunches about past or future events when factual information is not available. Jung says, "Whenever you have to deal with strange conditions where you have no established values or established concepts, you will depend upon the faculty of intuition" (1968, p. 14).

Thinking and feeling are called *rational* functions, because they make judgments and evaluations about experiences. In addition, thinking and feeling are considered polar opposites since, as Jung says, "when you think, you must exclude feeling, just as when you feel you must exclude thinking" (1968, p. 16). Likewise, sensation and intuition, the *irrational* functions, are thought to be polar opposites.

Ideally, the attitudes and functions would be equally developed, and all would work in harmony, but this is seldom the case. Usually one attitude and one function become dominant, and the other attitude and the other three functions remain undeveloped and unconscious. For the functions, the one opposite the dominant conscious one is the least developed, but the other two are subservient to the dominant function and in that way may become somewhat developed. For example, in a person whose thinking function is highly developed, the other three functions, especially feeling (the opposite of thinking), will be relatively undeveloped on the unconscious level and may be expressed in dreams, fantasies, or in odd and disturbing ways.

By combining the two attitudes and the four functions, Jung described eight different types of people. It should be noted, however, that these eight types probably never exist in pure form, because each person possesses both attitudes and all four functions, and which is conscious and which is unconscious is a matter of personal development.

The eight pure types are listed below with a brief description of what the person would tend to be like:

Thinking Extrovert. Lives according to fixed rules. Objective and cold. Positive and dogmatic in one's thinking. Feeling is repressed.

Feeling Extrovert. Very emotional and respectful of authority and tradition. Sociable person who seeks harmony with the world. Thinking is repressed.

Sensing Extrovert. Pleasure-seeking, jolly, and socially adaptive. Constantly seeking new sensory experiences. Probably interested in such things as good food and art. Very realistic. Intuition is repressed.

Intuiting Extrovert. Decisions guided by hunches rather than by facts. Very changeable and creative. Has trouble staying with one idea very long, rather moves from one idea to another very rapidly. Knows much about one's own unconscious. Sensation is repressed.

Thinking Introvert. Intense desire for privacy. Socially inhibited with poor practical judgment. Very intellectual person who ignores the practicalities of everyday living. Feeling is repressed.

Feeling Introvert. Quiet, thoughtful, and hypersensitive. Childish enigmatic, and indifferent to the feelings and opinions of others. Very little expression of emotion. Thinking is repressed.

Sensing Introvert. Life guided by just what happens. Artistic, passive, and calm. Detached from human affairs since one's main concern is over what happens. Intuition is repressed.

Intuiting Introvert. The odd, eccentric daydreamer who creates new but "strange" ideas. Seldom understood by other people but this is not a source of concern. Life guided by inner experiences rather than outer ones. Jung would be an example.

Here we see Jung's principles of equivalence, opposites, and entropy in operation. Because there is only so much libidinal energy available to the individual, if an abundance of it is invested in a particular component of the psyche, there will be little left for the other components (principle of equivalence). When something is conscious, its opposite is unconscious and vice versa (principle of opposites). There is a constant tendency for the libidinal energy to equalize itself across all components and levels of the psyche (principle of entropy). The components of the psyche that we have discussed in this section can be summarized as follows:

Attitudes	*Functions*		*Levels*
	Rational	*Irrational*	
Introversion	Thinking	Sensing	Conscious
Extroversion	Feeling	Intuiting	Unconscious

STAGES OF DEVELOPMENT

Stages of development were not as important to Jung as they were to Freud, but he did talk about them in very general terms. Jung's stages were defined in terms of the focus of libidinal energy. We saw earlier that Jung disagreed with Freud over the nature of the libido. Freud felt that it was mainly sexual in nature and that the cathexes formed within the first five years of life determined, to a large extent, what a person's adult personality would be like. Jung, on the other hand, felt that libidinal energy was directed simply toward whatever was important to the person at the time, and what was important changed as a function of maturation. Jung's stages of development can be summarized as follows:

Childhood (from birth to adolescence). During the early portion of this period, libidinal energy is expended on the learning of such things as walking, talking, and other skills necessary for survival. After the fifth year, more and more libidinal energy is directed toward sexual activities and reaches its peak during adolescence.

Young Adulthood (from adolescence to about forty). During this stage, libidinal energy is directed toward such things as learning a vocation, getting married, raising children, and relating in some way to community life. During this stage, the individual tends to be outgoing, energetic, impulsive, and passionate.

Middle Age (from about forty to later years of life). This was for Jung the most important stage of development. The person is transformed from an energetic, extroverted, and biologically oriented person to one with more cultural, philosophical, and spiritual values. The person is now much more concerned with wisdom and with life's meaning. The needs that must be satisfied during this stage are just as important as those of the preceding stages, but they are different kinds of needs.

> It is a great mistake to suppose that the meaning of life is exhausted with the period of youth and expansion . . . the afternoon of life is just as full of meaning as the morning; only its meaning and purpose are different. . . . We are here outside the range of Freudian and Adlerian reductions; we are no longer concerned with how to remove the obstacles to a man's profession, or to his marriage, or to do anything that means a widening of his life, but are confronted with the task of finding a meaning that will enable him to continue living at all. (Jung 1956, p. 74)

Since it is during middle age that a person first begins to determine the meaning of life, it is a time when religion becomes important. Jung believed that every person possesses a spiritual need which must be satisfied just as the need for food must be satisfied. However, Jung's definition of religion included any systematic attempt to deal with God, spirits, demons, laws, or ideals.

The steady evolution of the psyche toward understanding, harmony, and wisdom is called *progression.* Progression occurs when libidinal energy causes growth. *Regression* occurs when libidinal energy "flows backward" away from the external environment and inward toward the unconscious. Jung felt that regression was not necessarily bad. For example, if one confronts a barrier in life and is, therefore, frustrated, one may regress and sample information in the unconscious that will solve the problem. This can be diagrammed as follows:

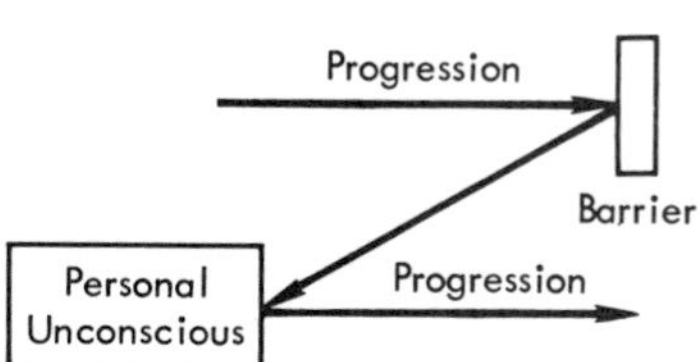

Time and time again Jung suggested that the proper use of the unconscious mind can be beneficial; it is ignoring it that can be dangerous.

LIFE'S GOAL

The goal of life is the harmony of the psyche but before this is possible, the different parts of the psyche must be known to a person. The differentiation of the various parts of the personality is called *individua-*

tion. The process of individuation is becoming aware of such things as the anima or animus, the shadow, the persona, the functions of thought, and all other components of the psyche. Only when these previously hidden components are recognized can they find expression, and, as we have seen, such recognition is not likely before middle age.

As the components of the psyche are discovered, there is a tendency to synthesize them. Jung called this tendency the *transcendent function.* The transcendent function is a constant striving for unity, for wholeness and for the integration of the personality. All of this moves toward the realization of the *self*. Earlier in this chapter, we mentioned that the self was an archetype that represented the integration of the psyche. If, after the differentiation process occurs, the transcendent function is completely effective, the person becomes self-actualized. In other words, the person can be self-actualized only if all the many components of the psyche are known and then placed in perfect harmony by the transcendent function. A rare occurrence indeed.

Jung felt that the self was symbolized by a *mandala,* which is the Sanskrit word meaning circle. The self is thought to be at the center of the circle or midway between the many polarities that make up the psyche. Jung found variations of the mandala in different cultures all over the world, indicating to him its universality. As with all archetypes, the self creates a sensitivity to certain experiences, which in this particular case, manifests itself in symbols of balance and harmony like the circle. An example of a mandala appears below:

Where does that leave all of us who are not self-actualized? According to Jung, we are in various degrees of trouble. The degree of our problem depends on how lopsided our development has been.

> Modern man does not understand how much his "rationalism" (which has destroyed his capacity to respond to numinous symbols and ideas) has put him at the mercy of the psychic "underworld." He has freed himself from "superstition" (or so he believes), but in the process he has lost his spiritual values to a positively dangerous degree. His moral and spiritual tradition has disintegrated, and he is now paying the price for this break-up in world-wide disorientation and dissociation. . . . As scientific understanding has grown, so our world has become dehumanized. Man feels himself isolated in the cosmos, because he is no longer involved in nature and has lost his emotional "unconscious identity" with natural phenomena. These have slowly lost their symbolic implications. Thunder is no longer the voice of an angry god, nor is lightning his

> avenging missile. No river contains a spirit, no tree is the life principle of a man, no snake the embodiment of wisdom, no mountain cave the home of a great demon. No voices now speak to man from stones, plants, and animals, nor does he speak to them believing they can hear. His contact with nature has gone, and with it has gone the profound emotional energy that this symbolic connection supplied. (Jung 1964, pp. 94, 95)

Obviously, Jung believed there is more to life than being rational. In fact, he believed that ignoring the irrational part of the psyche has caused many of our current problems.

> . . . [Contemporary man] is blind to the fact that, with all his rationality and efficiency, he is possessed by "powers" that are beyond his control. His gods and demons have not disappeared at all; they have merely got new names. They keep him on the run with restlessness, vague apprehensions, psychological complications, an insatiable need for pills, alcohol, tobacco, food—and, above all, a large array of neuroses. (Jung 1964, p. 82)

Again, the goal of Jungian therapy is to help the person on the way to selfhood.

CAUSALITY, TELEOLOGY, AND SYNCHRONICITY

Freud explained adult personality strictly in terms of prior experiences, and this is called *causality*. According to Jung, not only is such a belief incomplete, but it also gives one a feeling of despair and hopelessness, since it maintains that what a person will become is a function of what one already has been. Although Jung did not discount causality altogether, he felt *teleology* must be added to it in order to have a complete picture of human motivation. Teleology means that human behavior has a purpose; that is, that our behavior is drawn by the future as much as it is pushed by the past. In other words, to understand a person truly, one must understand his or her goals and aspirations for future attainment. This is on the personal level; on a more general level, all humanity is being drawn into the future by its collective unconscious. The sensitivities to certain experiences caused by the archetypes, in a sense, guide human behavior in the direction of further understanding and ultimately acting upon the contents of the collective unconscious. On the individual level, one's life is greatly influenced by personal goals and aspirations, but all humans are driven by the self archetype toward greater understanding of their personalities and toward the harmonious blending of all its components. Jung's general view of human motivation can be represented schematically as follows:

Past Experiences → Push → Person → Future Goals → Pull

Synchronicity Jung referred to synchronicity as *meaningful coincidence,* as when one dreams of a person and shortly thereafter the person appears, or when one fantasizes an event and the event occurs. According to Jung, such events are of such great importance to one's life that they must be more clearly understood. Synchronicity is one of Jung's more complex concepts, and we will discuss it only briefly here. In order for synchronicity to take place, there needs to be two events occurring independently of each other. That is, the two events have their own causality, but they are not causally related to each other. Then, at some point, an individual experiences them together, and in combination they have meaning to that person, whereas if they were experienced separately, they would not. It is this coming together in a meaningful way of two otherwise meaningless events that defines synchronicity. Progoff gives the following example of synchronicity from the life of Abraham Lincoln:

> There is a synchronistic event that occurred in the life of Abraham Lincoln that may say a great deal to us about the nature of Synchronicity and its future. During his early years, as we know, Lincoln found himself in a very difficult and conflicting situation. He had intimations of the fact that there was a meaningful work for him to do in the world. He realized, however, that that work would require him to develop his intellect and to acquire professional skills. In conflict with these subjective feelings was the fact that, in Lincoln's frontier environment, intellectual tools for professional study were very difficult to find. He had reason to believe that his hopes would never be fulfilled.
>
> One day a stranger came to Lincoln with a barrel full of odds and ends. He said that he was in need of money and that he would be much obliged if Lincoln would help him out by giving him a dollar for the barrel. The contents, he said, were not of much value; they were some old newspapers and things of that sort. But the stranger needed the dollar very badly. The story tells us that Lincoln, with his characteristic kindness, gave the man a dollar for the barrel even though he could not imagine any use that he would have for its contents. Some time later, when he went to clear out the barrel, he found that it contained almost a complete edition of Blackstone's *Commentaries.* It was the chance, or synchronistic, acquisition of these books that enabled Lincoln to become a lawyer and eventually to embark on his career in politics. (1973, pp. 170–171)

Note that the two events that came together were not causally related to each other but had their own lines of causality. On the one hand, we had an ambitious Lincoln who was frustrated because of the lack of needed materials, and on the other hand, we had a stranger with odds and ends who needed a dollar. Only when the two came together at a particular moment in Lincoln's life did they take on meaning. We might say that both Lincoln and the stranger were "lucky" to run into each other.

In a more complex way the concept of synchronicity can be applied to the relationship between the collective unconscious and various experiences we have. As we have seen, each archetype can be regarded as a predisposition to respond to a certain class of environmental events. In fact, an archetype can be considered a need to have certain kinds of experiences. Under these circumstances, when we have an experience that gives symbolic expression to an archetype, the experience is as satisfying as finding food is to a hungry person. This would explain why humans react emotionally to certain music, art forms, and various symbols in their lives. According to Jung, we all have archetypes and when our experiences give them expression, the result is emotionally satisfying. Since the archetypes have one causal heritage and the environmental events that give them symbolic expression have another, their coming together is coincidental and thus an example of synchronicity.

Examples of synchronicity can be found easily in everyone's life, but Jung is the only theorist who has explored the phenomenon. For a much more detailed description of synchronicity see Progoff's book, *Jung, Synchronicity, and Human Destiny: Noncausal Dimensions of Human Experience* (1973).

RESEARCH TECHNIQUES

We have already viewed Jung's research using his word-association test; this was his most scientifically orthodox research. The other sources of evidence he used to support his theory were more controversial. For example, he studied in depth his own dreams and visions. He studied the contents of the hallucinations of psychotic patients. He studied the religions, rituals, myths, and symbols of various cultures from various eras. He traveled to such places as Arizona, New Mexico, and Kenya, to do so. He studied theology, philosophy, mythology, literature, and poetry. He studied all forms of art and language. In short, he studied every major category of human existence, and everywhere he found support for his contention that humans are born with predispositions to respond to the world in certain ways. He felt that he found symbols corresponding to the content of the collective unconscious everywhere, symbols with powerful influences, yet not completely understood by those responding to them.

Like Freud, Jung looked upon dreams as one of the most important sources of information about the unconscious mind. Although both men looked upon dreams as important sources of information, Jung interpreted dreams much differently than Freud did. We now will consider Jung's method of dream analysis.

Jung's Analysis of Dreams First of all, Jung disagreed with Freud's distinction between manifest and latent contents of a dream. To Jung, the content of a dream is just what it appears to be.

> I have long maintained that we have no right to accuse the dream of, so to speak, a deliberate maneuver calculated to deceive. Nature is often obscure or impenetrable, but she is not, like man, deceitful. We must therefore take it that the dream is just what it pretends to be, neither more nor less. (Jung 1956, p. 100)

Later Jung stated:

> I have spent more than half a century in investigating natural symbols, and I have come to the conclusion that dreams and their symbols are not stupid and meaningless. On the contrary, dreams provide the most interesting information for those who take the trouble to understand their symbols. The results, it is true, have little to do with such worldly concerns as buying and selling. But the meaning of life is not exhaustively explained by one's business life, nor is the deep desire of the human heart answered by a bank account. (1964, p. 102)

Jung's statements are a bit misleading, however, since the contents of dreams can include fragments of ancient symbols and myths and may require considerable knowledge of history, religion, and anthropology to comprehend them.

One of the most important functions of the dream, according to Jung, is to *compensate* for neglected parts of the psyche. For example, if the shadow is not given an opportunity to express itself consciously, it will manifest itself in dream content, and one's dreams will be characterized by demons, devils, monsters, and passionate, immoral impulses. In other words, the person will have an abundance of nightmares. One way, therefore, to detect undeveloped portions of the psyche is to analyze the contents of dreams.

Clearly, Jung was not restricted by ordinary methods of science, and he felt no need to apologize since he believed that traditional methods of science could not be applied to the richness of the human psyche. He felt that one's methods had to be as complex and as flexible as what was being studied, and to be sure, the methods of laboratory science did not qualify. According to Jung, the arena of human experience is the proper place to study the human psyche, not the laboratory.

JUNG'S VIEW OF HUMAN NATURE

Certainly Jung's view of human nature is among the most complex ever portrayed. The human psyche is embedded in the past, present, and future; it consists of conscious and unconscious elements, masculine and feminine traits, rational and irrational impulses, spiritualistic and animalistic tendencies, and a tendency to bring all these contradictory tendencies and impulses into harmony with each other. Self-actualization is achieved when such harmony exists, but self-actualization must be sought; it does not occur automatically. The Jungian analyst helps the person to differentiate and recognize the components of the psyche, which is a prerequisite to harmonizing them.

To Jung, the spiritual need must be satisfied, which usually happens during middle age when many of the components of the psyche have been discovered. Religion, to Jung, was a major vehicle in the journey toward self-actualization. If Freud was pessimistic about human destiny, Jung was optimistic. However, Jung's optimism was contingent upon humans coming to grips with their unconscious mind; if this is not accomplished, the projections of the unconscious mind will continue to cause gross irrationality in our lives and perhaps even a third world war. Jung's theory matches the complexity of our times; it is no wonder that its popularity is increasing.

EVALUATION

Jung's theory, like all the theories covered in this text, has not gone uncriticized. His antiscientific attitude prompted the most severe criticism. He has been justly accused of being friendly toward occultism, spirituality, mysticism, and religion, all areas thought by many to emphasize the irrational. Jung felt that he was vastly misunderstood on this issue, however, and insisted that studying these topics in no way implied a belief in them. Rather, he studied them in order to gain information about the collective unconscious. He, like many contemporary personality theorists, believed that if the scientific method could not be applied to the study of a complex topic, it should be the method that is discarded, not the topic. He felt that personality was an example of such a topic.

Jung's theory also has been attacked for being incomprehensible, unclear, inconsistent, and even contradictory. Also, his concept of self-actualization has been labeled elitist, since it is possible for only highly intelligent, well educated persons with an abundance of leisure time to arrive at the degree of individuation necessary for self-actualization. This omits the vast majority of people.

On the positive side, Jung's theory can be credited with many original concepts in personality theory. His was the first theory to discuss the process of self-actualization which is currently so popular among personality theorists (for example, Rogers and Maslow). His was the first theory to emphasize the importance of the future in determining human behavior. Related to this was his stress on the importance of purpose and meaning to one's life. This is a theme we now see emphasized in the existential-humanistic theories of personality. Jung's theory was optimistic about human destiny rather than pessimistic, as Freud's theory was. Jung's theory stressed the attainment of selfhood as a master motive in human behavior, rather than the sexual impulses and early experiences that Freud had stressed.

Somehow Jung's theory creates an image of the psyche that is believable in light of the times in which we live. He leaves us with an image of a psyche that is pushed by the past, pulled by the future, and is attempting to make sense out of itself in the present. It is a complex psyche struggling to give expression to its various components. Such a psyche would cause a wide range of behaviors and interests, some of which might even be considered bizarre.

SUMMARY

Biographical information portrays Jung as a very complex person who had had a troubled childhood. He originally intended to study archaeology, but a dream caused him instead to study psychology. Although when they first met Freud and Jung became close friends, theoretical differences between the two eventually caused them to terminate their association. A major disagreement between the two was over the nature of the libido. Freud saw it as mainly sexual energy, and Jung saw it as general energy that could be directed at various problems as they arose, whether they be sexual or spiritual.

Jung accepted the principle of equivalence, which states that the psyche consists of a finite amount of energy; the principle of entropy, which states that there is a constant tendency toward equalization of psychic energy among the various components of the psyche; and the principle of opposites, which states that for every mental trait that exists, its opposite also exists. According to Jung, the psyche contains an ego (similar to Freud's concept of ego), a personal unconscious consisting mainly of repressed experiences from one's life, and the collective unconscious, which is a racial memory. The personal unconscious contains clusters of interrelated thoughts called complexes, which Jung used his word-association test to study. The collective unconscious is made up of archetypes, which are inherited predispositions to respond emotionally to certain categories of experiences. Archetypes result from common human experiences through the eons. The more highly developed archetypes include the persona, which is the tendency to select only a part of ourselves to offer to the public; the anima, which is the female component of the male psyche; the animus, which is the male component of the female psyche; the shadow, which is the part of our psyche that we share with lower animals; and the self, which is each person's goal of psychic wholeness and harmony.

Jung postulated two major attitudes that a psyche could possess, introversion and extroversion. The introvert tends to be inwardly oriented, whereas the extrovert tends to be externally oriented. In addition to the attitudes, Jung discussed four functions of thought: sensing, which detects the presence of things; thinking, which tells us what a thing is; feeling, which tells us whether a thing is acceptable or unacceptable; and intuition, which allows us to make guesses about things in the absence of factual information. The thinking and feeling functions are rational, and the sensation and intuition functions are irrational. By combining the two attitudes and the four functions, a description of eight different types of people is possible: a thinking extrovert, a feeling extrovert, a sensing extrovert, and intuiting extrovert, a thinking introvert, a feeling introvert, a sensing introvert, and an intuiting introvert.

Three stages of development were discussed: childhood (from birth to adolescence), during which time the skills necessary for survival are learned, young adulthood (adolescence to about forty years old), when a person typically learns a vocation, gets married, and raises children, middle-age (from about forty years of age to the later years), which was considered by Jung the most important time of life because philosophical and spiritual values are stressed and the meaning of life is sought. Growth toward a greater understanding of one's psyche is called progression; backward growth is called regression. Jung used the term individuation to describe the tendency to become increasingly aware of the many components of the psyche. The transcendent function was the tendency to harmonize the various components of the psyche once they had been discovered. The self refers to a fully integrated psyche and is symbolized by a mandala.

Jung accepted both causality, which states that what we do is determined by our past, and teleology, which states that what we do is determined by our interpretation of the future. In addition, he accepted synchronicity or meaningful coincidence as a major influence in a person's life. The main function of dreams, according to Jung, was to compensate for an unevenly developed psyche by giving expression to those portions of the psyche that are unable to manifest themselves more directly.

Jung's view of human nature was much more optimistic than Freud's. Jung viewed humans as largely future-oriented with an innate tendency toward self-actualiaztion. In addition, each person has more or less the same collective unconscious which reflects common human experiences throughout our evolutionary past.

Discussion Questions

1. Describe the rise and fall of the relationship between Jung and Freud.
2. How did Freud and Jung differ in their definition of libido?
3. Explain the principles of equivalence, entropy, and opposites.
4. Describe Jung's use of the word-association test.
5. Describe Jung's concept of the collective unconscious. Be sure

to include in your answer a description of the most fully developed archetypes.

6. List as many opposites in Jung's theory as you can.
7. What does it mean to say that a person is deceived by his or her own persona?
8. In what way can the anima or the animus disrupt relationships with members of the opposite sex? In what way can they facilitate relationships?
9. Differentiate between introversion and extroversion.
10. Describe the four functions of thought.
11. Summarize the stages of human development as seen by Jung.
12. Differentiate between Jung's concepts of progression and regression.
13. Describe one's "life's goal" as Jung saw it, and describe the steps that must be taken to attain it.
14. Differentiate between causality and teleology.
15. Describe Jung's concept of synchronicity, and give examples of it from your own life.
16. Summarize Jung's research techniques.
17. Contrast Jung's method of dream analysis with Freud's.
18. Summarize Jung's view of human nature.
19. Compare and contrast Freud and Jung on each of the following: methodology, the nature of the unconscious mind, motivation, and religion.
20. Using Jung's concept of the collective unconscious, explain the widespread appeal of music and sports.

Glossary

Anima. The female component of the male psyche.

Animus. The male component of the female psyche.

Archetype. An inherited predisposition to respond to certain aspects of the world. All the archetypes taken together make up the collective unconscious.

Attitude. The general orientation the psyche takes when relating to the world. The two basic attitudes are introversion and extroversion.

Causality. The belief that a person's personality can be explained in terms of past experiences.

Childhood. The stage of development that lasts from birth to adolescence, during which time libidinal energy is invested in such things as learning the basic skills necessary for survival and sex.

Collective Unconscious. The inherited predispositions that humans have to respond to certain events. These predispositions come from the universal experiences humans have had throughout their evolutionary past. For example, since all humans have had mothers, we are born with the tendency to respond to the general concept of mother. What is inherited is a sensitivity to certain categories of experience rather than specific responses to those categories.

Complex. A set of interrelated ideas which are highly valued and which exist in the personal unconscious. A person with a power complex would spend a disproportionate amount of time and energy accumulating personal power.

Ego. For Jung, the ego is everything of which we are conscious and entails performing the functions related to everyday life.

Extroversion. The tendency to be externally oriented, confident, outgoing, and gregarious.

Feeling. The function of thought that determines whether a thing is acceptable or unacceptable.

Functions of Thought. Determines how a person perceives the world and deals with information and experience. The four functions of thought are sensing, thinking, feeling, and intuiting.

Individuation. The process of becoming aware of the various components of the psyche.

Inflation of the Persona. A condition that exists when one's persona is too highly valued.

Introversion. The tendency to be internally oriented, quiet, subjective, and nonsocial.

Intuiting. The function of thought that makes hunches about things when factual information is not available.

Libido. According to Jung, the general life energy that can be directed to any problem that arises, be it biological or spiritual.

Middle-Age. The stage of development that lasts from about forty years of age to the later years of life, during which time libidinal energy is invested in philosophical and spiritual pursuits. According to Jung, this is the most important stage of development.

Persona. That superficial aspect of the psyche which a person displays publicly. It includes the various roles one must play in order to survive in a society.

Personal Unconscious. Consists of material that was once conscious and then repressed or material that was not vivid enough to make a conscious impression at first.

Principle of Entropy. The second law of thermodynamics which states that there is a constant tendency toward the equalization of energy within a system.

Principle of Equivalence. The first law of thermodynamics which states that the amount of energy in a system is fixed and, therefore, if some is removed from one part of the system, it must show up in another part.

Principle of Opposites. The contention that each component of the psyche has an opposite. For example, the rational is the opposite of the irrational; the conscious is the opposite of the unconscious; and introversion is the opposite of extroversion.

Progression. The steady evolution of the psyche toward understanding and harmony.

Psyche. A term that Jung equated with personality.

Regression. The opposite of progression. Occurs when the psyche develops backward instead of forward.

Self. The component of the psyche that attempts to harmonize all other components. Self-actualization is achieved when such a harmony is attained.

Self-Actualization. A state of balance and harmony that is reached when the various components of the psyche are recognized and given expression.

Sensing. The function of thought that detects the presence of things.

Shadow. The deepest part of the collective unconscious which contains all the animalistic urges that characterized our prehuman existence.

Synchronicity. Meaningful coincidence. When two independent events come together in a meaningful way.

Teleology. The belief that a person's personality can be best understood in terms of that person's future goals.

Thinking. The function of thought that tells what a thing is.

Transcendent Function. The continuous tendency of the psyche to achieve harmony and unity among its component parts.

Value. Varies as the amount of libidinal energy invested varies. Those components of the personality that have an abundance of libidinal energy invested in them are valued more than components with less energy invested in them.

Word-Association Test. A research technique that Jung used to explore the complexes within the personal unconscious. It consisted of reading one hundred words one at a time and having a person respond as quickly as possible with a word of his or her own.

Young Adulthood. The stage of development that lasts from adolescence to about forty years of age. During this time libidinal energy is invested in such things as learning a vocation, getting married, raising children, and participating in community life.

PART THREE

SOCIO-CULTURAL PARADIGM

chapter 4

alfred adler

Alfred Adler was born in a suburb of Vienna, Austria on February 17, 1870. His father, Leopold, was a moderately successful grain merchant. Adler grew up under comfortable physical circumstances and was able to enjoy the open spaces, relative freedom from want, and a city (Vienna) that was one of the great cultural centers of Europe. In addition, he was able to share his love of music with his entire family.

In spite of its apparent physical comfort, however, Adler looked upon his childhood as miserable. He thought of himself as undersized and ugly. He was the second of six children and had a severe rivalry with his older brother, who apparently was very athletic and a model child. Adler's mother seemed to prefer his older brother to him, but Adler got along very well with his father.

Adler's views of himself were not without foundation. He was a sickly child who was unable to walk until he was four years old. He suffered from rickets, which prevented him from engaging in any strenuous physical activity. Bottome relates one of Adler's early recollections:

> One of my earliest recollections is of sitting on a bench bandaged up on account of rickets, with my healthy elder brother sitting opposite me. He could run, jump, and move about quite effortlessly, while for me, movement of any sort was a strain and an effort. Everyone went to great pains to help me and my mother and father did all that was in their power to do. (1957, pp. 30–31)

When he was five, he caught pneumonia and almost died. In fact, he heard the doctor say to his parents, "Your boy is lost" (Orgler 1963). This illness, the death of a younger brother in a bed next to his when he was three, and being run over twice himself convinced him that he should become a medical doctor when he grew up.

Contrary to what one may think, Adler remained a friendly, sociable child with a genuine love for people (traits that he retained all his life). His unhappiness continued in school where he began as a poor student (especially in mathematics). One of his teachers counseled his parents to train him as a shoemaker, because he apparently was not qualified for anything else. Eventually, however, Adler became one of the best students in his class.

Adler's childhood ambition was realized when he obtained his medical degree from the University of Vienna (Freud's alma mater) in 1895. He first specialized in opthalmology (diseases of the eye) and later changed to general practice and finally to psychiatry. Two years after his graduation from medical school, he married Raissa Tinofejewa, a rich Russian girl who came to Vienna to study. Raissa was a particularly liberated, domineering woman, a fact that some have seen as causally related to Adler's concept of "masculine protest."

Adler read Freud's book, *The Interpretation of Dreams,* and wrote a paper defending Freud's theoretical position. On the basis of this defense, Adler was invited by Freud to join the Vienna Psychoanalytic Society in 1902. Adler accepted Freud's invitation, thereby becoming one of Freud's earliest colleagues. Adler became president of the Society in 1910, just one year before his official break from the Freudian group. It appears now that joining the group may have been a mistake to begin with, since Adler had little in common with Freud. This incompatibility became increasingly obvious and in 1911, while he was still president of the Vienna Psychoanalytic Society and after a nine-year association with Freud, he resigned from the society. The two men never met again. The differences between Adler and Freud which caused this separation were numerous and will be reviewed at the end of this chapter, but the following quotation from Ernest Jones lists a few of Adler's beliefs that were contrary to Freud's:

> Sexual factors, particularly those of childhood, were reduced to a minimum: a boy's incestuous desire for intimacy with his mother was interpreted as the male wish to conquer a female masquerading as sexual desire. The concepts of repression, infantile sexuality, and even that of the unconscious itself were discarded. . . . (1955, p. 131)

Freud characteristically had a low tolerance for "defectors," and he remained hostile to Adler all his life. Adler was the pigmy in Freud's statement, "I made a pigmy great." Adler said of Freud's theory that it was founded on the mythology of sex and that psychoanalysis was stimulated by the selfishness of a pampered child. Freud, who could not understand the grief a friend was suffering over the death of Adler, said: "I don't understand your sympathy for Adler. For a Jewish boy out of a Viennese suburb a death in Aberdeen is an unheard of career in

Alfred Adler. The Bettmann Archive, Inc.

itself and a proof of how far he had got on. The world really rewarded him richly for his service in having contradicted psychoanalysis" (Scarf 1971, p. 47).

After breaking with the Freudians, Adler and his followers formed a group which they first called the Society of Free Psychoanalytic Research, but they settled on the term "individual psychology" to describe their work. Unfortunately, individual psychology can be easily misunderstood, and there is a section in this chapter which attempts to clarify its meaning.

Adler served as a physician in the Austrian Army during World War I and, following his release, he was asked by the government to open a number of child guidance clinics in Vienna. This was one of Adler's early efforts to apply his theory to the problems of child rearing, education, and other everyday problems. Many of his books, articles, and lectures (of which there were hundreds) were directed either toward teachers or toward the general public. Adler's fame quickly spread and, in Vienna, he was surrounded by many students, friends, and admirers. Freud, disturbed by all this, proclaimed (incorrectly) that Adler's theory was actually nothing but psychoanalytic knowledge, which Adler has labeled his own by changing its terminology.

In 1926, Adler first visited the United States and was warmly received by educators. In 1927, he was appointed lecturer at Columbia University, and in 1932 he became a professor of medical psychology at the Long Island College of Medicine in New York. In 1935, partially because of the Nazi take-over in Europe, Adler made the United States his permanent home. He died on May 28, 1937 in Aberdeen, Scotland while on a lecture tour there.

There was one peak of popularity for Adlerian psychology in 1930 at the fifth International Congress of Individual Psychology in Berlin, which had over two thousand participants (Ansbacher 1977). Another peak seems either to be here or on the way. According to Ansbacher

> The Adlerian movement today numbers several thousand members in the United States, Canada, and European countries, especially Germany. It is composed of psychiatrists, psychologists, social workers, counselors, and educators, as well as lay people who accept the theory and apply the method of Adlerian psychology to family life and personal development. (1977, p. 49)

Adler's theory continues to be promoted today by the *American Journal of Individual Psychology* and by the American Society of Individual Psychology. Heinz and Rowena Ansbacher have summarized many of Adler's ideas in two volumes (1956, 1964). Adler's daughter Alexandra and his son Kurt are practicing Adlerian psychiatrists in New York. Adler was a strong believer in bringing his ideas to nonprofessionals, a task that is currently being perpetuated by Rudolf Dreikurs (1957, 1964).

INDIVIDUAL PSYCHOLOGY

In many ways, Adler's theory of personality is the opposite of Freud's. Whereas Freud saw individuals constantly in conflict with one another and with society, Adler saw them seeking companionship and harmony; whereas Freud ignored questions concerning life's meaning and the effects of future aspirations on one's life, Adler made these questions a central part of his theory; and whereas Freud saw the mind as consisting of different components often in conflict with one another, Adler looked upon the mind as an integrated whole working to help attain the future goals of the individual. So by choosing the term "individual psychology" for his theory, Adler by no means intended to imply that people are selfishly motivated to satisfy their own biological drives. Rather, he meant that although individuals are unique, they are characterized by inner harmony and a striving to cooperate with fellow humans.

Adler's theory is related to humanism because of its concern with the positive relationships among humans. His theory is related to existentialism because of its concern with questions concerning the meaning of human existence. Adler, like the modern existentialists, believed that humans are future-oriented (a belief shared with Jung), at least partially free to determine their own fate, and concerned with the meaning of life.

Adler's theory is related to Gestalt psychology because it emphasizes wholes and not parts. Such statements as "The whole is more than the sum of its parts," and "To dissect is to distort," characterize the beliefs of the Gestalt psychologist, and they are statements with which

Adler would agree. As already mentioned, Adler did not believe the mind to be divided into various components which were constantly warring with each other. Rather, he believed all aspects of the individual to be organized around a common purpose, a purpose that existed in the future and that had to be attained while working harmoniously with others and with society. Clearly, there is little similarity between Adler's individual psychology and Freud's psychoanalysis.

ORGAN INFERIORITY AND COMPENSATION

In 1907, Adler published his now famous essay entitled "Organ Inferiority and Its Physical Compensation." In this essay, Adler put forth the idea that people are especially vulnerable to disease in organs that are less developed or "inferior" to other organs. For example, some individuals are born with weak eyes, others with weak stomachs, others with weak hearts, and still others with damaged limbs. These biological deficiencies cause problems in the person's life because of the stresses put on them by the environment. These organic weaknesses inhibit the person from functioning normally and, therefore, must be dealt with in some way.

Since the body acts as an integrated unit, a person can *compensate* for a weakness either by concentrating on its development or by emphasizing other functions which make up for the weakness. For example, someone with a frail body may work hard to overcome this frailty. Likewise, a blind person may concentrate on the development of auditory skills. In both cases, a biological weakness was compensated.

In some cases, a person may *overcompensate* by converting a biological weakness into a strong point. This was the case when Teddy Roosevelt, who was an extremely frail child, became a hardy outdoorsman, and when Demosthenes overcame a speech impediment to become a great orator. At this early stage in the development of his theory, Adler emphasized biological inferiority, compensation, and overcompensation.

FEELINGS OF INFERIORITY

In 1910 Adler shifted his emphasis from actual physical inferiority to "subjective inferiority," or *feelings of inferiority*. Now, compensation or overcompensation was directed toward either real or imagined inferiorities. At this point in his theorizing, Adler left the biological sciences and entered psychology. Anything that caused inferiority feelings was a worthwhile topic to study.

Adler pointed out that all humans start life with feelings of inferiority, since we all are completely dependent upon adults for our survival. Children feel completely helpless compared to the powerful adults upon whom they depend. This feeling of being weak, impotent, and inferior stimulates in the child an intense desire to seek power, thereby overcoming feelings of inferiority. At this point in the evolution of Adler's theory, he stressed aggression and power as a means of overcoming feelings of inferiority.

Unfortunately, but mainly because of cultural conditions at the time that Adler was writing, he equated power and strength with masculinity and weakness and inferiority with femininity.

> . . . any form of uninhibited aggression, activity, potency, power, and the traits of being brave, free, rich, aggressive or sadistic can be considered masculine. All inhibitions and deficiencies, as well as cowardliness, obedience, poverty, and similar traits, can be considered as feminine. (Adler 1910/1956, p. 47)

At this point in the evolution of Adler's theory, to become more powerful meant to become more masculine and, consequently, less feminine. He referred to this striving to become more masculine as the *masculine protest*. Since both males and females seek to become powerful in order to overcome inferiority feelings, they both attempt to approximate the cultural ideal of masculinity. In other words, both males and females engage in the masculine protest.

Are feelings of inferiority bad? No, says Adler. In fact, to be a human being means to feel inferior. It is a condition common to all humans and, therefore, is not a sign of weakness or abnormality. In fact, such feelings are the primary motivating force behind all personal accomplishments. One feels inferior and is therefore driven to accomplish something. There is a short-lived feeling of success after such an accomplishment, but in light of the accomplishments of others, one again feels inferior and again is motivated to accomplish more, and on it goes without end.

But even though feelings of inferiority act as a stimulus for all positive growth, they also can create neurosis. A person can become overwhelmed by feelings of inferiority, at which point he or she is prevented from accomplishing anything. Under these circumstances, feelings of inferiority act as a barrier rather than as a stimulus for positive accomplishment. Such as person is said to have an *inferiority complex.* According to Adler, all humans experience the feeling of being inferior, but in some it stimulates neurosis and in others it creates a need to succeed. We will have something to say about what makes the difference later in this chapter.

STRIVING FOR SUPERIORITY

Adler's final theoretical position was that it is not more aggression, power, or masculinity that we constantly seek but superiority or perfection. Adler now referred to the striving for superiority as *the funda-*

mental fact of life. Although Adler retained striving for superiority as the master motive in his theory, he later changed from striving for individual superiority to striving for a superior or perfect society.

> It runs parallel to physical growth. It is an intrinsic necessity of life itself. . . . All our functions follow its direction; rightly or wrongly they strive for conquest, surety, increase. The impetus from minus to plus is never-ending. The urge from "below" to "above" never ceases. Whatever premises all our philosophers and psychologists dream of—self-preservation, pleasure principle, equalization—all these are but vague representations, attempts to express the great upward drive. . . . a fundamental category of thought, the structure of our reason, . . . *the fundamental fact of our life.* (Adler 1930, pp. 398–399)

Adler's theory had evolved from the point at which it emphasized compensation for organ inferiority, to that at which subjective inferiority was compensated through aggression and power, to that at which the fundamental fact of life is that all humans strive for superiority-perfection. What is the origin of this striving for perfection? According to Adler, it is innate; it is "built in" all humans at birth.

As we have seen, Adler believed that feelings of inferiority could result in positive growth or in an inferiority complex. Adler also believed that striving for superiority could be beneficial or harmful. If a person concentrates exclusively on his or her own superiority while ignoring the needs of others and of society, he or she may develop a *superiority complex.* A person with a superiority complex tends to be domineering, vain, boastful, arrogant, and to depreciate others. According to Adler, such a person lacks social interest and is, indeed, undesirable.

STYLE OF LIFE

All humans have the same ultimate goal, to strive for superiority, but how superiority is sought depends upon a person's unique circumstances. The means by which a particular individual attempts to gain superiority is called the *style of life.*

> The goal of superiority, with each individual, is personal and unique. It depends upon the meaning he gives to life; and this meaning is not a matter of words. It is built up in his style of life and runs through it like a strange melody of his own creation. . . . Understanding a style of life is similar to understanding the work of a poet. A poet must use words; but his meaning is more than the mere words he uses. The greatest part of his meaning must be guessed at; we must read between the lines. . . . The psychologist must learn to read between the lines; he must learn the art of appreciating life-meanings. (Adler 1931, pp. 57–58)

A person's life style determines which aspects of life are focused on and how; it gives an individual an identity; it determines how problems are solved; it determines what is perceived and what is ignored; and it specifies a person's future goals and how they are to be attained. A healthy life style will allow a person to approximate perfection and to get along harmoniously with others, and will contribute to the advancement of society's goals. A "mistaken" life style is based upon selfishness and is contrary to the aims of society.

When is one's life style formulated? Here there is some agreement between Adler and Freud. Adler said that one's life style was fairly well crystallized by the age of four or five.

Again, what life style a child develops depends on his or her personal circumstances. If a child has a particular reason (real or imagined) for feelings of inferiority, the life style could be aimed at compensating or overcompensating for that inferiority. Or a life style could develop when a child models himself or herself after someone perceived to be highly influential and effective.

> . . . Children look for the strongest person in their environment and make him their model or their goal. It may be the father, or perhaps the mother, for we find that even a boy may be influenced to imitate his mother if she seems the strongest person. . . . Later on, the ideal may become the doctor or the teacher. For the teacher can punish the child and thus he arouses his respect as a strong person. (Adler 1929a/1969, p. 54)

There is a considerable agreement between Adler and learning theorists on the concept of life style. The only difference is that Adler claimed that a life style evolves early in life as a means of overcoming feelings of inferiority or as a means of striving for perfection, whereas the learning theorist (see chapters 13, 14, and 15 for more detail) would say that a person's life style develops because it becomes a reliable source of reward. For example, Hergenhahn said:

> To have a life style is to have an identity and to have an identity is to have a number of interdependent behavior patterns that are successful in reliably bringing about rewarding experiences. For example, if a child's life style begins to develop in the direction of athletic interests, a whole class of events becomes potentially rewarding to him. (1972, p. 128)

In our discussion of Erik Erikson's theory of personality in chapter 6, we will see that he is another theorist who uses the concept of identity to describe the unifying theme that holds an individual's life together. The major difference between Adler and Erikson on this issue is that Adler believed that this identity (life style) developed in early childhood, whereas Erikson believes that it develops sometime during late adolescence.

FICTIONAL FINALISM

In 1911, Hans Vaihinger wrote a book entitled *The Philosophy of "As If."* Vaihinger's contention was that the lives of individuals are guided by fictions made up by them to make life significant and organized. Although these subjective beliefs have no counterpart in reality, they are very useful to the person attempting to grapple with the problems of existence. The person who believes there is a God acts "as if" there really is one and lives as if the soul will be judged on the basis of that behavior. Other fictions by which humans live would include "When I have enough money I will be happy," "To have a good wife and to raise children gives life its meaning," "If only I can get my Ph.D., everything will fall into place," "If I could only write a book, my financial problems would be over."

Adler embraced Vaihinger's thesis enthusiastically and made it an important part of his theory. He made fictional finalism the unifying principle of personality. Everything a person does, said Adler, is related to the final fictional goal. For Adler the future became much more important than the past to understanding human behavior. Adler felt that the idea of a fictional goal guiding behavior freed his theory from the determinism that characterized Freud's theory.

> Individual Psychology insists on the indispensability of finalism for the understanding of all psychological phenomena. Causes, powers, instincts, impulses, and the like cannot serve as explanatory principles. The final goal alone can. Experiences, traumata, sexual development mechanisms cannot yield an explanation, but the perspective in which these are regarded . . . which subordinates all life to the final goal, can do so. (Adler 1956, p. 92)

The concept of fictional finalism, which Adler later called "a guiding self-ideal," gave Adler's theory a strong teleological (future-oriented) component, but it did not ignore the past altogether. Now we can view the individual as pushed by feelings of inferiority or imperfection toward perfection using his or her unique style of life as a means of attaining some future goal.

Adler emphasized that these future goals or ideals were convenient fictions invented to make life more significant than it otherwise would be. Healthy people, according to Adler, change fictions when circumstances warrant it. Neurotic individuals, on the other hand, cling to their fictions at all costs. In other words, according to Adler, healthy individuals use fictional goals or ideals as tools in dealing with life. Life is unbearable without meaning, so they invent meaning. Life is chaotic without a plan for living, so healthy individuals invent such a plan. For healthy individuals, such goals, ideas, or plans are means of living a more effective, constructive life. For the neurotic, the idea that these things are only tools is lost. The goals, ideals, or plans become ends in themselves, rather than means to an end. As such, they are retained even when they have become ineffective in dealing with reality. Thus, for Adler, an important difference between the healthy person and the neurotic is the ease with which a fictional life plan can be dispensed with if circumstances warrant it. The healthy or normal person never loses sight of reality, whereas for neurotic persons the fictional life plan becomes reality.

We are reminded here of why Adler's theory is called individual psychology. Not only does the individual "invent" a life style but also invents the ultimate goal toward which the life style is directed. All of this invention implies a great deal of personal freedom, an implication we will explore further when we discuss "the creative self" later in this chapter.

SOCIAL INTEREST

Adler's earlier theory had been criticized because it portrayed humans as selfishly motivated to strive for personal superiority. With his concept of *social interest*, Adler put such criticism to rest. Social interest was, according to Adler, an innate need of all humans to live in harmony and friendship with others and to aspire toward the development of the perfect society. *The attainment of the perfect society replaced perfection of the individual as the primary motivation.* A well developed social interest relates to almost all aspects of one's life.

> It is almost impossible to exaggerate the value of an increase in social feeling. The mind improves, for intelligence is a communal function. The feeling of worth and value is heightened, giving courage and an optimistic view, and there is a sense of acquiescence in the common advantages and drawbacks of our lot. The individual feels at home in life and feels his existence to be worthwhile just as far as he is useful to others and is overcoming common, instead of private, feelings of inferiority. Not only the ethical nature, but the right attitude in aesthetics, the best understanding of the beautiful and the ugly, will always be founded upon the truest social feeling. (Adler 1956, p. 155)

However, what we inherit, according to Adler, is the *potential* for social interest. If that potential is not realized, the person will live a most unfortunate life. Simply put, those without well-developed social interest are neurotic or even worse than neurotic. "In all human failure, in the waywardness of children, in neurosis and neuropsychosis, in crime, suicide, alcoholism, morphinism, cocainism, in sexual perversion, in fact in all nervous symptoms, we may read lack of proper degree of *social feeling*" (Adler 1930, p. 401).

According to Adler, each individual must solve three major problems in life, all of which require a well developed social interest: (1) *Occupational Tasks.* Through constructive work the person helps to advance society; (2) *Societal Tasks.* This requires cooperation with fellow humans. Adler said: "It was only because man learned to cooperate that the great discovery of the division of labor was made, a discovery which is the chief security for the welfare of mankind" (1933, p. 132); (3) *Love and Marriage Tasks.* The relationship between this task and the continuance of society is clear. Adler said: "On his approach to the other sex and on the fulfillment of his sexual role depends his part in the continuance of mankind" (1956, p. 132).

What determines whether a person will have a well developed social interest or not? Primarily the mother. According to Adler, the first major social situation that the child encounters is in relation to the mother. The mother-child relationship acts as a model for subsequent social relationships with others. If the mother maintains a positive, cooperative atmosphere, the child will tend to develop social interest. If, however, the mother binds the child exclusively to herself, the child will learn to exclude other people from his or her life and will develop a low social interest. For Adler, it is the nature of the mother's early interactions with her child that primarily determine whether or not the child will have a healthy, open attitude toward other people.

It is interesting to note that several major personality theorists have seen the relationship among infant and mother and subsequent adjustments in life. Of course, Freud wrote extensively on this relationship but concentrated mainly on the satisfaction or frustration of the child's biological needs. As we saw above, Adler felt that either the mother instills social interest in her child or the child is likely to become a neurotic adult. Karen Horney, whose theory we will cover in the next chapter, believed that either a child had his or her needs consistently and lovingly satisfied or developed basic anxiety, a prerequisite to adult neuroses. Erik Erikson (chapter 6) feels that if the child does not experience the satisfaction of biological and emotional needs, he or she will develop basic mistrust, which vastly increases the likelihood of subsequent adjustment problems. Adler, Horney, and Erikson all agree that the child's early experiences with biological, emotional, and social need satisfaction relate to the presence or absence of adjustment problems later in life. In addition, all three stress the role of the mother, since she is usually the person who is primarily responsible for the satisfaction or frustration of the child's needs. In fact, in the following quotation we see that Adler felt the mother's job was monumental:

> After she [the mother] has succeeded in connecting the child with herself, her next task is to spread his interest towards his father, . . . the children of the family, to friends, relatives. . . . She must give the child his first experience of a trustworthy fellow being and she must then . . . spread this trust and friendship until it includes the whole of our human society. (1956, p. 373)

In the final version of Adler's theory, a person's life style and fictional goal must take the improvement of society into consideration. If they do not, the person will be neurotic.

MISTAKEN STYLES OF LIFE

Any style of life that is not aimed at socially useful goals is mistaken. We already have encountered two examples, the person who seeks personal superiority (superiority complex) and the person who is so overwhelmed by feelings of inferiority so as to accomplish nothing (inferiority complex). Both individuals lack social interest and, therefore, their life styles are mistaken or incorrect.

Adler delineated four types of people that were labeled according to their degree of social interest. The four types of people are: (1) *The Ruling-Dominant Type,* (2) *The Getting-Leaning Type,* (3) *The Avoiding Type,* and (4) *The Socially Useful Type.* The first type attempts to dominate or rule people. The second type expects everything from others and gets everything he or she can from them. The third type "succeeds" in life by avoiding problems; such a person avoids failure by never attempting anything. The fourth type confronts problems and attempts to solve them in a socially useful way. The first three types have faulty styles of life because they lack proper social interest. Only "the socially useful type" can hope to live a rich, purposeful life.

Where do faulty styles of life originate? Adler says in childhood, at the same time when a healthy style of life originates. Adler described three childhood conditions that tend to create a faulty style of life: *physical inferiority,* which can stimulate compensation or overcompensation which is healthy or can result in an inferiority complex which is unhealthy; *spoiling or pampering,* which makes a child who believes it is up to others to satisfy his or her every need. Such a child is the center of attention and grows up to be selfish with little, if any, social interest; *neglecting,* which causes the child to feel worthless and angry and to look upon everyone with distrust.

Adler looked upon Freud's theory as the creation of a pampered child.

> And, indeed, if we look closely we shall find that the Freudian theory is the consistent psychology of the pampered child, who feels that his instincts must never be denied, who looks on it as unfair that other people should exist, who asks always, "Why should I love my neighbor? Does my neighbor love me?" (Adler 1931, p. 97)

Placing the concept of "mistaken style of life" within the context of learning theory, it simply means that socially approved sources of reward are not available to the child so that he or she is driven to sources of reward that are antisocial in nature.

> If the "normal" ways of obtaining recognition, independence, and other forms of reward are not possible, the child may be driven to uncommon means of gaining an identity (life style). For example, if for some reason the child is not in a position of being rewarded for being scholarly, athletic, humorous, or attractive, he may be driven to a subgroup that will

reward him if he steals, lies, or cheats. Being known as a delinquent is at least being known, and being known (having an individual identity) seems to be important to every child. (Hergenhahn 1972, p. 129)

Erikson (chapter 6) uses the term "negative identity" to describe approximately what Adler called a mistaken style of life.

THE CREATIVE SELF

Hall and Lindzey call Adler's concept of the *Creative Self* his "crowning achievement as a personality theorist." They go on to say: "Here at last was the prime mover, the philosopher's stone, the elixir of life, the first cause of everything human for which Adler had been searching" (1970, p. 127).

With his concept of the creative self, Adler was saying that humans are not simply passive recipients of environmental or genetic influences. Rather, each individual is free to act upon these influences and combine them as he or she sees fit. Thus, no two people are ever the same even if the ingredients of their personalities are similar. We saw earlier that some individuals with physical inferiorities compensate and become socially useful. Others develop an inferiority complex and accomplish nothing. To Adler, the difference is a matter of choice. Thus, heredity and environment provide the raw materials from which personality is formed by the creative self. According to Adler, heredity and environment provide only the "bricks which he uses in his own 'creative' way in building up his attitude toward life. It is his individual way of using these bricks—or in other words, it is his attitude toward life—which determines his relationship to the outside world" (1935/1956, p. 206)

The idea of choosing one's destiny is very compatible with the philosophy of existentialism. With this new component of Adler's theory, we have the healthy person *choosing* a life style and an ultimate goal which agrees with the ideals of society. We see here another basic disagreement with Freud, who felt that human behavior was completely determined by biological and environmental influences and was in no way free.

Adler was the first personality theorist to suggest that human behavior was not completely determined. He insisted that each individual is free to determine his or her life. In other words, life, according to Adler, is open to many possible interpretations, and it is up to the individual to choose the most effective and the most comfortable one. Any given individual will have a certain biological heritage and a certain array of past experiences, but it is the creative self acting upon these variables and interpreting them that will determine the person's personality. This conception of Adler's has turned out to be prophetic, since it is a dominant theme among many modern personality theories.

Adler referred to birth order, first memories, and dreams as the three "entrance gates" to mental life, and he studied them extensively to discover the origins of life style and the individual's approach to problem solving.

Birth Order Adler concentrated his research on the first-born, the second-born, the youngest child, and the only child. The first-born child is the focus of attention until the next child is born, at which time he or she is "dethroned." According to Adler, the loss caused by the birth of a sibling is deeply felt by the first-born, because now the attention of the mother and father must be shared with a rival.

The second-born child has to be extremely ambitious since he or she is constantly attempting to catch up and surpass the older sibling. Of all the birth orders, Adler felt the second-born was the most fortunate (Adler was a second-born child). According to Adler, the second-born child behaves as if in a race, as if someone were a step or two in front, and he or she had to rush to get ahead.

The youngest child is, according to Adler, the second worse position after the first-born. Adler stated that the reason for this:

> . . . generally lies in the way in which all the family spoils them. A spoiled child can never be independent. He loses courage to succeed by his own effort. Youngest children are always ambitious; but the most ambitious children of all are the lazy children. Laziness is a sign of ambition joined with discouragement; ambition so high that the individual sees no hope of realizing it. (1931, p. 151)

The only child is like a first-born child that is never dethroned, at least by a sibling. The shock for the only child usually comes later (for example, in school), upon learning that he or she cannot remain the center of attention.

> Only children are often very sweet and affectionate, and later in life they may develop charming manners in order to appeal to others, as they train themselves in this way, both in early life and later. . . . We do not regard the only child's situation as dangerous, but we find that, in the absence of the best educational methods, very bad results occur which would have been avoided if there had been brothers and sisters. (Adler 1929b/1964, pp. 168–169).

All of these statements on the effects of birth order must be considered only general tendencies, however, since it is always possible for a child to convert a bad situation into a good one, or a good one into a bad one. Also, it should be noted that modern research on the effects of birth order yields equivocal results; some of it supports Adler's theory, but much of it does not.

First Memories Adler felt that one way of discovering the origins of one's life style is to ask an individual to describe earliest recollections.

> There are no "chance memories": out of the incalculable number of impressions which meet an individual, he chooses to remember only those which he feels, however darkly, to have a bearing on his situation. Thus his memories represent his "Story of My Life"; a story he repeats to himself to warn him or comfort him, to keep him concentrated on his goal, and to prepare him by means of past experiences to meet the future with an already tested style of action. (Adler 1931, p. 73)

Adler's own first memories were of his illness at the age of five and his decision to become a doctor. He asked over one hundred medical doctors for their earliest memories, and most of them were of either serious illness or a death in the family.

Dream Analysis Adler agreed with Freud on the importance of dreams but disagreed thoroughly with Freud's interpretation of them. To Adler, dreams provided a vicarious way of dealing with life's problems. They provided a means of trying different solutions to problems and of planning for the future. By analyzing how problems are approached in dreams and how future events are planned, a great deal could be learned about a person's life style.

In addition to these things, Adler also would observe how a client generally behaved. He observed various mannerisms such as how the client walked, spoke, dressed, and where he or she sat; all were regarded as valuable sources of information about the client's life style.

THE GOAL OF PSYCHOTHERAPY

Healthy individuals have well-developed social interest, unhealthy individuals do not. But individuals who have faulty life styles are likely to continue having them since life styles tend to be self-perpetuating. As we saw earlier, a life style focuses a person on one way of looking at things, and this mode of perception persists unless the person runs into major problems or is made to understand his or her life style through education or psychotherapy.

> These foundations of every individual development do not alter, unless perchance some harmful errors of construction are recognized by the subject and corrected. Whoever has not acquired in childhood the necessary degree of social sense, will not have it later in life, except under the above-mentioned special conditions. No amount of bitter experience can change his style of life, *as long as he has not gained understanding*. The whole work of education, cure, and human progress can be furthered only along lines of better comprehension. . . .
>
> Individual psychology considers the essence of therapy to lie in making the patient aware of his lack of cooperative power, and to convince

> him of the origin of this lack in early childhood maladjustments. What passes during this process is no small matter; his power of cooperation is enhanced by collaboration with the doctor. His "inferiority complex" is revealed as erroneous. Courage and optimism are awakened. And the "meaning of life" dawns upon him as the fact that proper meaning must be given to life. (Adler 1930, pp. 403–404)

By using an analysis of birth order, first memories, dreams, and mannerisms, Adlerians trace the development and manifestation of a mistaken life style, one that necessitates therapy because it is ineffective in dealing with life's problems. The therapist, along with the patient, seeks a new life style which contains social interest and therefore will be more functional.

SUMMARY OF THE DIFFERENCES BETWEEN ADLER AND FREUD

The major differences between Adler and Freud can be summarized as follows:

Adler	*Freud*
Emphasized conscious mind	Emphasized unconscious mind
Future goals important source of motivation	Future goals unimportant
Social motives primary	Biological motives primary
Optimistic about human existence	Pessimistic about human existence
Dreams used in problem solving	Dreams used to detect contents of unconscious mind
Humans at least partially free to determine their own personality	Personality completely determined by heredity and environmental factors
Minimized importance of sex	Maximized importance of sex
Goal of therapy to encourage life style incorporating social interest	Goal of therapy to discover repressed early memories

EVALUATION

As mentioned in the introduction to this chapter, Adler's theory is once again becoming popular. It is currently embraced by large numbers of educators, counselors, and therapists and has stimulated a considerable amount of research, for example, on the effects of birth order on personality. In fact, more and more influential people regard Adler's contribution to psychology as even greater than Freud's. For example, Albert Ellis says:

> Alfred Adler, more even than Freud, is probably the true father of modern psychotherapy. Some of the reasons are: He founded ego psychology, which Freudians only recently rediscovered. He was one of the first humanistic psychologists. . . . He stressed holism, goal-seeking, and the enormous importance of values in human thinking, emoting, and acting. He correctly saw that sexual drives and behavior, while having great importance in human affairs, are largely the result rather than the cause of man's non-sexual philosophies. . . .
>
> It is difficult to find any leading therapist today who in some respect does not owe a great debt to the Individual Psychology of Alfred Adler. (1970, p. 11)

It should be pointed out that although Ellis attributes the founding of the ego psychology to Adler, with considerable justification, that honor is usually given to either Anna Freud or Erik Erikson. As we shall see in chapter 6, it was Erikson who really detailed the functions of ego more than anyone else had done previously. It is true, however, that Adler's theory did release the individual from the id and did augment the importance of conscious experience; both of which were directly in accordance with what was later called ego psychology.

Viktor Frankl stated that Adler's opposition to Freud:

> . . . was no less than a Copernican switch. No longer could man be considered as the product, pawn and victim of drives and instincts; on the contrary, drives and instincts form the material that serves man in expression and in action.
>
> Beyond this, Alfred Adler may well be regarded as an existential thinker and as a fore-runner of the existential-psychiatric movement. (1970, p. 12)

Adler's theory was very much in tune with the spirit of the times and no doubt will remain a force in psychology for some time to come.

SUMMARY

Adler spent much of his childhood suffering from a number of physical ailments, feelings of inferiority, and in a losing competition with his older brother. He was one of Freud's earliest associates, but numerous differences caused them to terminate their relationship, which made Freud bitter toward Adler until Adler's death. Adler disputed Freud's notions of repression, infantile sexuality, and the importance of the unconscious. Adler's point of view, called individual psychology, stressed the wholeness and uniqueness of each individual in the attempt to work toward a better society in harmony with other people. Adler's theory is compatible with Gestalt psychology which emphasizes wholeness and interrelatedness, with existentialism which is concerned with the meaning of human existence, and with humanism which stresses the goodness of humans.

In the earliest version of his theory, Adler believed that people were motivated to compensate for actual physical weaknesses by emphasizing those things which would make up for those weaknesses. In some cases, he felt that a person could overcompensate and convert a weakness into a strength. Later, Adler extended his theory to include not only real physical weaknesses but imagined ones as well. Now compensation or overcompensation was directed at the feelings of inferiority resulting from either real or imagined inferiorities. In his early writing, Adler equated inferiority with femininity and superiority with masculinity. The striving to become more masculine in order to become more powerful was called the masculine protest. According to Adler, feeling inferior is not necessarily bad; in fact, such feelings are the motivating force behind all personal accomplishments. Some individuals, however, are not stimulated to growth by their feelings of inferiority. Rather, they are overcome by them, and they become a barrier to personal growth; such individuals are said to have an inferiority complex.

Adler's final theoretical position was that humans are primarily motivated to seek superiority or perfection. However, the superiority sought is compatible with society and not a selfish, individual superiority. A person who selfishly seeks personal superiority while ignoring the needs of other people and of society is said to have a superiority complex. The means by which an individual attempts to gain superiority is called his or her style of life.

Adler believed that individuals must insert meaning into their lives by inventing ideals or fictional goals which give them something for which to live and around which to organize their lives. Such fictions are called fictional finalisms. Healthy individuals use such fictions as tools for living a more significant, effective life. For healthy individuals, these fictions can easily be discarded if circumstances call for it. For neurotics, however, these fictions are confused with reality and therefore are retained at all costs.

Adler theorized that all individuals have an innate need to live in harmony with other people; he called this need social interest. Each person must solve three major problems in life, and each requires a strong social interest: (1) occupational tasks, (2) societal tasks, and (3) love and marriage tasks. Adler believed that the nature of a child's interaction with the mother determined to what extent the child developed social interest. Any life style not characterized by a strong social interest was labeled a mistaken style of life. Three types of people with a mistaken style of life are: the ruling-dominant type, the getting-leaning type, and the avoiding type. The socially useful type has a strong social interest, and therefore his or her life style is not mistaken. Three childhood conditions that can cause a mistaken style of life are: physical inferiority, spoiling or pampering, and neglecting.

Adler did not believe that personality was completely determined by biological inheritance, early experiences, or the environment. He felt that each individual is free to interpret life in any number of ways. The creative self allows us to be what we choose to be. Adler's research methods included the influence of birth order, first memories, and dream analysis. The major goal of psychotherapy was to correct a faulty style of life and to encourage social interest in its place.

Some of the major premises that differentiated Adler's theory from Freud's were Adler's emphasis on the conscious mind, social motives, one's future goals, personal freedom, dreams as aids in problem solving, and his de-emphasis on sexual motivation. In addition, Adler was optimistic about the human condition, whereas Freud was pessimistic.

Adler's theory seems to be increasing in popularity and can be regarded as a forerunner of the modern humanistic-existential personality theories.

Discussion Questions

1. List as many things as you can about Adler's early life that ultimately became part of his theory of personality.
2. Why did Adler call his theory "Individual Psychology"?
3. Trace the evolution of Adler's theory from its concern with organ inferiority to its concern with social interest.
4. Describe Adler's early concept of "masculine protest."
5. Distinguish between feelings of inferiority and an "inferiority complex."
6. Explain why a "superiority complex" exemplifies a mistaken style of life.
7. What is a style of life? Describe in as much detail as you can your own style of life.
8. Discuss Adler's concept of "fictional finalism." List any fictional goals you may have in your life.
9. Discuss Adler's concept of "social interest." Give a few examples of how the concept is used by Adler in this theory.
10. What is a "mistaken style of life"? Give a few examples of how such a style of life can occur.
11. Discuss Adler's concept of the "creative self."
12. Summarize Adler's views on the effects of birth order on personality.
13. Describe your first memories and note their relationship to your style of life. Do the same for a few of your acquaintances.
14. According to Adler, what is the goal of psychotherapy?
15. List the major differences between Adler's theory of personality and Freud's theory.

Glossary

Avoiding Type Person. A person exhibiting the mistaken life style of avoiding the attempt to solve life's problems, thereby escaping possible defeat. Such a person lacks social interest.

Compensation. Making up for a weakness, such as organ inferiority, either by overcoming it through concentrated effort or by emphasizing functions that substitute for the weakness.

Creative Self. The free element of the personality that allows the person to choose between alternative life styles and between fictional goals. It is the differential exercise of this creative power that is mainly responsible for individual differences.

Dream Analysis. Adler felt that dreams provided the dreamer a means of vicariously testing various prolem-solving techniques. Since problem-solving techniques are dictated by one's life style, Adler analyzed dreams in order to study indirectly a person's life style. The supposed meaning of dreams varied greatly from Adler to Freud.

Fictional Finalism. The fictional future goal to which a person aspires. This goal is the end to which the person is aspiring, and his or her life style is the means to that end.

First-Born Child. This child is the focus of attention until the birth of a sibling "dethrones" him or her. The loss felt by the first-born child when the second child is born often creates bitterness that causes problems later in life. Adler considered this to be the most troublesome birth position.

First Memories. Adler's research technique of asking a person to describe earliest recollections. Adler felt that such recollections gave evidence of the origins of one's style of life.

Getting-Leaning Type Person. A person exhibiting the mistaken style of life which expects everything to be given to him or her by others. Such a person lacks social interest.

Individual Psychology. Adler's term to describe his theory. The term "individual" was used to stress his belief that each person is an integrated whole striving to attain future goals and attempting to find meaning in life while working harmoniously with others.

Inferiority Complex. The psychological condition that exists when an individual is overwhelmed by feelings of inferiority to the point at which nothing can be accomplished.

Inferiority Feelings. The feelings that one has of being inferior, whether or not these feelings are justified by real circumstances. Such feelings, according to Adler, can lead either to positive accomplishments or to an inferiority complex.

Masculine Protest. Attempting to become more powerful by being more masculine and thereby less feminine. According to Adler's earlier theorizing, both males and females attempt to gain power by becoming more like the cultural ideal of the male.

mistaken

Mistaken Style of Life. Any style of life that is not aimed at socially useful goals. In other words, any life style not including social interest.

Neglecting. A procedure which causes the child to feel worthless and angry and to look upon everyone with distrust.

Only Child. This child is like a first-born child who was never dethroned. Only children, according to Adler, are often sweet, affectionate, and charming in order to appeal to others. Adler did not consider this birth position nearly as dangerous as the first-born's position.

Organ Inferiority. The condition that exists when some organ of the body does not develop normally. Such a condition can stimulate compensation or overcompensation, which is healthy, or can result in an inferiority complex, which is unhealthy.

3 possible results

Overcompensation. The process by which, through considerable effort, a previous weakness is converted into a strong point. An example would be when a frail child works hard to become an athlete.

Ruling-Dominant Type Person. A person exhibiting the mistaken style of life which dominates and rules people. Such a person lacks social interest.

Second-Born Child. This child is very ambitious since he or she is constantly attempting to catch up and surpass the older sibling. Of all the birth orders, Adler felt that the second-born had the best.

Sibling Rivalry. Competition between children in the same family.

Social Interest. The innate potential to live in harmony and friendship with others and to aspire to the development of a perfect society.

Socially Useful Type Person. A person exhibiting a life style containing a healthy amount of social interest. Such a life style is not "mistaken."

Spoiling or Pampering. Procedures that create a child who believes it is up to others to satisfy his or her needs.

Striving for Superiority. What Adler called "the fundamental fact of life." According to Adler's final theoretical position, it is not the search for the power necessary to overcome feelings of inferiority that motivates humans, rather, it is the constant search for perfection or superiority. However, it was the perfection of society that Adler stressed, rather than individual perfection.

Style of Life. The means by which an individual seeks to gain superiority. The person's life style is the main theme running through his or her life and thus influences almost every thing that person does. Life style can be equated roughly with the term "identity."

Superiority Complex. The psychological condition that exists when a person concentrates too much on his or her own need to succeed while ignoring the needs of others. Such a person tends to be vain, domineering, and arrogant.

Youngest Child. According to Adler, the second worst birth position after the first-born. This child is often spoiled and therefore loses courage to succeed by his or her own efforts.

chapter 5

karen horney

Karen Horney was born Karen Danielson in a small village near Hamburg, Germany on September 16, 1885 (the year that Freud was studying hypnotism with Jean Charcot in Paris). Her father was a Norwegian sea captain and her mother was Dutch. Horney's father, who was seventeen years older than her mother, had a personality considerably different from that of her mother. He was a very religious and quiet man. Her mother, on the other hand. was spirited, attractive, and liberal in her attitudes. Horney recalled her father as a frightening person who belittled her by making derogatory statements about her appearance and intelligence. She also felt that her mother rejected her in favor of her older brother.

When she was twelve years old, Horney was treated by a doctor who so impressed her that she decided then to become a doctor herself. Her father so bitterly opposed the idea of her becoming a medical doctor that her mother left him. In spite of her father's opposition and her own feelings of worthlessness, Horney maintained her aspiration, to become a medical doctor.

In 1909 (the year Freud and Jung gave a series of lectures at Clark University in the United States) when Horney was twenty-four, she married a Berlin lawyer named Oscar Horney, and they had three children. In 1926 she and her husband were divorced.

Horney's lifelong dream of becoming a doctor came true when she entered medical school at the University of Berlin, from which she received her M.D. in 1913. From 1914 to 1918, she received psychoanalytic training at the Berlin Psychoanalytic Institute. She become a practicing psychoanalyst at the age of thirty-three. From 1918 to 1932, she taught at the Berlin

Psychoanalytic Institute, besides having a private practice. During this time, Horney wrote several articles about feminine psychology and about her disagreements with Freud's theory.

In 1932, she accepted an invitation from Franz Alexander to come to the United States and become an associate director of the Chicago Institute for Psychoanalysis. Two years later, she moved to New York where she established a private practice and trained analysts at the New York Psychoanalytic Institute. The differences between her and the traditional Freudians became so great that she gave up her membership in the New York Institute and created her own organization called the American Institute for Psychoanalysis, which she headed until her death on September 14, 1952.

Horney was trained in the Freudian tradition, and all her work was influenced by that training. In fact, while at the Berlin Psychoanalytic Institute, she was psychoanalyzed by Karl Abraham and Hans Sachs, two of the most prominent Freudian analysts of that time. However, as time went on, Horney found it more and more difficult to apply Freudian notions to her work. She completely disagreed with Freud's notions of the Oedipal complex and his division of the mind into the id, ego, and superego. She felt that Freud's theory reflected a different

Karen Horney. Courtesy the Association for the Advancement of Psychoanalysis of the Karen Horney Psychoanalytic Institute and Center.

country and a different time. To state it simply, Horney found that Freud's theory did not fit the problems that people were having during the depression years in the United States. Sexual problems were secondary to a number of other problems that those special environmental conditions had created. Instead of sexual problems, people were worried about losing their jobs and not having enough money to pay the rent, to buy food, or to provide their children with needed medical care.

Horney reasoned that because there are such major differences in the kinds of problems that people experience from one country to another or from one time in history to another, they must be *culturally* determined, rather than biologically determined as Freud had assumed. So, although Horney was trained in the Freudian tradition and although she was deeply influenced by that training, her theory ended up being quite different from Freud's. To Horney, what a person experiences socially determines whether or not he or she will have psychological problems and, if so, what kind they will be. The conflict is caused by environmental conditions, not by opposing components of the mind (id, ego, and superego) as Freud had believed.

As we shall see, Horney did not abandon Freud's theory completely, but her point of view is much more compatible with Adler's than with Freud's.

BASIC HOSTILITY AND BASIC ANXIETY

In her book *The Neurotic Personality of Our Time* (1937), Horney elaborated her contention that neuroses are caused by disturbed human relationships. More specifically, she maintained that the rudiments of neurotic behavior are found in the relationship between parent and child. This is a point of agreement with Freud's theory, since Horney also stressed the importance of early childhood experience to personality development. Horney, however, did not accept Freud's notion of the psychosexual stages of development. Like Adler, Horney believed that the child started life with a feeling of helplessness relative to the powerful parents. She believed that the two basic needs in childhood were *safety* and *satisfaction,* and that the child was completely dependent upon the parents for their satisfaction.

Although each child is in fact helpless and dependent upon the parents during the early years, this need not necessarily create a psychological problem. Horney did not agree with Adler's earlier view that each child feels helpless and inferior and spends the rest of his or her life compensating or overcompensating for this feeling. She felt that the condition of helplessness was a necessary but not a sufficient condition for the development of neurosis. Two things can happen: (1) The parents can demonstrate genuine affection and warmth toward the child, thereby satisfying the need for safety, or (2) the parents can demonstrate indifference, hostility, or even hatred toward the child, thereby frustrating the child's need for safety. The former condition leads to normal development, and the latter condition leads to neurotic development.

Horney called the behavior of parents that undermines a child's security the "basic evil." A sample of such behavior is:

Indifference toward the child
Rejection of the child
Hostility toward the child
Obvious preference for a sibling
Unfair punishment
Ridicule
Humiliation
Erratic behavior
Unkept promises
Isolation of the child from others

A child who is abused by the parents in one or more of the ways above experiences *basic hostility* toward his or her parents. The child is now caught between dependence on the parents and hostility toward them, a most unfortunate situation. Since the child is in no position to change the situation, he or she must repress the hostile feelings toward the parents in order to survive. This repression of the child's basic hostility is motivated by feelings of helplessness, fear, love, or guilt (Horney 1937, p. 85). The child who represses basic hostility because of feelings of helplessness seems to be saying: "I have to repress my hostility because I need you" (Horney 1937, p. 86). The child who represses basic hostility because of fear seems to be saying: "I have to repress my hostility because I am afraid of you" (Horney 1937, p. 86).

In some homes, real love for a child may be lacking, but at least there is some effort to make the child seem wanted. For example, verbal expressions of love and affection may be substituted for real love and affection. The child, according to Horney, has little trouble telling the difference but clings to the "substitute" love because that is all there is. This child says: "I have to repress my hostility for fear of losing love" (Horney 1937, p. 86). In our culture, the child may also repress basic hostility because of having been made to feel guilty about having any negative feelings about his or her parents. Such a child feels sinful or unworthy in feeling hostile toward the parents and therefore represses such feelings.

Unfortunately the feeling of hostility caused by the parents does not remain isolated; instead, it generalizes to the entire world and all the people in it. The child is now convinced that everything and everyone is potentially dangerous. At this point, the child is said to be experiencing *basic anxiety,* one of Horney's most important concepts. Horney described basic anxiety and its relationship to basic hostility as follows:

> The condition that is fostered or brought about by the factors I have mentioned . . . is an insidiously increasing, all-pervading feeling of being lonely and helpless in a hostile world. . . . This attitude as such does not constitute a neurosis but it is the nutritive soil out of which a definite neurosis may develop at any time. Because of the fundamental role this attitude plays in neuroses I have given it a special designation: the basic anxiety; it is inseparably interwoven with a basic hostility. (1937, p. 89)

About basic anxiety and the conditions that cause it, Horney stated that it is:

> . . . the feeling a child has of being isolated and helpless in a potentially hostile world. A wide range of adverse factors in the environment can produce this insecurity in a child: direct or indirect domination, indifference, erratic behavior, lack of respect for the child's individual needs, lack of real guidance, disparaging attitudes, too much admiration or the absence of it, lack of reliable warmth, having to take sides in parental disagreements, too much or too little responsibility, overprotection, isolation from other children, injustice, discrimination, unkept promises, hostile atmosphere, and so on and so on. (1945, p. 41)

According to Horney, the origins of neurotic behavior are to be found in parent-child relationships. If the child experiences love and warmth, he or she will feel secure and probably develop normally. In fact, Horney felt that if a child were truly loved, he or she could survive a variety of abuses, such as periodic beatings and premature sexual experiences, without ill effects. If, however, the child did not feel loved, there would be hostility toward the parents, and this hostility will eventually be projected onto everything and everyone and become basic anxiety. According to Horney, a child with basic anxiety is well on the way to becoming a neurotic adult.

ADJUSTMENTS TO BASIC ANXIETY

Since basic anxiety causes the feelings of helplessness and fear, the person experiencing it must find ways to keep it to a minimum. Originally, Horney (1942) described ten strategies for minimizing basic anxiety, which she called neurotic trends or neurotic needs. As you read through these neurotic needs, you will note that they are needs that almost everyone has and that is an important point. The normal person, in fact, has many or all of these needs and pursues their satisfaction freely. In other words, when the need for affection arises, one attempts to satisfy it. When the need for personal admiration arises, one attempts to satisfy that need, and so forth. The neurotic person, however, does not pass easily from one need to another as conditions change. Rather, the neurotic focuses on one of the needs to the exclusion of all the others. The neurotic makes one of these needs the focal point of life. Unlike the normal person, the neurotic person's approach to satisfying one of these needs is all out of proportion to reality, disproportionate in intensity, and indiscriminate in application, and when the need goes unsatisfied, it stimulates intense anxiety. "If it is affection that a person must have, he must receive it from friend and enemy, from employer and bootblack" (Horney 1942, p. 41).

The ten neurotic trends or needs are (Horney 1942, pp. 54–60):

1. *The Neurotic Need for Affection and Approval.*
   Such an individual lives to be loved and admired by others.
2. *The Neurotic Need for a Partner Who Will Run One's Life.*
   Such an individual needs to be affiliated with someone who will protect him or her from all danger and fulfill all his or her needs.
3. *The Neurotic Need to Live One's Own Life within Narrow Limits.*
   Such a person is very conservative, avoiding defeat by attempting very little.
4. *The Neurotic Need for Power.*
   Such a person glorifies strength and despises weakness.
5. *The Neurotic Need to Exploit Others.*
   Such a person dreads being taken advantage of by others but thinks nothing of taking advantage of them.
6. *The Neurotic Need for Social Recognition.*
   Such a person lives to be recognized, for example, to have his or her name in the newspaper. The highest goal is to gain prestige.
7. *The Neurotic Need for Personal Admiration.*
   Such a person lives to be flattered and complimented. This person wants others to see him in accordance with the idealized image he has of himself.
8. *The Neurotic Need for Ambition and Personal Achievement.*
   Such a person has an intense interest in becoming famous, rich, or important, regardless of the consequences.
9. *The Neurotic Need for Self-sufficiency and Independence.*
   Such a person goes to great extremes to avoid being obligated to anyone and does not want to be tied down to anything or anyone. Enslavement is to be avoided at all costs.
10. *The Neurotic Need for Perfection and Unassailability.*
    Such a person attempts to be flawless because of hypersensitivity to criticism.

Again, normal people experience most, if not all of the above needs, and when they do, deal with them in proper perspective. For example, normal people's need for power is not intense enough to cause a conflict with other needs, such as the need for affection. Normal people are in a position of satisfying all their needs because they do not have an intense emotional investment in any one of them. The neurotic, on the other hand, has made *one* of the needs "a way of life." The neurotic's whole life is spent attempting to satisfy just one of the needs at the expense of all the others. Because it is important that many of the other needs be satisfied, the neurotic is locked into a "vicious circle." The more the one "neurotic need" is emphasized as a means of coping with basic anxiety, the more other important needs go unsatisfied. The more these other needs go unsatisfied, the more basic anxiety the neurotic feels, and the more anxious this person feels, the deeper he or she burrows into the single strategy in order to cope with the anxiety. And on it goes.

MOVING TOWARD, AGAINST OR AWAY FROM OTHER PEOPLE

In her book, *Our Inner Conflicts* (1945), Horney summarized her list of ten neurotic needs into three general categories. Each of the three categories described the neurotic's adjustment to other people. These three categories of adjustment are considered by many to be Horney's most significant contribution to personality theory.

Moving toward People This adjustment pattern includes the neurotic needs for affection and approval, for a dominant partner to control one's life and to live one's life within narrow limits. This person, whom Horney called *the compliant type* seems to say, "If I give in I shall not be hurt" (Horney 1937, p. 97).

> In sum, this type needs to be liked, wanted, desired, loved; to feel accepted, welcomed, approved of, appreciated; to be needed, to be of importance to others, especially to one particular person; to be helped, protected, taken care of, guided. (Horney 1945, p. 51)

It should be noted that like the ten neurotic needs, these adjustments to other people also are based on basic anxiety, which is based on basic hostility. So, although a person may adjust to basic anxiety by moving toward people and by apparently seeking love and affection, the person still is basically hostile. Thus, the compliant person's friendliness is superficial and is based on repressed aggressiveness.

Moving against People In most ways, this person is the opposite of the compliant type. This adjustment pattern combines the neurotic needs for power, for exploitation of others, for prestige, and for personal achievement. This person, whom Horney called *the hostile type* seems to say, "If I have power, no one can hurt me" (Horney 1937, p. 98).

> Any situation or relationship is looked at from the standpoint of "What can I get out of it?"—whether it has to do with money, prestige, contacts, or ideas. The person himself is consciously or semiconsciously convinced that everyone acts this way, and so what counts is to do it more efficiently than the rest. (Horney 1945, p. 65)

The hostile type is capable of acting polite and friendly, but it is always a means to an end. The origin of this adjustment technique is the same as for the compliant type, basic anxiety which was originally based on feelings of insecurity.

Moving away from People This adjustment pattern includes the neurotic needs for self-sufficiency, independence, perfection, and unassailability. This person whom Horney called *the detached type* seems to be saying, "If I withdraw, nothing can hurt me" (Horney 1937, p. 99).

> What is crucial is their inner need to put emotional distance between themselves and others. More accurately, it is their conscious and unconscious determination not to get emotionally involved with others in any way, whether in love, fight, co-operation, or competition. They draw around themselves a kind of magic circle which no one may penetrate. (Horney 1945, p. 75)

The relationship between the ten neurotic needs and the three major adjustment patterns to other people is summarized in Figure 5–1. As with the ten neurotic needs, the normal person utilizes all three adjustments to other people, depending upon which one is appropriate at the time. Neurotic individuals cannot. They emphasize one of the three adjustments at the expense of the other two. This causes further anxiety, since all humans at various times need to be aggressive, to be compliant, and to be detached or withdrawn. The lopsided development of the neurotic causes further anxiety, which causes further lopsided development. Thus we have the vicious circle again.

It should be noted that the three adjustment patterns are basically incompatible. For example, one cannot move toward people and away from people at the same time. For both the neurotic and the normal person, the three adjustment patterns are in conflict with each other. For the normal person, however, the conflict is not as emotionally charged as it is for the neurotic. Therefore, the normal person has much greater flexibility, being able to move from one adjustment mode to another as conditions change. The neurotic person must meet all of life's problems utilizing only one of the three adjustment patterns whether that pattern is appropriate or not. It follows that the neurotic person is far less flexible and is therefore less effective in dealing with life's problems than the normal person is.

THE RELATIONSHIP BETWEEN THE REAL SELF AND THE IDEAL SELF

For everyone there is a difference between the *real self* and the *ideal self.* The real self includes those things that are true about us at any particular time. The ideal self reflects what we would like to become. For normal people, the ideal self is a goal that they would like to reach in the future; it is something around which they can organize their lives and

"Solutions" to Neurotic Conflict

Self-Effacing Solution: *Love* *"Moving Toward" (Compliance)*	*Expansive Solution:* *Mastery* *"Moving Against" (Aggression)*	*Resignation Solution:* *Freedom* *"Moving Away" (Detachment)*
Need for: 1. Affection and approval 2. Partner to take control 3. Restriction of life to narrow borders *"If you love me, you will not hurt me."*	Need for: 4. Power and omnipotence and perfection 5. Exploitation of others 6. Social recognition and prestige 7. Personal admiration 8. Personal achievement *"If I have power, no one can hurt me."*	Need for: 3. Restriction of life to narrow borders 9. Self-sufficiency 10. Perfection and unassailability *"If I withdraw, nothing can hurt me."*
Identification with the despised real self	Identification with the ideal self	Vacillation between despised real self and ideal self

Figure 5–1 The relationship between the three major adjustment techniques and the ten neurotic needs. (From Monte 1977, p. 226.) Based on Horney, 1945, chaps. 3, 4, 5; 1942, chap. 2; and 1950, chap. 3.

to which they can aspire. For the normal person, the real self and the ideal self are always closely related and not too far apart. The normal person seems to be saying, "Based upon where I am now and what I am now, this is where I can reasonably hope to be in the future." For such an individual, as the real self changes, as it inevitably must, the idealized self also changes. Also, as ideals are attained new ones replace the old. For the normal person, then, aspirations are realistic and dynamic.

For the neurotic person, according to Horney, the relationship between the real self and the ideal self is a problem. In the first place, the neurotic's impression of the real self is distorted. These people's whole lives have been based on the assumption that the real self is lowly and despicable; why else would they have experienced the abuse suffered as children? So, for the neurotic, the ideal self becomes more of an escape from the real self than a realistic extension of it. For the neurotic, the ideal self is a wish instead of reality. For the neurotic, the idealized self is an unrealistic, immutable dream.

When one's life is directed to an unrealistic ideal self image, one is driven by what *should be*, rather than what is. Horney refers to this as the *tyranny of the should:*

> Forget about the disgraceful creature you actually are; this is how you should be; and to be this idealized self is all that matters. You should be able to endure everything, to understand everything, to like everybody, to be always productive—to mention only a few of these inner dictates. Since they are inexorable, I call them "the tyranny of the should." (1950, pp. 64–65)

Horney goes on to specify a number of the "shoulds" governing the life of the person whose real self has been displaced by an unrealistic idealized self:

> He should be the utmost of honesty, generosity, considerateness, justice, dignity, courage, unselfishness. He should be the perfect lover, husband, teacher. He should be able to endure everything, should like everybody, should love his parents, his wife, his country; or, he should not be attached to anything or anybody, nothing should matter to him, he should never feel hurt, and he should always be serene and unruffled. He should always enjoy life; or, he should be above pleasure and enjoyment. He should be spontaneous; he should always control his feelings. He should know, understand, and foresee everything. He should be able to solve every problem of his own, or of others, in no time. He should be able to overcome every difficulty of his as soon as he sees it. He should never be tired or fall ill. He should always be able to find a job. He should be able to do things in one hour which can only be done in two or three hours. (1950, p. 65)

The neurotic is locked into the illusion of the ideal self, an illusion that does not reflect reality and one that tends to be unchanging. The more intensely the neurotic chases this ideal, the further the individual is driven from the real self and the more intense the neurosis becomes. For such an individual, the only hope is a well-trained analyst.

Normal people, on the other hand, have dreams but they are realistic and changeable. Normal people experience both success and failure and both influence changes in their aspirations. Neurotic people experience mainly failure since their ideals tend to be incompatible with their real selves.

SECONDARY ADJUSTMENT TECHNIQUES

Horney referred to the tendencies to move toward, against, or away from people as major adjustment techniques, since one of the three tends to penetrate an individual's entire life. The eight adjustment techniques were called secondary because they tended to be used on a more limited basis than the tendencies relative to people were.

Blind Spots This is denying or ignoring certain aspects of experience, because they are not in accordance with one's idealized self-image. For example, if one looks upon oneself as extremely intelligent, one will tend to overlook experiences that suggest he is stupid, as when a student challenges the wisdom of a teacher. Often teachers cannot even recall such incidents at the end of the day. This is not to say the student was wrong; it is just that, in this case, the experience was not in accordance with the teacher's idealized self-image, and thus the teacher was blinded to it. This is compatible with Freud's notion of repression in which something that is contrary to the values of the superego is denied conscious expression because it would be disruptive to one's value structure. Blind spots, like repression, allow one to maintain the consistency of one's self-image by ignoring experiences not compatible with it.

Compartmentalization This is dividing one's life up into various components with different rules applying to them. For example, one set of rules applies to one's family life and another set to one's business life. Thus, one can act in accordance with Christian principles at home and be ruthless in one's business dealings. A teacher can be violently opposed to cheating in the classroom and yet not be opposed to cheating in golf or at bridge. A student may say no to an alcoholic beverage offered by an uncle at home but say yes when one is offered by a roommate at college. One sees no conflict here since "the situations are different."

Rationalization Horney saw rationalization mostly as Freud did. It is giving "good" (but faulty) reasons to excuse conduct that otherwise would be anxiety provoking.

Excessive Self-control This is guarding against anxiety by controlling any expression of emotion. The goal here is to maintain rigid self-control at all costs. This secondary adjustment technique is very close to the neurotic need to live one's life within narrow limits.

Externalization This is similar to Freud's ego defense mechanism of projection but is much more general. Externalization is the feeling that all the major influences in one's life are external to the self. The person is no longer responsible for himself or herself, because "it" or "they" are causing that person's actions. The person seems to be saying, "How can you hold me responsible? How can you attribute that failure to me?" or "Why should I feel humiliated when it was those out there that made me do what I did?" Some individuals seem to be incapable of accepting criticism. If they fail a test, it is because they were tired, the book was misleading, the teacher was confusing, or the test was replete with "trick questions." If they lose a job it is because they were discriminated against, someone was out to get them, or they belonged to the wrong religion or political party. The causes of all the unfortunate things that happen to them is "out there," not inside of themselves. Such individuals are said to be externalizing.

Arbitrary Rightness To the person utilizing this adjustment technique, the worst thing a person can be is indecisive or ambiguous. When issues arise that have no clear solution one way or the other, the person arbitrarily chooses one solution, thereby ending debate. An example would be when a mother says "You're not going out Friday night and that's the end of it." A person using this adjustment will arrive at a position and when doing so all debate ends. The position the person takes becomes the truth and therefore cannot be challenged. The person no longer needs to worry about what is right and wrong or what is certain and uncertain.

Elusiveness This technique is the opposite to arbitrary rightness. The elusive person never makes a decision about anything. If one is never committed to anything, one can never be wrong, and if one is never wrong, one can never be criticized. If a person decides to go to college and fails, there is no excuse. If, however, the decision to go to college is postponed because of lack of money, wanting to travel, wanting to get married, or just wanting to experience "the real world," one has at least delayed potential failure.

Cynicism Whereas the elusive person believes that going to college is important but postpones the decision to do so, the cynic does not believe in the value of a college education. In fact, cynics do not believe in anything. They take pleasure in pointing out the meaninglessness of the beliefs of others. Horney believed that this technique probably grew out of repeated failures with previous beliefs. By not believing anything, cynics are immune to the disappointment that comes from being committed to something that is shown to be false. Also, they are spared the difficult task of arriving at their own system of beliefs. They simply say *nothing* is worth believing.

Again, the difference between normal people and neurotics is one of degree. Normal people will undoubtedly use each of these secondary adjustment techniques at one time or another. Neurotics, however, will *overuse* one or more of them, thus reducing their flexibility and efficiency in solving life's inevitable problems.

THE GOAL OF PSYCHOTHERAPY - create a realistic relationship between real and ideal self.

To Horney, all therapy was self-therapy since no changes could take place without the involvement of the client. The goal of therapy, according to Horney, is to create a realistic relationship between the real self and the ideal self; to make the clients accept themselves for what they really are and thus develop realistic goals for the future. Such a process releases people from the "tyranny of the shoulds" and allows them to experience the successes and failures of normal people. Horney was optimistic about the human ability to change. Human interactions caused the problem, she said, and human interactions could solve the problem. On this issue she was in direct conflict with Freud.

> Freud's pessimism as regards neuroses and their treatment arose from the depths of his disbelief in human goodness and human growth. Man, he postulated, is doomed to suffer or to destroy. . . . My own belief is that man has the capacity as well as the desire to develop his potentialities and become a decent human being . . . I believe that man can change and go on changing as long as he lives. (Horney 1945, p. 19)

Although Horney looked upon the early childhood years as crucial to stimulating either normal or neurotic development, she believed the effects of these experiences to be reversible. According to Horney, change, even major change, is possible throughout one's life.

In her book *Self-analysis* (1942), Horney expressed the belief that people can go a long way in solving their own problems. After all, she asked, "How did humans ever solve their emotional problems before psychotherapy was available?" Her point is that obviously many people do not have emotional problems. Somehow, they have learned to solve problems, to minimize conflict, to maintain a reasonable relationship between their real and ideal self, and to embrace life with spontaneity. The role of the therapist is to help the neurotic learn to respond in these ways and to go on acting in these ways after therapy is terminated. By self-analysis, Horney meant the analysis of one's own life; she did not mean that all people are equipped to solve deep emotional problems in either themselves or in others. For example, severely neurotic people are not in a position to solve their own problems, and attempts to do so may do more harm than good.

A COMPARISON OF HORNEY AND FREUD

Early Childhood Experience Both Freud and Horney felt that early childhood experiences were extremely important. The reasons that these experiences were important were different for the two, however. Freud believed that there were universal stages of development, and fixation at any particular stage strongly influenced one's adult personality. Also, the various cathexes made in one's early life tended to remain intact throughout life. For Horney, it was the child's relationship to the parents that was important, since it was this relationship that determined whether or not the child would develop basic anxiety.

Unconscious Motivation Both Horney and Freud emphasized the importance of unconscious motivation. For Horney, it was repressed hostility which led to basic anxiety, which led to neurosis. Thus, the basis of all neurotic behavior is repressed basic hostility which, of course, is unconscious.

Biological Motivation Freud emphasized biological motivation. To him, all conflicts are derived from attempts to satisfy biological drives. His theory emphasized the sex drive only because it was so difficult to satisfy in modern Western civilization. Horney de-emphasized biological motivation by stressing the importance of the child's need for a feeling of security. Thus, we say that Freud's is a biological theory and Horney's is a social theory.

"Anatomy is Destiny" Horney strongly disagreed with Freud that females were destined to possess certain personality traits like sexual ambivalence, simply because they had a female anatomy. Many of Horney's early papers, written while she was in Germany, were attempts to reinterpret such Freudian notions as the Oedipus complex, penis envy, and castration anxiety. These papers have been compiled in her book *Feminine Psychology* (1967). For example, Horney's explanation of the Oedipus complex:

> . . . If a child, in addition to being dependent on his parents, is grossly or subtly intimidated by them and hence feels that any expression of hostile impulses against them endangers his security, then the existence of such hostile impulses is bound to create anxiety. . . . The resulting picture may look exactly like what Freud describes as the Oedipus Complex: passionate clinging to one parent and jealousy toward the other or toward anyone interfering with the claim of exclusive possession. . . . But the dynamic structure of these attachments is entirely different from what Freud conceives as the Oedipus complex. They are an early manifestation of neurotic conflicts rather than a primarily sexual phenomenon. (1939, pp. 83–84)

Horney said that in her observation men are just as likely to have "womb envy" as women are to have "penis envy." More importantly, however, is the fact that what is supposed to be masculine and what is supposed to be feminine is *culturally* determined rather than *biologically* determined.

Prognosis for Personality Change Freud, of course, felt that personality was formulated early in life, and major changes thereafter were extremely difficult to make. Horney agreed that personality is stongly influenced by early experiences but that it remained changeable throughout life. Thus, she was much more optimistic than Freud. "Our daring to name such high goals rests upon the belief that the human personality can change. It is not only the young child who is pliable. All of us retain the capacity to change, even to change in fundamental ways, as long as we live" (Horney 1945, p. 242).

EVALUATION

Like so many personality theories, it is difficult to offer much "scientific" evidence to support Horney's theory. This should not necessarily be taken as a criticism. A theory can be useful in many different ways. For example, it can act as a guide in the therapeutic process, and Horney's theory has certainly been that.

We see in Horney's theory another beam of light in the darkness. She found that her early training in Germany was not applicable to the problems she encountered in the United States and thus changed her notions. It must be realized that departing from Freudian dogma at that time was no easy matter. In fact, those that did so were excommunicated just as if they had violated religious dogma. Horney, of course, was excommunicated because she dared to contradict the Master. Thanks to Karen Horney's intelligence, courage, and creativity, we now have a theory of personality that illuminates facts missed by all the other theories that preceded hers. For example, her thoughts on feminine psychology were among the first in an area which is so popular today.

SUMMARY

Although Karen Horney was trained in the Freudian tradition, she departed from that tradition in a number of important ways. She stressed the importance of early parent-child relationships in her theory of personality development. If these relationships are positive, warm, and based on genuine love, the child will tend to develop normally. Normal people are flexible and spontaneous, and their goals are tied realistically to their abilities. If, however, parents react to a child with indifference, superficiality, or aggression, the child will feel basic hostility toward the parents, which must be repressed because of the child's feelings of helplessness, dependence, fear, or guilt. The repressed hostility that the child feels for the parent is projected upon the world in general, becoming basic anxiety. Basic anxiety is the feeling of being alone and helpless in a hostile world.

In order to combat basic anxiety, individuals adopt one of three adjustments relative to other people. They either move toward them, against them, or away from them. Normal individuals display all three adjustments toward other people depending on the circumstances. The neurotic's life, however, is dominated by one of the adjustments, and therefore, the other two go unsatisfied, causing greater conflict and anxiety. For neurotics, the real self is displaced by the ideal self, and their lives are governed by a list of unrealistic "shoulds" instead of goals based upon their own experiences.

Besides the major adjustment techniques of moving toward, against, or away from people, Horney also postulated the following secondary adjustment techniques: blind spots, in which inconsistencies in one's life are ignored; compartmentalization, in which one applies different values to different situations; rationalization, in which one gives logical but erroneous explanations for wrongdoings or shortcomings; excessive self-control, in which one minimizes failure by living within a narrow, predictable range of events; externalization, in which one sees failures as having outside causes; arbitrary rightness, in which one takes a stand which becomes equated with truth and therefore cannot be challenged; elusiveness, in which one avoids failure by postponing decisions; and cynicism, in which one believes nothing is worth commitment.

Horney agreed with Freud that much behavior is unconsciously motivated but disagreed with him on the importance of biological motivation. Horney felt the social need for security was much more important than the need for sexual satisfaction.

Just as many psychological problems are caused by culture, so are many of the differences between males and females. Horney felt that many female characteristics that Freud attributed to anatomy should be regarded as culturally determined.

Discussion Questions

1. Explain why Freud's theory of personality is called a biological theory and why Horney's is called a social theory.
2. Differentiate between those childhood experiences that Horney thought conducive to normal development and those she thought conducive to neurotic development.
3. Describe "basic hostility" and "basic anxiety" and explain how the two are related.
4. List a few examples of what Horney called the neurotic needs or

trends, and describe the difference between the normal person's adjustment to these needs and that of the neurotic individual.

5. Summarize the three major adjustment patterns relative to other people. Describe yourself in terms of these patterns; for example, do you use one more than the others and if so, which one?
6. Describe the difference between the real and the ideal self. Explain the difference in the relationship between the real and ideal selves for the normal person versus the neurotic person.
7. List as many differences as you can between neurotic and normal people, according to Horney.
8. Give a brief definition and an example of each of the following secondary adjustment techniques: blind spots, compartmentalization, rationalization, excessive self-control, externalization, arbitrary rightness, elusiveness, and cynicism.
9. Describe the process of psychotherapy as Horney views it.
10. Compare Horney's theory of personality with Freud's theory.

Glossary

Arbitrary Rightness. Exemplified when issues arise that have no clear solution one way or the other, and a person arbitrarily chooses one solution, thereby ending debate.

Basic Anxiety. The psychological state that exists when basic hostility is repressed. It is the general feeling that everything and everyone in the world are potentially dangerous.

Basic Hostility. The feeling that is generated in a child if needs for safety and satisfaction are not consistently and lovingly satisfied by the parents.

Blind Spots. Denying or ignoring certain aspects of experience because they are not in accordance with one's idealized self-image.

Compartmentalization. Dividing one's life up into various components with different rules applying to the different components.

Compliant Type Person. A person who uses "moving toward people" as the major means of reducing basic anxiety.

Cynicism. The strategy in which a person believes in nothing and is therefore immune to the disappointment that comes from being committed to something that is shown to be false.

Detached Type Person. A person who uses "moving away from people" as the major means of reducing basic anxiety.

Elusiveness. Opposite to arbitrary rightness. The elusive person never makes decisions about anything. Without a commitment to anything this person can never be wrong.

Excessive Self-Control. Guarding against anxiety by denying oneself emotional involvement in anything.

no emotional involvement, no anxiety

Externalization. Similar to Freud's ego defense mechanism of projection.

The belief that all the major influences in one's life are external to oneself.

Hostile Type Person. A person who uses "moving against people" as the major means of reducing basic anxiety.

Ideal Self. What a person hopes to become sometime in the future.

Moving against People. A major adjustment to basic anxiety which utilizes the tendency to exploit other people and to gain power over them. Horney referred to the person using this adjustment technique as the hostile type.

Moving away from People. A major adjustment to basic anxiety which utilizes the need to be self-sufficient. Horney referred to the person using this adjustment technique as the detached type.

Moving toward People. A major adjustment to basic anxiety which utilizes the need to be wanted, loved, and protected by other people. Horney referred to the person using this adjustment technique as the compliant type.

Neurotic Need for a Partner Who Will Run One's Life. The attempt to escape basic anxiety by affiliating oneself with a partner who will run one's life.

Neurotic Need for Affection and Approval. The attempt to escape basic anxiety by making love and affection the central theme in one's life.

Neurotic Need for Ambition and Personal Achievement. The attempt to escape basic anxiety by becoming famous, rich, or important.

Neurotic Need to Exploit Others. The attempt to escape basic anxiety by taking advantage of other people.

Neurotic Need for Perfection and Unassailability. The attempt to escape basic anxiety by striving to become flawless.

Neurotic Need for Personal Admiration. The attempt to escape basic anxiety by continuously seeking compliments.

Neurotic Need for Power. The attempt to escape basic anxiety by gaining power over the environment and over other people.

Neurotic Need for Self-Sufficiency and Independence. The attempt to escape basic anxiety by avoiding all obligations.

Neurotic Need for Social Recognition. The attempt to escape basic anxiety by gaining social prestige.

Neurotic Need to Live within Narrow Limits. The attempt to escape basic anxiety by living a very conservative life.

Neurotic Trends. Ten strategies for minimizing basic anxiety. Also called neurotic needs.

Rationalization. Giving "good" but erroneous, reasons to excuse conduct that would otherwise be anxiety provoking. Horney used this term in much the same way that Freud did.

Real Self. Things that are actually true about a person at any given time.

Safety. One of the two childhood needs that must be met if basic hostility and basic anxiety are to be avoided.

Satisfaction. One of two childhood needs that must be met if basic hostility and basic anxiety are to be avoided.

Self-Analysis. The process of self-help that Horney believed people themselves could apply themselves to solve life's many problems, to maintain a reasonable relationship between the real self and the ideal self, and to minimize conflict. She did feel, however, that severe emotional problems needed to be treated by a professional analyst.

Tyranny of the Should. Refers to the fact that when one's ideal self is substituted for the real self, one's behavior is governed by a number of unrealistic "shoulds."

chapter 6

erik erikson

Erik Erikson was born of Danish parents in Frankfurt, Germany in 1902. His father abandoned the home before Erikson was born, and three years later his mother married his pediatrician, Dr. Theodore Homberger. The fact that Dr. Homberger was not Erik's real father was kept a secret throughout his childhood, but he still developed the feeling that somehow he did not belong to his parents and fantasized about being the son of "much better parents." Erikson used his stepfather's surname for many years and even wrote his first articles using the name Erik Homberger. It was only when he became a United States citizen in 1939 that he changed his last name to Erikson.

Erikson's feeling of not belonging to his family was amplified by the fact that both his mother and stepfather were Jewish and he was, because of his Scandinavian heritage, tall with blue eyes and blond hair. In school he was referred to as a Jew, while at his stepfather's temple, he was called a "goy" (the Yiddish word for gentile). Is it any wonder why the concept of "identity crisis" was later to become one of Erikson's most important theoretical concerns?

After graduating from a gymnasium, roughly equivalent to an American high school, he rebelled against his stepfather's desire for him to become a doctor by studying art and roaming freely around Europe. Generally, Erikson was not a good student in school but did have artistic ability.

The year 1927 was a turning point in Erikson's life. In that year, he was invited by an old school friend, Peter Blos, to come to Vienna to work at a small school attended by the children of Freud's patients and friends. He was hired first as an artist, then as a tutor, and finally he was asked by Anna Freud if he would like to be trained as a child analyst. Erikson accepted the offer and received his psychoanalytic training under Anna Freud for which she charged him seven dollars per month. Anna Freud's particular brand of psychoanalytic theory, which differed in several ways from her father's, had a profound influence on Erikson, and in 1964 he showed his appreciation by dedicating his book *Insight and Responsibility* to her.

The situation was perfectly suited to Erikson. He was asked to join a group of people who were considered at that time to be outside the medical establishment. By joining this group of "outcasts," he could maintain his identity as the "outsider." On the other hand, because it was the function of the group to help disturbed people, he could at least indirectly satisfy his stepfather's desire for him to become a medical doctor.

His graduation from the gymnasium, a Montessori diploma, and his training as a child analyst by Anna Freud are the only formal training Erikson ever had. Because Erikson earned no advanced degrees, he is a clear example of Freud's contention that one need not be trained as a medical doctor in order to become a psychoanalyst.

In 1929, Erikson married Joan Serson, a Canadian woman who was also a teacher at the school at which Erikson worked. In 1933, in response to the increasing Nazi threat, the Eriksons (now with two sons) moved first to Denmark and then to Boston, Massachusetts, where he entered private practice as a child analyst.

Besides his private practice, Erikson was a research fellow under the supervision of Henry Murray in the Department of Neuropsychiatry at the Harvard Medical School. Erikson enrolled at Harvard as a Ph.D. candidate in psychology but dropped out of the program within a few months.

Between 1936 and 1939, Erikson held a position in the Department of Psychiatry at the Yale University Medical School where he worked with both normal and emotionally disturbed children. It was also about this time when Erikson came in contact with the anthropologists Ruth Benedict and Margaret Mead, and in 1938 he went on a field trip to the Pine Ridge Reservation in South Dakota to observe the child rearing practices of the Sioux Indians. Anthropological studies such as this one increased Erikson's awareness of the importance of social and cultural variables to personality development, an awareness that ultimately was to permeate his entire theory of personality.

In 1939 Erikson moved to California where he became a research associate at the Institute of Child Welfare at the University of California. By 1942 he was a professor of psychology but lost his professorship in 1950 when he refused to sign a loyalty oath. Later, when the University of California found him "politically reliable," he was offered his job back but refused to accept it because other professors had been dismissed for the same "crime."

Erik Erikson. The Bettmann Archive, Inc.

In 1950, the same year he left the University of California, Erikson published his now famous book, *Childhood and Society,* which strongly emphasized the importance of social and cultural factors to human development. This book also greatly elaborated the functions of the ego, which launched what is now called "ego psychology." We will have much more to say about ego psychology later in this chapter.

Between 1951 and 1960, Erikson lived in Stockbridge, Massachusetts where he was both a senior staff consultant at the Austin-Riggs Center (a treatment center for disturbed adolescents) and a professor in the Department of Psychiatry at the University of Pittsburgh Medical School.

In 1960, Erikson returned to the Harvard Medical School where he was a professor of human development and taught "The Human Life Cycle," an extremely popular undergraduate course.

As we shall see in this chapter, Erikson has made several contributions to psychology. One is the application of his theory of development to the study of major historical figures. Such an endeavor has been labeled *psychohistory.* Thus far, Erikson has analyzed such historical figures as Adolf Hitler, Maxim Gorky, Martin Luther, and Mahatma Gandhi. Erikson's book, *Gandhi's Truth* (1969) was awarded both a Pulitzer Prize and a National Book Award in philosophy and religion.

Throughout most of his writings, Erikson insists that there is a strong relationship between his theory and Freud's, but one gets the impression that this is mostly a tribute to Freud. Although it is true that there are some similarities between the theories of Erikson and Freud, the differences between the two are more important. Erikson's theory, for example, is much more optimistic about the human capacity for positive growth. We will compare Erikson's theory to Freud's throughout this chapter, but for now we will point out one common feature of the theories. Both have transcended the bounds of psychology and have influenced a variety of other fields such as religion, philosophy, sociology, and anthropology.

ANATOMY AND DESTINY

The closest that Erikson comes to traditional Freudian theory is in the chapter "The Theory of Infantile Sexuality" in his book *Childhood and Society*. In this chapter, Erikson summarizes his research on ten, eleven, and twelve year old boys and girls in California. The children were instructed by Erikson to "construct on the table an exciting scene out of an imaginary moving picture" (p. 98). The children were to use toy figures and various-shaped blocks. Much to Erikson's surprise, in over a year and a half, about 150 children constructed about 450 scenes, and not more than about six were scenes from a movie. For example, only a few of the toy figures were given names of actors or actresses. But if the children were not following Erikson's suggestion in creating their scenes, what was guiding their activities? The answer to this question came when Erikson noted that the common themes or elements in the scenes created by boys were quite different from those created by girls.

Erikson observed, for example, that the scenes created by girls typically included an enclosure which sometimes had an elaborate entrance and which contained such things as people and animals. The scenes created by girls tended to be static and peaceful, although often their scenes were interrupted by animals or dangerous men. The scenes created by boys often had high walls around them and had many objects such as high towers or cannons protruding from them. The scenes created by boys also had relatively more people and animals outside the enclosure. The boys' scenes were dynamic and included fantasies about the collapse or downfall of their creation.

Examples of scenes created by boys and girls are shown in Figure 6–1. Erikson concluded that the scenes created by the children were outward manifestations of their genital apparatus. This tendency was so reliable that Erikson was surprised and uneasy when there was a departure from it. For example, Erikson stated:

> One day, a boy arranged . . . a "feminine" scene, with wild animals as intruders, and I felt that uneasiness which I assume often betrays to an experimenter what his innermost expectations are. And, indeed, on departure and already at the door, the boy exclaimed, "There is something wrong here," came back, and with an air of relief arranged the animals along a tangent to the circle of furniture. Only one boy built and left

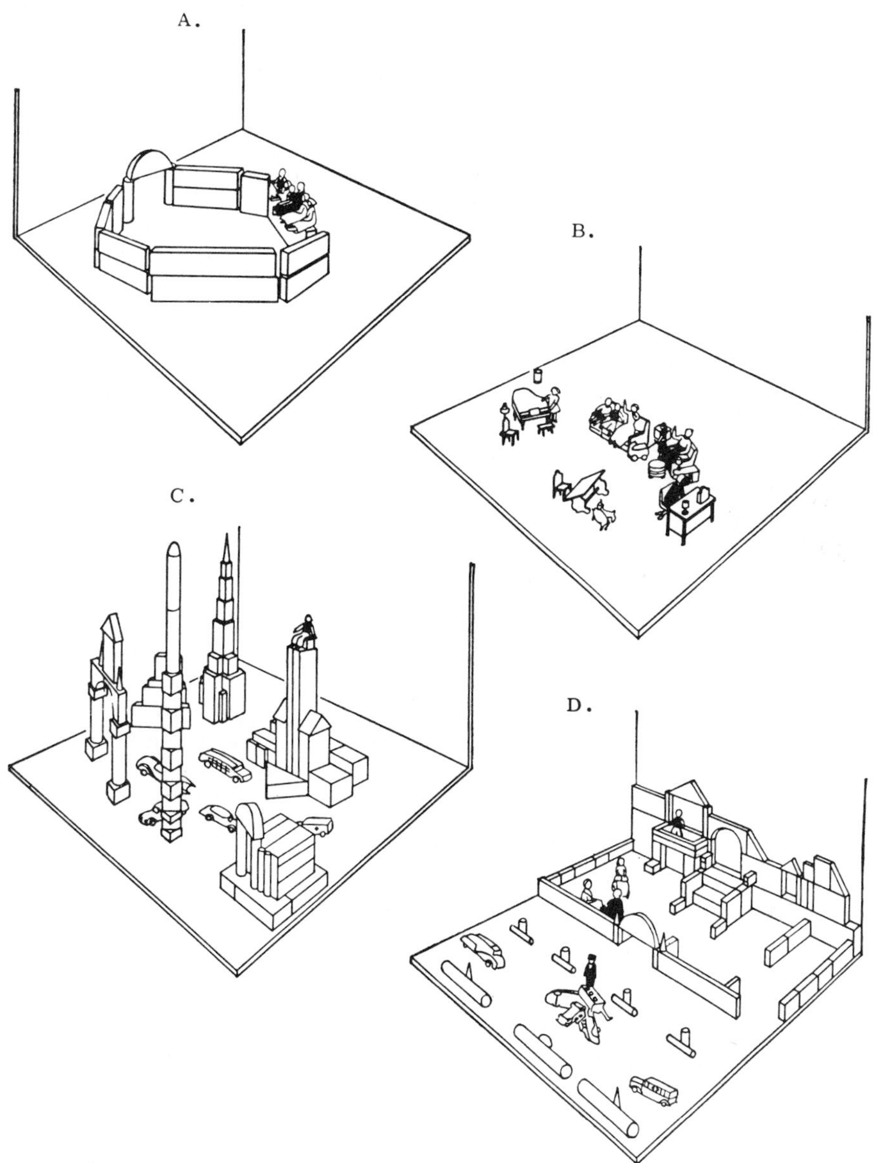

Figure 6–1 A and B exemplify scenes created by girls, and C and D exemplify scenes created by boys. (From Erikson 1963, pp. 100–105.)

> such a configuration, and this twice. He was of obese and effeminate build. As thyroid treatment began to take effect, he built, in his third construction (a year and a half after the first) the highest and most slender of all towers—as was to be expected of a boy. (1963, p. 101)

It should be emphasized, however, that Erikson never said that biology was the *only* factor that determined how a person perceives and acts upon the world. Social factors are also important. We are told by our culture how boys and girls are supposed to act and think, and these cultural dictates will obviously influence our outlook.

> Am I saying, then, that "anatomy is destiny"? Yes, it is destiny, insofar as it determines not only the range and configuration of physiological functioning and its limitations but also, to an extent, personality configurations. The basic modalities of woman's commitment and involvement naturally also reflect the ground plan of her body. . . . [But] a human being, in addition to having a body, is *somebody,* which means an indivisible personality and a defined member of a group. . . . In other words, anatomy, history, and personality are our combined destiny. (Erikson 1968, p. 285)

Needless to say, Erikson's views of male-female differences have not gone uncriticized. One reaction came from Naomi Weisstein (1971) in her article "Psychology Constructs the Female, or the Fantasy Life of the Male Psychologist (with Some Attention to the Fantasies of His Friends, the Male Biologist and the Male Anthropologist)." Weisstein argues that psychology does not really know what either men or women are really like, because it deals with only the cultural stereotypes of both. She then questions the validity of the research that is supposed to demonstrate innate determinates of personality as a function of sex. Lastly, she insists that what has been called biologically determined differences in behavior between the sexes is really better explained as the result of social expectations. She concludes that insofar as there are differences between the sexes, they are the result of cultural expectations and the prejudices of male social scientists.

Erikson reacted to criticism such as this in his essay entitled "Once More the Inner Space" (1975). Essentially he said that (1) psychoanalytic truths are often disturbing and that he can understand people being upset by them, and (2) biology is only one strong determinent of personality; culture is obviously another.

Another important point should be made about Erikson's view of sexual differences. He never says that males are better than females or vice versa. Rather, he says that there are important differences between males and females and that male traits and female traits complement each other. It is true that in some cultures such as ours, the male role has been glorified relative to the female role, but Erikson finds this unfortunate. He feels that both men and women are hurt by current cultural stereotypes. Erikson stated that "only a renewal of social creativity can liberate both men and women from reciprocal roles which, in fact, have exploited both" (1975a, p. 237).

EGO PSYCHOLOGY

Erikson's view of the relationship between biology and personality exemplifies a point on which he was in close agreement with Freud. In this section, we will review the part of Erikson's theory that most disagrees with Freud.

According to Freud, the job of the ego was to find realistic ways of satisfying the impulses of the id while not offending the moral demands of the superego. Clearly, Freud looked upon the ego as operating "in the service of the id" and as the "helpless rider of the id horse." The ego, according to this view, had no needs of its own. The id was the energizer of the entire personality, and everything a person did was ultimately reduced to its demands. As we saw in chapter 2, Freud looked upon enterprises such as art, science, and religion as mere displacements or sublimations of basic idinal desires.

The first shift away from Freud's position came from his daughter Anna in her book *The Ego and the Mechanisms of Defense* (1936). Anna Freud suggested that instead of emphasizing the importance of the id, psychoanalysis should "acquire the fullest possible knowledge of all the three institutions [that is, id, ego, superego] of which we believe the psychic personality to be constituted and to learn what are their relations to one another and to the outside world" (1936, pp. 4–5). Erikson was obviously influenced by his teacher Anna Freud, but he felt that she did not go far enough. Roazen stated:

> Erikson respects Anna Freud's *The Ego and the Mechanisms of Defense* for having conclusively organized the nature of the defensive ego. The problem for Erikson was that Anna Freud had described the ego's functions in terms of warding off quantities of drives, whereas Erikson wanted to go further and extend his reach beyond mere defensiveness to adaptation. (1976, p. 22)

Erikson gave the ego properties and needs of its own. The ego, according to Erikson, may have started out in the service of the id but in the process of serving it, developed its own functions. For example, it was the ego's job to organize one's life and to assure continuous harmony with one's physical and social environment. This conception emphasizes the influence of the ego on healthy growth and adjustment and also as the source of the person's self-awareness and identity. This contrasts sharply with the earlier Freudian view that the ego's sole job was to minimize the id's discomfort. Because Erikson stresses the autonomy of the ego, his theory exemplifies what has come to be called *ego psychology*. Although, as we saw in chapter 4, there are those who credit Alfred Adler with the founding of ego psychology, it is an honor generally given to Erikson since he actually emphasized the term ego in his theory. Adler indeed described behaviors and adjustment patterns that were independent of biological drives (for example, striving for superiority and social interest), but he did not stress the difference between idinal functions and ego functions. Although there is a choice between Adler and Erikson as to who founded ego psychology, more votes are usually given to Erikson than to Adler.

Indeed, Erikson's entire theory can be viewed as a description of how the ego gains or loses strength as a function of developmental experiences. Clearly, the most famous aspects of Erikson's work are his descriptions of the eight developmental stages through which he feels all humans pass and what happens to the ego during each of these stages. It is to this aspect of Erikson's work that we turn next.

THE EIGHT STAGES OF HUMAN DEVELOPMENT

Erikson sees life as consisting of eight stages which stretch from birth to death. The first five stages closely parallel Freud's proposed psychosexual stages of development in the time at which they are supposed to occur. As to what is supposed to occur during these stages, however, there is little agreement between Erikson and Freud. The last three stages are Erikson's own and represent one of his major contributions to psychology.

According to Erikson, the *sequence* of the eight stages is genetically determined and thus is unalterable. Such a genetically determined sequence of development is said to follow the *epigenetic principle,* a term which Erikson borrowed from biology. Erikson describes this principle as follows:

> Whenever we try to understand growth, it is well to remember the *epigenetic principle* which is derived from the growth of organisms *in utero*. Somewhat generalized, this principle states that anything that grows has a ground plan, and that out of this ground plan the parts arise, each part having its special ascendancy, until all parts have arisen to form a functioning whole. (1968, p. 92)

Each stage of development is characterized by a *crisis*. The word crisis is used by Erikson as it is used by medical doctors, that is, to connote an important turning point. Thus, the crisis characterizing each stage of development has a positive resolution and a negative one. A positive resolution contributes to the strengthening of the ego and therefore to greater adaptation. A negative resolution weakens the ego and inhibits adaptation. Furthermore, a positive crisis resolution in one stage increases the likelihood that the crisis characterizing the next stage will be resolved positively. A negative resolution in one stage lowers the probability that the next crisis will be resolved effectively.

Although biology determines when the stages will occur, since the maturational process determines when experiences become possible, it is the *social* environment that determines whether or not the crisis associated with any given stage is resolved positively. For this reason, the stages proposed by Erikson are called *psychosocial* stages of development to contrast them with Freud's *psychosexual* stages.

One last point needs to be made before we list the stages. Erikson does not believe that a solution to a crisis is either completely positive or completely negative. Rather, he says the resolution of a crisis has both positive and negative elements. It is when the *ratio* of positive to negative is higher in favor of the positive that the crisis is said to be resolved positively. We will say more about this in our discussion of the first stage of development, to which we now turn.

1. Basic Trust versus Basic Mistrust Notice that each stage is named for the crisis that it creates. This stage lasts from birth through the first year and corresponds closely to Freud's oral stage of psychosexual development.

This is the time when children are most helpless and thus most dependent on adults. If those caring for infants satisfy their needs in a loving and consistent way, they will develop a feeling of basic trust. If, however, their mothers are rejecting and satisfy their needs in an inconsistent manner, they will develop a feeling of mistrust.

If care is loving and consistent, infants learn that they need not worry about a loving, reliable mother and therefore are not overly disturbed when she leaves their sight.

> The infant's first social achievement, then, is his willingness to let the mother out of sight without undue anxiety or rage, because she has become an inner certainty as well as an outer predictability. Such consistency, continuity, and sameness of experience provide a rudimentary sense of ego identity which depends, I think, on the cognition that there is an inner population of remembered and anticipated sensations and images which are firmly correlated with the outer population of familiar and predictable things and people. (Erikson 1963, p. 247).

The basic trust versus basic mistrust crisis is resolved when the child develops more trust than mistrust. Remember, it is the ratio of the two solutions that is important. A child who trusted everyone and everything would be in trouble. A certain amount of mistrust is healthy and conducive to survival. However, it is the child that has a predominance of trust who has the courage to take risks and who is not overwhelmed by disappointments and setbacks.

Erikson says that when the crisis characterizing a stage is positively resolved, a *virtue* emerges in one's personality. A virtue can be considered something that adds strength to one's ego. In this stage, when the child has more basic trust than basic mistrust, the virtue of *hope* emerges. Erikson defines hope as "the enduring belief in the attainability of fervent wishes, in spite of the dark urges and rages which mark the beginning of existence" (1964, p. 118).

We can say that trusting children dare to hope, a process which is future-oriented, whereas children lacking enough trust cannot hope since they must worry constantly about whether their needs will be satisfied or not and therefore are tied to the present.

2. Autonomy versus Shame and Doubt This stage occurs from about the end of the first year to about the end of the third year and corresponds to Freud's anal stage of psychosexual development.

During this stage, children rapidly develop a wide variety of skills. They learn to walk, climb, push, pull, and talk. More generally, they learn how to hold on and to let go. Not only does this apply to physical objects but to feces and urine as well. In other words, children now can "willfully" decide to do something or not to do it. Thus, children now are engaged in a battle of wills with their parents.

The parents must perform the delicate task of controlling the child's behavior in socially acceptable directions, without injuring the child's sense of self-control or autonomy. In other words, the parents must be reasonably tolerant but still be firm enough to assure behavior that is socially approved. If the parents are overly protective or unjust in their use of punishment, the child will be doubtful and experience shame. "From a sense of self-control without loss of self-esteem comes a lasting sense of good will and pride; from a sense of loss of self-control and of foreign overcontrol comes a lasting propensity for doubt and shame" (Erikson 1963, p. 254).

About shame Erikson said: "Shame supposes that one is completely exposed and conscious of being looked at: in one word, self-conscious. One is visible and not ready to be visible . . . " (1963, p. 252).

If the child develops more autonomy than shame and doubt during this stage, the virtue of *will* emerges. Erikson defined will as: "the unbroken determination to exercise free choice as well as self-restraint, in spite of the unavoidable experience of shame and doubt in infancy" (1964, p. 119).

Notice that the virtues emerging as the result of positive crises resolutions are *ego functions*. For example, the virtues of hope and will have some influence on the quality of one's life but little on survival. Individuals without much hope or will, will survive; that is, they will be able to satisfy their biological (idinal) needs, but they probably would not be flexible, optimistic, or generally as happy as those with more hope and will.

3. Initiative versus Guilt This stage occurs from about the fourth year to about the sixth year and corresponds to Freud's phallic stage of psychosexual development.

During this stage the child is capable of still more detailed motor activity, more refined use of language, and a more vivid use of imagination. These skills allow the child to *initiate* ideas, actions, and fantasies, and to *plan* future events. According to Erikson, the child during this stage "is apt to develop an untiring curiosity about differences in sizes in general, and sexual differences in particular . . . his learning is now eminently intrusive and vigorous: it leads away from his own limitations and into future possibilities" (1959, p. 76).

In the preceding stages children learned that they were people. Now they begin to explore what kind of person they can become. During this stage, limits are tested in order to find out what is permissible and what is not. If parents encourage children's self-initiated behaviors and fantasies, the children will leave this stage with a healthy sense of initiative. If, however, parents ridicule the children's self-initiated behavior and imagination, they will leave this stage lacking self-sufficiency. Instead of taking the initiative, they will tend to feel guilty when pondering such behavior and therefore will tend to live within the narrow limits that others set for them.

If children develop more initiative during this stage than guilt, the virtue of *purpose* will emerge. Erikson defined purpose as "the courage to envisage and pursue valued goals uninhibited by the defeat of infantile fantasies, by guilt and by the foiling fear of punishment" (1964, p. 122). Children who have met the crisis of the first three stages possess the positive virtues of hope, will, and purpose.

*4. **Industry versus Inferiority*** This stage lasts from about the sixth year to about the eleventh year and corresponds to Freud's latency stage of psychosexual development. Most children attend school throughout this stage.

It is during this stage that children learn the skills necessary for economic survival, the technological skills that will allow them to become productive members of the community.

> . . . The inner stage seems all set for "entrance into life," except that life must first be school life, whether school is field or jungle or classroom. The child must forget past hopes and wishes, while his exuberant imagination is tamed and harnessed to the laws of impersonal things—even the three R's. For before the child, psychologically already a rudimentary parent, can become a biological parent, he must begin to be a worker and potential provider. (Erikson 1963, pp. 258–259)

School is the place where children are trained for future employment in and adjustment to their culture. Because in most cultures, including our own, surviving requires the ability to work cooperatively with others, social skills are among the important lessons taught by the schools.

The most important lesson that children learn during this stage is "the pleasure of work completion by steady attention and persevering diligence" (Erikson 1963, p. 259). From this lesson comes a sense of industry which prepares children to look confidently for productive places in society among other people.

If children do not develop a sense of industry, they will develop a sense of inferiority which causes them to lose confidence in their ability to become contributing members of society. Such children are more likely to develop a "negative identity," a concept that will be explained later in this chapter.

There is another danger associated with this stage, and that is that children will overvalue their places in the work force. For such people, work is equated with life, and they thus are blinded to the many other important aspects of human existence. "If he accepts work as his only obligation, and 'what works' as his only criterion of worthwhileness, he may become the conformist and thoughtless slave of his technology and of those who are in a position to exploit it" (Erikson 1963, p. 261). According to Erikson, the skills necessary for future employment must be encouraged during this stage but not at the expense of several other important human attributes.

If children's sense of industry is greater than their sense of inferiority, they will leave this stage with the virtue of *competence.* "competence . . . is the free exercise of dexterity and intelligence in the completion of tasks, unimpaired by infantile inferiority" (Erikson 1964, p. 124). Like the other virtues discussed above, competence comes from loving attention and encouragement. A sense of inferiority comes from ridicule or lack of concern by those individuals most important to the children.

5. *Identity versus Role Confusion* This stage occurs between about twelve years to twenty years of age and corresponds roughly to Freud's genital stage of psychosexual development.

It is for his description of this psychosocial stage that Erikson is known best, for it contains his now famous concept of *identity crisis.*

Erikson felt that this stage represented the transition period between childhood and adulthood. In the preceding stages, children were learning what they were and what it was possible for them to do, that is, the various roles that were available to them. During this stage children must ponder all this accumulated information about themselves and their society and ultimately commit themselves to some strategy for life. When they have done this, they have gained an identity and have become adults. Gaining a personal identity marks the satisfactory end of this stage of development. However, the stage itself is seen as a time of searching for an identity but not of having one. Erikson called this period a *psychosocial moratorium,* by which he meant an interval between youth and adulthood.

Erikson has used the term identity (sometimes called ego identity) in a variety of ways. For example, it is "a feeling of being at home in one's body, a sense of 'knowing where one is going,' and an inner assuredness of anticipated recognition from those who count" (Erikson, 1959, p. 118). Erikson discusses the relationship between identity and earlier experiences:

> The growing and developing youths, faced with this physiological revolution within them, and with tangible adult tasks ahead of them, are now primarily concerned with what they appear to be in the eyes of others as compared with what they feel they are, and with the question of how

> to connect the roles and skills cultivated earlier with the occupational prototypes of the day. . . . The integration now taking place in the form of ego identity is more than the sum of the childhood identifications. It is the accrued experience of the ego's ability to integrate all identifications with the vicissitudes of the libido, with the aptitudes developed out of endowment and with the opportunities offered in social roles. The sense of ego identity, then, is the accrued confidence that the inner sameness and continuity prepared in the past (one's ego in the psychological sense) are matched by the sameness and continuity of one's meaning for others, as evidenced in the tangible promise of a "career." (1963, pp. 261–262)

Erikson made no apology for using the term identity in a variety of ways. Since it is a complex concept, he felt it must be approached from many angles.

If young adults do not leave this stage with an identity, they leave it with *role confusion* or perhaps with a *negative identity*. Role confusion is characterized by the inability to choose a role in life, thus prolonging the psychological moratorium indefinitely or to make superficial commitments which are soon abandoned. Negative identities are all those things that children are warned not to become. Erikson defined negative identity as: "an identity perversely based on all those identifications and roles which, at critical stages of development, had been presented to the individual as most undesirable or dangerous, and yet also as most real" (1959, p. 131). Erikson gave an example:

> A mother who is filled with unconscious ambivalence toward a brother who disintegrated into alcoholism may again and again respond selectively only to those traits in her son which seem to point to a repetition of her brother's fate, in which case this "negative" identity may take on more reality for the son than all his natural attempts at being good: he may work hard on becoming a drunkard. . . . (1959, p. 131)

For Erikson, the concepts of role confusion and negative identity explain much of the unrest and hostility expressed by adolescents in this country. In his analysis of Malcolm X, the American black leader in the 1950s and 1960s, Erikson made the following point:

> . . . should a child feel that the environment tries to deprive him too radically of all the forms of expression which permit him to integrate the next step in his ego identity, he will resist with the astonishing strength encountered in animals who are suddenly forced to defend their lives. Indeed, in the social jungle of human existence, there is no feeling of being alive without a sense of identity. (1964, p. 24)

The adolescent may lash out at those identities that do not fit him.

> The loss of a sense of identity often is expressed in a scornful and snobbish hostility toward the roles offered as proper and desirable in one's family or immediate community. As part or aspect of the required role, or all parts, be it masculinity or feminity, nationality or class membership,

> can become the main focus of the young person's acid disdain. (Erikson 1959, p. 129)

Why should an adolescent choose a negative identity if a positive one were not available? Erikson said because he would "rather be nobody or somebody bad, or indeed, dead—and this totally, and by free choice—than be not-quite somebody" (1959, p. 132).

If young adults emerge from this stage with a positive identity rather than with role confusion or a negative identity, they also will emerge with the virtue of *fidelity*. Erikson defines fidelity as "the ability to sustain loyalties freely pledged in spite of the inevitable contradictions of value systems" (1964, p. 125).

The stages preceding this provided the child with the "stuff" from which an identity could be derived. In this stage, the individual has to assimilate this information. The development of an identity marks the end of childhood and the beginning of adulthood. From this point on, life is a matter of acting out one's identity. Now that the individual "knows who he or she is," the task of life becomes one of carrying "that person" optimally through the remaining stages of life.

The reader has probably noted the similarity between Erikson's concept of identity and Adler's concept of life style. The major difference between the two seems to be when they develop. For Adler, life style is a means of gaining superiority and perfection which develops in early childhood. As we have just seen, Erikson uses the term identity to describe the synthesis of earlier experiences into the major role one will play the rest of one's life. Both the terms life style and identity refer to the major theme around which a person's life is organized; the major difference is when the theme develops.

6. Intimacy versus Isolation This stage is called early adulthood and lasts from about twenty years to about twenty-four years of age. For this and the remaining psychosocial stages, there is no corresponding Freudian psychosexual stage of development.

Freud once defined a healthy person as one who loves and works; Erikson agrees with this definition. However, only the person who has a secure identity can risk entering into a love relationship with another. The young adult with a strong identity eagerly seeks intimate relationships with others.

> . . . the young adult, emerging from the search for and the insistence on identity, is eager and willing to fuse his identity with that of others. He is ready for intimacy, that is, the capacity to commit himself to concrete affiliations and partnerships and to develop the ethical strength to abide by such commitments, even though they may call for significant sacrifices and compromises. (Erikson 1963, p. 263)

People who do not develop a capacity for productive work and intimacy withdraw into themselves, avoid close contacts, and thus develop a feeling of isolation.

Erikson lists what an intimate relationship should be in order for it to be beneficial to both the individual and society:

1. Mutuality of orgasm
2. With a loved partner
3. Of the other sex
4. With whom one is able and willing to share a mutual trust
5. And with whom one is able and willing to regulate the cycles of
   a. work
   b. procreation
   c. recreation
6. So as to secure to the offspring, too, all the stages of a satisfactory development (1963, p. 266).

If individuals develop a greater capacity for intimacy than for isolation during this stage, they also will emerge with the virtue of *love*. Erikson defines love as: "the mutuality of devotion forever subduing the antagonisms inherent in divided function" (1964, p. 129).

Erikson's theory has been criticized for moralizing. It should be clear that what Erikson defined as the positive adjustments to the crises at various stages of development are clearly in accordance with Christian ethics and with existing social institutions. The danger in this (as in all theories) is that Erikson may be describing what he hopes will be rather than what is. It is important, therefore, to know what the biases of a theorist are so that one can spot them when they show up in the theory. Roazen (1976) reasons:

> The preachiest features of Erikson's work have emerged relatively recently. It is undoubtedly better for a thinker to make explicit his commitments, rather than for latent convictions to exert an unwitting influence. But as one reflects on the implications of Erikson's ego psychology, with its deferential attitude toward the benefits of preexisting social institutions, a consistent ethical mood does emerge: marriage, heterosexuality, and the raising of children are unquestionably part of what he takes the good life to consist of. (p. 171)

7. Generativity versus Stagnation This stage occurs from about twenty-five to about sixty-five years of age and is called middle adulthood.

If one has been fortunate enough to develop a positive identity and to live a productive, happy life, one attempts to pass on the circumstances that caused these things to the next generation. This can be done either by interacting with children directly (they need not be one's own), or by producing or creating things that will enhance the lives of those in the next generation.

> Generativity, then, is primarily the concern in establishing and guiding the next generation, although there are individuals who, through mis-

> fortune or because of special and genuine gifts in other directions, do not apply this drive to their own offspring. And indeed, the concept generativity is meant to include such more popular synonyms as *productivity* and *creativity,* which, however, cannot replace it. (Erikson 1963, p. 267)

The person who does not develop a sense of generativity is characterized by "stagnation and interpersonal impoverishment" (Erikson 1963, p. 267).

If the ratio of generativity to stagnation is in favor of the former, one leaves this stage with the virtue of *care* which Erikson defines as "the widening concern for what has been generated by love, necessity, or accident; it overcomes the ambivalence adhering to irreversible obligation" (1964, p. 131).

8. Ego Integrity versus Despair This stage occurs from about the age of sixty-five to death and is called late adulthood. Erikson defines ego integrity as follows:

> Only in him who in some way has taken care of things and people and who has adapted himself to the triumphs and disappointments adherent to being, the originator of others or the generator of products and ideas—only in him may gradually ripen the fruit of these seven stages—I know no better word for it than ego integrity. (1963, p. 268)

According to Erikson, it is only the person who can look back on a rich, constructive, happy life who does not fear death. Such a person has a feeling of completion and fulfillment. The person who looks back on life with frustration experiences despair. As strange as it may seem, the person experiencing despair is not as ready for death as the person with a sense of fulfillment, since the former has not yet achieved any major goals in life.

Not only are the eight stages progressively related to each other, but the eighth stage is directly related to the first. In other words, the eight stages are interrelated in a circular fashion. For example, the adult's attitude toward death will directly influence the young child's sense of trust. Erikson believes that "it seems possible to further paraphrase the relation of adult integrity and infantile trust by saying that healthy children will not fear life if their elders have integrity enough not to fear death" (1963, p. 269). If the individual has more ego integrity than despair, his or her life will be characterized by the virtue of *wisdom,* which Erikson defines as "detached concern with life itself, in face of death itself" (1964, p. 133).

No theory of personality is without its critics and Erikson's is no exception. For example: Roazen finds Erikson's description of the last stage of life his least satisfactory:

> This final stage of the life cycle, about which Erikson has written relatively little, seems least satisfactory of all. Why should wisdom be defined by the acquiescence in the inevitable? It can just as well be argued that wisdom should also lead to dissatisfaction, even rage, at past personal mistakes, unfortunate chance, or uncorrected social injustices. Any old person is likely to be emotionally less elastic than in younger years. Not all development results in gains. As a matter of fact, there would be something peculiar if aging did not involve depression—not only does an older person lose some of his powers, but loved ones die. Whatever satisfactions can be foreseen in what has been, in Erikson's terms, generated for the future, death is lonely and often painful. (1976, p. 116)

In spite of some criticism, Erikson's description of the eight stages of human development has been highly influential and promises to be for a long time. The eight stages of development and the virtues they produce are summarized in Figure 6–2.

1. Trust vs Mistrust (Birth–1)
   If the crisis is successfully resolved hope emerges.
   If the crisis is unsuccessfully resolved fear emerges.
2. Autonomy vs Shame and Doubt (1–3)
   If the crisis is successfully resolved self-control and will power emerge.
   If the crisis is unsuccessfully resolved self-doubt emerges.
3. Initiative vs Guilt (4–5)
   If the crisis is successfully resolved direction and purpose emerge.
   If the crisis is unsuccessfully resolved feelings of unworthiness emerge.
4. Industry vs Inferiority (6–11)
   If the crisis is successfully resolved competence emerges.
   If the crisis is unsuccessfully resolved incompetence emerges.
5. Identity vs Role Confusion (12–20)
   If the crisis is successfully resolved fidelity emerges.
   If the crisis is unsuccessfully resolved uncertainty emerges.
6. Intimacy vs Isolation (20–24)
   If the crisis is successfully resolved the capacity for love emerges.
   If the crisis is unsuccessfully resolved promiscuity emerges.
7. Generativity vs Stagnation (25–65)
   If the crisis is successfully resolved care emerges.
   If the crisis is unsuccessfully resolved selfishness emerges.
8. Ego Integrity vs Depair (65–Death)
   If the crisis is successfully resolved wisdom emerges.
   If the crisis is unsuccessfully resolved feelings of despair and meaninglessness emerge.

Figure 6–2 The eight crises corresponding to Erikson's eight stages of development and the traits that emerge if they are successfully or unsuccessfully resolved.

THE GOAL OF PSYCHOTHERAPY

Erikson stresses that his psychotherapeutic practices differ from those of traditional psychoanalysis because modern times have created different kinds of disorders. For example, Erikson explained that "the patient of today suffers most under the problem of what he should believe in and who he should—or, indeed, might—be or become; while the patient of early psychoanalysis suffered most under inhibitions which prevented him from being what and who he thought he knew he was" (1963, p. 279).

For Erikson, the main focus in the therapeutic process is the patient's ego which must be strengthened to the point at which it can cope with life's problems. "Rehabilitation work can be made more effective and economical if the clinical investigation focuses on the patient's shattered life plan and if advice tends to strengthen the resynthesis of the elements on which the patient's ego identity was based" (1959, p. 43).

Erikson felt that the traditional technique of releasing the contents of the unconscious mind could do more harm than good. Erikson said that the psychoanalytic method "may make some people sicker than they ever were . . . especially if, in our zealous pursuit of our task of 'making conscious' in the psychotherapeutic situation, we push someone who is leaning out a little too far over the precipice of the unconscious" (1968, p. 164).

Erikson had his patients sit across from him in an easy chair rather than lie down on a couch because the former creates a more equitable situation for the patient than the latter did. He minimized dream analysis saying that "even a periodic emphasis on dreams today is wasteful and may even be deleterious to therapy" (1954, p. 131).

Briefly stated, the healthy individual is one whose ego is characterized by the eight virtues resulting from the positive solution of each crisis in the eight stages of development. The purpose of psychotherapy is to encourage the growth of whatever virtues are missing, even if it means going back and helping the person to develop a sense of basic trust. *For Erikson, the outcome of every crisis resolution is reversible.* For example, the person leaving the first stage of development without basic trust may later gain it, and the person having it may lose it.

A COMPARISON OF ERIKSON AND FREUD

The major areas in which Erikson and Freud differ are listed next.

Development Freud concentrated his studies on the psychosexual stages of development coming before the age of six, because he felt that most of what is important to personality development occurs by then. Erikson studied development as it occurred throughout life. Although Jung, too, believed that important developments occurred throughout one's life, Erikson's description of the development process was much more detailed than Jung's.

Ego Psychology Erikson shifted attention away from the id and toward the ego. Rather than seeing the individual as warring with society, Erikson saw society as a potential source of strength. Corsini explained this as follows:

> Instead of viewing the individual as the plaything of social forces, Erikson presents the concept of the emerging individual, challenged by the crises of life, from which he can emerge victorious and strengthened. This means that he views the person as in charge, the captain of his fate rather than a crew member who has to do another's bidding. Erikson has an optimistic-creative view of personality. (1977, p. 413)

The Unconscious Mind Although Erikson's theory emphasizes the conscious ego, he does not neglect unconscious mechanisms completely. In fact, although the ego gains strength from certain social experiences, the experiences themselves are largely unconscious.

Psychotherapy We have seen that Erikson considered people healthy if they successfully traversed the eight stages of life, acquiring the virtues of hope, will, purpose, competence, fidelity, love, care, and wisdom. If people do not acquire these virtues, their ego will be weaker than it otherwise would be, and it is the job of the therapist to help provide the circumstances under which the virtues can develop. This is in marked contrast to Freud's belief that therapy facilitates the understanding of unconscious mechanisms using techniques such as dream analysis and free association.

Religion Freud took a dim view of religion, saying that it was merely a collective neurosis based on infantile fears and desires. Erikson totally disagrees. For him, religion is something that many people truly need. For centuries humans have used religion to make the events of their lives more understandable and therefore less threatening. Without it, according to Erikson, the lives of millions of individuals would be filled with uncertainty. In this respect, Erikson agrees with Jung and Adler.

We see that although Erikson calls himself a Freudian, his theory has little in common with Freud's. In addition, his conception of human nature is in marked contrast to Freud's. Perhaps, as we have already suggested, Erikson's insistence that his theory is closer to Freud's than it really is reflects Erikson's deep appreciation that the Freudians took him into their camp, thus solving his own severe identity crisis.

EVALUATION

Like so many personality theories, Erikson's theory cannot be evaluated on the basis of laboratory investigations, at least not yet. Erikson did not create his theory with the researcher in mind. He attempted to classify conceptually several items related to personality development, and one either feels that they are clarified or they are not; either his theory is a useful guide to understanding personality or it is not. "The proof lies in the way in which the communication between therapist and patient 'keeps moving,' leading to new and surprising insights and to the patient's greater assumption of responsibility for himself" (1964, p. 75).

The point is that Erikson feels that there are ways other than laboratory investigations to evaluate a personality theory. In spite of Erikson's feelings about the need to verify his theory scientifically, others have taken it upon themselves to do just that. For example, Ciaccio (1971) asked 120 male white children to make up stories about five pictures. The children were equally divided into three groups consisting of five, eight, and eleven year olds. With the help of several judges, the stories the children told were categorized sentence by sentence according to which stage of development it best corresponded. The percentages of each child's sentences that expressed concern with the first four of Erikson's stages were recorded. The data tended to support Erikson's theory. The four year olds showed the greatest number of themes corresponding to Stage II (46%), next was Stage III (42%). The eight year olds showed the greatest number of themes corresponding to Stage III (56%), with Stage II second (20%). The eleven year olds showed the greatest number of themes corresponding to Stage IV (44%), with Stage III second (26%).

As mentioned earlier in this chapter, Erikson has utilized his theory to analyze the lives of several well known historical figures; for example, Hitler, George Bernard Shaw, Mahatma Gandhi, Maxim Gorky, and Martin Luther. His efforts have created a new discipline called *psychohistory*. One might ask how accurate is Erikson's analysis of an historical figure. Erikson answered that his analysis is based on *disciplined subjectivity* and may be "half-legend." Erikson remarked on his analysis of Martin Luther:

> If some of it is legend, so be it; the making of legend is as much part of the scholarly re-writing of history as it is part of the original facts used in the work of scholars. We are thus obliged to accept half-legend as half-history, provided only that a reported episode does not contradict other well-established facts; persists in having a ring of truth; and yields a meaning consistent with psychological theory. (1958, p. 37)

It is because of Erikson's lack of scientific rigor that Roazen cautions us to:

> . . . be aware that what he has presented us with is a set of theories, not facts. And it is partly because of his own acknowledged lack of theoretical-mindedness that many of his readers come away with the belief, despite his declared intentions, that he has uncovered an ineluctable piece of science rather than constructed a valuable point of view. (1976, p. 120)

In spite of Erikson's lack of scientific rigor, his theory is considered by many to be one of the most useful ever developed. Henceforth, when you encounter the terms psychosocial development, ego strength, psychohistory, identity, identity crisis, and life cycle, keep in mind that they all are concepts that were first articulated by Erik Erikson and have since become an important part of psychology.

SUMMARY

Though Erikson had only the equivalent of a high school diploma, he was invited to work in a small school established to care for children who either were receiving therapy from Anna Freud or who had parents who were receiving therapy from Sigmund Freud. Erikson worked as a tutor for a while but eventually went into training to become a child analyst under the supervision of Anna Freud. Anna Freud's interest in the ego had a lasting effect on Erikson, who is usually credited with founding ego psychology. Ego psychology emphasizes the autonomous functions of the ego and de-emphasizes the importance of the id to personality development.

Erikson agrees with Freud that one's sex markedly influences one's personality but does not believe that masculine traits are better or worse than feminine traits. Rather, he believes that masculine and feminine traits complement each other.

The most widely known aspect of Erikson's theory is his description of the eight stages of human development. Each of the eight stages is characterized by a crisis which can be resolved positively or negatively. The crises characterizing the various stages are: (1) basic trust versus basic mistrust, (2) autonomy versus shame and doubt, (3) initiative versus guilt, (4) industry versus inferiority, (5) identity versus role confusion, (6) intimacy versus isolation, (7) generativity versus stagnation, and (8) ego integrity versus despair.

If a crisis is resolved positively, a virtue will be gained which strengthens the ego. If the crises characterizing the eight stages of development are resolved positively, the person will live later years with the virtues of hope, will, purpose, competence, fidelity, love, care, and wisdom. Such a person is called healthy by Erikson, since he or she looks back on life with positive feelings and does not fear death. Children familiar with older people with these attributes are more likely to develop basic trust than basic mistrust. Not only are all the stages of development interrelated, but they are interrelated in a circular fashion.

One of the most important stages of development is the fifth stage because it is when the identity crisis occurs. It is during this stage when people attempt to find out who they are and where they are going in life. If people find answers to these questions, they will leave this stage with an identity; if not, they will leave this stage with role confusion. It is also possible for people to develop a negative identity, which is the antithesis of a role that society has deemed desirable.

For Erikson, the outcomes of the experiences during the stages of development are reversible; that is, a favorable outcome can become unfavorable and an unfavorable outcome can become favorable. In fact, Erikson looked upon the therapeutic process mainly as a means of reversing the outcomes of various stages of development. For Erikson, the goal of therapy was to strengthen the conscious ego, rather than to understand the contents of the unconscious mind, as was the case with Freud. There are many other differences between Freud's theory and Erikson's. For example, Freud viewed religion as a collective neurosis based on infantile desires, fear, and ignorance. Erikson, on the other hand, sees religion as a necessity of life and conducive to healthy adjustment.

Although Erikson's theory is difficult to evaluate experimentally, it has made significant contributions to such areas as psychotherapy, education, child rearing, and the analysis of historical figures.

Discussion Questions

1. Describe Erikson's early experiences that you think may have stimulated his later interest in the concept of "identity crisis."
2. Describe the relationship between anatomy and destiny as viewed by Erikson.
3. Compare ego psychology with traditional psychoanalytic theory.
4. Why are Erikson's stages of development labeled psychosocial rather than psychosexual?
5. Summarize the eight stages of development suggested by Erikson. Include in your summary the crisis that characterizes each stage and the virtue that emerges if the crisis is resolved positively.
6. In what ways are the psychosocial stages interrelated?
7. Summarize as many of the major differences between Erikson and Freud as you can.
8. Erikson has been accused of being unduly influenced by Christian ethics in his theorizing. Respond to this accusation.
9. Describe as many of Erikson's contributions to psychology as you can.
10. Discuss anything about yourself or others that Erikson's theory has made clearer to you. For example, does the concept of identity crisis have any personal meaning to you?

Glossary

Anatomy and Destiny. Freud felt that many important personality traits were determined by one's sex. Erikson believed the same but felt that one's culture was another powerful influence on one's personality. Although Erikson believed males and females had different personality characteristics, he did not consider one set of characteristics better than the other.

Autonomy. The sense of being relatively independent of external control that arises if the crisis characterizing the second stage of development is resolved positively.

Basic Mistrust. The lack of trust of the world and the people in it that arises if the crisis characterizing the first stage of development is resolved negatively.

Basic Trust. The general feeling of trust of the world and the people in it that arises if the crisis characterizing the first stage of development is resolved positively.

Care. The virtue that arises when a person leaves the seventh stage of development with a greater sense of generativity than of stagnation.

Competence. The virtue that arises if a child leaves the fourth stage of development with a greater sense of industry than of inferiority.

Crisis. A problem that characterizes a stage of development that can be resolved positively, thus strengthening the ego, or resolved negatively, thus weakening the ego. Each crisis, therefore, is a turning point in one's development.

Despair. The lack of satisfaction with life and the fear of death that characterize the person who has negatively resolved the crisis which occurs during the eighth and final stage of development.

Disciplined Subjectivity. The term used by Erikson to describe his approach to analyzing an historical figure. He meant that such an analysis was based partly on facts and partly on educated guesses.

Ego Integrity. The satisfaction with life and the lack of fear of death that characterize the person who has positively resolved the crisis which occurs during the eighth and final stage of development.

Ego Psychology. A theoretical system that stresses the importance of the ego as an autonomous part of the personality instead of looking at the ego as merely the servant of the id.

Epigenetic Principle. The principle that states that a sequence of growth is genetically determined and that each stage, once developed, gives rise to the next.

Fidelity. The virtue that arises at the end of the fifth stage of development if one has a sense of identity instead of role confusion.

Generativity. The impulse to help members of the next generation that arises when the crisis characterizing the seventh stage of development is resolved positively.

Guilt. The general feeling that develops in a child if the crisis characterizing the third stage of development is resolved negatively.

Hope. The virtue that arises if a child leaves the first stage of development with more basic trust than basic mistrust.

Identity. The sense of knowing who you are and where you are going in life that develops when the fifth stage of development is resolved positively. The emergence of an identity marks the end of childhood and the beginning of adulthood. Probably Erikson's most famous concept.

Identity Crisis. The crisis that characterizes the fifth stage of development which results either in the person gaining an identity (positive resolution) or in role confusion (negative resolution).

Industry. The sense of enjoyment from work and from sustained attention that arises if the crisis characterizing the fourth stage of development is resolved positively.

Inferiority. The loss of confidence in one's ability to become a contributing member of one's society that arises if the crisis characterizing the fourth stage of development is resolved negatively.

Initiative. The general ability to initiate ideas and actions and to plan future events that arises if the crisis characterizing the third stage of development is resolved positively.

Intimacy. The ability to merge one's identity with that of another person that arises if the crisis characterizing the sixth stage of development is resolved positively.

Isolation. The inability to share one's identity with that of another person that results if the crisis characterizing the sixth stage of development is resolved negatively.

Love. The virtue that arises if one leaves the sixth stage of development with a greater sense of intimacy than of isolation.

Negative Identity. An identity that is contrary to the goals of society. Negative identities are all those things that a child is warned *not* to become.

Psychohistory. The term used to describe Erikson's utilization of his developmental theory of personality to analyze historical figures.

Psychosocial Moratorium. The time during the fifth stage of development when the adolescent is searching for an identity.

Psychosocial Stages of Development. Erikson's eight stages of human development, so-named to emphasize the importance of social experience to the resolution of the crises that characterize each stage.

Purpose. The virtue that arises if a child leaves the third stage of development with a greater sense of initiative than of guilt.

Role Confusion. The state produced by not acquiring an identity during the fifth stage of development. The state is characterized by an inability to choose a role in life and represents the negative resolution of the identity crisis.

Shame and Doubt. The feelings that develop instead of the feeling of autonomy when the crisis characterizing the second stage of development is resolved negatively.

Stagnation. The lack of concern about the next generation that characterizes the person whose crisis during the seventh stage of development was resolved negatively.

Virtue. An ego strength that arises when the crisis characterizing a stage of development is resolved positively.

Will. The virtue that arises if the child leaves the second stage of development with a greater sense of autonomy than of shame and doubt.

Wisdom. The virtue that arises if a person has more ego integrity than despair during the eighth and final stage of development.

PART FOUR

TRAIT PARADIGM

chapter 7

gordon allport

Allport was born in Montezuma, Indiana on November 11, 1897, making him the first American-born personality theorist covered thus far in this text. Allport was the youngest of four sons. His father was a physician, his mother was a school teacher, and both had a strong, positive influence on him. In his brief autobiography he said:

> My mother had been a school teacher and brought to her sons an eager sense of philosophical questing and the importance of searching for ultimate religious answers. Since my father lacked adequate hospital facilities for his patients, our household for several years included both patients and nurses. Tending office, washing bottles, and dealing with patients were important aspects of my early training. . . . Dad was no believer in vacations. He followed rather his own rule of life, which he expressed as follows: If every person worked as hard as he could and took only the minimum financial return required by his family's needs, then there would be just enough wealth to go around. Thus it was hard work tempered by trust and affection that marked the home environment (1967, pp. 4–5)

Allport credited experiences like those described to his lifelong concern with human welfare and with his strong humanistic psychology.

Although Allport was born in Indiana, he grew up in Cleveland, Ohio, where he attended public schools. At the urging of his older brother Floyd (who himself became a famous psychologist), who had graduated from Harvard two years earlier, Gordon Allport entered Harvard in 1915. He barely passed the entrance examination, and his early grades were *Cs* and *Ds*. He worked hard, however, and finished the year with straight *As*. He graduated from Harvard in 1919 with a major in economics and philosophy.

Apparently not sure of what to do next and still seeking his personal identity, he spent the next year teaching English and sociology at Robert College in Istanbul, Turkey. Allport enjoyed teaching so much that he decided to accept a fellowship offered to him by Harvard to do graduate work in psychology.

On his way back to the United States, Allport stopped in Vienna to visit one of his brothers. While there he had an experience that was to have a profound effect on his later theorizing. He wrote to Freud asking for permission to visit with him and permission was granted. Allport described his brief visit with Freud:

> Soon after I had entered the famous red burlap room with pictures of dreams on the wall, he summoned me to his inner office. He did not speak to me but sat in expectant silence for me to state my mission. I was not prepared for silence and had to think fast to find a suitable conversational gambit. I told him of an episode on the tram car on my way to his office. A small boy about four years of age had displayed a conspicuous dirt phobia. He kept saying to his mother, "I don't want to sit there . . . don't let that dirty man sit beside me." To him everything was *schmutzig* [filthy]. His mother was a well-starched *Hausfrau,* so dominant and purposive looking that I thought the cause and effect apparent.

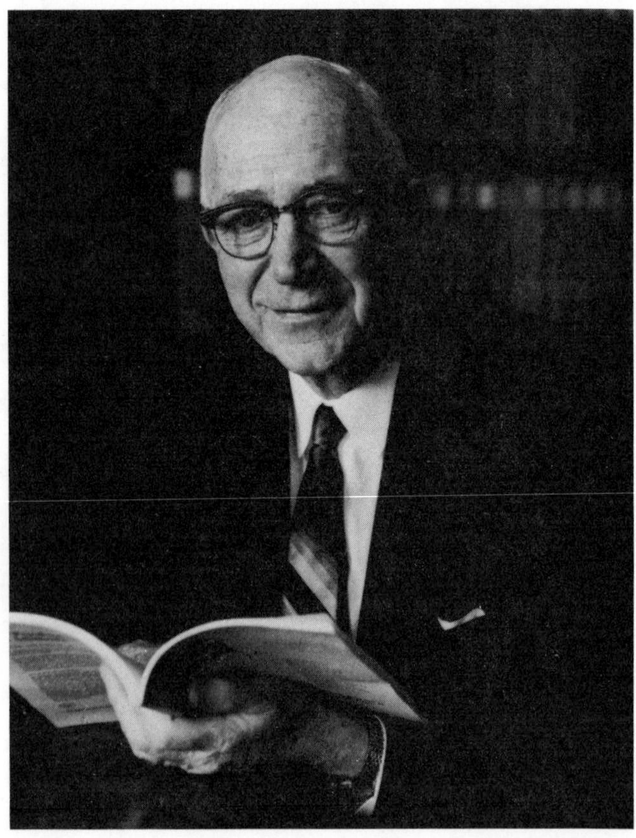

Gordon Allport. Courtesy Harvard University News Office.

> When I finished my story Freud fixed his kindly therapeutic eyes upon me and said, "And was that little boy you?" Flabbergasted and feeling a bit guilty, I contrived to change the subject. While Freud's misunderstanding of my motivation was amusing, it also started a deep train of thought. I realized that he was accustomed to neurotic defenses and that my manifest motivation (a sort of rude curiosity and youthful ambition) escaped him. For therapeutic progress he would have to cut through my defenses, but it so happened that therapeutic progress was not here an issue. (1968, pp. 383–384)

Allport learned from this experience that it is possible for "depth" psychology to dig so deeply that more important truths may be overlooked. Allport felt that he had perfectly valid, conscious reasons for visiting Freud and for telling him his little story, which were completely missed by Freud in his attempt to arrive at a "deeper" truth. As we shall see throughout this chapter, Allport believed the best way to discover what a person's true motives are, is to ask the person. Throughout his life, Allport displayed a dislike for psychoanalytic theory.

Allport returned to Harvard where he earned his M.A. in 1921 and his Ph.D. in 1922, at the age of twenty-four. His early work was indeed indicative of what was to become Allport's own brand of personality theory. His first publication was coauthored by his brother Floyd and was entitled "Personality Traits: Their Classification and Measurement" (Allport & Allport 1921). His Ph.D. dissertation was entitled "An Experimental Study of the Traits of Personality."

Aided by a traveling fellowship, Allport spent the school year from 1922 to 1923 at the University of Berlin and the University of Hamburg, and the school year from 1923 to 1924 in England at Cambridge University. In 1924, he then returned to Harvard where he offered the first course on personality ever offered in the United States. The course was entitled "Personality: Its Psychological and Social Aspects."

Allport married Ada Lufkin Gould on June 30, 1925, and their one child, Robert Brandlee, now is a pediatrician. Except for a four-year appointment at Dartmouth College from 1926 to 1930, Allport was at Harvard for his entire professional career. Allport died on October 9, 1967, one month before his seventieth birthday.

As we shall see, Allport was truly an eclectic theorist, taking the best from a wide variety of other theories of personality. However, Allport was the first to criticize what he considered the worst in those theories. At one time or another, Allport took issue with psychoanalysis, behaviorism (S-R psychology), animal research designed to provide information about humans, and statistical methods of studying personality, such as factor analysis. For example, Allport said that psychologists like Freud and Jung had created:

> . . . a kind of contempt for the "psychic surface" of life. The individual's conscious report is rejected as untrustworthy, and the contemporary thrust of his motives is disregarded in favor of a backward tracing of his

> conduct to earlier formative stages. The individual loses his right to be believed. And while he is busy leading his life in the present with a forward thrust into the future, most psychologists have become busy tracing it backward into the past. (1960, p. 96)

Allport believed strongly that the principles governing the behavior of lower animals or neurotic humans are different from those governing the behavior of healthy adult humans, therefore, little can be learned about one by studying the other. "Some theories of becoming are based largely upon the behavior of sick and anxious people or upon the antics of captive and desperate rats. Fewer theories have derived from the study of healthy human beings, those who strive not so much to preserve life as to make it worth living" (Allport 1955, p. 18).

Indeed, Allport battled with any point of view in psychology that obscured human individuality or dignity. Clearly, if one had to isolate the dominant theme running through all of Allport's works, it is *the importance of the individual.* This theme, of course, put Allport in a position contrary to "scientific" psychology, because it was considered the job of science to find the general laws governing all behavior. Science was interested in what is generally true, and Allport was interested in what is specifically true.

Allport felt strongly that psychological research should have practical value, and in addition to his books on personality theory, which we will consider in this chapter, he wrote such books as:

The Individual and His Region (1950)
The Nature of Prejudice (1954)
The Psychology of Rumor (1947) with L. Postman

WHAT IS PERSONALITY?

In his 1937 book *Personality: A Psychological Interpretation,* Allport introduced the study of personality to America. From the very beginning, Allport was opposed to the established viewpoints of psychoanalysis and behaviorism. Allport's early theorizing was influenced mainly by Gestalt psychology, which he encountered in Germany after his graduation from Harvard, and by his strong humanistic tendencies developed early in his life. As we saw in chapter 4, Gestalt psychology emphasized the wholeness and interrelatedness of conscious experience and was appalled by any attempt to subdivide it in order to study it more thoroughly. Gestalt psychology also ignored the unconscious mind almost completely. Allport said that Gestalt psychology was "the kind of psychology I had been longing for but did not know existed" (1968, p. 387). In fact, Allport distrusted science as a source of information about personality. He was more comfortable with the traditional descriptions of humans found in literature and philosophy. This is not to say that Allport ignored information provided by the scientific method;

clearly he did not. However, he did not want to be restricted to scientific method in his efforts to understand personality. He felt that much useful nonscientific information had accumulated through the years and that it would be foolhardy not to make use of that information.

In 1937, Allport reviewed the history of the word personality, beginning with its ties to the Greek word *persona,* which means mask. He then reviewed fifty definitions of personality before arriving at his own now famous definition: "Personality is the dynamic organization within the individual of those psychophysical systems that determine his unique adjustments to his environment" (1937, p. 48).

In 1961 Allport changed the phrase "unique adjustments to his environment" to "characteristic behavior and thought" (p. 28). Since Allport's definition of personality acts as a summary of most of his major concepts, we shall examine its key components more carefully.

Dynamic Organization This refers to the fact that personality, though always organized, is constantly changing. Personality, according to Allport, is never something that is, rather, it is something that is *becoming.* Although there is enough similarity in people to maintain their identity from one experience to another, in a sense they never are quite the same people they were before a particular experience. Allport borrowed this idea from the ancient Greek philosopher Heraclitus who said "Nothing is, everything is becoming," and "No man can step into the same river twice." It is the same with personality; it has organization and continuity within the person, but it is constantly changing or becoming something different.

Psychophysical Systems According to Allport: "The term 'psychophysical' reminds us that personality is neither exclusively mental nor exclusively neural. The organization entails the operation of both body and mind, inextricably fused into a personal unit" (1937, p. 48).

Determine According to Allport, personality was not an abstraction or a convenient fiction; it actually existed: "Personality *is* something and *does* something. . . . It is what lies *behind* specific acts and *within* the individual" (1937, p. 48). Allport believed that the person is by no means simply a passive reactor to the environment. Rather, a person's behavior is generated from within by the personality structure.

Characteristic Behavior and Thought It has been mentioned that Allport revised his definition of personality in 1961 by deleting the phrase "unique adjustments to the environment" and replacing it with "characteristic behavior and thought." He did so because he felt the earlier statement placed too much emphasis on survival and thus on the satisfaction of biological needs. His revised definition covered *all* behavior and thought whether or not they were related to adaptation to the environment. One's dreams for the future, for example, are just as important as satisfying the hunger drive, but they have little or nothing to do with biological survival.

Both versions of Allport's definition of personality stress the importance of individuality. In the 1937 definition, the word "unique" was used, in the 1961 definition, the word "characteristic" was used. Indeed, as we have seen, the emphasis on studying individual human beings rather than on the laws governing all human beings was a constant theme running through all of Allport's work. Over and over he said that no two humans are alike, and therefore *the only way to ever learn about a particular individual is to study that particular individual.*

Allport distinguished among the terms personality, character, temperament, and type.

Character Allport was bothered by the term "character" because it implied the moral judgment of a person, such as when it is said that a person has "a good character." Allport preferred: "to define *character* as *personality evaluated*, and *personality* as *character devaluated*" (1961, p. 32).

Temperament Allport referred to temperament, intelligence, and physique as the *raw materials* from which personality is shaped; all three are genetically determined. Temperament is the emotional component of the personality, which Allport described as:

> . . . the characteristic phenomena of an individual's emotional nature, including his susceptibility to emotional stimulation, his customary strength and speed of response, the quality of his prevailing mood, and all peculiarities of fluctuation and intensity in mood, these phenomena being regarded as dependent upon constitutional makeup, and therefore largely hereditary in origin. (1961, p. 34)

Type A type is a category in which one person can be placed by another person. In other words, we use the word type when we are describing other people. Types, therefore, are ways of categorizing people. If a person continually acts aggressively, we may say he or she is the aggressive type, which is to say that his or her behavior fits into this category. Personality, on the other hand, is something that is within a person causing him or her to behave in certain ways. We can say that personality generates behavior patterns that can be described as types.

CRITERIA FOR AN ADEQUATE THEORY OF PERSONALITY

In 1960, Allport described five characteristics that he felt any good theory of personality should possess.

1. An adequate theory will view personality as contained within the person According to Allport, those theories that explain personality in terms of the various roles people play or in terms of behavior patterns elicited by environmental circumstances are inadequate. In other words, personality must be explained in terms of internal mechanisms, rather than of external mechanisms. Clearly, and not so surprisingly, Allport's theory meets this criterion.

2. An adequate theory will view the person as filled with variables that contribute to his or her actions This statement, which is very much related to point 1, was made to show Allport's disdain of those behaviorists who assumed, for methodological reasons, that the human organism was empty. To these S-R psychologists (discussed in chapters 9 and 10), the proper way to study human behavior was to make a "functional analysis" of stimulating conditions (S) and responses to those conditions (R). Such psychologists prided themselves on studying the *empty organism* (B. F. Skinner led this group). Allport, of course, felt that this position was especially distasteful and dehumanizing: "Any theory of personality pretending adequacy must be dynamic and, to be dynamic, must assume a well-stocked organism" (Allport 1960, p. 26). Again, Allport's theory of personality fulfills this requirement for an adequate theory of personality.

3. An adequate theory will seek motives for behavior in the present instead of in the past Here Allport is expressing his dissatisfaction with psychoanalytic theory which traces adult motives to childhood experiences. According to Allport, neurotics may be prisoners of their past, and psychoanalytic methods may be useful in dealing with them, but the motives for healthy, mature adults are found in the present. Furthermore, healthy, normal adults are aware of their motives and can describe them accurately if asked to do so.

> When we set out to study a person's motives, we are seeking to find out what that person is trying to do in this life—including, of course, what he is trying to avoid and what he is trying to be. I see no reason why we should not start our investigation by asking him to tell us the answers as he sees them. (Allport 1960, p. 101)

We will see in our discussion of functional autonomy, later in this chapter, that Allport saw adult motivation as separate from earlier experiences.

4. The units of meaure employed by an adequate personality theory must be capable of "living synthesis" According to Allport, the integrity of the total personality must never be lost. People are more than a collection of test scores or conditioned reflexes. Whatever units of measure are used to describe a person, they must be capable of describing the whole, dynamic personality:

> To say that John Brown scores in the eightieth percentile of the "masculinity-feminity" variable, in the thirtieth percentile on "need for achievement" and at average on "introversion-extroversion" is only moderately

> enlightening. Even with a more numerous set of dimensions, with an avalanche of psychometric scores, patterned personality seems to elude the psychodiagnostician. (Allport 1960, p. 30)

Allport's theory never lost sight of the whole person. As we shall see, the unit of measure that he felt made this possible is the "trait."

5. An adequate theory will adequately account for self-awareness Humans are the only animals aware of their own awareness, and this fact, according to Allport, must be considered in any adequate account of personality. We shall explore Allport's attempt to deal with this difficult problem when we discuss the "proprium" later in this chapter.

We see that Allport's theory is five for five in terms of meeting his own criteria for an adequate theory of personality. Other theorists, of course, would have their own criteria which Allport's theory would not fit.

ALLPORT'S CONCEPT OF TRAIT

We have seen that Allport felt an adequate theory of personality would employ units of measure capable of "living synthesis." For Allport, that unit was the *trait.* To help describe the various traits that people may possess, Allport and Odbert (1936) examined 17,953 adjectives that have been used to characterize people. However, Allport certainly did not equate traits with names. Traits, for Allport, were real biophysical structures. In 1937, Allport said that he did not believe that:

> . . . every trait-name necessarily implies a trait; but rather that behind all confusion of terms, behind the disagreement of judges, and apart from errors and failures of empirical observation, there are none the less *bona fide* mental structures in each personality that account for the consistency of its behavior. (p. 289)

Allport defined a trait as: "a neuropsychic structure having the capacity to render many stimuli functionally equivalent, and to initiate and guide equivalent (meaningfully consistent) forms of adaptive and expressive behavior" (1961, p. 347).

Traits account for the consistency in human behavior. Because no two people possess exactly the same traits, each confronts environmental experiences differently. A person possessing the trait of friendliness will react to a stranger differently than a person possessing the trait of suspiciousness. In both cases the stimulus is the same but the reactions are different because different traits are involved. Or, as Allport explained, "The same fire that melts the butter hardens the egg" (1937, p. 102).

People's traits organize experiences since people confront the world in terms of their traits. For example, if people are basically aggressive, they will be aggressive in a wide range of situations. Traits will guide their behavior because people can respond to the world only in terms of their traits. Traits, therefore, both initiate and guide behavior. How a trait influences the way one will react to various situations is shown in Figure 7–1.

Obviously traits cannot be observed directly, and therefore their existence must be inferred. Allport suggested the following criteria for assuming the existence of a trait:

> . . . the *frequency* with which a person adopts a certain type of adjustment is one criterion of a trait. A second criterion is the *range of situations* in which he adopts this same mode of acting. A third criterion is the *intensity* of his reactions in keeping with this "preferred pattern" of behavior. (1961, p. 340)
>
> It is only the repeated occurrence of acts having the same significance (equivalence of response) following upon a definable range of stimuli having the same personal significance (equivalence of stimuli) that makes necessary the inference of traits and personal dispositions. These tendencies are not at all times active, but are persistent even when latent, and have relatively low thresholds of arousal. (1961, p. 374)

Traits are not Habits Habits are more specific than traits. For example, one may have the habits of brushing one's teeth, putting on clean clothing in the morning, brushing one's hair, washing one's hands, and cleaning one's nails. However, one has all these habits because one has

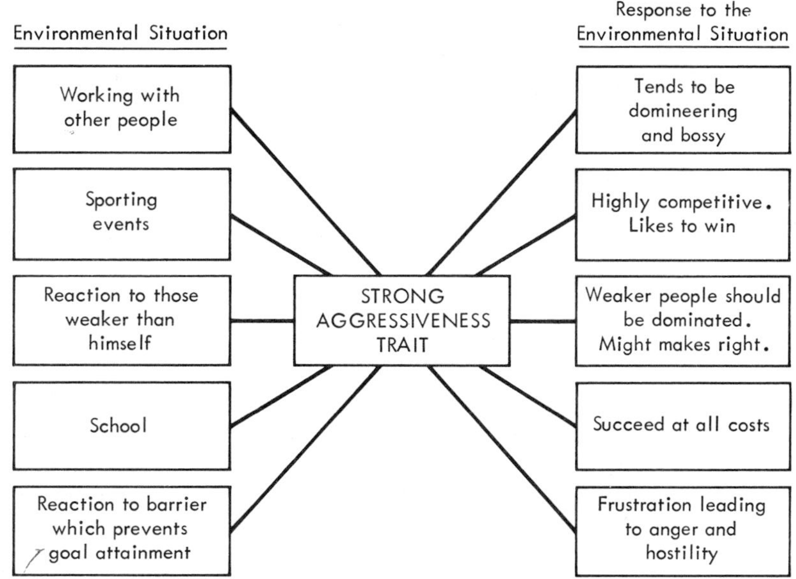

Figure 7–1 How one might react to various situations if one had a strong aggressive trait.

the trait of cleanliness. In other words, a trait synthesizes a number of specific habits. This can be diagrammed as follows:

Specific Habits	*Trait*
Brushing Hair	
Brushing Teeth	
Washing Hands	Cleanliness
Wearing Clean Clothing	
Cleaning Nails	

Traits are not Attitudes Attitudes, like habits, are more specific than traits. A person has an attitude toward something, for instance, a certain person, a brand of automobile, or travel. A trait, on the other hand, is much more general. For example, if a person is basically aggressive, he or she will act aggressively toward strangers, acquaintances, animals, world affairs, and the like. A second distinction between attitudes and traits is that attitudes usually imply evaluation; that is, attitudes are usually for or against something; they are either positive or negative; and they imply either acceptance or rejection of something. Traits, on the other hand, are responsible for all behavior and cognitions whether or not evaluation is involved.

KINDS OF TRAITS

First, Allport distinguished between *individual* traits and *common traits.* As their names imply, individual traits are those possessed by a particular individual, and common traits are those shared by a number of individuals. The distinction between individual and common traits is determined mainly by what is being specified. Any group can be described by its traits. For example, a group can be described as friendly, aggressive, or intelligent. Likewise, any individual can be described by his or her traits; one can be described as friendly, aggressive, or intelligent. When traits are used to describe a group, they are called common traits; when they are used to describe an individual, they are called individual traits. Although recognizing the existence of both kinds of traits, Allport felt strongly that the personality theorist should focus on individual traits.

Borrowing his terms from the philosopher W. Windelband, Allport insisted that the personality theorist use the *idiographic* method of research, which is the intense study of a single case, and avoid the *nomothetic* method, which studies groups of individuals and analyzes averages. Allport felt that averages were merely abstractions and really described no single individual accurately. In other words, Allport felt that the only way to learn about a particular person is to study that person, since no two people have exactly the same configuration of traits.

Later in the evolution of his theory, Allport came to feel that using the term trait to describe both group and individual characteristics was confusing. He therefore retained the term common traits to describe characteristics of groups but changed the term individual trait to *personal disposition*, which he defined as: "a generalized neuropsychic structure (peculiar to the individual), with the capacity to render many stimuli functionally equivalent, and to initiate and guide consistent (equivalent) forms of adaptive and stylistic behavior" (1961, p. 373). Note that the definition of personal disposition is essentially the same as the definition of trait listed earlier.

Having decided upon the study of personal dispositions, it was clear to Allport that not all the dispositions that a person possesses have the same impact on personality. He therefore distinguished among cardinal, central, and secondary dispositions.

Cardinal Dispositions If one possesses a cardinal disposition, it influences almost everything one does. When one thinks of Don Juan, for example, one thinks of a man possessed by romance, and when one thinks of Florence Nightingale one thinks of a person driven by human compassion. Both individuals exemplify cardinal dispositions. Clearly, cardinal dispositions are observed in only a small number of people.

Central Dispositions Think of a person you know quite well. Now pretend you have been asked to write an honest letter of recommendation for that person. Jot down the person's characteristics that you would mention in such a letter. Those terms on your list describe that person's central dispositions and summarize the consistencies in the person's behavior. Examples might be punctual, neat, highly creative, and persistent.

Allport believed that each person possesses surprisingly few central dispositions. "When psychology develops adequate diagnostic methods for discovering the major lines along which a particular personality is organized (personal dispositions), it may turn out that the number of such foci will normally vary between five and ten" (1961, p. 367).

Secondary Dispositions Secondary dispositions apply to a much narrower range of stimuli than do either cardinal or central dispositions. Secondary dispositions are close to habits or attitudes but are still more general than either. These would include a person's idiosyncrasies like preferences for certain kinds of food or clothing.

THE PROCESS OF BECOMING

Earlier we saw that Allport defined personality as a "dynamic organization." We also saw that Allport believed personality to consist of biological as well as psychological structures, such as personal dispositions.

The fact that all of the diverse aspects of personality are continuous and are organized, implies the existence of an organizing agent. In ancient times this agent was called the soul. Later it was called the self or ego. Allport felt that all of these terms were too nebulous and renamed the organizer of the personality the *proprium.* The proprium includes all the facts about a person that makes him or her unique. Allport defined proprium as follows:

> Personality includes these habits and skills, frames of reference, matters of fact and cultural values, that seldom or never seem warm and important. But personality includes what is warm and important also—all the regions of our life that we regard as peculiarly ours, and which for the time being I suggest we call the *proprium.* The proprium includes all aspects of personality that make for inward unity. (1955, p. 40)

This inward organization and self-awareness are not present at birth but, rather, evolve slowly over time. Allport believed that full propriate functioning characterizes only the final stage of an eight-stage developmental sequence that starts at birth and continues until adulthood.

1. ***The Sense of the Bodily "Me"*** (first year). Infants learn that their bodies exist because of the many sensations they experience.

2. ***The Sense of Self-identity*** (second year). With this sense comes the realization that there is self-continuity over time. That is, children come to realize that they are the same people although there are changes in their sizes and experiences. The development of language is directly related to the development of self-identity. Specifically, children learn their name which acts as an anchor for their identity through a variety of experiences. "By hearing his name repeatedly the child gradually sees himself as a distinct and recurrent point of reference. The name acquires significance for him in the second year of life. With it comes awareness of independent status in the social group" (Allport 1961, p. 115.)

3. ***The Sense of Self-esteem*** (third year). This is the feeling of pride that emerges when children learn they can do things on their own. During this stage children often seek complete independence from adult supervision.

4. ***The Sense of Self-extension*** (fourth year). During this stage children learn the meaning of the word "mine." Now they realize that not only do their bodies belong to them, but so do certain toys, games, parents, pets, sisters, and so on. At this time the sense of self is extended to external objects.

5. The Emergence of Self-image (four to six years). During this stage children develop a conscience which acts as a frame of reference for "the good me" and "the bad me." Now children can compare what they do with the expectations others have of them. To use Horney's terms, children now have a real self (what they do) and an ideal self (what others expect them to be like). It is also during this stage that children begin to formulate future goals for themselves.

6. The Emergence of the Self as a Rational Coper (six to twelve years). At this stage children recognize "thinking" as a means of solving life's problems. In a sense children begin to think about thinking.

7. The Emergence of Propriate Striving (twelve years through adolescence). At this stage of development, people become almost completely future-oriented. Long-term goals are created which give organization and meaning to life. According to Allport, the primary objective in life is not *need reduction,* as so many theorists would have us believe. Rather, it is *need induction* that is important. In other words, healthy adults create problems by formulating future goals which, in many cases, are unattainable.

> Propriate striving confers unity upon personality, but it is never the unity of fulfillment, of repose, or of reduced tension. The devoted parent never loses concern for his child; the devotee of democracy adopts a lifelong assignment in his human relationships. The scientist, by the very nature of his commitment, creates more and more questions, never fewer. Indeed, the measure of our intellectual maturity, one philosopher suggests, is our capacity to feel less and less satisfied with our answers to better and better problems. (Allport 1955, p. 67)
>
> The possession of long-range goals, regarded as central to one's personal existence, distinguishes the human being from the animal, the adult from the child, and in many cases, the healthy personality from the sick. (Allport 1955, p. 51)

8. The Emergence of the Self as Knower (adulthood). The final stage of development occurs when the self is aware of, unifies, and transcends the preceding seven aspects of the self. In other words, the self as knower synthesizes all of the propriate functions. The term proprium refers to all eight aspects of the self. The development of the proprium is summarized in Figure 7–2.

FUNCTIONAL AUTONOMY

Allport had four requirements for an adequate theory of motivation.

1. It must recognize the contemporary nature of motives. As we have seen, Allport did not believe that the child is the father of the man as

Period of Development	Propriate Development
1. First year	The infant learns that he exists through the many sensations he experiences.
2. Second year	The child learns that his identity remains intact although circumstances change.
3. Third year	The feeling of pride that results from individual accomplishments.
4. Fourth year	The child extends his self-image by recognizing that certain objects belong to him.
5. Fourth to sixth year	Develops a conscience or a superego. Now can deal with the concepts of right and wrong.
6. Sixth to twelfth year	Child uses reason and logic to solve complex problems.
7. Twelfth year through adolescence	Child formulates future goals and begins to organize his life around them.
8. Adulthood	An individual who is the synthesis of the preceding stages of development emerges.

Figure 7–2 The eight stages of development of the proprium and the functions associated with them.

the psychoanalysts believed. According to Allport, in order for a motive to be a motive it must exist in the present.

2. It must allow for the existence of several kinds of motives. Allport felt that to reduce all human motivation to one factor such as drive reduction or aspiring for superiority was foolhardy. "Motives are so diverse in type that we find it difficult to discover the common denominator" (1961, p. 221).

3. It must recognize the importance of cognitive processes. To Allport, it was impossible to truly understand a person's motives without knowing his or her plans, values, and intentions. He felt that perhaps the best way to understand a person's personality structure is to ask "What do you want to be doing five years from now?" No other theorist covered thus far put nearly as much trust in a person's cognitive processes as Allport did.

4. It must recognize that each person's pattern of motivation is unique. Just as no two people have the same configuration of traits, neither do they have the same configuration of motives. Because Allport believed that traits initiated behavior, they can be equated with motives. Allport asked: "What is the relation between units of motivation and units of personality? I would suggest that all units of motivation are at the same time units of personality" (1960, p. 118).

Allport introduced a motivational concept that he felt satisfied the above requirements. This was *functional autonomy,* which he defined as "any acquired system of motivation in which the tensions involved are not of the same kind as the antecedent tensions from which the acquired system developed" (1961, p. 229).

Functional autonomy, which is probably Allport's most famous concept, simply means that the reasons why an adult now engages in some form of behavior are not the same reasons which originally caused him or her to engage in that behavior. In other words, past motives are not functionally related to present motives. Allport offered the following example:

> . . . a student who first undertakes a field of study in college because it is required, because it pleases his parents, or because it comes at a convenient hour may end by finding himself absorbed in the topic, perhaps for life. The original motives may be entirely lost. What was a means to an end becomes an end in itself. (1961, p. 235)

Allport felt that when motives became part of the proprium they were pursued for their own sake and not for external encouragement or reward. Such motives are self-sustaining because they have become part of the person. To say that healthy adults pursue goals because they are rewarded or reinforced for doing so was, to Allport, ridiculous. For example, Allport commented:

> How hollow to think of Pasteur's concern for reward, or for health, food, sleep, or family, as the root of his devotion to his work. For long periods of time he was oblivious to them all, losing himself in the white heat of research. And the same passion is seen in the histories of geniuses who in their lifetimes received little or no reward for their work. (1961, p. 236)

Allport distinguished between two kinds of functional autonomy: (1) *Perseverative functional autonomy* refers to repetitious activities in which one blindly engages and which once served a purpose but no longer do so. These activities occur independently of reward and independently of the past but are low-level activities of little importance. An example would be when a man still rises at 7:30 each morning although he has been retired for some time. (2) *Propriate functional autonomy* refers to an individual's interests, values, goals, attitudes, and sentiments.

Allport suggested that propriate functional autonomy was governed by three principles.

1. The Principle of Organizing the Energy Level This principle states that when one needs no longer to be concerned with survival and early adjustments in life, a considerable amount of energy becomes available to that person. Since this energy is no longer needed for basic adaptation, it can be diverted into propriate striving, for instance, future goals.

2. The Principle of Mastery and Competence There is an innate need for healthy adults to increase their efficiency and effectiveness and to aspire to greater mastery. In other words, according to Allport, healthy humans have a need to become better and better at more and more things. This is another case of drive induction, instead of drive reduction.

3. The Principle of Propriate Patterning The person's proprium is the frame of reference which determines what is pursued in life and what is rejected. This means that, although motives become functionally independent of the past, they do not become independent of the proprium. In other words, all motives must be compatible with the total self (proprium). This assures the consistency and the integration of the personality.

Of course, not all behavior is caused by functionally autonomous motives. Much human behavior is stimulated by biological drives, reflex action, reinforcement, and habit. Allport recognized this but felt that behavior under the control of functionally autonomous motives was characteristically human and therefore should be the personality theorist's focus of study.

THE HEALTHY, MATURE ADULT PERSONALITY

Clearly Allport's theory did not grow out of psychoanalysis. In fact, he was not a psychotherapist and was not interested in emotionally disturbed people. He felt strongly that the principles governing the healthy, adult personality could not be learned by studying animals, children, the past, or neurotics. According to Allport, the difference between a neurotic and a healthy person is that the former's motives lie in the past while the latter's lie in the future.

The concern that Allport had for studying healthy humans instead of neurotics is remarkably close to the position taken more recently by Maslow (see chapter 13). Maslow felt that psychologists, by being overconcerned with emotionally disturbed individuals, were incapable of understanding healthy, exceptional individuals. Maslow attempted to correct the situation by exploring the lives of what he called self-actualizing people. The list of characteristics that Maslow found such individuals to possess is very similar to the following list of attributes which Allport felt characterized the normal, healthy adult:

1. The Capacity for Self-extension Healthy adults participate in a wide range of events. They have many friends and hobbies and tend to be active politically and/or religiously.

2. The Capacity for Warm Human Interactions Healthy adults are capable of intimate relationships with others without being possessive or jealous. Such people are compassionate as evidenced by their ability to tolerate major differences in values and beliefs between themselves and others.

3. Demonstrates Emotional Security and Self-acceptance Healthy adults have the tolerance necessary to accept the conflicts and frustrations inevitable in life. They also have a positive image of themselves. This is contrasted with the immature person who is filled with self-pity and who has a negative self-image.

4. Demonstrates Realistic Perceptions Healthy adults see things as they are, not as they hoped they would be. Such individuals display good common sense when appraising a situation and in determining adjustments to it.

5. Demonstrates Self-objectification Healthy adults have an accurate picture of their own assets and liabilities. They understand the difference between their real selves and their ideal selves and know the difference between what they think of themselves and what others think of them.

The person possessing this self-insight, according to Allport, also will have a good sense of humor. Humor necessitates the ability to laugh at what one cherishes, including oneself. Individuals who are not sure of themselves see nothing funny about jokes directed at them or at what they believe.

6. Demonstrates a Unifying Philosophy of Life According to Allport the lives of healthy adults are "ordered or steered toward some selected goal or goals. Each person has something quite special to live for, a major intention" (1961, pp. 294–295).

Allport, like Jung and Erikson and to a somewhat lesser degree like Adler, placed great importance on religion and like Jung, Allport believed that the importance of religion can be realized only in adulthood. Allport believed that all healthy adults have a need for some unifying orientation, and although this orientation is commonly religious in nature it does not need to be.

> Psychologically speaking we should point to the close analogy that exists between a religious orientation and all other high-level schemata that influence the course of becoming. Every man, whether he is religiously inclined or not, has his own ultimate presuppositions. He finds he cannot live his life without them, and for him they are true. Such presuppositions, whether they be called ideologies, philosophies, notions, or merely hunches about life, exert creative pressure upon all conduct that is subsidiary to them (which is to say, upon nearly *all* of a man's conduct). (Allport 1955, pp. 95–96)

Whereas Freud looked upon the need for religion as characteristic of the neurotic, Allport saw some form of religious orientation as a necessary part of the healthy adult personality.

Given Allport's emphasis on the individual, how does one go about attempting to understand a specific person's personality? Allport felt that one of the best ways was to use personal documents such as diaries, autobiographies, letters, or interviews. Allport's most thorough utilization of personal documents to describe an individual's personality was of a collection of 301 letters written by Jenny Grove Masterson (a pseudonym) over an eleven-year period. The final version of this study was published as *Letters from Jenny* in 1965, although Allport had worked on the case for a number of years prior to that time.

Jenny was born in Ireland in 1868 and moved to Canada when she was five. She had five younger sisters and one younger brother, all of whom were very dependent on her since her father had died when she was eighteen. Jenny outraged her family when she married a railway inspector who had been married previously. She and her husband moved to Chicago where she described life as boring. Her husband died in 1897 when she was twenty-nine years old. Shortly after her husband's death, Jenny gave birth to her only child, whom she named Ross. She worked hard and devoted herself to Ross. Until Ross was seventeen, he and his mother were very close, but at that time he left to go to Princeton. In his sophomore year Ross enlisted in the army in the Ambulance Corps. Before his going overseas to France, Jenny visited Ross at Princeton and met two of his friends, Glenn and Isabel. It was with Glenn and Isabel whom Jenny was later to correspond.

When Ross returned home, he had changed completely and, except for finishing his degree at Princeton, his life was characterized by a series of failures and quarrels with his mother. The most intense quarrel followed Jenny's discovery of Ross's secret marriage. On this Allport commented: "On his first visit to her following her discovery she drove him out of her room with violent denunciations and a threat to have him arrested if he ever tried to see her again" (1965, p. 6).

Following this encounter, Jenny contacted Ross's old friends, Glenn and Isabel, who were now married and teaching in an eastern college town. They offered "to keep in touch" with Jenny, and the result was 301 letters. The correspondence started in March, 1926 when Jenny was fifty-eight and continued until October, 1937 when Jenny died at the age of seventy. She outlived her son Ross by eight years.

The letters are intriguing, and the reader is urged to read all of them. Two samples are given below to indicate the tone of the correspondence. In a letter dated January 5, 1927, she described her childhood as follows:

> . . . My father dropped dead one day, and had no provision made for his family—7 of them, all under 18. Not one in the house capable of earning a penny. It was my salary that kept the house going. . . . No

> one ever denied it, or pretended to think otherwise, and when I dared to marry the man I had been in love with for years, but dreaded to take my money out of their house . . . why, they said I was like the cow that gave the milk and then kicked the pail. (Allport 1965, p. 27)

Jenny displays pessimism in a letter she wrote in June, 1928:

> . . . Anyway I am firmly convinced that I am "through" and ought to step out. I have done all, of any use, that it is possible for me to do in this world. Whether it was for good or bad it is over and done and nothing can change it now, "The moving finger writes, and having writ moves on" and my days for possible usefulness are past. I should step out, but am a coward. To suppose that Ross needs me would be indeed a joke. (Allport 1965, p. 50)

Allport had thirty-six judges read the letters in sequence and they, along with Allport, used 198 trait names to describe Jenny, but when synonymous traits were lumped together, it was observed that Jenny could be described accurately using eight trait names. They were:

1. Quarrelsome—suspicious
2. Self-centered
3. Independent
4. Dramatic
5. Artistic
6. Aggressive
7. Cynical
8. Sentimental

Using a computer, Paige (1966) made a complex statistical factor analysis of Jenny's letters and isolated eight "factors" characterizing them.

1. Aggression
2. Possessiveness
3. Need for Affiliation
4. Need for Autonomy
5. Need for Familial Acceptance
6. Sexuality
7. Sentience (love of art, literature, etc.)
8. Martyrdom

Upon reviewing Paige's study, Allport concluded that nothing had been gained by using a computer but felt that the subjective impressions of the judges were more informative.

There is probably no better example of what Allport meant by idiographic research than his analysis of Jenny's letters. It is because of this type of research that Allport has been accused of being more of an artist than a scientist.

Besides his studies of religion, prejudice, rumor, and his extensive idiographic study of Jenny through her letters, Allport also investigated expressive behavior and values. Both his studies of expressive behavior and of values retained his emphasis on the importance of the individual. His research on expressive behavior, for example, investigated a person's unique facial expressions, style of walking, speech mannerisms, and handwriting (see Allport & Vernon 1933; Allport & Cantril 1934). His *Study of Values,* first published with Vernon in 1931, is now in its third edition. To study values, Allport and his collaborators (Allport, Vernon, & Lindzey 1960) devised a scale that attempted to determine the extent to which a person emphasized the following values in his or her life:

1. *The Theoretical.* The person emphasizing this value is primarily concerned with the search for truth.
2. *The Economic.* The person emphasizing this value is very pragmatic and interested in the relevance of knowledge.
3. *The Aesthetic.* The person emphasizing this value is strongly inclined toward artistic experiences.
4. *The Social.* The person emphasizing this value gives high priority to developing and maintaining warm human relationships.
5. *The Political.* The person emphasizing this value is primarily interested in attaining power.
6. *The Religious.* The person emphasizing this value gives great importance to seeking unity and harmony in the universe.

Allport, Vernon, and Lindzey (1960) report that the scale produced the expected results; for example, clergymen scored highest on the religious value, art students scored highest on the aesthetic value, and business students scored highest on the economic value.

EVALUATION

In many ways, Allport's theory was the forerunner of the existential-humanistic theories that we will cover in chapters 11, 12, and 13. All humanistic personality theories have in common the emphasis on the uniqueness of the individual, the belief that human motives are not merely biological in nature, that humans are future-oriented, and that psychology should be socially relevant. Clearly, Allport believed all of these things. In fact, Allport resisted many extremely powerful trends in psychology because he felt that they caused humans to lose their individuality.

Allport had many critics. He was consistently criticized for being unscientific. Because all sciences seek to discover general laws, usually by using nomothetic methods, Allport's emphasis on the idiographic method, in which the single case is studied intensively, seemed unscientific. It is perhaps ironic that the other theorist covered in this text who utilized the idiographic approach is B. F. Skinner (chapter 9), a rigorous scientist who has done most of his research on nonhuman subjects. Allport was also criticized for assuming a discontinuity between animals and humans, between child and adult, and between normal and abnormal. He was criticized for placing too much emphasis on the conscious mind at the expense of the unconscious mind and for stressing internal causes of behavior at the expense of external causes. His theory also was criticized for not generating verifiable hypotheses as any good scientific theory should.

Probably Allport's most severely criticized concept was functional autonomy. When most, if not all, accepted points of view in psychology were attempting to determine the relationship between early experience and adult personality, Allport claimed that such a relationship did not exist. He claimed that motivation for present behavior was in the present, not in the past. This notion was attacked as not being verifiable and therefore scientifically meaningless.

There is little doubt that Allport's theory was instrumental in developing what we now call humanistic psychology. His concern with the dignity of each human and with the creation of optimal sociological conditions for human development are clearly seen in the following statement:

> Psychology is truly itself only when it can deal with individuality. . . . We study the human person most fully when we take him as an individual. He is more than a bundle of habits, more than a point of intersection of abstract dimensions. He is more than a representative of his species, more than a citizen of the State, more than an incident in the movements of mankind. He transcends them all. The individual, striving ever for integrity and fulfillment, has existed under all forms of social life—forms as varied as the nomadic and feudal, capitalistic and communistic. No society holds together for long without the respect man shows to man. The individual today struggles on even under oppression, always hoping and planning for a more perfect democracy where the dignity and growth of each personality will be prized above all else. (Allport 1961, p. 573)

SUMMARY

Allport was America's first personality theorist. In his famous 1937 definition of personality, he emphasized that personality was dynamic, organized, and unique. He also said that personality was real in that it both initiates and guides behavior. He distinguished between personality and character, which implies evaluation; and temperament, which with intelligence and physique are the "raw materials" from which personality is constructed; and type, which is a classification used by one person to categorize another person. Allport theorized that traits provided the structure, the uniqueness, and the motivation which characterize a person's personality. Common traits are those shared by a number of individuals. What Allport originally called individual traits are those possessed by only one person. He later renamed them personal dispositions, to avoid their confusion with common traits. Nomothetic methods are used to examine what people have in common, and the idiographic method is used to discover what is true about the individual. Since not all personal dispositions have the same influence on one's behavior, Allport distinguished between cardinal traits, which influence just about everything a person does; central dispositions, of which everyone has five to ten; and secondary dispositions, which are only slightly more general than a complex habit.

Allport believed that the mature adult personality matured slowly, through eight stages. The major attributes that emerge during each stage are: (1) the bodily self, (2) self-identity, (3) self-esteem, (4) self-extension, (5) self-image, (6) self as rational coper, (7) propriate striving; and (8) self as knower. Allport's most controversial concept was functional autonomy, which stated that although one set of circumstances may have originally explained the existence of a motive, that motive can exist in an adult independent of those earlier circumstances. In other words, what was once a means to an end can become an end in itself.

Allport was not very interested in animals, children, or neurotics. He was interested in healthy, adult humans whom he felt had the following characteristics: (1) self-extension, (2) warm human interactions, (3) emotional security and self-acceptance, (4) realistic perceptions, (5) self-objectification, and (6) a unifying philosophy of life. *Letters to Jenny* (1965) summarized a major idiographic research project in which a woman's traits were studied through the 301 letters she had written over an eleven-year period.

Allport's theory can be considered current in light of today's emphasis on psychology's humanistic theories. His theory has been called nonscientific because it is not easily verified and because he insisted on studying the single case rather than group averages.

Discussion Questions

1. First state Allport's definition of personality, as best you can, and then discuss each of the definition's major components.
2. Distinguish among the terms personality, character, temperament, and type.
3. Outline Allport's criteria for an adequate personality theory.
4. Describe Allport's concepts of trait and personal disposition. In your answer describe the various kinds of personal dispositions.
5. Distinguish among personal dispositions, habits, and attitudes.
6. Distinguish between nomothetic and idiographic research techniques.

7. List and describe the various stages in the development of the proprium.
8. Discuss Allport's concept of functional autonomy.
9. List and describe the six characteristics of a normal, healthy, mature adult.
10. Summarize Allport's idiographic study of Jenny.
11. List several positive and several negative aspects of Allport's theory.
12. Explain why Allport had the attitude he did toward the use of lower animals, children, and neurotics as sources of information about personality.

Glossary

Attitude. Attitudes, like habits, are much more specific than traits. One can, for example, have a favorable attitude toward boxing, but this is only a single manifestation of the more general trait of aggressiveness.

Becoming. Allport's description of the process by which the proprium develops. According to Allport, personality is never static; rather, it is always becoming something else.

Bodily "Me". The attribute that emerges during the first stage in the evolution of the proprium. At this stage, infants learn that their bodies exist because of their sensory experiences.

Capacity for Self-extension. The participation in a wide range of events that characterizes the healthy, mature adult.

Capacity for Warm Human Interactions. The ability to have intimate relationships with others without being possessive or jealous. Such an ability characterizes the healthy, mature adult.

Cardinal Dispositions. "A ruling passion" that influences most everything a person does. Only a few individuals possess a cardinal diposition.

Central Dispositions. Those things about a person that you would mention in a letter of recommendation. The five to ten characteristics that summarize a particular person's personality.

Character. A description of an individual that includes a value judgment. Whereas a person's character can be "good" or "bad," a personality cannot be.

Common Traits. Traits shared by a number of individuals.

Emotional Security and Self-acceptance. Two of the characteristics of a healthy, mature adult.

Functional Autonomy. A motive that existed once for some practical reason later exists for its own sake. In other words, a motive that was once a means to an end becomes an end in itself. Allport's most famous and controversial concept.

Habit. A specific mode of responding, for example, putting on clean clothing in the morning, that develops because a more general trait exists, for example, the trait of cleanliness.

Idiographic Method. A research method that studies a single case in great detail and depth.

Individual Traits. Traits possessed by a particular individual. Later in the evolution of his theory, Allport changed the term individual trait to personal disposition.

Need Induction. The creation of needs rather than their reduction. Allport believed that the healthy human lives in accordance with long-term goals which create more problems than they solve. Thus, his theory is said to emphasize need induction rather than need reduction.

Need Reduction. The satisfaction of a basic need. To many theorists, the elimination or reduction of needs is the primary goal in life. Allport did not agree.

Nomothetic Method. A research method that studies groups of individuals and therefore concentrates on average performance rather than on the performance of a single individual.

Perseverative Functional Autonomy. Low-level habits retained even though they are no longer functional.

Personal Disposition. Identical to an individual trait. The term individual trait was changed to personal disposition to avoid confusion with the term common trait.

Personal Documents. To Allport, one of the best ways to study an individual's personality was to examine personal documents such as diaries, autobiographies, and letters.

Personality. According to Allport, personality is the dynamic organization within the individual of those psychophysical systems that determine characteristic behavior and thought.

Principle of Mastery and Competence. The principle that states that there is an innate need for humans to aspire to greater mastery and competence.

Principle of Organizing the Energy Level. The principle that states that energy which was once used for survival can be changed into concern for the future, when survival is no longer an issue.

Principle of Propriate Patterning. The principle that states that the proprium is the frame of reference which is used by a person in determining what is worth pursuing and what is not.

Propriate Functional Autonomy. The important motives around which one organizes one's life. Such motives are independent of the conditions that originally produced them.

Propriate Striving. The attribute that emerges during the seventh stage in the evolution of the proprium. At this stage, the adolescent becomes almost completely future-oriented.

Proprium. All the facts about a person that make him or her unique.

Raw Materials of the Personality. Temperament, intelligence, and physique.

Realistic Perceptions. Those accurate perceptions that characterize the healthy, mature adult.

Secondary Dispositions. More specific than cardinal or central dispositions but still more general than habits and attitudes. A secondary disposition may be a person's preference for loud clothing or for sweet food.

Self as a Rational Coper. The attribute that emerges during the sixth stage in the evolution of the proprium. At this stage, the child begins to use complex mental operations (thinking) to solve problems.

Self as Knower. The attribute that emerges during the eighth and final stage in the evolution of the proprium. At this stage, the proprium is aware of, unifies, and transcends the preceding seven aspects of the proprium.

Self-esteem. The attribute that emerges during the third stage in the evolution of the proprium. At this stage, the child develops a feeling of pride by doing things on his or her own.

Self-extension. The attribute that emerges during the fourth stage in the evolution of the proprium. At this stage, the child's self-identity generalizes to external objects.

Self-identity. The attribute that emerges during the second stage in the evolution of the proprium. At this stage, the child develops a self-identity; for example, realizing that he or she is the same person although conditions change.

Self-image. The attribute that emerges during the fifth stage in the evolution of the proprium. At this stage, the child develops a conscience and begins to formulate future goals.

Self-objectification. The honest appraisal of one's assets and liabilities that characterizes the healthy, mature adult. A person with self-objectification typically has a good sense of humor.

Temperament. One of the raw materials from which personality is shaped. Temperament is the emotional component of the personality.

Trait. A mental structure that initiates and guides reactions and thus accounts for the consistency in one's behavior.

Type. A category into which one person can be placed by another person. To label a person as "an aggressive type" is to place him or her in a descriptive category based on behavior.

Unifying Philosophy of Life. The unifying theme that holds together the life of a healthy, mature adult and gives it meaning. Such a theme is often religious in nature, but, according to Allport, it does not need to be.

chapter 8

raymond b. cattell

Raymond B. Cattell was born in Staffordshire, England in 1905. He remembers his childhood as a happy one, with an abundance of such activities as exploring caves, swimming, and sailing. He does report considerable competition with his brother, however, who was three years older. The fact that England entered World War I when Cattell was nine years old had a major effect on his life. Seeing hundreds of wounded soldiers treated in a nearby house that had been converted into a hospital taught him that life could be short and that one should accomplish as much as possible while one could. As we shall see, this sense of urgency about work has characterized Cattell throughout his academic life.

At sixteen Cattell entered the University of London where he majored in physics and chemistry. He graduated at nineteen with high honors. Throughout his undergraduate years Cattell became increasingly concerned with social problems and increasingly aware that his background in the natural sciences had not prepared him to deal with those problems. These realizations prompted him to enter graduate school in psychology at the University of London where he ultimately earned his M.A. and Ph.D. degrees. While in graduate school, he worked with the famous psychologist-statistician Charles E. Spearman, who invented the technique of factor analysis and applied it to the study of intelligence. As we shall see, Cattell used factor analysis extensively in his study of personality.

After receiving his Ph.D., Cattell had great difficulty finding work doing what he had been trained to do, so he accepted a number of what he called "fringe" jobs. He was a lecturer at the University of Exeter in England (1927 to 1932), and he was the founder and director of a psychology clinic in the school system in the city of Leicester, England (1932 to 1937). In 1937 he was invited by the prominent American psychologist, Edward L. Thorndike, to come to America to become his research associate at Columbia University. Cattell accepted Thorndike's invitation and remembers his first year in New York as depressing because he deeply missed England.

From 1938 to 1941 Cattell was the G. Stanley Hall Professor of Genetic Psychology at Clark University in Worcester, Massachusetts. In 1941 he moved to Harvard where he was a lecturer until 1944.

In the years following graduate school, Cattell never lost interest in applying the statistical technique of factor analysis to the study of personality. Finally at the age of forty, in 1945, Cattell was offered a position at the University of Illinois as research professor and director of the Laboratory of Personality and Group Analysis. Cattell's professional output while he was at the University of Illinois (1945 to 1973) was almost unbelievable.

Cattell married Monica Rogers on December 1, 1930 and had one son who is now a surgeon. His wife left him a few years after their marriage because of their poverty and because of his total dedication to his work. He married again on April 2, 1946 to Alberta Karen Schuetter and had four children.

As already mentioned, Cattell developed early in life the belief that one should work hard and not waste time. Thus far, Cattell has published over three hundred professional articles and more than twenty books. Cattell's first article was published in 1928 when he was twenty-three years old. This means that he has published an average of a book

Raymond B. Cattell. Courtesy Raymond B. Cattell.

or an article every other month for the last fifty years. It is not only the quantity of Cattell's work that is impressive, but its quality as well. His work at the Laboratory of Personality and Group Analysis has won him worldwide recognition as a personality theorist.

In 1953, Cattell wrote an essay on the psychology of the researcher, which won the Wenner-Gren prize given by the New York Academy of Science, and has held the Darwin Fellowship for Genetic Research. The scope of Cattell's research interests is evident in that he has published articles in American, British, Australian, Japanese, Indian, and African journals.

In 1973 he established the Institute for Research on Morality and Self-realization in Boulder, Colorado. It is here where Cattell is currently pursuing his lifelong interest in social problems.

FACTOR ANALYSIS

It seems fair to say that Cattell's theory of personality has not become overwhelmingly popular among those studying personality. His theory is indeed highly informative and in many ways unique among the personality theories, but its lack of wide acceptance can be explained by two facts. First, the sheer bulk of Cattell's work has made it impossible for the "outsider" to digest. For example, Wiggins said in the 1968 edition of the *Annual Review of Psychology*:

> Cattell occupies such a unique position in the field of personality structure that his work demands separate consideration. In the three years under review (May 1964–May 1967) Cattell has published four books, 12 chapters and 40 articles, a total of almost four thousand pages that must somehow be summarized. In addition, he has found time to launch a new journal (*Multivariate Behavioral Research*) and edit a massive handbook (*Handbook of Multivariate Experimental Psychology*). This alone would warrant separate consideration but there is more. The appearance of so many major works and especially the publication of his *Collected Papers* (*Personality and Social Psychology*) has once again forced an evaluation of a body of literature so vast, uneven, and demanding that many American workers have simply tended to ignore it. (p. 313)

All that one could reasonably do with Cattell's theory would be to sample parts of it and hope that his most important concepts are included in that sample. Such a sample is offered in this chapter. Secondly, Cattell relies heavily on *factor analysis*. There is no doubt that the apparent complexities of this technique have caused many to overlook Cattell's theory. We contend, however, that factor analysis is only *apparently* complex and that the logic behind it is simple and straightforward.

Because in most important ways, to understand factor analysis is to understand Cattell's theory of personality, we begin our discussion of his theory of personality with a rudimentary discussion of factor analysis.

The cornerstone of factor analysis is the concept of *correlation.* When two things vary together they are said to be correlated, that is, co-related. For example, there is a correlation between height and weight, because when one increases the other will also tend to increase. The stronger the tendency is for two variables to vary together, the stronger is the correlation between them. The strength of the relationship between two variables is expressed mathematically by a *correlation coefficient.* A correlation coefficient can vary in magnitude from + 1.00 to – 1.00. A coefficient of + 1.00 indicates a perfect positive relationship between two variables; that is, as measures on one variable increase, so will measures on the second variable. A coefficient of – 1.00 indicates a perfect negative relationship between two variables; that is, as measures on one variable increase, measures on the other variable will decrease. A correlation coefficient of + .80 indicates a strong positive relationship between two variables, but not a perfect one. That is, there is a tendency for the two variables to vary positively together. A coefficient of – .56 indicates a moderate negative relationship.

Cattell's procedure is to measure a large number of individuals in as many ways as possible. For example, he records the everyday behavior of various individuals, such as how many accidents they had, the number of organizations to which they belonged, and the number of social contacts they had. He calls the information gathered by such observations *L-Data,* the *L* for "life record." He gives his subjects questionnaires on which they rate themselves on various characteristics. He calls the information gathered by such a technique *Q-Data* the *Q* for questionnaire. Lastly, he uses what he calls objective tests to elicit responses from his subjects, which are then analyzed. For example, subjects take a word association test to which they respond with a word each time the experimenter says a word. Information gathered using this technique is called *T-Data,* the *T* for test.

The next step is to intercorrelate all of the test scores, creating a *correlation matrix.* A simplified correlation matrix is shown in Figure 8–1.

Tests	A	B	C	D	E
A	—	1.00	1.00	.00	.00
B	1.00	—	1.00	.00	.00
C	1.00	1.00	—	.00	.00
D	.00	.00	.00	—	1.00
E	.00	.00	.00	1.00	—

Figure 8–1 A hypothetical correlation matrix showing all of the possible intercorrelations among five tests.

Next the following assumptions are made:

1. Two tests that measure the same thing must give similar results. In other words, tests measuring the same ability will tend to be correlated.
2. The extent of agreement (correlation) between two tests will indicate the extent to which the two tests are measuring the same thing.

With these assumptions in mind, the correlation matrix is examined in order to find which tests are highly correlated with each other. In other words, clusters of correlations are sought. Such a search is called a *cluster analysis*. When a cluster of tests showing high correlation with each other is observed, the tests are considered to be measuring the same ability or characteristic. An ability discovered in such a way is called a *factor*, and in Cattell's theory the term factor can be equated with the term *trait*. For Cattell, factor analysis is a method used to discover traits, which he regarded as the building blocks of personality.

The procedures in Cattell's version of factor analysis can be summarized as follows:

1. Measure a large number of people in a variety of ways.
2. Correlate performance on each measure with performance on every other measure. This creates a correlation matrix.
3. Determine how many factors (traits) need to be postulated in order to account for the various intercorrelations (clusters) found in the correlation matrix.

In the hypothetical correlation matrix depicted in Figure 8–1, it is clear that Tests *A*, *B*, and *C* have a great deal in common with each other since they are perfectly correlated, but they have nothing in common with Tests *D* and *E*. On the other hand, Tests *D* and *E* have a great deal in common since they are perfectly correlated with each other, but they have nothing in common with Tests *A*, *B*, and *C*. Under these circumstances our correlation matrix has detected two separate factors or traits. One is measured by Tests *A*, *B*, and *C*, and the other is measured by Tests *D* and *E*.

A sample of the ways in which the three tests could be related to each other is shown in Figure 8–2. The upper left-hand corner of the picture shows what would happen if the three tests all measure separate factors. The upper right-hand corner shows that Tests *A* and *B* tend to measure a common factor, but Test *C* measures a different factor. The lower left-hand corner of the figure indicates that all three tests are measuring a common factor. The lower right-hand corner of the figure shows Test *A* measuring one factor and Tests *B* and *C* measuring another factor.

Factor analysis, then, is a technique, based on the methods of cor-

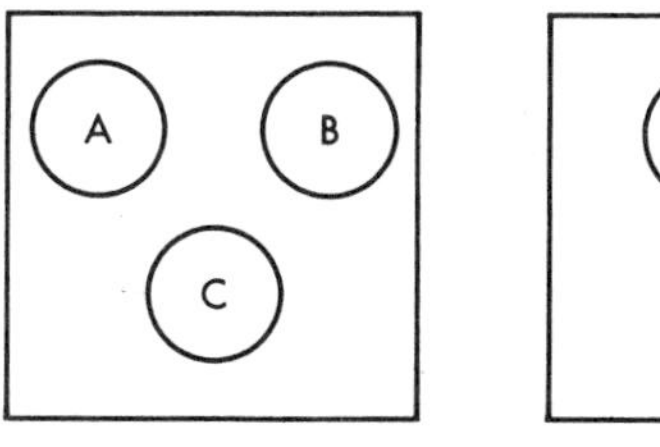

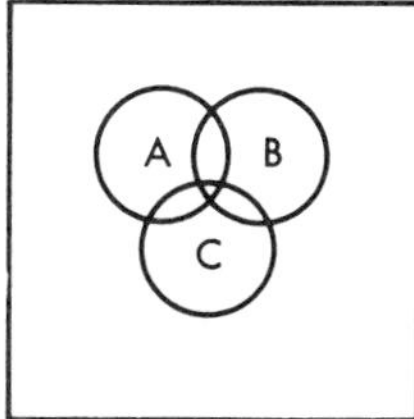

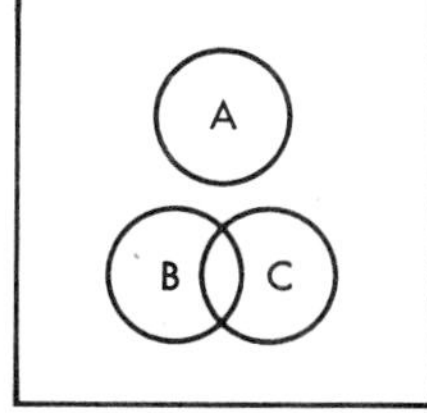

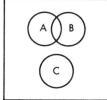

Figure 8–2 Examples of how three tests can be related to each other. See text for explanation.

relation, which attempts to account for the interrelationships found among numerous measures. The technique is certainly not confined to the study of personality. As mentioned earlier, Cattell's mentor, Charles Spearman, used factor analysis to study intelligence, and Cattell, in addition to using it to study personality, used factor analysis to study the characteristics of groups, institutions, and even nations.

CATEGORIES OF TRAITS

As already mentioned, Cattell considers traits as the building blocks of personality, and clearly the concept of trait is the most important concept in his theory. Most of his factor analytic research has been a search for personality traits, and that search has uncovered several categories of traits which we will review next.

Unique Traits and Common Traits Cattell agrees with Allport that there are traits shared by all members of a community (common traits) and those which characterize a single individual (unique traits). Cattell believes that all members of a community share the same traits, but that these traits differ in strength from person to person. In fact, Cattell found that trait strengths differ *in the same person* from time to time. The kind of factor analysis that we described, in which many subjects are measured on many variables and the scores intercorrelated, is called the *R-technique*. The kind of factor analysis that traces the strength of several traits over a period of time for *the same individual* is called the *P-technique*. Figure 8–3 shows the outcome of one P-technique study. This study measured the same individual eighty times on eight traits over a forty-four-day period. The person being studied kept a diary

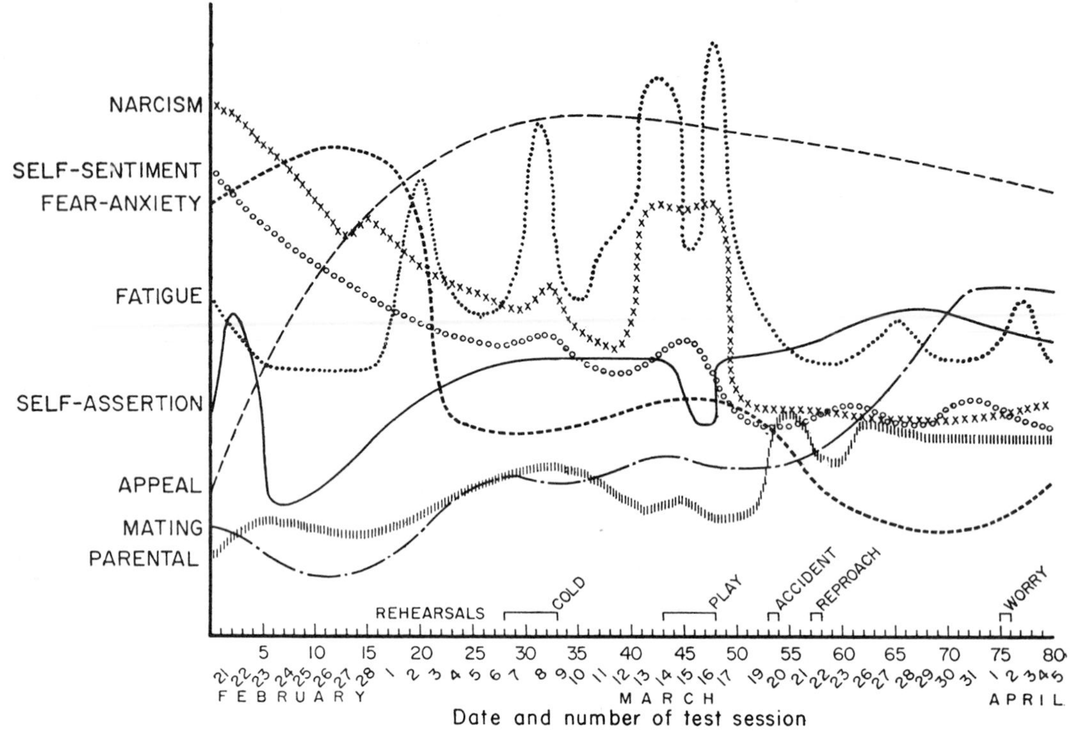

Figure 8–3 An example of Cattell's P-technique in which certain traits that a person possesses are measured over time. (From Cattell 1957, p. 553.)

during the experiment, and several of his major experiences are indicated along the baseline of Figure 8–3. For example, he had to rehearse for a play in which he was to play the lead role, he had a cold, the play for which he rehearsed was held, his father was in an accident, an aunt criticized him for not helping his family enough, and he was worried because his academic advisor was apparently hostile toward him. We can clearly see from Figure 8–3 that the various traits that one possesses will manifest themselves with varying strength as one's life circumstances change.

Surface Traits and Source Traits The difference between surface traits and source traits is probably the most important distinction made in Cattell's theory. Surface traits are groups of observations that are correlated. For example, people with more formal education may go to the movies less than people with less formal education do. Such observations are superficial in that they explain nothing. They are simply a statement of what kind of characteristics tend to be grouped together (correlated). Such characteristics can, and probably do, have many causes.

Source traits, on the other hand, are the causes of behavior. They constitute the most important part of a person's personality structure and are ultimately responsible for all of a person's consistent behavior. Thus, every surface trait is caused by one or more source traits, and a source trait can influence several surface traits.

For Cattell, the search for source traits starts by measuring everything one can measure about a large group of people. The measures are then intercorrelated, and a cluster analysis indicates which measures tend to be measuring the same things. Such a factor analysis yields surface traits. The surface traits are then analyzed to see which of them tend to be related to each other, in other words, stimulated by the same source. Such an analysis provides information about source traits.

Another way to describe the difference between source traits and surface traits is to say that the latter are always manifestations of the former. The source traits can be considered the elements of personality in that everything we do is influenced by them. Cattell concluded that all individuals possess the same source traits but do so in varying degrees. For example, all people possess intelligence (a source trait), but all people do not possess the same amount of intelligence. The strength of this source trait in a given individual will influence many things about that person; for example, what the person reads, who his or her friends are, what he or she does for a living, and the person's attitude toward a college education. All of these outward manifestations of the source trait of intelligence are surface traits. Another example would be all of the outward things a person does in response to being hungry, such as going to the store, buying food, going home, preparing the food, and then eating. All of the observable behaviors related to eating exemplify surface traits, while the hunger drive which causes them all exemplifies a source trait. However, our examples are somewhat misleading, since, as we have seen, hardly anything that a person does is caused by only one source trait.

After extensive research through the years, Cattell concluded that there are approximately sixteen source traits on which people can be compared, and they are listed in Figure 8–4.

Cattell (with Saunders and Stice) constructed his now famous *Sixteen Personality Factor Questionnaire* (1950) around the sixteen source traits that his research had yielded. This test has been used to compare a wide variety of groups. The performance of several different groups on the sixteen Personality Factor Questionnaire is shown in Figure 8–5.
Cattell's *Sixteen Personality Factor Questionnaire* has also been widely used to predict vocational and academic success or failure.

Constitutional and Environmental-mold Traits Some source traits are genetically determined and are called constitutional source traits, and others result from experience and are called environmental-mold traits.

	High Score Indicates A Tendency Toward:	*Low Score Indicates A Tendency Toward:*
Factor A.	*Cyclothymia* Socially Adjusted Easygoing Warm Hearted Frank	*Schizothymia* Socially Hostile Indifferent Secretive
Factor B.	*Intelligence* Alert Imaginative Thoughtful Wise	*Unintelligent* Dull Stupid Unimaginative
Factor C.	*Ego Strength* Unworried Mature Stoic Patient	*Ego Weakness* Anxious Infantile Worried Impatient
Factor E.	*Domination* Confident Boastful Aggressive Forceful	*Subordination* Unsure Modest Complacent Timid
Factor F.	*Surgency* Talkative Genial Cheerful Responsive Alert	*Desurgency* Silent Brooding Depressed Seclusive
Factor G.	*Superego Strength* Conscientious Responsible Persevering Loyal	*Superego Weakness* Unscrupulous Frivolous Irresolute Undependable
Factor H.	*Parmia* Carefree Overtly interested in sex Brave	*Threctia* Careful Overtly disinterested in sex Cowardly
Factor I.	*Premsia* Introspective Sensitive Sentimental Intuitive	*Haria* Insensitive Practical Logical Self-sufficient
Factor L.	*Protension* Suspicious Jealous Skeptical Wary	*Security* Credulous Trustful Unsuspecting Gullible
Factor M.	*Autia* Eccentric Placid Complacent Self-absorbed	*Praxernia* Practical Conventional Poised Earnest

	High Score Indicates A Tendency Toward:	Low Score Indicates A Tendency Toward:
Factor N.	*Shrewdness* Socially Alert Insightful regarding others Expedient Calculating	*Naiveté* Socially Clumsy Crude Indifferent Apathetic
Factor O.	*Guilt Proclivity* Timid Worrysome Depressed Moody	*Guilt Rejection* Self-Confident Cheerful Without Fear Self Sufficient
Factor Q(1).	*Radicalism* Encourages Change Rejects Convention Freethinking	*Conservatism* Rejects Change Disgusted by Foul Language Conservative
Factor Q(2).	*Self-Sufficiency* Temperamentally Independent Prefers working with a few assistants rather than a committee Prefers reading to classes Prefers textbooks to novels	*Group-Sufficiency* Seeks Social Approval Group Dependent Prefers to travel with others Believes there are more nice people than foul
Factor Q(3).	*Controlled Will* Believes in insurance rather than luck Sensitive to uncertainty Does not make promise he cannot keep Does not say things which he later regrets	*Uncontrolled Will* Careless Rapidly changing interests Tries several approaches to the same problem Does not persevere in the face of obstacles
Factor Q(4).	*ID-Significance* Free-Floating Anxiety Unexpected lapses of memory Suffers frustration because of unsatisfied physiological needs	*ID-Insignificance* Relaxes Composed Few periods of depression Disinclined toward worry

Figure 8–4 The factors that Cattell concluded were the building blocks of the personality. Note that each factor is bipolar. A high score on a particular factor indicates a tendency to possess the traits on the left of the diagram, and a low score indicates a tendency to possess the traits listed on the right side of the diagram.

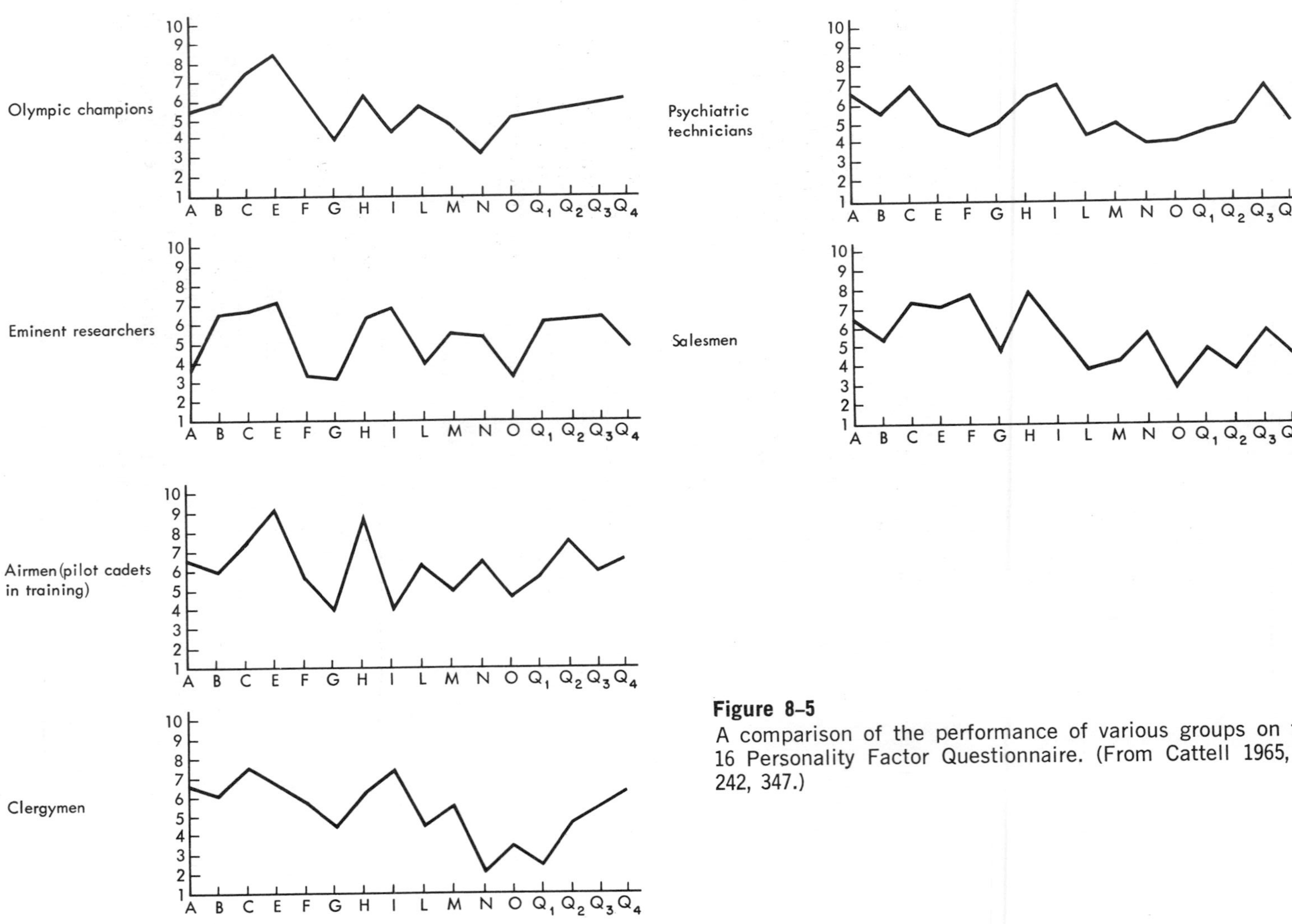

Figure 8–5
A comparison of the performance of various groups on the 16 Personality Factor Questionnaire. (From Cattell 1965, p. 242, 347.)

> If source traits found by factorizing are pure, independent influences, as present evidence suggests, a source trait could not be due both to heredity and environment but must spring from one or the other. . . . Patterns thus springing from *internal* conditions or influences we may call *constitutional source traits*. . . . On the other hand, a pattern might be imprinted on the personality by something external to it. . . . Such source traits, appearing as factors, we may call *environmental-mold traits*, because they spring from the molding effect of social institutions and physical realities which constitute the cultural pattern. (Cattell 1950, pp. 33–34)

Thus, some of the sixteen source traits are determined genetically and some are culturally determined.

Ability Traits Some source traits that a person possesses determine how effectively he or she works toward a desired goal; such traits are called ability traits. One of the most important ability traits is intelligence. Recently, Cattell has distinguished between two kinds of intelligence, *crystallized* and *fluid*. He defines fluid intelligence as "that form of general intelligence which is largely innate and which adapts itself to all kinds of material, regardless of previous experience with it" (1965, p. 369). Cattell defines crystallized intelligence as "a general factor, largely in a type of abilities learned at school, representing the effect of past application of fluid intelligence, and amount and intensity of schooling; it appears in such tests as vocabulary and number ability measures" (1965, p. 369).

Cattell believes that too often a person's intelligence is equated with crystallized intelligence which most traditional IQ tests attempt to measure. To help remedy the situation, Cattell developed the *Culture Fair Intelligence Test* which was designed to measure fluid intelligence.

Cattell's research has led him to believe that 80 percent of a person's intelligence is determined by heredity (for example: Cattell, Stice & Kristy 1957). He feels that what we call intelligence is 80 percent a genetically determined aptitude (fluid intelligence) and 20 percent an experientially determined achievement (crystallized intelligence). But much to Cattell's dismay, it is the latter which is typically measured by standard IQ tests, rather than the former.

Temperament Traits These are genetically determined characteristics which determine a person's general "style and tempo." Temperament traits determine the speed, energy, and emotion with which a person responds to a situation. They determine how mild mannered, irritable, or persistent a person is. Temperament traits, therefore, are constitutional source traits that determine a person's emotionality.

Dynamic Traits Whereas other traits are the building blocks of personality, dynamic traits set the personality in motion. Dynamic traits set the person in motion toward some goal; they therefore are the motivational elements of personality. Cattell elaborated four different dynamic or motivational traits: ergs, metaergs, sentiments, and attitudes. We will consider each.

ERGS, METAERGS, SENTIMENTS, AND ATTITUDES

Ergs An erg is a dynamic, constitutional source trait. An erg is very similar to what other theorists have called drives, needs, or instincts. Cattell chose the term erg (from the Greek *ergon* meaning energy), because he felt the other motivational terms were too ambiguous. The ergs provide the energy for all behavior. Cattell defines erg as:

> An innate psycho-physical disposition which permits its possessor to acquire reactivity (attention, recognition) to certain classes of objects more readily than others, to experience a specific emotion in regard to them, and to start on a course of action which ceases more completely at a certain specific goal activity than at any other. (1950, p. 199)

It can be seen from this definition that an erg has four aspects:

1. It causes selective perception; that is, it causes some things to be attended to more than others. For the hungry person, food-related events are attended to more than events unrelated to food.
2. It stimulates an emotional response to certain objects. For example, the thought of eating is a pleasant one.
3. It stimulates goal-directed behavior. For example, the hungry person will do whatever is necessary to come into contact with food.
4. It results in some sort of consummatory response. That is, when one comes into contact with food one will eat it.

Cattell's research has revealed eleven ergs, which are listed on the right-hand side of Figure 8–6.

Metaergs A metaerg is a dynamic source trait with an environmental origin. In other words, a metaerg is an environmental-mold, dynamic source trait. Thus, a metaerg is the same as an erg except for its origin. Both ergs and metaergs cause motivational predispositions toward certain environmental objects. But ergs are innate whereas metaergs are learned. Metaergs are divided into *sentiments* and *attitudes*. According to Cattell, sentiments are "major acquired dynamic trait structures which cause their possessors to pay attention to certain objects or classes of objects, and to feel and react in a certain way with regard to them." (1950, p. 161). Cattell believes that sentiments are usually centered on such things as one's career or profession, sports, religion, one's parents, one's spouse or sweetheart, or oneself. The most powerful sentiment of all, according to Cattell, is the *self-sentiment* which organizes the entire personality.

> In the first place, the preservation of the self as a physically healthy and intact going concern is obviously a prerequisite for the satisfaction of any sentiment or erg which the individual possesses! So also is the preservation of the social and ethical self as something which the community respects. . . . Dynamically, the sentiment towards maintaining the self correct by certain standards of conduct, satisfactory to community and super-ego, is therefore a *necessary instrumentality* to the satisfaction of most other of our life interests. . . . It contributes to all sentiment and ergic satisfactions, and this accounts also for its dynamic strength in controlling, as the 'master sentiment,' all other structures. (Cattell 1965, pp. 272–273)

A sentiment is an acquired predisposition to respond to a class of objects or events in a certain way. An *attitude* is more specific but is derived from a sentiment which, in turn, is derived from an erg. An attitude, according to Cattell, is a tendency to respond in a particular way in a particular situation to a particular object or event. Cattell (1957, p. 444) describes the manifestation of an attitude:

In these circumstances (Stimulus situation)	I (organism)	want so much (Interest-need, of a certain intensity)	to do this (Specific goal, course of action)	with that. (Object concerned in action)

Thus an attitude is an interest, of a certain intensity, in doing something with something in a certain situation.

Subsidiation By the term subsidiation Cattell meant simply that sentiments are subsidiary to ergs (that is, dependent on them), and attitudes are subsidiary to sentiments. This arrangement is diagrammed in what Cattell called the *dynamic lattice,* shown in Figure 8–6.

It can be seen in Figure 8–6 that ergic desires are seldom satisfied directly. Instead, one usually goes about satisfying a basic need indirectly. For example, one may develop skills in order to get a job, in order to get married, or in order to satisfy one's sex drive. Cattell called this indirect satisfaction of an ergic impulse *long-circuiting*. Also, it can be seen that each sentiment is a function of, or subsidiary to, a number of ergs. For example, the sentiment toward wife seems to reflect the ergs of sex, gregariousness, protection, and self-assertion. The most important point about the dynamic lattice is that it demonstrates the complexity of human motivation. Attitudes, sentiments, and ergs are constantly interacting and are constantly reflecting not only current circumstances, but also an individual's future goals.

PERSONALITY DEVELOPMENT

Like most personality theorists, Cattell believes personality development to be a function of both motivation and learning. Motivation is responsible for many changes in perceptual and behavioral capabilities.

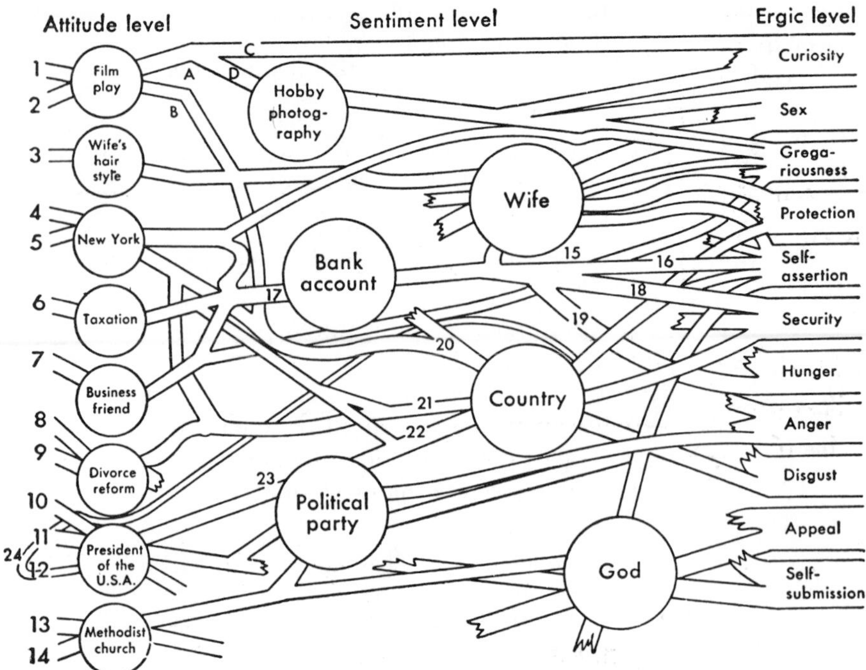

Figure 8–6 A dynamic lattice showing the relationship among ergs, sentiment, and attitudes. (From Cattell 1950, p. 158.)

Learning allows changes in the ways ergs are satisfied; that is, learning is responsible for the development of sentiments and attitudes.

Cattell believes that there are three kinds of learning: *classical conditioning, instrumental conditioning, and structured learning.* He defines classical conditioning as a situation in which "a new stimulus gets attached to an old response by occurring a moment before the old stimulus" (1965, p. 266). Instrumental conditioning (also called reward learning or operant conditioning) is learning to perform a response that will produce a reward.

Cattell feels that both classical and instrumental conditioning are relatively unimportant because they deal with only one stimulus or one response at a time. He feels a third kind of learning, which he calls *personality* or *structured learning,* is much more important. According to Cattell, the learning process, as it occurs in real life, cannot be neatly divided into conditioned reflexes. Rather, it typically is a change in a person's entire constellation of traits. In other words, when something is learned, it influences one's entire personality structure in one way or another; thus the name "structured learning," indicating that one personality structure existed before learning took place, and that another personality structure existed after learning took place.

As an example of how structured learning is produced, Cattell shows the many adjustments that are possible if the satisfaction of an erg is blocked. He describes the various adjustment possibilities as a series of *dynamic crossroads*, which are summarized in Figure 8–7. It can be seen in Figure 8–7 that the arousal of ergic tension can result in anything from immediate satisfaction to pathological disorders, depending on the circumstances. In any case, one's trait structure is modified somewhat from the experience, and therefore structured learning has taken place.

SYNTALITY

Cattell feels that since much of people's behavior is determined by their group affiliations, it is important to know as much as possible about the groups to which people belong. Whereas the term personality summarizes an individual's traits, the term *syntality* summarizes a group's traits. Cattell studied groups such as various religions, schools, peer groups, and nations in the same way that he studied people. For example, in one study (Cattell, Breul, & Hartman 1952) forty countries

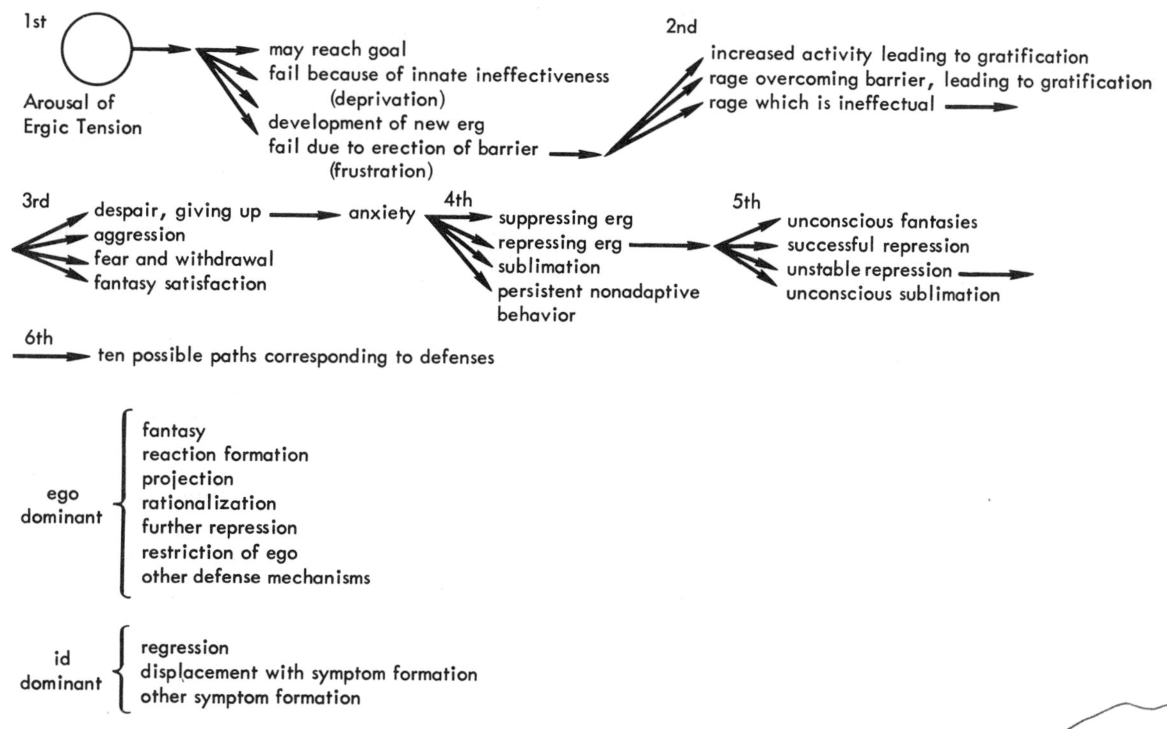

Figure 8–7 The adjustment possibilities or dynamic crossroads that follow the arousal of ergic tension. (Summarizes information from Cattell 1950, pp. 209–247.)

were evaluated on seventy-two variables. All measures were intercorrelated and factor analyzed. It was found that the major differences between the countries could be explained using the following four factors:

Factor 1: Enlightened Affluence versus Narrow Poverty
Factor 2: Vigorous Order versus Unadapted Rigidity
Factor 3: Cultural Pressure and Complexity versus Direct Ergic Expression
Factor 4: Size

Bischof summarized several of Cattell's studies of group characteristics:

> 1. Differences appear to exist in variability of the crystallized and fluid intelligence. Crystallized intelligence is probably less variable in cultures with school systems such as our own.
> 2. In a study of Hawaiian children, approximately half of whom were of Japanese extraction, Cattell found a commonality or corresponding agreement of the Primary Personality Factors in both American and Japanese extraction children.
> 3. Other data indicate that citizens of the United States have lower emotional scores than other national groups. The averages for French citizens and Asiatic Indians were approximately twice as high in degrees of emotionality. Emotionality scores for British, Japanese, and Italian subjects fell, in the average, somewhere between the French and American emotionality measurements. Cattell tentatively concluded that people living in nations which bordered free enterprise and communist nations had the highest scores on emotionality.
> 4. In a comparison between American and British university undergraduate students, there was a significantly higher level of anxiety among the Americans. American university students seemed to be more extraverted than the British. The undergraduates in Britain indicated higher ego strength than the American group. The American group indicated a higher superego development than the British group. Further work with second order factors gave some indication that the American students were more emotionally sensitive and far more radical than their British counterparts. The British students also seemed to be less anxious and more conservative.
> 5. Cattell found that both large and small groups, when given the choice of working with or without a leader after some experience, always decided to elect a leader. Cattell's concern has been not with how or when they picked a leader but with the very poor method of leader selection that he found in the groups he studied. Most of the leaders were extremely inefficient and widely prone to making errors. (1970, p. 472)

Thus the groups that influence people have traits, too, and these traits can be uncovered by factor analysis just as the traits characterizing people can be discovered using that technique. Once group or national traits have been discovered, a wide variety of comparisons can be made.

This kind of research is certainly one of Cattell's most remarkable contributions.

THE SPECIFICATION EQUATION

Like Allport, Cattell is mainly interested in normal people. He is interested in being able to predict with considerable accuracy how people will respond in various situations. In arriving at his predictions, Cattell is very much a *determinist.* That is, he believes that behavior is a function of a finite number of variables, and if those variables are completely known, human behavior can be predicted with complete accuracy. Such a belief characterizes determinism. Of course, Cattell and other determinists realize that all of the variables influencing behavior can never be known, so the prediction of behavior will always be probabilistic. Realizing this, the determinist says that as more is known about the variables influencing human behavior, predictions of human behavior will become more accurate. According to Cattell, this is also true in the realm of personality research. The more we know about the various traits of a particular person, the better we will be able to predict his or her behavior.

What, then, is personality to Cattell? It is that which provides consistency, thus making prediction possible.

> *Personality is that which permits a prediction of what a person will do in a given situation.* The goal of psychological research in personality is thus to establish laws about what different people will do in all kinds of social and general environmental situations. . . . Personality is . . . concerned with *all* the behavior of the individual, both overt and under the skin. (Cattell 1950, pp. 2–3)

In general, Cattell's position can be symbolized as follows:

$$R = f(P,S)$$

in which:

R = the person's reaction
P = the person's personality
S = the situation

In other words, how a person behaves is a function of both the person's personality and the given situation.

Obviously, this formula is an oversimplification of Cattell's point of view. In order to predict accurately a person's performance, what was symbolized *P* (personality) must be spelled out in greater detail. What exactly is a person's personality? According to Cattell, it is all of the traits that he or she possesses. Thus, a measure of each of a person's traits must be included in the formula. Also, since the importance of a person's traits will vary from situation to situation, the importance or weight of each trait must be specified in each situation. Such a specification is called the trait's *factor loading.* In addition to a person's stable traits, other more temporary conditions may influence behavior at certain times. For example, he or she may be sick or fatigued. Likewise, certain situations may require that the person play a role, and such a requirement will strongly influence behavior. Temporary body states such as fatigue, illness, anxiety, and required social roles are called *situational modulators,* since they are thought to modulate behavioral expressions.

Now it becomes clear how complicated it is to predict a person's behavior. We must know what traits a person possesses, how important they are to the situation of interest, the person's present bodily state, and what roles the situation will stimulate him or her to play. The general formula just given becomes the following formula, which Cattell calls the specification equation (Cattell 1965, p. 265):

$$P_j = s_{j_A} A \ldots + s_{j_T} T \ldots + s_{j_E} E \ldots + s_{j_M} M \ldots + s_{j_R} R \ldots + s_{j_S} S$$

Where:

- P_j = performance in situation j
- A = ability traits
- T = temperament traits
- E = ergic tensions present
- M = metaergs (sentiments and attitudes)
- R = roles called for in the situation
- S = temporary bodily states such as fatigue, illness or anxiety
- s_j = a weight or "loading" indicating the importance of each of the above influences in situation j.

This formula simply restates Cattell's assumption of determinism; if you want to know how a person will react to a certain situation, list his or her traits and weigh each one in terms of their relevance to the situation. For example, if the person were in a problem-solving situation, the ability trait of intelligence would be given great weight or a high factor loading. When this is done with each of a person's traits and when the situational modulators are taken into consideration, the person's behavior is thought to be highly predictable.

EVALUATION

Cattell's theory, like most theories of personality, has received mixed reviews. On the positive side, many feel that too much personality research has been unscientific, and therefore Cattell's effort to quantify personality is most welcome. There is no doubt that Cattell has been a careful researcher in one of psychology's more complex areas. His use of factor analysis has necessitated the clear and unambiguous definition of his concepts. However, as one may expect, there are those who look upon Cattell's attempt to quantify personality as negative rather than positive, saying that scientific method is not appropriate to the study of human attributes.

Allport was disturbed by Cattell's emphasis on groups rather than on individuals. Allport felt that Cattell's method yielded average traits which no individual actually possessed.

> An entire population (the larger the better) is put into the grinder, and the mixing is so expert that what comes through is a link of factors in which every individual has lost his identity. His dispositions are mixed with everyone else's dispositions. The factors thus obtained represent only *average* tendencies. Whether a factor is really an *organic* disposition in any one individual life is not demonstrated. All one can say for certain is that a factor is an empirically derived component of the *average* personality, and that the average personality is a complete abstraction. This objection gains point when one reflects that seldom do the factors derived in this way resemble the dispositions and traits identified by clinical methods when the *individual* is studied intensively. (Allport 1937, p. 244)

We find Cattell's theory refreshingly different and very much in tune with the times. Perhaps it is the only theory that uses a research technique as complicated as its object of study. No one denies that human personality is complex, and it makes sense that our most sophisticated statistical technique (factor analysis) should be used to study it. It makes even more sense now that computers are available to aid in the analysis. Remember, it is no longer important for us to find *the* correct theory of personality. Instead, our search is for theories that cumulatively aid in our understanding of the complex phenomenon called personality. Cattell's theory illuminates still other aspects of personality which otherwise would remain in darkness.

SUMMARY

Cattell's approach to the study of personality first measures a large group of individuals in as many ways as possible. The measures then are intercorrelated and displayed in a correlation matrix. The measures that are moderately or highly correlated are thought to be measuring the same attribute. This procedure is called factor analysis, and the attributes it detects are called factors or traits. Cattell describes a number of different kinds of traits. For example, he feels that common traits are shared by all members of a community and that unique traits are possessed only by a specific individual. Unlike Allport, Cattell is mainly concerned with common traits. His most important distinction is between surface traits and source traits. Surface traits are those that are actually measured and are, therefore, expressed in overt behavior of some kind. Source traits are those that are the underlying causes of overt behavior. He feels that most people have about sixteen source traits. Some source traits are genetically determined and are called constitutional traits. Other source traits are shaped by one's culture and are called environmental-mold traits. Cattell also distinguishes among ability, temperament, and dynamic traits. Ability traits determine how well a task is performed. The most important ability trait is intelligence of which Cattell describes two kinds. Fluid intelligence is general problem-solving ability and is thought to be genetically determined. Crystallized intelligence is the cumulated knowledge of the kind learned in school and is thus gained through experience. Temperament traits are constitutional and determine a person's emotional make-up. Dynamic traits are those that set the person in motion toward a goal; in other words, they determine a person's motivational make-up. Cattell distinguishes two categories of dynamic traits: ergs and metaergs. Ergs are roughly equivalent to instincts, biological needs, or primary drives. Metaergs are learned drives, divided into sentiments and attitudes. Sentiments are predispositions to act in certain ways to classes of objects or events. Attitudes are specific responses to specific objects or events. Since ergs are at the core of one's motivational patterns, sentiments are said to be subsidiary to ergs, and since attitudes are dependent on sentiments, attitudes are said to be subsidiary to sentiments. Cattell diagrams the relationships among ergs, sentiments, and attitudes in what he calls the dynamic lattice. The fact that humans almost inevitably take indirect routes to satisfy ergic tensions is referred to as long-circuiting.

To explain how personality develops, Cattell postulates three kinds of learning: classical and instrumental conditioning and structured learning. The latter is by far the most important kind of learning, since it involves a change in one's entire personality. Cattell exemplifies structured learning by showing what happens at a number of choice points following the arousal of ergic tension. A series of such choice points is called dynamic crossroads.

Whereas factor analysis yields personality traits when applied to humans, it yields syntality when applied to the study of specific groups. Cattell is very much a determinist in that he believes that when an individual's traits are specified, when these traits are weighted or loaded according to their importance in a given situation, and when temporary influences such as fatigue, illness, or anxiety are taken into consideration, a person's behavior can be predicted with considerable accuracy. Prediction is made by including as much information about a person as possible in a specification equation.

Cattell's theory is probably the only theory of personality that employs a research technique as complicated as that which it is designed to study. He has been praised for his scientific approach to the study of personality and criticized by those who feel certain human attributes are not quantifiable.

Discussion Questions

1. Describe the technique of factor analysis as Cattell used it to study personality.
2. Distinguish between surface traits and source traits.
3. Distinguish among ability, temperament, and dynamic traits.
4. Distinguish between fluid and crystallized intelligence.
5. Discuss ergs, metaergs, and the dynamic lattice.
6. What is meant by subsidiation?
7. What is meant by long-circuiting?
8. Discuss Cattell's concept of structured learning. Include a discussion of the dynamic crossroads in your answer.
9. Disuss Cattell's concept of syntality. Give a few examples of what Cattell found when he studied the characteristics of various groups.
10. Report and elaborate on as many of the components of the specification equation as you can.
11. Differentiate between the *R* and *P* factor analytic techniques.
12. Respond to the statement "Factor analysis is only as good as the information fed into it."
13. Summarize, as best you can, the essence of Cattell's theory of personality.
14. What is Allport's major criticism of Cattell's theory?

Glossary

Ability Trait. A trait that determines how effectively a person works toward a desired goal. Intelligence is such a trait.

Attitude. A learned tendency to respond in a particular way in a particular situation to a particular object or event. Attitudes derive from sentiments which in turn derive from ergs. An attitude is one kind of metaerg.

Classical Conditioning. The kind of learning in which a stimulus that did not originally elicit a response is made to do so. An example would be when a dog is made to salivate at the sound of a buzzer which had been associated with food.

Cluster Analysis. The systematic search of a correlation matrix in order to discover factors.

Common Trait. A trait shared by all members of a community.

Constitutional Trait. A trait that is genetically determined.

Correlation. The condition that exists when values on two variables vary together in some systematic way.

Correlation Coefficient. A mathematical expression indicating the extent to which two variables are correlated. Correlation coefficients can vary from + 1.00, indicating a perfect positive correlation, to − 1.00, indicating a perfect negative correlation.

Correlation Matrix. A display of the many correlation coefficients that results when a large number of sources of information are intercorrelated.

Crystallized Intelligence. The kind of intelligence that comes from formal education or from general experience. This is the kind of intelligence that most intelligence tests attempt to measure.

Culture Fair Intelligence Test. A test designed to measure fluid intelligence rather than crystallized intelligence.

Determinism. The belief that behavior is a function of a finite number of variables, and if those variables were completely known, behavior could be predicted with complete accuracy.

Dynamic Crossroads. The many possible behavior patterns that result when ergic satisfaction is blocked.

Dynamic Lattice. A diagram showing the relationships among ergs, sentiments, and attitudes.

Dynamic Trait. A motivational trait that sets a person in motion toward a goal. Cattell postulated the existence of two kinds of dynamic traits: ergs and metaergs.

Environmental-mold Trait. A trait that is determined by experience rather than by heredity.

Erg. A constitutional dynamic source trait that provides the energy for all behavior. Much the same as what other theorists call a primary drive. Hunger and thirst are examples of ergs.

Factor. An ability or characteristic that is thought to be responsible for consistent behavior.

Factor Analysis. A complex statistical technique based on the concept of correlation which Cattell used to discover and investigate personality traits.

Factor Loading. The weight given to a factor based on its importance to a given situation.

Fluid Intelligence. A general problem-solving ability that is largely innate.

Instrumental Conditioning. Learning to make a response that either will make a reward available or remove an aversive stimulus.

L-Data. Information about a person's everyday life. The "*L*" stands for "life record."

Long-Circuiting. The indirect satisfaction of an erg. An example is a man developing athletic ability in order to be desirable to a female who will satisfy his sexual desires.

Metaerg. An environmental-mold, dynamic source trait. Much the same as what other theorists called secondary or learned drives.

Negative Correlation. The condition that exists when, as values on one variable tend to increase, values on a second variable tend to decrease, and vice versa.

Positive Correlation. The condition that exists when values on two variables tend to increase and decrease together.

P-Technique. The kind of factor analysis that studies how a single individual's traits change over time.

Q-Data. Information provided by people filling out a questionnaire on which they rate themselves on various characteristics.

R-Technique. The kind of factor analysis that studies many things about many people in the hope of finding common traits.

Self-sentiment. The concern for oneself which is a prerequisite to the pursuit of any goal in life.

Sentiment. A learned predisposition to respond to a class of objects or events in a certain way. A sentiment is one kind of metaerg.

Situational Modulators. The temporary conditions, such as fatigue or illness, that influence how a person will respond in a given situation.

Source Traits. These traits constitute a person's personality structure and are thus the ultimate causes of behavior. Source traits are causally related to surface traits.

Specification Equation. A formula listing the various factors influencing behavior in a given situation.

Structured Learning. The kind of learning that results in the rearrangement of one's personality traits. Accoding to Cattell, this is the most important kind of learning.

Subsidiation. The fact that sentiments depend on ergs and attitudes depend on sentiments.

Surface Traits. The outward manifestations of source traits. These are the characteristics of a person that can be observed and measured.

Syntality. The description of the traits that characterize a group or a nation.

T-Data. Information obtained about a person from the performance on a projective test. The "*T*" stands for "test."

Temperament Trait. A constitutional source trait that determines a person's emotionality.

Trait. For Cattell, the term trait can be equated with the term factor. Both refer to an underlying ability or characteristic responsible for consistency in behavior.

Unique Trait. A trait possessed by a single individual. Unlike Allport, Cattell de-emphasized unique traits in his research.

PART FIVE

LEARNING PARADIGM

chapter 9

burrhus f. skinner

B. F. Skinner was born on March 20, 1904 in Susquehanna, Pennsylvania. He was the older of two sons, but his younger brother died at the age of sixteen. Skinner's father was a lawyer who wanted his son to follow in his footsteps, but that was never to be. He was raised according to strict standards but was physically punished only once.

> I was never physically punished by my father (a lawyer) and only once by my mother. She washed my mouth out with soap and water because I had used a bad word. My father never missed an opportunity, however, to inform me of the punishments which were waiting if I turned out to have a criminal mind. He once took me through the county jail, and on a summer vacation I was taken to a lecture with colored slides describing life in Sing Sing. As a result I am afraid of the police and buy too many tickets to their annual dance. (Skinner 1967, pp. 390–391)

Perhaps this unusually small amount of physical punishment influenced Skinner's later theoretical emphasis on the positive rather than on the aversive control of behavior. As we have seen throughout this text, it is not unusual to find the seeds of a theory in the theorists' early childhood experiences.

Skinner's aptitude for creative apparatus building, for which he is now widely known, was evident in his childhood.

> I was always building things. I built roller-skate scooters, steerable wagons, sleds, and rafts to be poled about on shallow ponds. I made see-saws, merry-go-rounds, and slides. I made slingshots, bows and arrows, blow guns and water pistols from lengths of bamboo, and from a discarded water boiler a steam cannon with which I could shoot plugs of potato and carrot over the houses of our neigh-

> bors. I made tops, diabolos, model airplanes driven by twisted rubber bands, box kites, and tin propellers which could be sent high into the air with a spool-and-string spinner. I tried again and again to make a glider in which I myself might fly.
>
> I invented things, some of them in the spirit of the outrageous contraptions in the cartoons which Rube Goldberg was publishing in the *Philadelphia Inquirer* (to which, as a good Republican, my father subscribed). For example, a friend and I used to gather elderberries and sell them from door to door, and I built a flotation system which separated ripe from green berries. I worked for years on the design of a perpetual motion machine. (It did not work.). (Skinner 1967, p. 388)

In high school, Skinner earned money by playing in a jazz band and with an orchestra. He went to Hamilton College, a small liberal arts school in Clinton, New York. He felt that he never fit into the life of the college student, because he was terrible at sports and was "pushed around" by unnecessary requirements like daily chapel. He wrote highly critical articles about the faculty and administration in the school paper and disrupted the campus with a number of tricks. For example, he caused the campus and the local railroad station to be jammed with people by falsely announcing a lecture by Charlie Chaplin. The college president told Skinner to quit his antics or he would not graduate. Skinner graduated with a Phi Beta Kappa Key and an A.B. degree in English literature. It is interesting to note that Skinner never took a course in psychology as an undergraduate.

Skinner left college with a burning desire to be a writer. Part of this desire is explained by the fact that the famous American poet, Robert Frost, had favorably reviewed three of Skinner's short stories. Skinner's first attempt at writing was in the attic of his parents' home.

B. F. Skinner

John Broadus Watson. Courtesy Clark University.

This attempt failed. His next attempt was in Greenwich Village in New York City. This attempt also failed. After two years of trying, Skinner concluded that he "had nothing important to say" and gave up the idea of becoming a writer. He spent the next summer in Europe.

While in Greenwich Village, Skinner read the works of Ivan Pavlov and J. B. Watson which greatly influenced him. Upon returning from Europe in 1928, he enrolled in the graduate program in psychology at Harvard. He at last had found his niche (or as Erikson would say, his identity), and he pursued his studies with extreme intensity. Skinner described his daily routine at Harvard:

> I would rise at six, study until breakfast, go to classes, laboratories, and libraries with no more than fifteen minutes unscheduled during the day, study until exactly nine o'clock at night and go to bed. I saw no movies or plays, seldom went to concerts, had scarcely any dates and read nothing but psychology and physiology. (1967, p. 398)

This high degree of self-discipline characterizes Skinner's work habits to this day.

Skinner earned his M.A. in two years (1930), his Ph.D. in three years (1931) and then remained at Harvard for the next five years as a postdoctoral fellow. He began his teaching career at the University of Minnesota in 1936 and remained there until 1945. It was during this time that Skinner established himself as a nationally prominent experimental psychologist by publishing his famous book *The Behavior of Organisms* (1938).

In 1945 Skinner moved to Indiana University as chairman of the psychology department until 1948 when he returned to Harvard where he has remained ever since.

Skinner has been highly productive, to say the least. In 1948 he published *Walden Two,* which described a society that functioned in accordance with his principles of learning. In 1953 he published *Science and Human Behavior,* which, in this writer's opinion, is the best overall presentation of his theory. *Verbal Behavior* was published in 1957, and in that same year he published (along with Charles B. Ferster) *Schedules of Reinforcement.* Recently he wrote *Beyond Freedom and Dignity* (1971), which became a best seller and garnered reactions from a wide variety of sources, including an extremely negative one from the then vice-president of the United States, Spiro T. Agnew.

Skinner was disturbed that his position had been misunderstood by so many (including many psychologists), so he wrote another book, *About Behaviorism* (1974), which attempted to clarify his position. Of course, the titles listed above represent only a sample of Skinner's many articles and books.

BEHAVIORISM

It is impossible to understand fully Skinner's view of personality without first understanding the school of psychology to which he belongs, which is *behaviorism.* In order to understand behaviorism we must briefly discuss two other schools of psychology. Psychology's first school of thought was *structuralism,* which developed in Germany. The main goal of the structuralists was to study the nature of consciousness through the use of introspection or self-analysis. A well-trained subject was shown an object and was asked to describe the various sensations that the object caused. It was hoped that this process would eventually uncover the elements of thought from which all conscious experience is derived. Structuralism was short-lived for several reasons, but the main one was the growing influence of Darwinism. American psychologists embraced the doctrine of evolution enthusiastically and created America's first school of psychology around it, which was *functionalism.* As the name implies, the functionalist was concerned primarily with discovering how various processes are related to survival. For example, they studied how thinking and behaving functioned in one's adaptation to the environment. It is important to note that the functionalist studied both behavior *and* cognitive processes but did so with the goal of discovering how they enhanced adjustment to the environment.

John B. Watson took the next step. According to Watson, if psychology wanted to be truly scientific, it would have to have a subject matter that could be reliably and objectively studied. This could not be consciousness, because the study of consciousness had been notoriously unreliable and because it could be studied only indirectly through introspection. The subject matter on which Watson insisted was behavior, and he thus founded the school of *behaviorism.* Watson insisted that the study of consciousness be abandoned completely. He also wanted to end explanations of human behavior in terms of instincts. Likewise, he felt that setting man artificially apart from the other animals made no sense. The behavior of both, he said, is governed by the same principles.

Watson believed that, with the exception of a few basic emotions which are inherited, behavior patterns are learned through experience. Therefore, if you can control an individual's experiences, you can create any kind of individual you wish. Watson's following statement of this belief is one of the most famous (or infamous) statements ever made by a psychologist:

> Give me a dozen healthy infants, well-formed, and my own specified world to bring them up in and I'll guarantee to take any one at random and train him to become any type of specialist I might select—doctor, lawyer, artist, merchant, chief, and yes, even beggarman and thief, regardless of his talents, penchants, tendencies, abilities, vocations, and race of his ancestors. (1926, p. 10)

Behaviorism became the rage in American psychology, and although there are signs that its popularity is diminishing, behaviorism still is a dominant force in American psychology. This brings us back to B. F. Skinner, who is no doubt the most famous behaviorist in the world today.

Like most behaviorists, Skinner bypasses the internal workings of the organism (for instance, cognitive and physiological processes) and concentrates on the relationship between environmental events and behavior. For this reason, Skinner's approach has been characterized as the "empty organism" approach. Skinner feels that no information is lost by making a *functional analysis* between measurable experiences and measurable behavior and leaving out the intervening activities. In fact, he said, all of the problems inherent in a study of consciousness can be avoided:

> The mentalistic problem can be avoided by going directly to the prior physical causes while bypassing intermediate feelings or states of mind. The quickest way to do this is to confine oneself to what an early behaviorist, Max Meyer, called the "psychology of the other one": consider only those facts which can be objectively observed in the behavior of one person in its relation to his prior environmental history. If all linkages are lawful, nothing is lost by neglecting a supposed nonphysical link. Thus, if we know that a child has not eaten for a long time, and if we know that he therefore feels hungry and that because he feels hungry he then eats, then we know that if he has not eaten for a long time, he will eat. (Skinner 1974, p. 13)

As we shall see throughout this chapter, Skinner believes strongly that a behavioral technology based on behavioristic principles can solve many of the world's major problems. He believes, however, that many nonscientific explanations of the causes of behavior are inhibiting the utilization of such a technology. His book *Beyond Freedom and Dignity* (1971) describes this problem in great detail. The following quotation from that book nicely summarizes Skinner's concerns:

> The environment is obviously important, but its role has remained obscure. It does not push or pull, it *selects,* and this function is difficult to discover and analyze. The role of natural selection in evolution was formulated only a little more than a hundred years ago, and the selective role of the environment in shaping and maintaining the behavior of the individual is only beginning to be recognized and studied. As the interaction between organism and environment has come to be understood, however, effects once assigned to states of mind, feelings, and traits are beginning to be traced to accessible conditions, and a technology of behavior may therefore become available. It will not solve our problems, however, until it replaces traditional prescientific views, and these are strongly entrenched. (p. 25)

In the following section, we will examine how, according to Skinner, the environment *selects* some behaviors and not others.

RESPONDENT AND OPERANT BEHAVIOR

It should be clear from what has preceded that both John B. Watson and B. F. Skinner represent the behavioristic camp. Although it is true that they both are behaviorists, they are different kinds of behaviorists because each emphasizes a different kind of behavior. Watson accepted the principles of learning developed by Ivan Pavlov as a model for his brand of behaviorism. Pavlov's work on learning contains the following ingredients:

Conditioned Stimulus (CS)—A stimulus that, at the beginning of training, does not elicit a predictable response from an organism.

Unconditioned Stimulus (UCS)—A stimulus that elicits an automatic, natural, and predictable response from an organism.

Unconditioned Response (UCR)—The natural and automatic response elicited by the unconditioned stimulus.

Pavlov found that if the conditioned stimulus were paired several times with the unconditioned stimulus, it gradually would develop the capacity to elicit a response similar to the unconditioned response; such a response was called a *conditioned response* (CR). Pavlovian or *Classical Conditioning* can be diagrammed as follows:

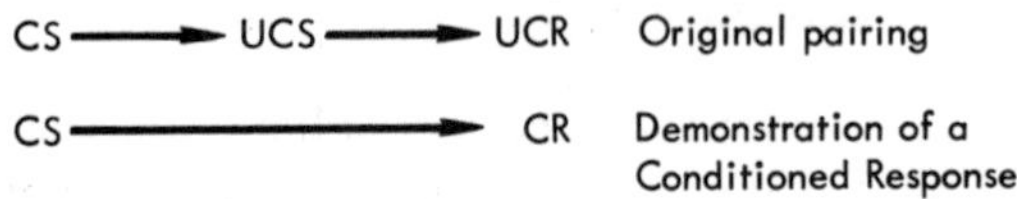

Skinner refers to behavior elicited by a known stimulus as *respondent behavior,* and all conditioned and unconditioned responses are examples. He calls Pavlovian or classical conditioning *type S* conditioning to stress the importance of the stimulus. The important thing to remember about respondent behavior is that there is a direct link between its occurrence and the stimulus that preceded it. In other words, there is a direct stimulus-response association. All reflexes, such as pupillary constriction when light intensity is increased or pupillary dilation when light intensity is decreased, are examples of respondent behavior.

Unlike Pavlov and Watson, Skinner does not emphasize respondent behavior in his theory. Rather, he emphasizes behavior that is *not* linked to any known stimulus. He emphasizes behavior that appears to be simply emitted by the organism rather than elicited by a known stimulus. This is labeled *operant behavior.* Skinner believes that operant behavior is indeed caused by stimulation, but the source of that stimulation is not known, so that behavior *appears* to be emitted. Skinner also said that it is not important to know the origins of operant behavior. The most important characteristic of operant behavior is that it is under the control of its consequences. In other words, it is what happens *after* operant behavior is emitted that determines its fate. The name "operant" now might make more sense; operant behavior operates on the environment so as to change it in some way. The changes in the environment that it causes will determine the subsequent frequency with which the response is made. We will have much more to say about this in the next section, but for now suffice it to say that the conditioning of operant behavior is called *type R* conditioning, to emphasize the importance of the response. Skinner's work has been, and is, primarily on the area of operant conditioning.

OPERANT CONDITIONING

Operant conditioning has been used in psychotherapy, education, and child rearing and has been proposed as a means of redesigning cultures. A technique this powerful must be complex and not readily available, right? Wrong! Operant conditioning is summarized in the following statement: "If the occurrence of an operant is followed by presentation of a reinforcing stimulus the strength is increased" (Skinner 1938, p. 21). Putting this in slightly different form, we can say, if a response is followed by a reward, the response will be strengthened. This enormously powerful rule could not be more simple: *If you want to strengthen a certain response or behavior pattern, reward it!*

How do we know what will act as a reinforcer or reward for a particular organism? Only through its effect on behavior. If a stimulus strengthens behavior, it is a reinforcer; if it does not, it is not.

In order to modify behavior, two things are necessary—behavior and a reinforcer. Having defined operant or type *R* conditioning, we will look in more detail at its characteristics. It should be kept in mind as we go through these characteristics that, according to Skinner, personality is nothing more than consistent behavior patterns that have been strengthened through operant conditioning. As we look more carefully at the principles of operant conditioning, we are at the same time examining Skinner's theory of personality.

Acquisition In order to demonstrate operant conditioning, Skinner invented a small experimental chamber for use with small animals, such as rats or pigeons, that has come to be called a "Skinner box." Typically, the chamber contains a lever, a light, a food cup, and a grid floor. The apparatus is arranged so that when the lever is depressed, a feeder mechanism is activated which delivers a pellet of food into the food cup. In this box the lever press reponse is the operant response of interest and the food pellet is the reinforcer. Even before the reinforcer is introduced into the situation, the animal will probably press the lever now and then just as part of its random activity. The frequency with which an operant response occurs *before* the introduction of a reinforcer is called the *operant level* of that response. When the response is followed by a reinforcer, the frequency with which it is made increases, which is what Skinner meant when he said a response has been strengthened. Operant conditioning is measured by the change in *rate of responding*. Under the conditions described above, the rate with which the lever press response is made will increase (relative to its operant level), by which operant conditioning is said to have been demonstrated. Note that the origins of the initial lever press responses are not known, nor do they need to be. The situation is arranged so that when a lever press response is made, it is reinforced, and when it is reinforced, it is strengthened in that the frequency with which it is made increases.

Summary

So much for rats in Skinner boxes; now how about people? Remember, the behaviorist does not believe that there is one set of learning principles for humans and another set for nonhumans. It is assumed that the same principles apply to all living organisms. Obviously such an assumption has not gone unchallenged. Greenspoon (1955) hypothesized that the therapist's "mmm-hmm" is reinforcing in a situation in which a client is talking quietly. To verify this notion, Greenspoon tested a large number of subjects one at a time in a situation in which he uttered "mmm-hmm" each time a plural noun was spoken by the subject. This arrangement subsequently increased the frequency with which plural nouns were spoken, even though none of the subjects was aware of the fact that his or her verbal behavior was being modified.

Verplanck (1955) had his experimental class at Harvard condition a wide range of simple motor responses using points as the reinforcer.

> . . . After finding a fellow student who was willing to be a subject, the experimenter instructed him as follows: "Your job is to work for points.

> You get a point every time I tap the table with my pencil. As soon as you get a point, record it on your sheet of paper. Keep track of your own points." With these instructions, it seemed likely that a tap, a "point," would prove to be a reinforcing stimulus. The method worked very well. Indeed, the experimenters were now able to condition a wide variety of simple motor behaviors, such as slapping the ankle, tapping the chin, raising an arm, picking up a fountain pen, and so on. They were further able to differentiate out, or shape, more complex parts of behavior, and then to manipulate them as responses. The data they obtained included the results on the manipulation of many of the variables whose effects were familiar in operant conditioning of rats and pigeons. Despite the fact that the experiments were carried out in a variety of situations, the experimenters were able to obtain graphical functions that could not be distinguished from functions obtained on the rat or the pigeon in a Skinner box. (Verplanck 1955, pp. 598–599)

Verplanck and his students went on to condition the response of stating opinions (for example, "I think that," or "I believe that").

> The results of these experiments were unequivocal. In the first experiment, on opinion-statements, every one of 23 subjects showed a higher rate of giving opinion-statements during the 10-minute period when the experimenter reinforced each of them by agreeing with it, or by repeating it back to him in paraphrase, than he showed in the first 10-minute period when the experimenter did not reinforce. (Verplanck 1955, p. 600)

Verplanck, like Greenspoon, found that conditioning did not depend on the subject's awareness of what was happening. Most of Verplanck's subjects were totally unaware of the experimental conditions governing their behavior.

The Greenspoon and Verplanck studies represent only a sample of the hundreds of studies that have confirmed that operant principles apply to human behavior as well as to nonhuman behavior. These two studies were chosen for this book because they show the ease with which that is demonstrated.

Shaping What does one do if the response that one wants to strengthen is not in the organism's response repertoire? The answer is that it is shaped into existence. Assume that the lever press response is one that a rat would initially not make on its own in a Skinner box. Using the principles of operant conditioning already described, the lever press response can be developed through a series of several steps. Using an external hand switch to trigger the feeder mechanism, the rat would be reinforced only for behavior that brings it closer and closer to making the response that is ultimately wanted, which, in this case, is the lever press. We see that the shaping process has two components: *differential reinforcement,* which means that some responses are reinforced and some are not; and *successive approximation,* which means the responses that are reinforced are those that are increasingly close to the response ultimately desired. Hergenhahn listed the following steps as one way of shaping the bar-press response:

1. Reinforce the rat for being on the side of the test chamber containing the bar.
2. Reinforce him for moving in the direction of the bar.
3. Reinforce him for rising up in front of the bar.
4. Reinforce him for touching the bar.
5. Reinforce him for touching the bar with both paws.
6. Reinforce him for exerting pressure on the bar.
7. Reinforce him only for the bar-press response. (1974, p. 361)

Obviously a number of complex human skills need to be shaped into existence over time, since they do not appear initially in fully developed form. Reading is one example. Hergenhahn suggested the following shaping procedure to encourage reading in a young child:

1. Have a number of children's books available and leave them where the child is likely to come across them.
2. If a child avoids books, reward activities related to reading such as noticing signs, naming and/or labeling things, and so on.
3. As the activities in number 2 above are rewarded, the child will tend to do them more often, and when he does, one must become more rigorous in what is expected before giving additional rewards, for example, reading longer signs and attending to more detailed labels.
4. A next step could be to ask the child to get you certain books, such as the red one, the one with the duck on the cover, the one with the A, B, C's on it. When he does, he is rewarded.
5. The next step involves getting the child still more involved with the book, for example, asking him to find certain things like the red barn, the dog, and so on. Again, the child is rewarded in some way for doing this.
6. The above process is continued and refined until the child is reading on his own.
7. To maintain this interest in reading once it has been brought about through these procedures, it is important to go on rewarding the child even when he starts reading on his own, at least to begin with. Eventually, the content of the stories will begin to be enough of a reward to maintain the child's interest in reading. (1972, pp. 40–41)

According to operant theory, the best way to teach a complex skill is to divide it into its basic components and gradually shape it into existence one small step at a time. According to this point of view, the shaping process is extremely important to education and to child rearing. For example, Skinner gave the following example of how a mother may unknowingly shape undesirable behavior in her child:

> The mother may unwillingly promote the very behavior she does not want. For example, when she is busy she is likely not to respond to a call or request made in a quiet tone of voice. She may answer the child only when it raises its voice. The average intensity of the child's vocal behavior therefore moves up to another level. . . . Eventually the mother gets used to this level and again reinforces only louder instances. This

> vicious circle brings about louder and louder behavior. . . . The mother behaves, in fact, as if she has been given the assignment of teaching the child to be annoying. (1951, p. 29)

Extinction If operant behavior that is followed by a reinforcer is strengthened, it should follow that if the reinforcer is removed from the situation the operant behavior would be weakened. This is exactly what happens. If, for example, after the lever press response was conditioned, the feeder mechanism was disconnected, thus creating a situation in which a lever press response is no longer followed by a food pellet, eventually that response would return to its original operant level. In other words, when a reinforcer no longer follows a response, the frequency with which the response is made returns to the level before the reinforcer was introduced into the situation, and we say that *extinction* has taken place.

Extinction can be regarded as the counterpart of acquisition, and the two processes together, according to Skinner, explain much of what we call personality. Briefly stated, rewarded behavior persists, and nonrewarded behavior extinguishes. For example, an infant emits the sounds contained in every language on earth. From these random babblings the child's language is shaped. Those sounds that resemble words of the parents' language are noticed or reinforced in some way, and those utterances that are irrelevant to the parents' language are ignored. The reinforced verbal responses are strengthened and are shaped further, whereas the nonreinforced verbal responses are extinguished. So it is with all the behavior we refer to as personality.

Extinction is important to the Skinnerian view of behavior modification. This view is quite simple: *Reinforce desired behavior and ignore undesirable behavior.* Skinner looks upon extinction as the proper method of dealing with undesirable behavior, *not punishment.* Skinner gave the following example:

> The most effective alternative process (to punishment) is probably *extinction.* This takes time but is much more rapid than allowing the response to be forgotten. The technique seems to be relatively free of objectionable by-products. We recommend it, for example, when we suggest that a parent "pay no attention" to objectionable behavior on the part of his child. If the child's behavior is strong only because it has been reinforced by "getting a rise out of" the parent, it will disappear when this consequence is no longer forthcoming. (1953, p. 192)

We will have more to say about the problems associated with punishment later in this chapter.

Spontaneous Recovery Let us say that we have extinguished the lever press in a rat. That is, since the reinforcement for a lever press was discontinued, that response went back to its original operant level. Now we take the animal out of the Skinner box and put it back in its home cage for a period of time, say twenty-four hours. Next we put it back in the Skinner box. We usually would note that, although there was no additional training, the rate with which the lever press response is made again will increase. This renewed burst of response following a delay after extinction is called *spontaneous recovery*.

Behavioral theory must take spontaneous recovery into account. The therapist and patient, believing that an undesirable habit has been extinguished, both may be disappointed when it reappears, but the reappearance of the habit may simply be spontaneous recovery. In a way, the appearance of spontaneous recovery indicates that extinction was never complete in the first place. After several extinction sessions no spontaneous recovery will occur, even after a prolonged rest period. Like extinction, spontaneous recovery characterizes both classical (type *S*) and operant (type *R*) conditioning.

Discriminative Operants A discriminative operant is an operant response that is made under one set of circumstances but not under others. In describing the Skinner box, it was mentioned that it typically contains a light which is usually above the lever. The circuitry of the Skinner box can be arranged so that a lever press response is reinforced when the light is on but not reinforced when the light is off. Under these circumstances the rate with which the lever is pressed is much higher when the light is on than it is when the light is off. We say that the light has become a *discriminative stimulus* (S^D) for the lever press response. In other words, the light on condition becomes the *occasion* for the lever press response. With S^R symbolizing a reinforcing stimulus or simply a reinforcer, the situation can be diagrammed as follows:

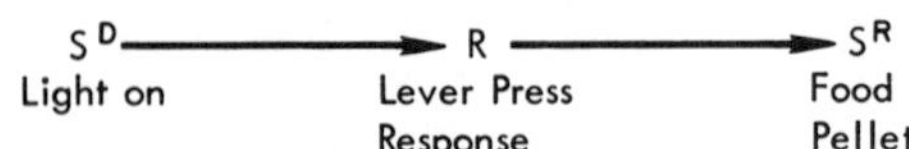

Everyday life is filled with discriminative operants. A few examples follow:

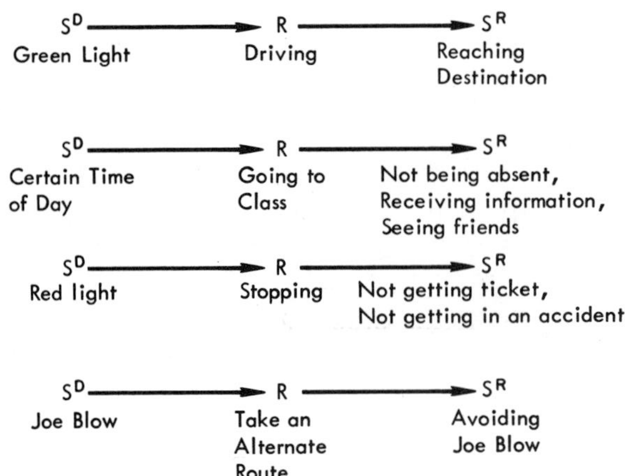

The reader may be wondering if we are not now talking about operant behavior as if it were respondent behavior, since the operant behavior now appears to be elicited by a known stimulus. The answer is that there are still important differences between a discriminative operant and respondent behavior. With respondent behavior a response is always a direct and automatic reaction to a stimulus, for example:

$$\text{UCS} \longrightarrow \text{UCR}$$
$$\text{or}$$
$$\text{CS} \longrightarrow \text{CR}$$

In the case of UCS, the UCR occurs automatically because of the way the organism is constructed; for instance, shining a light in a living organism's eye will automatically cause the pupil to constrict. Likewise, a CS will elicit a CR because of the CS's previous history with a UCS, just as a buzzer will elicit salivation because the buzzer previously had been paired with food. In other words, in the case of a CS the reinforcement occurred in the past; it will not occur after the CR has been made.

With a discriminative operant, the S^D is a signal that *if* a certain response is made it will be *followed* by reinforcement. The S^D alone does not cause the response, the reinforcement *following* the response is still necessary for the maintenance of the discriminative operant, which is not the case with respondent behavior.

Secondary Reinforcement At this point we must distinguish between a primary reinforcer and a secondary reinforcer. Primary reinforcers are things related to survival, like food, water, oxygen, elimination, and sexual activity. These things are not biologically neutral, because if an organism (or in the case of sex, a species) goes long enough without any one of them, it will not survive. Food for a hungry animal is a natural, powerful, primary reinforcer, as is water for a thirsty animal. Secondary reinforcers are stimuli that were originally biologically neutral and thus not reinforcing but that *acquired* their reinforcing properties through their association with a primary reinforcer. This principle can be stated as follows: *Any neutral stimulus that is consistently paired with a primary reinforcer takes on reinforcing properties of its own.*

It follows that each S^D that precedes a primary reinforcer, such as food, will become a secondary reinforcer. In our example in which a light was the occasion for a lever press response to be reinforced by food, the light became a secondary reinforcer. Once a stimulus takes on reinforcing properties it can be used to condition a new response or it can be used to maintain the response it was the occasion for. For example, the light in the example could be used to teach the animal a response other than the lever press response, for example, sticking its nose in a particular corner of the Skinner box. Likewise if the light followed the lever press response during extinction, the animal would go on responding far beyond the point at which it would stop if the light did not follow the lever press response.

According to Skinner, most human behavior is governed by secondary reinforcers. For example, since mothers are typically associated with the satisfaction of the child's basic needs, they become secondary reinforcers. Eventually the sight of the mother is enough to pacify temporarily a hungry or thirsty child. In fact, attention alone is a powerful secondary reinforcer, because it must precede the satisfaction of almost all, if not all, basic needs. Besides attention, which is a secondary reinforcer for children and adults alike, other common secondary reinforcers include:

kind words	awards
bodily contact	recognition
glances	gifts
money	privileges
medals	points

Secondary reinforcers that do not depend upon a particular motivational state are called *generalized reinforcers*. A mother, for example, is a generalized reinforcer since her presence is associated with several primary reinforcers. Her reinforcing properties do not depend upon the child being hungry or thirsty. Money is another generalized reinforcer since it, like a mother, usually is associated with several primary reinforcers.

There are two points of agreement in Skinner's theory and Allport's theory. First, they both believe the single individual should be intensively studied; that is, they both use the idiographic approach to research. For example, Skinner stated:

> A prediction of what the *average* individual will do is often of little or no value in dealing with a particular individual. . . . a science is helpful in dealing with the individual only insofar as its laws refer to individuals. A science of behavior which concerns only the behavior of groups is not likely to be of help in our understanding of the particular case. (1953, p. 19)

Second, they both accept the notion of functional autonomy. The notion was not nearly as important to Skinner as it was to Allport, but nonetheless, Skinner did accept it to a certain extent. This can be detected in the following statement by Skinner:

> Eventually generalized reinforcers are effective even though the primary reinforcers upon which they are based no longer accompany them. We play games of skill for their own sake. We get attention or approval for its own sake. Affection is not always followed by a more explicit sexual reinforcement. The submissiveness of others is reinforcing even though

we make no use of it. A miser may be so reinforced by money that he will starve rather than give it up. (1953, p. 81)

Chaining For the Skinnerians, much complex behavior is explained using the concept of *chaining*, which involves the concept of secondary reinforcement. We mentioned that any S^D that is the occasion for primary reinforcement becomes a secondary reinforcer. It is also true that all stimuli that consistently and immediately precede primary reinforcement will take on secondary reinforcing properties. In turn, stimuli associated with those stimuli will take on reinforcing properties, and so forth. In this way, stimuli far removed from the primary reinforcement can become secondary reinforcers, and as such can influence behavior. These secondary reinforcers develop two functions: they reinforce the response that preceded their appearance, and they act as an S^D for the next response. The secondary reinforcers act as S^Ds which ultimately bring the organism into contact with the primary reinforcer. It is the primary reinforcer that holds this entire chain of events together.

> One response can bring the organism into contact with stimuli that act as an S^D for another response, which in turn causes it to experience stimuli that cause a third response, and so on. This process is referred to as *chaining*. In fact, most behavior can be shown to involve some form of chaining. For example, even the lever press in the Skinner box is not an isolated response. The stimuli in the Skinner box act as S^Ds, causing the animal to turn toward the lever. The sight of the lever causes him to approach it and press it. The firing of the feeder mechanism acts as an additional S^D which elicits the response of going to the food cup. Consuming the food pellet acts as an S^D causing the animal to return to the lever and again press it. This sequence of events (chain) is held together by the food pellet, which, of course, is a primary positive reinforcer. It can be said that various elements of a behavioral chain are held together by secondary reinforcers, but that the entire chain depends upon a primary reinforcer. (Hergenhahn 1976, p. 99)

The process described in the preceding quotation is diagrammed in Figure 9–1.

Chained behavior also results when two people confront each other. Typically, what one person says acts as an S^D for a response from the

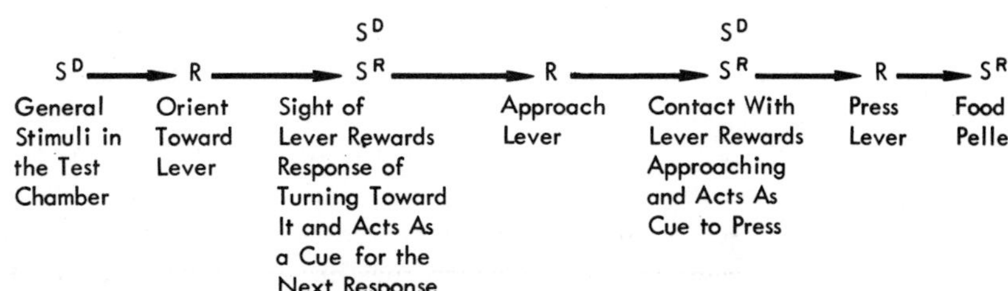

Figure 9–1 An example of simple chained behavior. (From Hergenhahn 1976, p. 100.)

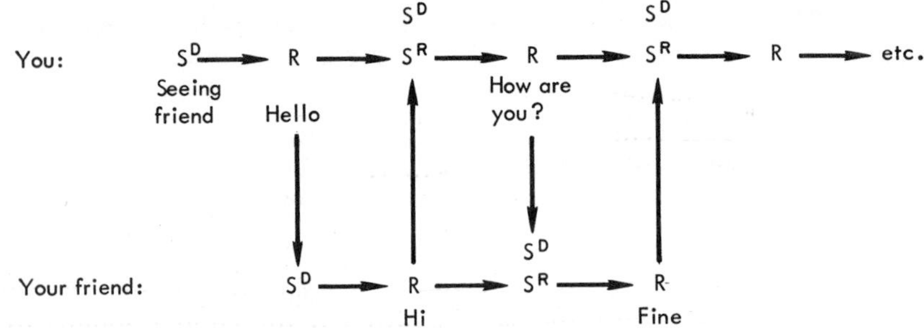

Figure 9–2 An example of chaining involving two people. (From Hergenhahn 1976, p. 100.)

second person, and the second person's response not only rewards the first person's response but also acts as an S^D for another response, and so forth. An example of this process is diagrammed in Figure 9–2. Skinner maintains that these principles also govern our behavior when we simply roam about or even when we mentally free associate.

> A response may produce or alter some of the variables which control another response. The result is a "chain." It may have little or no organization. When we go for a walk, roaming the countryside or wandering idly through a museum or store, one episode in our behavior generates conditions responsible for another. We look to one side and are stimulated by an object which causes us to move in its direction. In the course of this movement, we receive aversive stimulation from which we beat a hasty retreat. This generates a condition of satiation or fatigue in which, once free of aversion stimulation, we sit down to rest. And so on. Chaining need not be the result of movement in space. We wander or roam verbally, for example, in a casual conversation or when we "speak our thoughts" in free association. (Skinner 1953, p. 224)

Anyone who plays a musical instrument has experienced chained behavior: When into a musical piece, playing a note both reinforces the preceding response (S^R) and stimulates the next one (S^D).

VERBAL BEHAVIOR

As indicated in chapter 1, the nativism-empiricism controversy is an ancient one. The nativist maintains that important attributes, such as intelligence, creativity, or even personality, are mainly genetically determined. The empiricist, on the other hand, insists that such attributes are the product of experience and not of genes. As one might expect, both points of view are represented in the explanation of language.

Skinner falls squarely in the empiricist's camp. For him language is simply verbal behavior which is governed by the same principles as any other behavior is; reinforced behavior persists, nonreinforced behavior extinguishes. Skinner (1957) did describe various categories of verbal behavior which are distinguished by what is being done in order to be reinforced. The *mand* is a verbal command which specifies its own reinforcer. For example, the mand "pass the salt" is reinforced when the salt is passed. A *tact* is the accurate naming of something. For example, if a child says "doll" while holding a doll, he will be reinforced. *Echoic behavior* is repeating something verbatim. For example, in the early stages of language training, a parent may point to her mouth and say "mouth"; if the child responds by saying "mouth," she will be reinforced.

We see then that Skinner's explanation of language is simply an extension of his general principles of learning. Skinner's most severe critic has been Noam Chomsky (1959). Basically, Chomsky contends that language is simply too complex to be explained by learning. For example, it has been estimated that there are 10^{20} possible 20-word sentences in the English language, and it would take approximately one thousand times the estimated age of the earth just to listen to them all (Miller 1965). Thus, says Chomsky, a process other than learning must be operating. Chomsky's answer is that the brain is structured in a way that causes it to generate language. In other words, our verbal skills are genetically determined. Chomsky's nativistic explanation of language is, of course, diametrically opposed to Skinner's empirical explanation.

SCHEDULES OF REINFORCEMENT

So far we have talked as if it were necessary in modifying behavior to reinforce every desirable response that is made. That is, if we want to encourage children to read, they should be reinforced each time we observe them reading, or if we want a rat to continue to press a lever in a Skinner box, we should reinforce it with food each time it does so. If, indeed, each desirable response is followed by reinforcement, we say that the organism is on a 100 percent or *continuous reinforcement schedule.* Likewise, if a response that had been learned is now never followed by a reinforcement, we say that the organism is on a 0 percent reinforcement schedule which, of course, leads to extinction.

Skinner observed that everyday behavior is maintained on schedules somewhere between these two extremes.

> We do not always find good ice or snow when we go skating or skiing. . . . We do not always get a good meal in a particular restaurant because cooks are not always predictable. We do not always get an answer when we telephone a friend because the friend is not always at home. . . . The reinforcements characteristic of industry and education are almost always intermittent because it is not feasible to control behavior by reinforcing every response. (Skinner 1953, p. 99)

A response that is sometimes followed by a reinforcer and sometimes not followed by a reinforcer is said to be on a *partial reinforcement schedule*. Many believe that the research by Ferster and Skinner (1957) on schedules of reinforcement represents a major contribution to experimental psychology. Although Ferster and Skinner studied many schedules, four have become most representative of their work and they are described briefly.

1. Fixed Interval Reinforcement Schedule (FI) On this schedule, the organism is reinforced for a response that is made following a certain time interval. For example, only the response made following a thirty-second interval is reinforced. After an organism has been on this kind of schedule for a while, its behavior quickens toward the end of the time interval and then slows down drastically after reinforcement has been obtained. Individuals working for a fixed weekly or monthly salary are thought to be on this kind of schedule. Students preparing a term paper also will often wait until the deadline approaches before starting and then "work like mad" to finish. Such behavior is typical of a FI schedule. Note that with this schedule only one response is needed to obtain reinforcement, if the response is made at just the right time.

2. Fixed Ratio Reinforcement Schedule (FR) On this schedule the organism must make *x* number of responses before it is reinforced. For example, every fourth (FR4) or every fifth (FR5) response may be reinforced. Such a schedule produces extremely high rates of responding and is thought to characterize individuals doing piecework or working for a commission. In both cases the harder one works the more pay one receives, since reinforcement is response contingent instead of time contingent.

3. Variable Interval Reinforcement Schedule (VI) On this schedule the organism is reinforced at the end of variable time intervals. In other words, rather than the organism being reinforced after a fixed interval of say ten seconds, it is reinforced *on the average* of every ten seconds. For example, it may be reinforced for a response made after five seconds, then after twenty seconds, then after two seconds. Bosses who believe their workers should be periodically rewarded would place them on such a schedule. At various times as they were working, the boss would come along with a kind word, although they did nothing extra to deserve the kind word.

For interval schedules it is not the *number* of responses made that is important; rather, it is the *passage of time* which determines when a response will be reinforced. For ratio schedules, however, the frequency of responding has a direct relationship to the number of reinforcers the organism will receive. For ratio schedules, the faster the organism responds, the more often it will be reinforced.

4. Variable Ratio Reinforcement Schedule (VR) This, like the FR schedule, is response contingent; only on this schedule, the organism is reinforced on the basis of an average number of responses. That is, instead of being reinforced for *every* fourth response, it is reinforced on the *average* of every fourth response. Thus, reinforcements could be close together or fairly far apart. However, on this schedule the faster it responds the more reinforcement it will obtain. This schedule produces the highest rate of responding. Gambling behavior is under the control of a VR schedule, as is the behavior of salespersons. For example, the faster one pulls the handle of a slot machine, the more often one will receive a payoff (and the faster one will go broke). With salespersons, the more contacts they make, the more likely they will make a sale, although exactly when a sale will be made cannot be predicted. The salesperson's schedule of reinforcement may look as follows:

> No Sale, No Sale, Sale, No Sale, Sale, No Sale, No Sale, No Sale, No Sale, No Sale, Sale, Sale, and so on.

Partial reinforcement schedules have two important effects on behavior: (1) They influence rate of responding. The VR schedule produces the highest rate of responding, followed by the FR schedule, then the VI schedule, and finally the FI schedule. (2) They increase resistance to extinction. All partial reinforcement schedules produce greater resistance to extinction than does a 100 percent or continuous schedule of reinforcement, and this fact is named the *partial reinforcement effect* (PRE). That is, a response followed by reinforcement only some of the time will persist much longer when reinforcement is discontinued than will a response followed by reinforcement each time that it occurs. The PRE has obvious implications for education and child rearing. For example, even though a 100 percent schedule may be used in the early stages of training, a response should be switched to a partial reinforcement schedule as soon as possible. This will increase the perseverence of the response. In most cases, this will happen automatically since most behavior that occurs outide a laboratory is on some kind of partial reinforcement schedule.

SUPERSTITIOUS BEHAVIOR

When a response is responsible for making available a reinforcer, we say that the reinforcer is *contingent* on the response. In our earlier example, a rat had to press the lever in a Skinner box *in order to* obtain a pellet of food. This is called *contingent reinforcement;* if the appropriate response is not made, the reinforcer will not become available.

Now let us imagine what would happen if a Skinner box were

arranged so that the feeder mechanism would fire automatically, providing the animal with a pellet of food *regardless of what it was doing.* Let us imagine, for example, that the feeder mechanism is arranged so that it automatically provides a pellet of food on the average of every fifteen seconds. According to the principles of operant conditioning, whatever the animal is doing when the feeder mechanism fires will be reinforced and thus tend to be repeated. As that response is being repeated, the feeder mechanism will again fire, further reinforcing the response. The end result will be that whatever the animal was "caught" doing when the feeder mechanism first fired will become a very strong habit. Strange ritualistic behavior develops under these circumstances. For example, one animal may learn to turn in a circle, another may learn to bob its head, still another may learn to sniff air holes on the top of the Skinner box. Such behavior is called *superstitious behavior,* since it appears *as if* the animal believed its ritualistic response is responsible for producing the reinforcer, when in fact it is not. Reinforcement that occurs regardless of what the animal is doing is called *noncontingent reinforcement.* Superstititous behavior results from noncontingent reinforcement.

There are numerous examples of superstitious behavior on the human level. A baseball player, for example, who adjusts his hat a certain way just before hitting a home run will have a strong tendency to adjust his hat that way again the next time he comes up to bat. Many actors who are wearing a certain article of clothing before giving an outstanding performance will sometimes wear that same article of clothing whenever they perform. A native who beats on a drum in response to an eclipse of the sun may have a strong tendency to beat the drum the next time an emergency develops since his drum beating looked "as if" it brought the sun back.

KINDS OF REINFORCEMENT CONTINGENCIES

In this section we will discuss the various events that can follow a response and thus influence that response.

Positive Reinforcement As we have already seen, a *primary positive reinforcer* is something that is related to survival. If a response produces a primary positive reinforcer, the rate with which that response is made increases. We have seen too that any biologically neutral stimulus that is paired with a primary positive reinforcer takes on positive reinforcing characteristics of its own, thus becoming a *secondary positive reinforcer.* As with primary reinforcement, if a secondary positive reinforcer follows a response, the rate with which that response is made will go up.

Negative Reinforcement Whereas positive reinforcement presents the organism with something it "wants," negative reinforcement *removes* something it does not want. A *primary negative reinforcer* is a stimulus that is potentially harmful to the organism, such as an extremely loud noise, a very bright light, or an electric shock. Any response that removes or reduces one of these aversive stimuli will increase in frequency and is said to be negatively reinforced. This is labeled an *escape contingency,* since the organism's response allows it to escape from an aversive situation. Any neutral stimulus consistently paired with a primary negative reinforcer becomes a *secondary negative reinforcer,* and an organism will work to escape from it just as it does from a primary negative reinforcer. Both primary and secondary negative reinforcement involve escaping from an aversive situation.

It is important to note that both positive and negative reinforcement result in an increase in response probability or in rate of responding. Both result in something the organism wants. In the case of positive reinforcement, a response produces something the organism wants. In the case of negative reinforcement, a response removes something aversive.

Avoidance An *avoidance contingency* is engaging in behavior that prevents an aversive event from occurring. For example, opening an umbrella prevents getting wet, which is aversive. If a Skinner box is arranged so that a light precedes the onset of a shock, the animal will learn to respond to the light in such a way as to avoid the shock. With an avoidance contingency the organism's behavior prevents it from experiencing a negative reinforcer. As with our earlier example with Joe Blow:

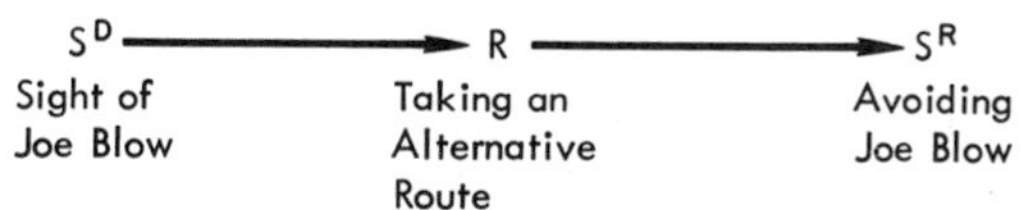

The sight of Joe Blow was a signal for an aversive encounter, and taking a route away from Joe Blow prevented or avoided that encounter. Whereas the reinforcement from negative reinforcement contingencies comes from *escaping* something aversive, the reinforcement from an avoidance contingency comes from *avoiding* an aversive experience.

Punishment Punishment is either removing a positive reinforcer or presenting a negative reinforcer. In other words, punishment is either taking away something an organism wants or giving it something it does not want.

Over and over Skinner emphasizes his belief that behavior should be controlled using positive contingencies. He feels strongly that positive reinforcement and punishment are not opposite in their consequences. That is, although positive reinforcement strengthens behavior, punishment does not necessarily weaken it.

> Punishment is designed to remove awkward, dangerous, or otherwise unwanted behavior from a repertoire on the assumption that a person who has been punished is less likely to behave in the same way again. Unfortunately, the matter is not that simple. Reward and punishment do not differ merely in the direction of the changes they induce. A child who has been severely punished for sex play is not necessarily less inclined to continue; and a man who has been imprisoned for violent assault is not necessarily less inclined toward violence. Punished behavior is likely to reappear after the punitive contingencies are withdrawn. (Skinner 1971, pp. 61–62)

Even if punishment is effective in eliminating undesirable behavior, why use it if the same thing can be accomplished with positive control? The use of punishment in controlling behavior appears to have several shortcomings. For example, it causes the punished person to become fearful; it indicates what the person should not do, instead of what he or she should do; it justifies inflicting pain on others; it often causes aggression; and it tends to replace one undesirable response with another, as when a child who is spanked for a wrongdoing now cries instead.

Skinner stresses positively reinforcing desirable behavior and ignoring undesirable behavior. This should be looked upon as an ideal, however, since there are times where punishing a child is strongly reinforcing to a parent. A child acting up in a supermarket may stop doing so immediately if spanked by a parent, and this will vastly increase the likelihood of the child being spanked again next time it acts up. Even parents are capable of learning. As Skinner says, there are always two organisms whose behavior is being modified in a learning situation, and sometimes it is difficult to know who is the experimenter and who is the subject. This point is made in the cartoon in Figure 9–3.

Figure 9–3 "Boy, have I got this guy conditioned! Every time I press the bar down he drops in a piece of food." (From Skinner 1959, p. 378.)

Malott, Ritterby, and Wolf (1973, p. 4–2) state our biggest problem as follows:

MAN'S BIGGEST PROBLEM IS THAT
HIS BEHAVIOR IS MORE EASILY
INFLUENCED BY
SMALL, BUT IMMEDIATE AND DEFINITE
REINFORCERS
THAN IT IS BY
LARGE, BUT DISTANT AND UNCERTAIN
REINFORCERS

It is the fact described in this quotation that keeps many people smoking cigarettes when they "know" they should not and overeating when they "know" that in the long run it will do them no good. The prospect of a long healthy life is no contest for a small amount of nicotine or the immediate taste of food in one's mouth.

The relatively greater effect of small immediate reinforcers compared to large distant ones is exemplified in Figures 9–4 and 9–5.

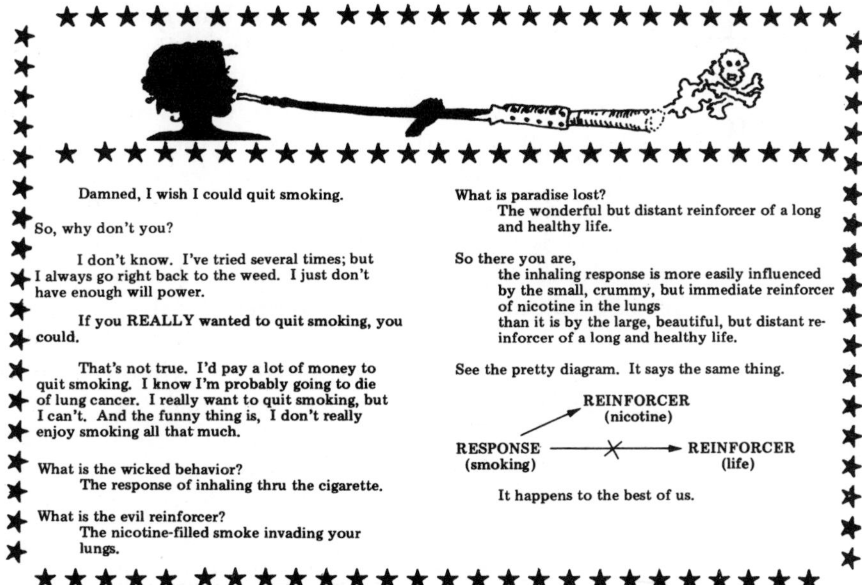

Damned, I wish I could quit smoking.
So, why don't you?
I don't know. I've tried several times; but I always go right back to the weed. I just don't have enough will power.
If you REALLY wanted to quit smoking, you could.
That's not true. I'd pay a lot of money to quit smoking. I know I'm probably going to die of lung cancer. I really want to quit smoking, but I can't. And the funny thing is, I don't really enjoy smoking all that much.
What is the wicked behavior?
The response of inhaling thru the cigarette.
What is the evil reinforcer?
The nicotine-filled smoke invading your lungs.
What is paradise lost?
The wonderful but distant reinforcer of a long and healthy life.
So there you are,
the inhaling response is more easily influenced by the small, crummy, but immediate reinforcer of nicotine in the lungs than it is by the large, beautiful, but distant reinforcer of a long and healthy life.
See the pretty diagram. It says the same thing.
REINFORCER
(nicotine)
RESPONSE
(smoking)
REINFORCER
(life)
It happens to the best of us.

Figure 9–4 The diagram shows that smoking is under the control of immediate reinforcers rather than of distant ones. (From Malott, Ritterby, & Wolf 1973, p. 4–3.)

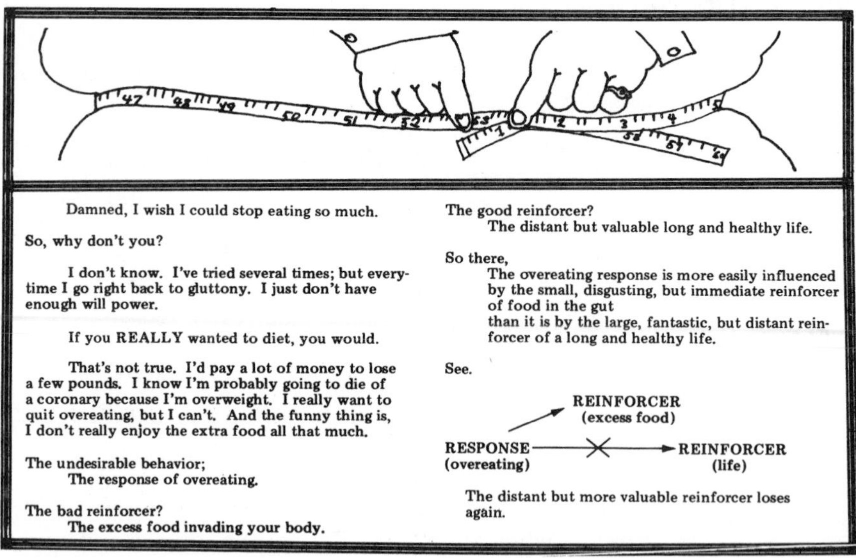

Damned, I wish I could stop eating so much.
So, why don't you?
I don't know. I've tried several times; but every-time I go right back to gluttony. I just don't have enough will power.
If you REALLY wanted to diet, you would.
That's not true. I'd pay a lot of money to lose a few pounds. I know I'm probably going to die of a coronary because I'm overweight. I really want to quit overeating, but I can't. And the funny thing is, I don't really enjoy the extra food all that much.
The undesirable behavior;
The response of overeating.
The bad reinforcer?
The excess food invading your body.
The good reinforcer?
The distant but valuable long and healthy life.
So there,
The overeating response is more easily influenced by the small, disgusting, but immediate reinforcer of food in the gut
than it is by the large, fantastic, but distant reinforcer of a long and healthy life.
See.
REINFORCER
(excess food)
RESPONSE
(overeating)
REINFORCER
(life)
The distant but more valuable reinforcer loses again.

Figure 9–5 The diagram shows that excessive eating is under the control of immediate reinforcers rather than distant ones. (From Malott, Ritterby, & Wolf 1973, p. 4–3.)

So how do we solve "our biggest problem?" One way is to make the future immediate, and one way to do that is through *contingency contracting*. Let us say you want to quit smoking but cannot seem to do it on your own. Let us assume further that one hundred dollars is a substantial amount of money for you. One thing you can do is to make an agreement with another person in which you turn over the one hundred dollars to that person with the stipulation that each week that you go without smoking you will get back ten dollars. If you have even one cigarette during the week, you will lose ten dollars. Such an agreement is called a contingency contract. Obviously, many variations are possible. For example, the payoff could come on a daily basis instead of on a weekly basis, and the object of value could be such things as records or clothing instead of money. The major point is that by such an agreement you have rearranged the reinforcement contingencies in your environment so that they now encourage desirable behavior and discourage undesirable behavior. In the case of smoking, rather than waiting for old age for the effects of nonsmoking to become manifest, you need wait only a day or a week. Now your behavior is under the control of more immediate reinforcers instead of distant ones.

What happens when the contract expires? Perhaps other reinforcement contingencies will support the desired behavior. In other words, it is hoped that nonsmoking will be functional in producing reinforcement. Both smoking and nonsmoking produce reinforcers. The problem is switching from one source of reinforcement to another. For example, the reinforcers that support smoking include nicotine and perhaps a degree of social approval from other smokers. The reinforcers for not smoking include saving money, feeling better, not suffering the abuse from anticancer commercials, and social approval from other nonsmokers. Both smoking and nonsmoking are functional in producing reinforcement, and it is mainly a matter of switching from one source of reinforcement to another. Contingency contracting is one way of making the switch.

IMPLICATIONS FOR CHILD REARING

The major lesson from Skinner's theory is quite clear: control reinforcement contingencies and you control behavior. This statement is especially important to child rearing, since parents have at least the potential for controlling the reinforcement contingencies governing their child's behavior. Hergenhahn summarizes how reinforcement theory can be used in child rearing:

> 1. Decide the major personality characteristics you want your child to possess as an adult. Let's say, for example, you want the child to grow up to be a creative adult.
> 2. Define these goals in behavioral terms. In this case you ask, "What is a child doing when he is being creative?"
> 3. Reward behavior that is in accordance with these goals. With this example, you would reward instances of creativity as they occurred.
> 4. Provide consistency by arranging the major aspects of the child's environment so that they too reward the behavior you have deemed important. (1972, pp. 152–153)

This plan of action oversimplifies the situation, however, since anyone attempting to follow it will run into at least the following problems:.

> 1. Often it will not be clear what behavior you want from the child.
> 2. Your ideas concerning what constitutes desirable behavior may change.
> 3. You may want different things at different times.
> 4. Just because you want certain things from your child does not mean everyone else will want the same things.
> 5. It is not always easy to know what will be rewarding to a child.
> 6. Often what you reward will depend upon your mood.
> 7. Sometimes you will get the behavior you want from the child, but at the wrong time or place.
> 8. It is difficult to reward others when you are not adequately rewarded yourself. (Hergenhahn 1972, pp. 16–17)

The situation is further complicated by the fact that children constantly are learning things from the television they watch, the books they look at and/or read, and the games they play. A major influence from television seems to come from *modeling*. Children will model or imitate the behavior of someone they see being reinforced; thus they receive *vicarious reinforcement*. If children see a gun fighter on television being reinforced with power, money, and recognition, they may imitate this behavior and in so doing experience those reinforcers indirectly. This means that parents wishing to direct their children's emerging personality will need to take into consideration all of the children's major experiences, which is clearly a monumental task.

According to the Skinnerians, it is never a question of whether children's lives should be controlled or not, since they always are controlled. It is simply a matter of who or what is going to do the controlling.

WALDEN TWO

contingency management

The purposive manipulation of reinforcement contingencies so that they encourage certain behaviors is called *contingency management*. We just saw how contingency management could be applied to child rearing. Skinner believes it can be used on a much larger scale. In fact, he defines culture itself as a set of reinforcement contingencies which encourages certain behaviors and discourages others. It follows that cultures, like experiments, can be designed to produce certain effects.

> A culture is very much like the experimental space used in the analysis of behavior. Both are sets of contingencies of reinforcement. A child is born into a culture as an organism is placed in an experimental space. Designing a culture is like designing an experiment; contingencies are arranged and effects noted. In an experiment we are interested in what happens, in designing a culture with whether it will work. (Skinner 1971, p. 153)

When contingency management is used to design a culture, the effort is an example of *cultural engineering*. In 1948, Skinner published a book called *Walden Two* in which he described a utopian culture designed in accordance with the principles of operant conditioning.

Walden Two is a fictitious community of one thousand people. A few of the community's characteristics are: There are no private homes, rather, the inhabitants live in apartment complexes; children do not live with their parents, they first live in a nursery and later in a dormitory, and they move to their own apartment when they are about thirteen years old; no living quarters have cooking facilities, all meals are in community dining halls, which assures a healthy diet and frees individuals from the drudgery of preparing meals; women of Walden Two are not burdened by cooking, cleaning, or mothering and are thus able to realize their full potential along with men; marriage and childbearing is encouraged in the mid-teens; marriages tend to last because couples are matched by interests, money is no problem, and child rearing is no burden; children do not live with their parents, rather they are raised by experts since average parents do not have the knowledge or the facilities to properly raise children. The goal is "to have every adult member of Walden Two regard all the children as his own and to have every child think of every adult as his parent" (Skinner 1948, p. 142).

Education is individualized in that every child progresses at his or her own pace. There is no "formal" education and teachers act only as guides. Education is provided in the actual workshop and laboratories in the community. Even at the college level, students are merely "taught to think" and left to get anything else on their own. There are no grades or diplomas.

There is virtually no money in Walden Two. Rather, each individual is responsible for 1,200 labor credits. This amounts to about four hours of work per day, although some jobs are worth more labor credits than others. For example, an unpleasant job like garbage collecting or sewer cleaning would be worth more labor credits than a more pleasant job would. Thus, by engaging in unpleasant work, the member would need to work fewer hours than someone doing more pleasant work.

Each member of the community is provided with all of his or her basic needs. For example, the following things all are provided: food, leisure activities, clothing, medical services, education, and security against old age and ill health. This allows the members to concentrate on such things as the arts, the sciences, the exercise of skills, the satisfaction of curiosities, and on self-actualization.

There are no prisons, no taverns, no unemployment, no narcotics, no mental institutions, no wars, and no crime. Is such an "ideal" society possible? Frazier, the hero of the novel, who, to many, represents Skinner himself, said:

> The one fact that I would cry from every housetop is this: the Good Life is waiting for us. . . . It does not depend on a change in government or on the machinations of world politics. It does not wait upon an improvement in human nature. At this very moment we have the necessary techniques, both material and psychological, to create a full and satisfying life for everyone. (1948, p. 193)

Several experimental communities have been designed according to the suggestions found in *Walden Two*. One of these communities, in Virginia, publishes a newsletter which describes its progress (Twin Oaks; Louisa, Virginia 23093). The history of this particular project is summarized in a book by K. Kinkade (1973).

BEYOND FREEDOM AND DIGNITY

Skinner believes strongly that cultural engineering need not be fictional, but before such engineering will be possible we need to develop a technology of behavior.

> What we need is a technology of behavior. We could solve our problems quickly enough if we could adjust the growth of the world's population as precisely as we adjust the course of a spaceship, or improve agriculture and industry with some of the confidence with which we accelerate high-energy particles, or move toward a peaceful world with something like the steady progress with which physics has approached absolute zero (even though both remain presumably out of reach). But a behavioral technology comparable in power and precision to physical and biological technology is lacking, and those who do not find the very possibility ridiculous are more likely to be frightened by it than reassured. That is how far we are from "understanding human issues" in the sense in which physics and biology understand their fields, and how far we are from preventing the catastrophe toward which the world seems to be inexorably moving. (Skinner 1971, p. 5)

What prevents the development of a technology of behavior? According to Skinner, the main barrier is the traditional view of human nature, which depicts people as autonomous. Autonomous people are free to do as they choose and therefore are worthy of praise and dignity when they accomplish something. If those same accomplishments could be ascribed to outside influences, they would lose their meaning.

> We recognize a person's dignity or worth when we give him credit for what he has done. The amount we give is inversely proportional to the conspicuousness of the causes of his behavior. If we do not know why a person acts as he does, we attribute his behavior to him. We try to gain additional credit for ourselves by concealing the reasons why we behave in given ways or by claiming to have acted for less powerful reasons. We avoid infringing on the credit due to others by controlling them inconspicuously. We admire people to the extent that we cannot explain what they do, and the word "admire" then means "marvel at." What we may call the literature of dignity is concerned with preserving due credit. It may oppose advances in technology, including a technology of behavior, because they destroy chances to be admired and a basic analysis because it offers an alternative explanation of behavior for which the individual himself has previously been given credit. The literature thus stands in the way of further human achievements. (Skinner 1971, pp. 58–59)

The trouble with the notion of autonomous people, according to Skinner, is that it explains nothing about human behavior; that is, in autonomous people the causes of behavior are mystical. As our knowledge about human behavior has increased, says Skinner, more and more of what once was attributed to autonomous people has been attributed to the environment. As we learn more, this trend will continue.

If it were autonomous people that needed to be understood and improved before we could solve our problems, then, says Skinner, we would be in trouble.

> Fortunately, the point of attack is more readily accessible. It is the environment which must be changed. A way of life which furthers the

> study of human behavior in its relation to that environment should be in the best possible position to solve its major problems. This is not jingoism, because the great problems are now global. In the behavioristic view, man can now control his own destiny because he knows what must be done and how to do it. (Skinner 1974, p. 251)

EVALUATION

Skinner's theory does much more than explain personality; it specifies the principles by which personality can be changed. Since consistent behavior patterns are under the control of reinforcement contingencies, if you change those contingencies, you change behavior. This rule is as true for maladaptive behavior as it is for adaptive behavior. The clinical approach called behavior therapy which grew out of this contention has been used successfully for a wide range of behavior problems, such as juvenile delinquency, psychotic behavior, alcoholism, drug addiction, thumb sucking, and the treatment of phobias. Entire programs at several mental institutions have been redesigned to reflect operant principles (see, for example, Ayllon & Azrin 1968, and Atthowe & Krasner 1968).

Skinner's ideas have been manifested in education through programmed learning, teaching machines, and in the recognized need for behaviorally defined educational objectives. Skinner also believes that if schools controlled behavior positively instead of negatively they would not stimulate as much escape and avoidance behavior as they now do.

The treatment and care of the mentally retarded and the autistic child have been revolutionalized by Skinner's theory. We have seen how his ideas are being utilized in child rearing and in the modification of personal behavior. More and more, his ideas are being used in prison reform in which positive control is being explored as an alternative to negative control (see, for example, Boslough 1972).

A good theory explains, synthesizes large amounts of information, generates new information, and can be used as a guide in solving practical problems. Skinner's theory gets high marks in all of these categories. The criticisms that he generalizes too readily from the animal level to the human level and from the laboratory to the "real world" seem minor when compared to what has been accomplished using his theory as a guide.

SUMMARY

Skinner's position falls into the behavioristic camp because it stresses the study of overt behavior and not internal mental or physiological events. He recognized two major categories of behavior; respondent behavior, which is elicited by a known stimulus, and operant behavior, which appears to be emitted rather than elicited. Respondent behavior is controlled by the events that *precede* it, and operant behavior is controlled by the events that *follow* it. Skinner's work has been mainly on operant behavior. If an operant response is followed by a reinforcer (either positive or negative), the rate with which it occurs will increase. An operant response is acquired by following the desired response with a reinforcer. If the desired response does not occur naturally, it can be shaped into existence using differential reinforcement and successive approximations. If the reinforcement for an operant response is discontinued, the rate eventually will return to its operant level, and extinction will have taken place. Following a delay after extinction, the conditioned operant response will again appear, which is called spontaneous recovery. The situation can be arranged so that an operant response will be made under one set of circumstances but not under another set of circumstances. For example, a rat could be trained to press the bar in a Skinner box when the light is on but not when it is off. Under these conditions, we say that the light has become the occasion or the discriminative stimulus (S^D) for the bar press response and that the rat has learned a discriminative operant. Any neutral stimulus consistently paired with a primary reinforcer becomes a secondary reinforcer, and thus all S^Ds become secondary reinforcers. A stimulus that is paired with more than one primary reinforcer becomes a generalized reinforcer.

Much complex behavior is explained using the concept of chaining. Chaining occurs when one response by an organism brings it into proximity of a reward which both reinforces that response and triggers the next one. Chaining can also involve two people when the response of one triggers the response in the other. Verbal behavior or language is thought to be governed by the same principles as any other behavior is. Those utterances that are reinforced are repeated, those that are not reinforced extinguish. Thus Skinner is on the empiricism side of the empiricism-nativism debate. A response that is followed by a reinforcer on only some occasions is said to be on a partial reinforcement schedule. A response that is reinforced each time it occurs is said to be on a continuous or 100 percent reinforcement schedule. A response that has been on a partial reinforcement schedule takes much longer to extinguish than one that has been on a continuous schedule, which is called the partial reinforcement effect (PRE).

When a response makes available a reinforcer, we say that the reinforcer is contingent upon the response. When a reinforcer appears independent of any response, we refer to it as a noncontingent reinforcement. The ritualistic responses labeled superstitious behavior result from noncontingent reinforcement. A primary positive reinforcer is something that contributes to survival. A secondary positive reinforcer is anything that has been consistently paired with a primary positive reinforcer. A primary negative reinforcer is anything that is physically harmful to the organism. A secondary negative reinforcer is anything that has been consistently paired with a primary negative reinforcer. Positive reinforcement occurs when a response adds a primary or secondary positive reinforcer to the situation. Negative reinforcement occurs when a response removes a primary or secondary negative reinforcer from the situation. Punishment occurs when a response adds a primary or secondary negative reinforcer to the situation or removes a primary or secondary positive reinforcer. Skinner opposes the use of punishment in the control of behavior and stresses control through positive reinforcement.

A major problem that humans have is that our behavior is controlled by small, immediate reinforcers instead of by larger, more distant reinforcers. One way to remedy this problem is to use contingency contracting which rearranges the reinforcement contingencies in the environment. The Skinnerians believe that behavior can be directed by controlling reinforcement contingencies, which seems to have special relevance to child rearing, since parents have considerable control over their child's environment. Skinner wrote a utopian novel entitled *Walden Two,* which described a society designed in accordance with the principles of operant conditioning. Skinner feels strongly, however, that cultural engineering need not be fictitious. We now have the knowledge that would allow us to develop a technology of behavior that could be used to solve many of our major problems. It is the traditional view of autonomous people with their freedom and dignity that is the major barrier to the development of such a technology of behavior.

Discussion Questions

1. Describe the essential features of behaviorism.
2. Differentiate between respondent and operant behavior and between type *S* and type *R* conditioning.
3. Discuss how you would go about shaping a response that an animal did not ordinarily make.
4. What is a discriminative operant? Give several examples from everyday life.
5. Discuss the concept of secondary reinforcement. Indicate its importance to the control of human behavior. Include in your answer a definition of generalized reinforcers, and give a few examples of them.
6. Discuss the concept of chaining, and give a few examples of chained behavior on the human level.
7. Describe the nativism-empiricism debate as it applies to verbal behavior. Summarize Skinner's explanation of verbal behavior.
8. Define as many schedules of reinforcement as you can. Describe the partial reinforcement effect, and discuss its relevance to everyday life.

9. What is superstitious behavior? Include in your answer a discussion of contingent and noncontingent reinforcement.
10. List and describe as many kinds of reinforcement contingencies as you can.
11. Discuss the concept of punishment from the Skinnerian point of view.
12. Describe "our biggest problem" and offer a possible way of solving it.
13. Describe how Skinner's theory might be applied to child rearing.
14. Discuss cultural engineering from Skinner's point of view. Give examples of what he feels could be done now.
15. According to Skinner, what must be done before we can begin to solve our major problems? What does Skinner feel is the major factor inhibiting us from making progress in this area?
16. Correlate the emotions of depression, sorrow, joy, and anxiety with the presence or absence of positive or negative reinforcers. For example, what emotion would one tend to experience if a source of positive reinforcement which had been missing for a while suddenly reappeared?
17. Describe how you might use poker chips to modify the behavior of patients in a mental institution.
18. Describe how Skinner's ideas could be used by a primary school teacher.
19. How, according to Skinner, should undesirable behavior be treated?
20. Pretending that you are Skinner, choose any other theory that has been covered in this text thus far and criticize it.

Glossary

Acquisition. That part of operant conditioning in which an operant response is followed by a reinforcer, thereby increasing the rate with which the response occurs.

Avoidance Contingency. The situation in which the organism can avoid an aversive stimulus by engaging in appropriate activity.

Behaviorism. A school of psychology, founded by J. B. Watson, whose members believe that the only scientifically valid subject matter for psychology is measurable behavior. The behaviorists feel that consciousness cannot be reliably studied and therefore should be ignored.

Chaining. The situation in which one response brings the organism into contact with stimuli which (1) reinforce that response and (2) stimulate the next response. Chaining can also involve other people; for example, one person's response can both reinforce another person's response and determine the next course of action.

Classical Conditioning. The kind of conditioning studied by Ivan Pavlov and used by J. B. Watson as a model for his version of behaviorism.

Conditioned Response (CR). A response similar to an unconditioned response which is elicited by a previously neutral stimulus (CS).

Conditioned Stimulus (CS). A stimulus which, before classical conditioning principles are applied, is biologically neutral; that is, it does not elicit a natural reaction from an organism.

Contingency Contracting. An agreement between two people that when one acts in an appropriate way the other one gives him or her something of value. For example, each time the first goes a week without smoking, the second gives him or her ten dollars.

Contingency Management. The purposive manipulation of reinforcement contingencies so that they encourage certain behaviors.

Contingent Reinforcement. The situation in which a certain response must be made before a reinforcer is obtained; that is, no response, no reinforcer.

Continuous Reinforcement Schedule. A schedule of reinforcement which reinforces a desired response each time that it occurs. Also called a 100 percent schedule of reinforcement.

Cultural Engineering. The use of contingency management in designing a culture.

Culture. According to Skinner, a set of reinforcement contingencies.

Differential Reinforcement. The situation in which some responses are reinforced and others are not.

Discriminative Operant. An operant response that is made under one set of circumstances but not under others.

Discriminative Stimulus (S^D). A cue indicating that if a certain response is made it will be followed by reinforcement.

Echoic Behavior. The accurate repeating of what someone else had said.

Escape Contingency. A situation in which an organism must respond in a certain way in order to escape from an aversive stimulus. All negative reinforcement involves an escape contingency.

Extinction. The weakening of an operant response by removing the reinforcer that had been following the response during acquisition. When a response returns to its operant level we say that it has extinguished.

Fixed Interval Reinforcement Schedule (FI). The reinforcement schedule that reinforces a response that is made only after a specified interval of time has passed.

Fixed Ratio Reinforcement Schedule (FR). The reinforcement schedule that reinforces every nth response. For example, every fifth response the organism makes is reinforced (FR5).

Functional Analysis. Skinner's approach to research which attempts to relate measurable environmental experiences to measurable behavior and bypasses cognitive and physiological processes altogether.

Functionalism. America's first school of psychology. The major goal of the functionalist was to relate various behavioral and psychological processes to survival.

Generalized Reinforcers. A class of secondary reinforcers that have been paired with more than one primary reinforcer. A mother, for example, is a generalized reinforcer because she is associated with the satisfaction of several biological needs.

Mand. A verbal response that demands something and is reinforced when what is demanded is obtained.

Modeling. The imitation of the behavior of someone who is seen obtaining reinforcement.

Negative Reinforcer. Anything that when removed from the situation by a response increases the rate with which that response is made.

Noncontingent Reinforcement. The situation in which there is no relationship between an organism's behavior and the availability of reinforcement.

Operant Behavior. Behavior that cannot be linked to any known stimulus and therefore appears to be emitted rather than elicited.

Operant Conditioning. The modification of response strength by manipulation of the consequences of the response. Responses that are followed by a reinforcer gain in strength; responses not followed by a reinforcer become weaker. Also called type *R* conditioning.

Operant Level. The frequency with which an operant response is made before it is systematically reinforced.

Partial Reinforcement Effect (PRE). The fact that a partially or intermittently reinforced response will take longer to extinguish than a response on a continuous or 100 percent schedule of reinforcement.

Partial Reinforcement Schedule. A schedule of reinforcement that sometimes reinforces a desired response and sometimes does not. In other words, the response is maintained on a schedule of reinforcement somewhere between 100 percent and 0 percent.

Positive Reinforcer. Anything that when added to the situation by a response increases the rate with which that response is made.

Primary Negative Reinforcer. A negative reinforcer which is related to an organism's survival; for example, pain or oxygen deprivation.

Primary Positive Reinforcer. A positive reinforcer which is related to an organism's survival, for example, food or water.

Primary Reinforcers. Things an organism must have in order to survive, for example, food, water, and oxygen.

Punishment. Either removing a positive reinforcer or presenting a negative reinforcer.

Rate of Responding. Used by Skinner to demonstrate operant conditioning. If a response is followed by a reinforcer, the rate or frequency with which it is made will go up; if a response is not followed by a reinforcer, its rate of frequency either will stay the same (if it is at its operant level) or will go down.

Respondent Behavior. Behavior that is elicited by a known stimulus.

Respondent Conditioning. Another term for classical or Pavlovian conditioning. Also called type S conditioning.

Secondary Negative Reinforcer. A negative reinforcer that derives its reinforcing properties through its association with a primary negative reinforcer.

Secondary Positive Reinforcer. A positive reinforcer that derives its reinforcing properties through its association with a primary positive reinforcer.

Secondary Reinforcer. Things that acquire reinforcing properties through their association with primary reinforcers.

Shaping. The gradual development of a response that an organism does not normally make. Shaping requires differential reinforcement and successive approximation.

Skinner Box. A small experimental chamber that Skinner invented in order to demonstrate operant conditioning.

Spontaneous Recovery. The reappearance of a conditioned response following a delay after extinction had taken place.

Structuralism. Psychology's first school of thought. The goal of the structuralist was to study the nature of consciousness through the use of introspection.

Successive Approximation. The situation in which only those responses that are increasingly similar to the one ultimately wanted are reinforced.

Superstitious Behavior. Behavior that develops under noncontingent reinforcement in which the organism looks as if it believes that there is a relationship between its actions and reinforcement, when in fact there is no such relationship.

Tact. That part of verbal behavior that accurately names objects and events in the environment.

Type R Conditioning. The term used by Skinner to describe the conditioning of operant or emitted behavior in order to emphasize the importance of the response (R) to such conditioning. Also called operant conditioning.

Type S Conditioning. The term Skinner used to describe classical conditioning in order to emphasize the importance of the stimulus (S) to such conditioning. Also called respondent conditioning.

Unconditioned Response (UCR). The natural, automatic response elicited by an unconditioned stimulus (UCS).

Unconditioned Stimulus (UCS). A stimulus that elicits an automatic, natural response from an organism. Also called a primary reinforcer, because conditioning ultimately depends upon the presence of a UCS.

Variable Interval Reinforcement Schedule (VI). The reinforcement schedule in which a certain average time interval must pass before a response will be reinforced. For example, the organism is reinforced on the average of every thirty seconds.

Variable Ratio Reinforcement Schedule (VR). The reinforcement schedule in which a certain average number of responses need to be made before reinforcement is obtained. For example, the organism is reinforced on the average of every fifth response.

Verbal Behavior. Skinner's term for language.

Vicarious Reinforcement. The kind of reinforcement that comes from modeling the behavior of someone who is seen engaging in activities which are reinforced.

Walden Two. The name of a novel written by Skinner to show how his learning principles could be applied to cultural engineering.

chapter 10

john dollard and neal miller

Neal E. Miller was born in Milwaukee, Wisconsin on August 3, 1909. He received his B.S. degree from the University of Washington in 1931. While at the University of Washington he studied with the famous learning theorist, Edwin Guthrie. He received his M.A. degree from Stanford in 1932 and his Ph.D. degree from Yale in 1935. While at Yale he studied with another famous learning theorist, Clark L. Hull. As we shall see, Hull had a major influence on Miller's theory of personality. Miller did what Hull himself expressed an interest in doing but never did, that is, explore the relationship between his (Hull's) theory of learning and Freud's theory of personality.

Shortly after obtaining his Ph.D., Miller went to Europe as a Social Science Research Council Traveling Fellow. While in Europe he was psychoanalyzed by Heinz Hartman at the Vienna Institute of Psychoanalysis. From 1936 to 1941 he was an instructor, assistant professor, and associate professor at Yale's Institute of Human Relations. From 1942 to 1946 he directed psychological research for the Army Air Force. In 1946 he returned to Yale, and in 1952 he became the James Rowland Angell Professor of Psychology.

Miller remained at Yale until 1966 when he went to Rockefeller University to become professor of psychology and head of the laboratory of physiological psychology. Through the years Miller has been a courageous researcher who has been willing to apply the rigorous methods of science to the more subjective aspects of human experience, such as conflict, language, and unconscious mechanisms. This boldness continues today at Rockefeller University where Miller is currently exploring the conditions under which individuals can learn to control their own internal environment. His pioneer research in this area of *biofeedback* is but one area in which Miller has stimulated research and to which he has made significant contributions.

John Dollard was born in Menasha, Wisconsin on August 29, 1900. He received his A.B. degree from the University of Wisconsin in 1922 and his M.A. in 1930 and Ph.D. in 1931 from the University of Chicago in sociology. In 1932 he became assistant professor of anthropology at Yale University, and in 1933 he became an assistant professor of sociology in the newly formed Institute of Human Relations at Yale. In 1935 he became research associate at the institute and in 1948 became research associate and professor of psychology. Dollard remained at Yale where he became professor emeritus in 1969.

Dollard is truly a generalist. Besides teaching anthropology, sociology, and psychology, he also was trained in psychoanalysis at the Berlin Institute. He wrote *Caste and Class in a Southern Town* (1937), which was concerned with the role of blacks in a community, and *Children of Bondage* (1940) with Allison Davis. During World War II, he conducted a psychological analysis of military behavior which resulted in two books: *Victory over Fear* (1942) and *Fear in Battle* (1943). This list is only a sample of Dollard's publications.

In 1939 Dollard and Miller (along with Doob, Mowrer, and Sears) published a book entitled *Frustration and Aggression,* which attempted to analyze frustration and its consequences in terms of learning principles. Shortly afterwards, Miller and Dollard published *Social Learning*

John Dollard. Courtesy John Dollard.

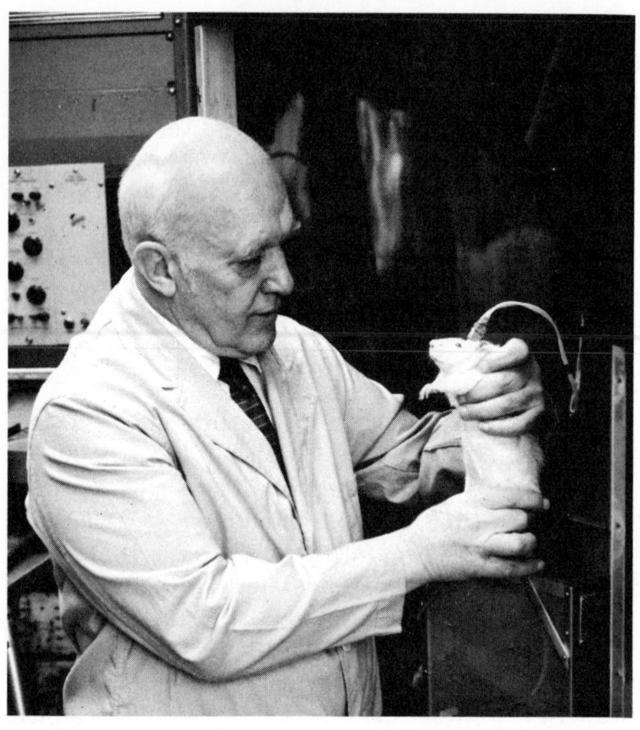

Neal Miller. Courtesy Neal Miller.

and Imitation (1941), which analyzed several complex behavior problems within the context of learning principles. In 1950, Dollard and Miller published *Personality and Psychotherapy: An Analysis in Terms of Learning, Thinking and Culture.* Much of this chapter is based on this latter book.

The combined efforts of Dollard and Miller created a framework within which complex topics such as personality and psychotherapy could be understood more clearly than they had ever been before. As we shall see, they took two preexisting systems, namely Freud's and Hull's, and synthesized them, thus creating a more comprehensive and more useful theoretical structure than either Freud's theory or Hull's theory alone had been.

THE GOAL OF DOLLARD AND MILLER

Dollard and Miller dedicated their 1950 book, *Personality and Psychotherapy* to "Freud, Pavlov and their students." The first paragraph of this book reads:

> This book is an attempt to aid in the creation of a psychological base for a general science of human behavior. Three great traditions, heretofore followed separately, are brought together. One of these is psycho-

> analysis, initiated by the genius of Freud and carried on by his many able students in the art of psychotherapy. Another stems from the work of Pavlov, Thorndike, Hull, and a host of other experimentalists. They have applied the exactness of natural-science method to the study of the principles of learning. Finally, modern social science is crucial because it describes the social conditions under which human beings learn. The ultimate goal is to combine the vitality of psychoanalysis, the rigor of the natural-science laboratory, and the facts of culture. We believe that a psychology of this kind should occupy a fundamental position in the social sciences and humanities—making it unnecessary for each of them to invent its own special assumptions about human nature and personality. (p. 3)

Dollard and Miller set as their goal combining the genius of Freud's insights with the rigors of scientific method as exemplified by the work of the learning theorists in order to understand more clearly human behavior in a cultural setting.

Why the emphasis on learning principles? It is because Dollard and Miller believe that most human behavior is learned. In their earlier book, *Social Learning and Imitation* (1941), which was dedicated to Clark Hull, they explained:

> Human behavior is learned; precisely that behavior which is widely felt to characterize man as a rational being, or as a member of a particular nation or social class, is acquired rather than innate. To understand thoroughly any item of human behavior—either in the social group or in the individual life—one must know the psychological principles involved in its learning and the social conditions under which this learning took place. It is not enough to know either principles or conditions of learning; in order to predict behavior both must be known. The field of psychology describes learning principles, while the various social science disciplines describe the conditions. (p. 1)

It is not just simple overt behavior that Dollard and Miller feel is learned, but also the complex processes such as language and the processes described by Freud such as repression, displacement, and conflict. Since they believe that most important behavior is learned, they also believe that an understanding of the principles of learning is essential if human behavior is to be understood.

HULL'S THEORY OF LEARNING

In the preceding chapter we saw that Skinner defined a reinforcer as anything that modified either the probability of a response or the rate of responding. Hull (1943) was more specific about the nature of reinforcement. He said that in order for a stimulus to be a reinforcer it must reduce a drive. Therefore Hull is said to have a *drive reduction* theory of learning. A stimulus capable of reducing a drive is a reinforc*er* and the actual drive reduction is the reinforce*ment*.

The cornerstone of Hull's theory is the concept of *habit*, which is an association between a stimulus and a response. If a stimulus (S) leads to a response (R) which, in turn, produces a reinforcer, the association between that stimulus (S) and that response (R) becomes stronger. We say that the habit of performing that response in the presence of that stimulus becomes stronger. Since habits describe relationships between stimuli and responses, Hull's theory has been called an S-R theory of learning.

In addition to the concepts of drive reduction and habit, Dollard and Miller borrowed many other concepts from Hull's theory of learning. Among them are the concepts of response hierarchies, stimulus generalization (which Hull borrowed from Pavlov), primary and secondary drives, primary and secondary reinforcers, anticipatory goal responses, and cue-producing responses.

A few of the Freudian concepts that Dollard and Miller attempt to explain or equate with learning principles are the pleasure principle, the relationship between frustration and aggression, the importance of early childhood experience to the formation of adult personality, conflict, suppression, and the importance of the unconscious mind to the generation and maintenance of neurotic behavior. Dollard and Miller also attempt to explain many of the effective procedures in psychotherapy in terms of Hullian learning principles.

For the remainder of this chapter we will review certain aspects of Freudian theory and place them within the context of Hull's theory of learning. First, however, we will note some similarities and differences between Hull's and Skinner's theories of learning.

RELATIONSHIP TO SKINNER'S POSITION

Skinner's position is very antitheoretical. His approach to research was to make a *functional analysis* between environmental conditions and behavior. He is said to study the "empty organism" because, for his purposes, he did not care about the physiological or cognitive processes that occur between environmental events and the behavior they produce. Skinner even refused to speculate on the nature of reinforcement.

Hull's approach to learning theory was *much* different. His formulations were highly theoretical. In fact, most of Hull's theory is concerned with hypothetical events that were believed to influence either learning or performance. Hull's theory attempted to explain both cognitive and behavioral events and, therefore, it provided a more useful framework for Dollard and Miller to use than a theory such as Skinner's could have. For example, it would have been impossible to explain concepts such as suppression without a theory that provided for mediational processes such as thinking and reasoning. Hull's theory provides such processes, Skinner's does not.

Like Skinner, the Hullians, including Dollard and Miller, see nothing wrong with studying lower animals, such as the rat, to learn about human behavior. In fact, Dollard and Miller feel rather strongly that two of the best sources of information about the normal human personality are the rat and neurotic humans who seek professional help. They feel that studying rats is useful because their histories (both genetic and environmental) can be controlled, they are less complex than humans, and the simple behavioral "units" found in rats are the ingredients of human behavior.

Dollard and Miller feel that studying neurotics is useful: They seek help and therefore can be observed under controlled conditions; their behavior can be systematically studied over a fairly long period of time; they are more willing than normal people to speak openly about sensitive and highly personal aspects of their lives; and the same variables govern both neurotic and normal behavior, but the variables appear in exaggerated form in neurotics, making them easier to observe. Dollard and Miller do caution, however, that any generalizations from rats or neurotics applied to normal humans should be checked empirically to test their validity. Dollard and Miller feel that a combination of psychotherapy and laboratory experimentation offers the best means of studying personality.

Like Skinner, Dollard and Miller also acknowledge the importance of culture to determining certain personality attributes. In the last chapter we saw that Skinner defined culture as a set of reinforcement contingencies; Dollard and Miller say about the same thing in the following quotation:

> No psychologist would venture to predict the behavior of a rat without knowing on what arm of a T-maze the feed or the shock is placed. It is no easier to predict the behavior of a human being without knowing the conditions of his "maze," i.e., the structure of his social environment. Culture, as conceived by social scientists, is a statement of the design of the human maze, of the type of reward involved, and of what responses are to be rewarded. It is in this sense a recipe for learning. This contention is easily accepted when widely variant societies are compared. But even within the same society, the mazes which are run by two individuals may seem the same but actually be quite different. . . . No personality analysis of two . . . people can be accurate which does not take into account these cultural differences, that is, differences in the types of responses which have been rewarded. (1941, pp. 5–6)

DRIVE, CUE, RESPONSE, AND REINFORCEMENT

Dollard's and Miller's theory of personality relies heavily on four concepts which they borrowed from Hull's theory of learning. The four concepts are drive, cue, response, and reinforcement. Each will be discussed.

Drive A drive is any strong stimulus that impels an organism to action and whose elimination or reduction is reinforcing. Drives may be *internal,* such as hunger or thirst, or they may be *external,* such as a loud noise or intense heat or cold. A drive may be *primary* in that it is directly related to survival, for example, hunger, thirst, pain, sex, and elimination, or it may be *secondary,* or learned, such as fear, anxiety, or the need to be successful and/or attractive. Secondary drives are usually culturally determined, whereas primary drives are not. It is important to note that primary drives are the building blocks of personality, and all acquired drives ultimately depend upon them. This is very similar to Freud's position, that many of the everyday behaviors we see in people are indirect manifestations of basic drives such as sex or aggression.

Drive is the motivational concept in Dollard's and Miller's theory. Drive is the energizer of personality. Obviously, the stronger the stimulus, the stronger the drive is and the greater the motivation.

> A drive is a strong stimulus which impels action. Any stimulus can become a drive if it is made strong enough. The stronger the stimulus, the more drive function it possesses. The faint murmur of distant music has but little primary drive function; the infernal blare of the neighbor's radio has considerably more. (Dollard & Miller 1941, p. 18)

Cue A cue is a stimulus that indicates the appropriate direction that an activity should take. Whereas drives energize behavior, cues guide behavior.

> The drive impels a person to respond. Cues determine when he will respond, where he will respond, and which response he will make. Simple examples of stimuli which function primarily as cues are the five o'clock whistle determining when the tired worker will stop, the restaurant sign determining where the hungry man will go, and the traffic light determining whether the driver will step on the brake or on the accelerator. (Dollard & Miller 1950, p. 32)

Any stimulus can be thought of as having certain drive properties depending on its strength and certain cue properties depending on its distinctiveness.

Response Responses are elicited by the drive and cues present, which are aimed at reducing or eliminating the drive. In other words, the hungry (drive) person seeing a restaurant (cue) must get into the restaurant (response) before the hunger drive can be reduced. In Dollard's and Miller's theory (and in Hull's) a response can be *overt;* it can be directly instrumental in reducing a drive or it can be *internal,* entailing the thinking, planning, and reasoning that will *ultimately* reduce a drive. Dollard and Miller refer to internal responses as cue-producing responses. We will have more to say about such responses later in the chapter.

Some responses are more effective than others in reducing a drive and are the ones that should occur when next the drive occurs. New responses must be learned to new situations, and old responses must be discouraged if they are no longer maximally effective. The rearrangement of response probabilities as new conditions emerge or as old conditions change is called *learning*. We will say more about the circumstances under which response probabilities change in the next section.

Reinforcement As we said earlier, reinforcement, according to Dollard and Miller, is equated with drive reduction. Any stimulus that causes drive reduction is said to be a reinforcer. A reinforcer can be primary, in which case it satisfies a need related to survival, or it can be secondary. A secondary reinforcer, as in Skinner's theory, is a previously neutral stimulus that has been consistently paired with a primary reinforcer. A mother, for example, becomes a powerful secondary reinforcer because of her association with the reduction of primary drives.

If a cue leads to a response and the response leads to reinforcement, the association between the cue and the response will be strengthened. If this process is repeated, eventually we can say that the organism has developed a strong habit.

It should be pointed out that the nature of reinforcement is a highly controversial issue among learning theorists, of which Dollard and Miller are aware. Like good scientists, they use the definition of reinforcement that they feel is the best available but would be happy to discard that definition if a better one came along.

> The stimulus-reduction hypothesis of reinforcement could be discarded without having an appreciable effect on the rest of my theoretical formulations. I take this occasion to urge attempts to formulate and rigorously test competing hypotheses, and time permitting, may even join in that activity myself. However unsatisfactory, the drive-reduction hypothesis is not likely to be abandoned as long as it is the best thing of its kind that we have. The decisive way to kill it is with a superior alternative. (Miller 1959, p. 257)

As we have seen, Dollard and Miller set as their goal the explanation of human personality in terms of learning theory. Having discussed the concepts of drive, cue, response, and reinforcement, we are now in a position to understand what, according to Dollard and Miller, learning theory is.

> What, then, is learning theory? In its simplest form, it is the study of the circumstances under which a response and a cue stimulus become connected. After learning has been completed, response and cue are bound together in such a way that the appearance of the cue evokes the response. . . . Learning takes place according to definite psychologi-

> cal principles. Practice does not always make perfect. The connection between a cue and a response can be strengthened only under certain conditions. The learner must be driven to make the response and rewarded for having responded in the presence of the cue. This may be expressed in a homely way by saying that in order to learn one must want something, notice something, do something, and get something. Stated more exactly, these factors are drive, cue, response and reward. These elements in the learning process have been carefully explored, and further complexities have been discovered. Learning theory has become a firmly knit body of principles which are useful in describing human behavior. (Dollard & Miller 1941, pp. 1–2)

There is no better summary anywhere of what the learning theorists call *reinforcement theory* than the preceding statement, "that in order to learn one must want something, notice something, do something, and get something."

RESPONSE HIERARCHIES

Every cue elicits a number of responses simultaneously, which vary in terms of their probability of occurrence. This group of responses elicited by a cue is what Hull called *the habit family hierarchy*, which can be diagrammed as follows:

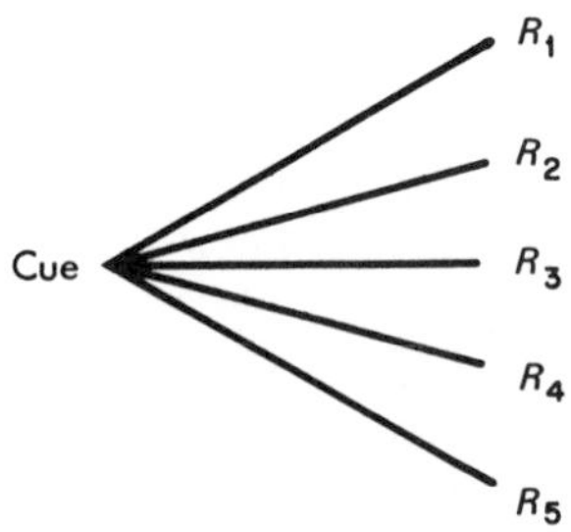

In the situation diagrammed above, R_1 is the most likely response to be made when the cue is encountered, R_2 is next likely, and so forth. If R_1 is prevented, R_2 would be made and if R_1 and R_2 were blocked, R_3 would be made, and so on.

When a newborn child experiences an irritation, a set of responses is triggered which, since no learning is involved, is called the *innate hierarchy of responses*. This hierarchy is a genetically determined set of responses that is triggered by certain drive conditions. The hungry infant first may become restless, then cry, and then toss violently while screaming. Note that the innate hierarchy of response exists for only a short period of time. As certain responses in the hierarchy are reinforced, they change their position in the hierarchy. The response most likely to occur is called the *dominant response* in the hierarchy and is the one that has been most successful in bringing about drive reduction.

most likely to occur

Learning is constantly rearranging responses in the various habit family hierarchies. Prior to a learning experience, the arrangement of responses elicited by a cue is called the *initial hierarchy of responses.* After learning has taken place, the revised arrangement of responses is called the *resultant hierarchy of responses.*

It is important to note that if the dominant response in a hierarchy always reduced the existing drive, no learning would ever take place. If, for example, the innate response of blinking always removed stray particles from one's eye, there would be no need to learn to rub the eye or roll it or wash it. According to Dollard and Miller, all learning, which we can now equate with the rearrangement of response hierarchies, depends on failure. This is labeled the *learning dilemma.* The concept of the learning dilemma has vast implications for both education and child rearing.

> In the absence of a dilemma, no new learning of either the trial-and-error or the thoughtful problem-solving type occurs. For example, a mother was worried because her child seemed to be retarded in learning to talk. Brief questioning revealed that she was adept at understanding the child's every want as expressed by its gestures. Having other successful means of responding, the child was not in a dilemma. He learned only his old habits of using gestures more thoroughly, and consequently he did not perform that type of random vocal behavior which would lead to speech. By gradually pretending to become more stupid at understanding gestures, the mother put the child in a dilemma and probably facilitated the learning of speech. At least, under these modified conditions, this child rapidly learned to talk.
>
> The absence of a dilemma is one of the reasons why it is often difficult to teach successful people new things. Old, heavily rewarded habits must be interrupted before new learning can occur. When the accustomed rewards are withdrawn by unusual circumstances such as revolution, new responses may occur and, if rewarded, may be learned; Russian Counts *can* learn to drive taxicabs and Countesses to become cooks. (Dollard & Miller 1950, pp. 45–46)

FEAR AS AN ACQUIRED DRIVE

We have looked in detail at the complexities of Dollard's and Miller's concepts of response and reinforcement. In this section we will focus on their concept of drive, and in the next section we will discuss in more detail some additional properties of cues.

We mentioned earlier that there are two kinds of drives—primary and secondary. Primary drives are biologically determined, and secondary drives are learned or culturally determined. One of the most important secondary drives is fear, since it is so important to both adaptive and maladaptive human behavior. Freud observed that fear could serve as a warning of impending danger. For example, events that accompanied a painful experience, when reencountered, would cause fear or anxiety, thus warning the person to be careful. For example, a child who was burned by a hot stove would experience fear when next seeing a stove even though there was no pain in merely seeing the stove.

In 1948a Miller performed his now famous experiment exploring the acquisition of fear. His apparatus consisted of an experimental chamber with black and white compartments. When a rat was allowed to roam freely, it showed no aversion to either the white or the black compartments. Next, Miller shocked the rat in the white compartment, and it was allowed to escape the shock by running into the black compartment. The rat quickly learned to escape the shock by leaving the white compartment. Later when the animal was placed in the white compartment without being shocked, it urinated, defecated, crouched, and ran into the black compartment. The animal had learned to fear the white compartment, because it had been associated with shock.

Miller next arranged the experiment so that the animal could escape the white compartment only by first turning a small wheel. The animal learned to do this, even though no additional shocks were given. Miller replaced the wheel with a lever and found the animal quickly extinguished the wheel-turning response, which was now ineffective, and learned the lever-pressing response, again with no further shocks. The animal had developed a *conditioned fear reaction* to the white chamber.

The most important thing about Miller's experiment is that it demonstrates that fear itself becomes a drive which can be reduced, resulting in reinforcement. It was the reduction of fear, not pain, that caused the animal to learn the wheel-turning and the lever-pressing responses. Such behavior is highly resistant to extinction because as long as fear is present, its reduction will be highly reinforcing. Note that, under these circumstances, the animal does not stay in the situation long enough to learn that it will not receive additional shocks and thereby extinguish its fear reaction. It keeps behaving "as if" it will be shocked again if it lingers in the situation.

It is Dollard's and Miller's contention that phobias, anxieties, and other irrational fear responses are produced by similar experiences on the human level. Such behavior looks irrational to the observer because the history of its development is not known as it is with the rat. It could be that because of harsh physical punishment for sexual behavior in early childhood, a person has an aversion to sexual activities and sexual thoughts. For this person, even approximating such activities and/or thoughts elicits fear, which is reduced by escape or avoidance. Like the rat in Miller's experiment, this person never dwells long enough in the anxiety-provoking situation to learn that he or she will no longer be punished for such thoughts or activities. Like with the rat, extinction of the fear reaction is impossible. As we shall see later in this chapter, the main job of psychotherapy, as Dollard and Miller see it, is to provide a situation in which the client is encouraged to experience threatening thoughts without punishment and, in that way, to finally extinguish them. This, of course, is very similar to what Freud was attempting to do when he used free association and dream analysis to discover repressed thoughts.

STIMULUS GENERALIZATION

If there is an association between S_1 and R_1, not only will S_1 elicit R_1, but so will a variety of stimuli similar to S_1. The greater the similarity of a stimulus to S_1, the greater will be the tendency for it to elicit R_1. This is called *stimulus generalization.* In Miller's experiment on fear, we would expect not only the white compartment to elicit fear but also various shades of gray compartments to elicit fear. However, the whiter the compartment, the greater will be the fear response since it was the white compartment that was originally associated with pain.

All learned responses generalize to other stimuli. If a child learns to fear snakes, she probably will also, at least at first, fear rope. If an adolescent fears his father, he will also tend to fear men who look like his father. A woman who is raped may shortly thereafter hate all men. With further experience, however, most normal humans learn to discriminate. *Discrimination* is the opposite of generalization. Thus, the child learns that some snakes are to be feared, but that ropes are safe. The adolescent learns that his father perhaps should be feared under some circumstances, but that men of similar appearance pose no threat, and the rape victim realizes that her attacker was not typical of all men. Therefore, generalization causes the initial tendency for learned responses to be elicited by a wide range of stimuli, but further experience allows the person to discriminate and thus respond selectively to stimuli. This is true at least of normal people. As we shall see later in this chapter, neurotics often lose their ability to discriminate and therefore tend to overgeneralize their anxieties.

Dollard and Miller distinguish two kinds of generalization: primary and secondary. *Primary generalization* is based on the physical similarity among stimuli. The closer two stimuli are in their physical attributes, the greater the probability is that they will elicit the same response. Primary generalization is innate and is governed by a person's sensory apparatus. *Secondary generalization* is based on verbal labels and not on the physical similarity among stimuli. Thus, one responds to all individuals labeled "friendly" in a similar way as are those labeled "hostile." Likewise, the word "dangerous" equates a large number of dangerous situations which tends to elicit similar kinds of responses. Secondary generalization is what Dollard and Miller call learned equivalence, which is mediated by language. It is important to realize that secondary generalization is not based upon physical attributes; in fact, it can counteract primary generalization by labeling one event "good" and another event "bad," although the two events are physically very similar.

CONFLICT

One of Freud's concepts that Miller studied intensively was that of *conflict*. Lewin (1935) had studied the concept earlier, and Miller borrowed from both Freud and Lewin. It was Miller who experimentally analyzed in depth the concept of conflict. Freud had talked about the continuous conflict between libidinal desires and the demands of the superego. To Freud a person could be both attracted to an object and repelled by it at the same time. This was later called an approach-avoidance conflict and is one of four kinds of conflict studied by Miller. Each of the four now will be described.

Approach-Approach Conflict Here the conflict is between two positive goals that are equally attractive at the same time. Such a conflict can be diagrammed as follows:

An approach-approach conflict exists when two equally atttractive people ask for a date on the same night or when one is both hungry and sleepy. Such conflicts can become severe—witness the proverbial ass that starved to death between two equally desirable bails of hay. Typically, however, this kind of conflict is easily solved by attaining first one goal and then the other; for example, one could first eat and then go to bed.

Avoidance-Avoidance Conflict Here the person must choose between two negative goals. For example, the child must eat her spinach or be spanked, the student must do his arithmetic homework or get low grades, a person must either go to a job he dislikes or lose his income. A person having such a conflict is "damned if he does and damned if he doesn't"; he can also be said to be "caught between the devil and the deep blue sea." Such a conflict can be diagrammed as follows:

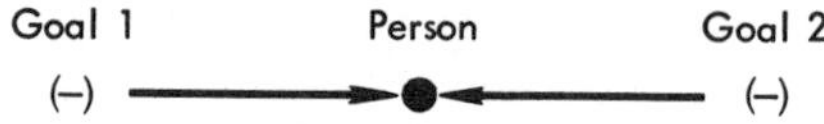

Two kinds of behavior typically characterize an organism having an avoidance-avoidance conflict: (1) vacillation or indecision and (2) escape. Escape can be either actually leaving the conflict situation, or it can be mental escape such as daydreaming or mental preoccupation with other thoughts.

Approach-Avoidance Conflict Here the person is both attracted to and repelled by the *same goal.* A job may be attractive because of the money it will earn but be unattractive because it is boring or because it keeps the person from doing more enjoyable things. The young woman may be attracted to the idea of marriage because of the security it would bring to her life but may be anxious about her sexual role in marriage. Such a conflict can be diagrammed as follows:

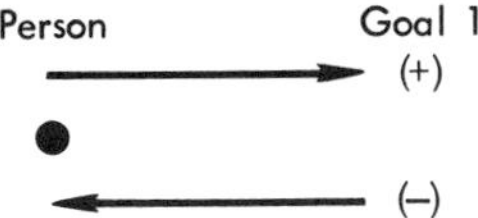

Miller listed the following as the most significant features of the approach-avoidance conflict:

(A) The tendency to approach a goal is stronger the nearer the subject is to it.

(B) The tendency to avoid a feared stimulus is stronger the nearer the subject is to it.

(C) The strength of avoidance increases more rapidly with nearness than does that of approach.

(D) The strength of tendencies to approach or avoid varies directly with the strength of the drive upon which they are based.

(E) Below the asymptote of learning, increasing the number of reinforced trials will increase the strength of the response tendency that is reinforced.

(F) When two incompatible responses are in conflict, the stronger one will occur. (1959, pp. 205–206)

It is on the approach-avoidance conflict that Miller has done his most extensive research (for example, 1944, 1959, & 1964). Figure 10–1 summarizes many of these characteristics of the approach-avoidance conflict.

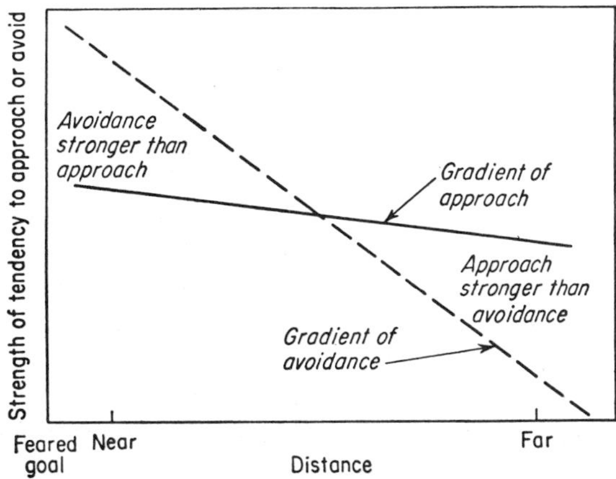

Figure 10–1 Diagram of an approach-avoidance conflict. (From Miller 1959, p. 206.)

Among the many deductions that can be made from Figure 10–1 is that as long as the approach gradient is higher than the avoidance gradient, the person will approach the goal. As soon as the avoidance gradient becomes higher the person will avoid the goal. Therefore, since the approach gradient becomes higher the farther one is from the goal, there will be a strong approach tendency. As one approaches the goal, however, the avoidance tendency increases and eventually is stronger than the approach tendency. At that point, the person will retreat from the goal. Thus, we would expect vacillation at the point at which the two gradients cross. We all know couples who have doubts about their relationship and who are constantly breaking up and going back together. While apart, the favorable aspects of their relationship are dominant, and therefore they are driven back together. Once reunited, however, they confront the negative aspects of their relationship and are once again driven apart.

We will have more to say about the approach-avoidance conflict in subsequent sections of this chapter.

Double Approach-Avoidance Conflict Here the person has ambivalent feelings about two goal objects. Such a conflict can be diagrammed as follows:

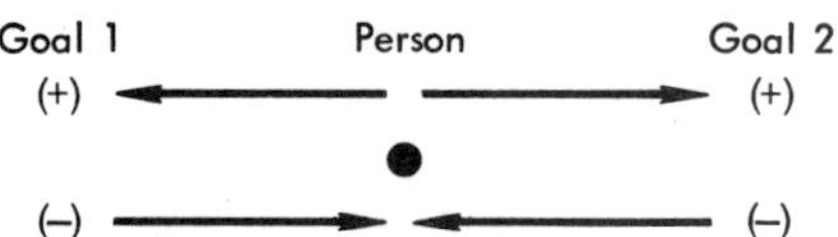

One example of a double approach-avoidance conflict comes from the female child's position relative to her parents in Freudian theory. She is attracted to her mother because the mother satisfies her biological needs but is repelled by the mother because she is thought responsible for denying the girl a penis. She is attracted to her father because he possesses the valued organ and yet is envious of him because he does. According to Freud, the female child has ambivalent feelings about both parents.

According to Dollard and Miller, most neurotic behavior involves conflict. For example, when a neurotic individual begins to engage in activities or thoughts that will lead to the reduction of a strong drive such as sex, he is overwhelmed with anxiety. The closer he comes to approaching a goal that will satisfy his need for sex, the stronger his anxiety will become until eventually he retreats from the goal. However, since his original need was not satisfied, he again approaches sex-related goals only to be eventually driven from them by anxiety, and on it goes. Only psychotherapy, or its equivalent, will rescue this person from this vicious circle.

DISPLACEMENT

Another Freudian concept that is explored thoroughly by Dollard and Miller is that of *displacement*. Clearly, one of the most important aspects of Freud's theory was his contention that frustrated drives did not simply go away but rather showed up in disguised form. In other words, if a need could not be satisfied directly, it was displaced and satisfied indirectly. As we saw in chapter 2, Freud's term for the displacement of the sex drive to more socially acceptable activities such as hard work, and creativity in general, was sublimation.

Miller's first step was to verify experimentally the phenomenon of displacement. To do this, Miller (1948b) placed two rats in an apparatus and shocked them both until they started fighting, at which point the shock was turned off. In other words, the aggressive act of fighting was reinforced by escape from shock. Training continued in this manner until the animals began fighting immediately after the shock was turned on. At this point, a doll was placed in the apparatus, and the animals were shocked. Again they fought with each other and ignored the doll. This is shown in Figure 10–2.

When only one animal was placed in the apparatus and shocked, however, it attacked the doll. This is shown in Figure 10–3. When the object of aggression was not available to the animal, it aggressed toward a substitute object, that is, the doll. Thus *displaced aggression* was demonstrated.

To show that displacement occurs is important, but it leaves unanswered questions as to what determines which objects are involved in

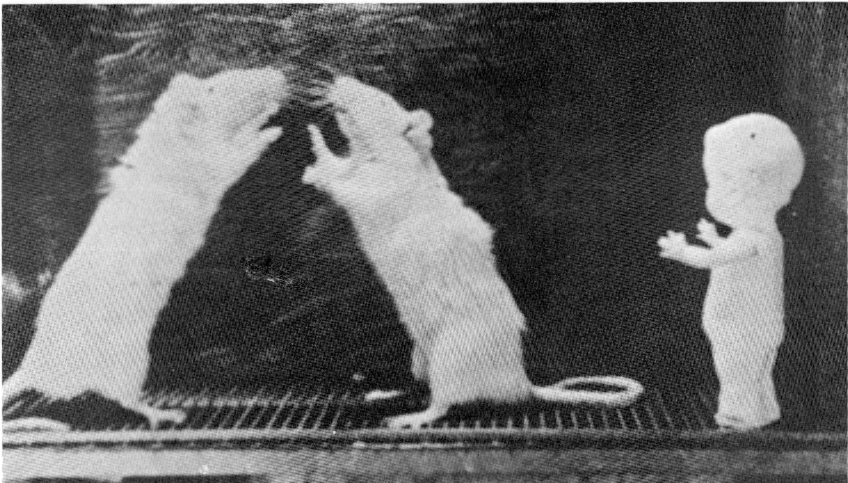

Figure 10–2 The figure shows two rats that have been trained to fight each other in order to terminate an electric shock. (From Miller 1948(b), p. 157.)

Figure 10–3 The figure shows the displacement of an aggressive response. (From Miller 1948(b), p. 157.)

displacement and why. For example, if an employee cannot aggress toward her boss after being refused a raise, toward what object or objects will she aggress toward? Miller (1959, pp. 218–219) reached the following conclusions about displacement:

1. When it is impossible for an organism to respond to a desired stimulus, it will respond to a stimulus which is most similar to the desired stimulus. For example, if a woman is prevented from marrying the man she loved because of his death, she will tend to marry someday a man very similar to him.
2. If a response to an original stimulus is prevented by conflict, displacement will occur to an intermediate stimulus. For example, if a girl leaves her boyfriend after a quarrel, her next boyfriend will tend to be similar to her original boyfriend in many ways and yet also different from him.
3. If there are strong avoidance tendencies to an original stimulus, displacement will tend to occur toward a very dissimilar stimulus. For example, if a girl's original romance were very negative, her next sweetheart would tend to be much different from the first.

If displacement occurs because of conflict, the strength of the conflicting responses will determine where displacement takes place. Figure 10–4 shows the nature of displacement when there is a weak conflicting response and when there is a strong conflicting response.

We can see in Figure 10–4, for example, that if there is a desire to aggress toward a goal and a weak fear of punishment, there will be a tendency to displace to an object similar to the original goal. However, if there is a desire to aggress toward a goal and a strong fear of punishment, the expression of aggression probably will be to objects very dis-

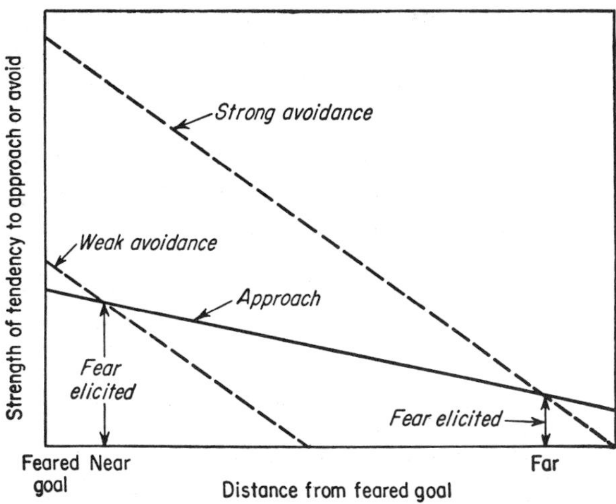

Figure 10–4 The figure shows that with a weak avoidance tendency, fear is not experienced until objects very near or very similar to the goal are encountered. When there is a strong avoidance tendency, however, fear is caused by objects more distant from and more dissimilar to the goal. (From Miller 1959, p. 208.)

similar to the original goal. In other words, increasing an individual's fear will decrease the tendency to displace the response to similar objects, and decreasing an individual's fear increases the tendency to displace the response to similar objects. For example, if an employee has no fear of her boss and her boss frustrates her, she will aggress directly toward the boss. If an employee has a mild fear of her boss and the boss frustrates her, she will not aggress toward the boss but will aggress toward someone very similar to the boss, for instance, the vice president or manager. If an employee has a strong fear of her boss and the boss frustrates her, she will aggress toward objects very dissimilar to the boss, like other cars on the way home from work, her husband and/or children, or perhaps her pet.

One could also expect students who are frustrated by poor academic performance and who are fearful of teachers and school authorities to be among those who would commit acts of vandalism against their school. Their aggression caused by the frustration of poor academic performance is displaced from those directly responsible for their frustration to an object that is related but less threatening, the school itself.

We see then that if an object of choice is not available and there is no conflict, displacement is simply a matter of stimulus generalization. That is, an object most like the one not available will be chosen. If there is a conflict, however, displacement will be governed by the net of the approach and avoidance tendencies.

THE FRUSTRATION-AGGRESSION HYPOTHESIS

In 1939 Dollard and Miller (along with Doob, Mowrer, and Sears) published their first book together, entitled *Frustration and Aggression.* In this book they analyzed the Freudian notion that frustration leads to aggression, better known as the frustration-aggression hypothesis. Dollard, Doob, Miller, Mowrer, and Sears made the following assumption:

> This study takes as its point of departure the assumption that *aggression is always a consequence of frustration.* More specifically, the proposition is that the occurrence of aggressive behavior always pre-supposes the existence of frustration and, contrariwise, that the existence of frustration always leads to some form of aggression. (1939, p. 1)

Frustration was defined as "that condition which exists when a goal-response suffers interference" (1939, p. 11), and *aggression* was defined as "an act whose goal-response is injury to an organism (or organism-surrogate)" (1939, p. 11). It was assumed that the disruption of goal-directed behavior causes frustration, and frustration causes aggression toward the person or object acting as a barrier between the person and his or her goal.

Dollard and others (1939, pp. 28–32) conclude that there are three main factors that determine how much aggression will result from frustration:

1. The drive level associated with the frustrated response In other words, the more intensely the person wants to attain a goal, the more frustrated he or she will be when the goal-directed activity is blocked, and thus the more aggressive that person will become.

2. The completeness of the frustration Goal responses that are only partially blocked will lead to less frustration and therefore less aggression than produced by goal responses that are completely blocked.

3. The cumulative effect of minor frustrations Minor frustrations or interferences will eventually add up to produce considerable frustration and therefore considerable aggression. If on the way to a restaurant to eat, for example, one first is interrupted by a friend who wants to chat, then by unusually heavy traffic, and then finds the restaurant closed, one is likely to become more frustrated than one would have been if one had gone directly to the restaurant and found it closed.

In all of these points, the message is always the same—the strength of aggression is a function of the magnitude of frustration.

In the last section we learned that as the threat of punishment for a direct act of aggression increases, the tendency for the act of aggression to be displaced to less threatening people or objects also increases. According to Dollard and others: "it follows that the *greater the degree of inhibition specific to a more direct act of aggression, the more probable will be the occurrence of less direct acts of aggression"* (1939, p. 40).

Through the years the relationship between frustration and aggression has been found to be less direct than originally thought. For example, Miller (1941) concluded that aggression is only one result of frustration. Other possible reactions to frustration are withdrawal or apathy, regression, and fixation (stereotyped behavior). Most researchers still believe, however, that aggression is one of the most common and important reactions to frustration and that the relationship between the two has many implications for penal reform, child rearing, and behavior modification in general.

THE IMPORTANCE OF LANGUAGE

Earlier in the chapter we listed "response" as one of the four essential ingredients in Dollard's and Miller's theory. The other three are drive, cue, and reinforcement. Two kinds of responding were mentioned, instrumental or overt and internal or thinking. Both kinds of responses were considered important by Dollard and Miller, which is a major distinction between their theory and Skinner's. It is not that Skinner avoided the topic of language, he did not. However, to him, language was simply verbal behavior which was governed by the same laws as any other behavior was. Dollard and Miller were much more willing to speculate on the nature of internal thought processes and their relationship to language than Skinner was. Furthermore, Dollard and Miller analyzed the Freudian notions of repression and neuroses in terms of internal response mechanisms. Dollard and Miller feel that people's ability to use language accounts for their higher mental processes, which are part of both neurotic and normal functioning.

Many years ago, Pavlov referred to physical stimuli that elicit conditioned responses as the *first signal system.* That is, through experience we learn to respond to certain environmental objects in certain ways, depending on the nature of our experience with them. For example, we avoid hot stoves and salivate when we are hungry and see food. In addition, according to Pavlov, we develop conditioned responses to *symbols of environmental events.* For example, we become fearful when we hear words like "fire," "danger," or "enemy." Likewise, we feel good when we hear the name of a loved one or hear such words as "love," "peace," or "friend." Pavlov called these conditioned responses the *second signal system.*

Dollard and Miller follow Pavlov in believing that language becomes a symbolic representation of reality. As this set of symbols develops, one can "think through" experiences without actually needing to have them. Thinking, then, is a kind of talking to oneself about a number of behavioral possibilities. Dollard and Miller call images, perceptions, and words, *cue-producing responses* because they generally determine what the next response in a sequence will be. Counting, for example, is a series of cue-producing responses because the response "one" triggers the response "two," and so forth. Thoughts constitute responses, but they also act as cues in eliciting further responses.

Two of the most useful functions of cue-producing responses are

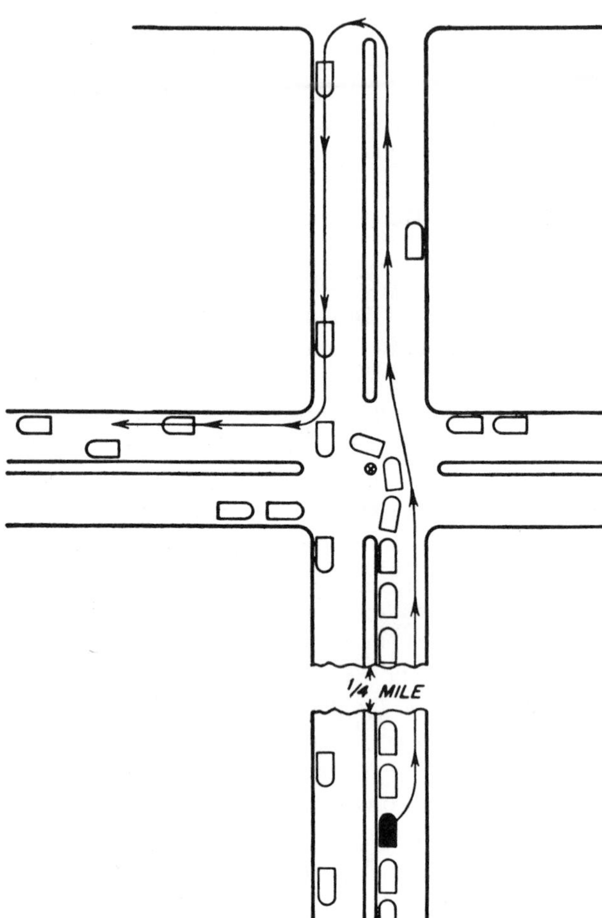

An example of reasoning. The driver in the black car is blocked from making a left turn by the traffic jam in the left lane. In the distance he sees the cars in the much lighter traffic coming from the opposite direction making the right turn easily on to the road he wants to take. He thinks, "If I were only going the other way." This stimulates him to think of how he could be going the other way. He pulls out into the right lane, passes the cars ahead, turns around, comes back the other way, and makes a right turn on to the highway. (The small circle at the center intersection indicates a traffic light.)

Figure 10–5 An example of how reasoning replaces behavioral trial and error in a problem-solving situation. (From Dollard & Miller 1950, p. 112.)

reasoning and *planning*. Reasoning replaces overt behavioral trial and error with cognitive trial and error. The latter is far more efficient because *mentally* a problem can be approached from a variety of points of view and no set sequence needs to be followed. Figure 10–5 shows the advantage of reasoning in problem solving.

When cue-producing responses are part of solving an immediate problem, the process is called reasoning. When the cue-producing responses are directed at the solution of a future problem, the process is called planning.

In this section we have emphasized Dollard's and Miller's analysis of language in normal functioning. Later in this chapter we will see how language functions in the mechanism of repression and in neuroses in general.

THE UNCONSCIOUS MIND

Like Freud, Dollard and Miller consider unconscious processes to be extremely important to determining behavior. They describe two major categories of unconscious material, (1) experiences that were never verbally labeled and (2) experiences that have been repressed.

Experiences that were never verbalized Learning that occurs before language is developed is not labeled or recorded in a way that allows it to be recalled and, therefore, such learning becomes part of the unconscious.

> According to our hypothesis, drives, cues, and responses that have never been labeled will necessarily be unconscious. One large category of this kind will be experiences that occurred before the child learned to talk effectively. Since the effective use of speech develops gradually and may not be established for certain categories until long after the child has learned to say "Mamma," the period during which major parts of social learning are unconscious extends over a considerable number of years and has no set boundaries. (Dollard & Miller 1950, p. 198)

At the time in life thought by Freud to be most crucial to adult personality development, experiences are unlabeled and thus cannot be recalled. These early experiences have a profound effect on one's later conscious life, and yet they themselves remain unconscious.

> The young child does not notice or label the experiences which it is having at this time. It cannot give a description of character traits acquired during the first year of life nor yet of its hardships, fears, or deep satisfactions. What was not verbalized at the time cannot well be reported later. An important piece of history is lost and cannot be elicited by questionnaire or interview. Nevertheless, the behavioral record survives. The responses learned occur and may indeed recur in analogous situa-

> tions thoughout life. They are elicited by unlabeled cues and are mutely interwoven into the fabric of conscious life. (Dollard & Miller 1950, p. 136)

Experiences that have been repressed Some thoughts are uncomfortable because they cause anxiety. A few examples would be: thinking about an automobile accident in which a loved one was killed or injured; thinking about sex after learning how evil such thoughts are; thinking about how you would like to steal something from a store; thinking about how you would like to steal away your best friend's boyfriend; or thinking about how you would like to caress your teacher or minister. Anxiety is a negative drive just like pain, hunger, or thirst, and therefore anything that reduces anxiety will be reinforcing. In other words, *anything that terminates an anxiety-provoking thought will be learned as a habit.*

If suddenly during a conversation you find yourself wanting your best friend's boyfriend, you may find such a thought anxiety provoking because of your early moral training. If so, you may respond by consciously "putting the thought out of your mind." Such a conscious and deliberate effort to stop an anxiety-provoking thought is called *suppression.* Suppression is learned just like any other response; that is, because it is followed by drive reduction (in this case, anxiety is reduced), it gains in strength. Suppression is a common way of stopping thoughts that cause one to be anxious.

Eventually the suppression of anxiety-provoking thoughts becomes *anticipatory* in that such thoughts are terminated automatically before they can cause anxiety. When a potentially painful thought is aborted before it enters consciousness the process is called *repression.* Repression is the learned response of *not-thinking* thoughts that are unpleasant. In repression, early thoughts act as signals that, if a line of thought is continued, it will result in the experience of anxiety, and therefore the line of thought is terminated long before it can become painful. For this reason, repression is said to be anticipatory, and because it prevents the experience of anxiety, it is said to be a conditioned avoidance response. Suppression allows *escape* from anxiety-provoking thoughts, whereas repression allows *avoidance* of them. In other words, repression is triggered when unacceptable material starts to emerge from the unconscious, and suppression is triggered when such material is already conscious. Both processes are learned responses which are maintained by the elimination, reduction, or prevention of anxiety.

It may appear that a process such as repression is beneficial because it allows a person to avoid many painful thoughts, and this certainly is true. Repression also has its negative side. A thought that is repressed cannot be treated rationally since it does not enter consciousness. As we saw in the preceding section, it is conscious mechanisms that are part of the problem-solving processes of reasoning and planning. If a category of experience is repressed, it cannot be considered logically, and the activities related to it will tend to be unreasoned and stupid. Furthermore, any attempt to bring repressed material into consciousness is typically met with great resistance, which is the case during psychoanalysis.

As the reader may have guessed by now, the mechanism of repression is thought by Dollard and Miller (as it was by Freud) to be causally related to most neurotic behavior. The goal of psychotherapy is to free certain thoughts from repression so that they may be treated logically and realistically.

NEUROSIS AND SYMPTOM FORMATION

Dollard and Miller follow Freud in assuming that conflict is at the heart of neurotic behavior and that this conflict is unconscious and usually learned in childhood.

> An intense emotional conflict is the necessary basis for neurotic behavior. The conflict must further be unconscious. As a usual thing, such conflicts are created only in childhood. How can it be that neurotic conflicts are engendered when there is no deliberate plan to do so? Society must force children to grow up, but it does not idealize neurosis and makes no formal provision in its system of training for the production of neurotic children. Indeed we deplore the neurotic and recognize him as a burden to himself and to others. How then does it happen? Our answer is that *neurotic conflicts are taught by parents and learned by children.* (Dollard & Miller 1950, p. 127, italics added)

Beyond stating that neurotic behavior is unconsciously motivated by a conflict with its origin in childhood, it is difficult to state further exactly what neurosis is.

> Most people, even scientists, are vague about neurosis. Neither the neurotic victim nor those who know him seem able to state precisely what is involved. The victim feels a mysterious malady. The witness observes inexplicable behavior. The neurotic is mysterious because he is *capable* of acting and yet he is *unable* to act and enjoy. Though physically capable of attaining sex rewards, he is anesthetic; though capable of aggression, he is meek; though capable of affection, he is cold and unresponsive. As seen by the outside witness, the neurotic does not make use of the obvious opportunities for satisfaction which life offers him. (Dollard & Miller 1950, p. 12)

Although the term neurosis is hard to define precisely, it is clear that the neurotic is miserable, stupid about certain aspects of his or her own existence and often develops physical symptoms which are only manifestations of the repressed conflict.

If children are severely punished for sexual activities, they will learn to repress sexual behaviors and thoughts as adults. They will therefore need to live with a sex drive that strongly impels them to engage in sexual activities but with a strong fear of punishment if they do so. As we saw in the last section, thoughts of sexual activity will be repressed under these circumstances, and as a result, this strong approach-avoidance conflict will remain unconscious so that language cannot be used to describe and analyze it.

> Without language and adequate labeling, the higher mental processes cannot function. When these processes are knocked out by repression, the person cannot guide himself by mental means to a resolution of his conflict. Since the neurotic cannot help himself, he must have the help of others if he is to be helped at all—though millions today live out their lives in strong neurotic pain and never get help. The neurotic, therefore, is, or appears to be, stupid because he is unable to use his mind in dealing with cetain of his problems. He feels that someone should help him, but he does not know how to ask for help since he does not know what his problem is. He may feel aggrieved that he is suffering, but he cannot explain his case. (Dollard & Miller 1950, p. 15)

The neurotic, therefore, is caught in an unbearable conflict between frustrated drives, on the one hand, and the fear connected with the approach responses that would bring about their satisfaction, on the other.

Symptom Formation Neurotics often develop symptoms such as phobias, inhibitions, avoidances, compulsions, and physical disorders such as paralysis or nervous tics. Although it is common for neurotics to think that their symptoms constitute their problem, they do not. Neurotic symptoms are only manifestations of a repressed conflict. As an example, Dollard and Miller (1950) cite the case of Mrs. A. who was an orphan, born of unknown parents in a southern city. She was raised by foster parents who gave her very repressive sex training. Although she had strong sexual appetites, sex became a dirty, loathsome thing about which it was painful for her to talk or think. Eventually she developed a number of phobias and a preoccupation with her heartbeat. In analysis it was learned that her preoccupation with her heartbeat was used as a means of preventing sex-related thoughts. Dollard and Miller summarized the case of Mrs. A. as follows:

> When on the streets alone, her fear of sex temptation was increased. Someone might speak to her, wink at her, make an approach to her. Such an approach would increase her sex desire and make her more vulnerable to seduction. Increased sex desire, however, touched off both anxiety and guilt, and this intensified her conflict when she was on the street. . . . When sexy thoughts came to mind or other sex stimuli tended to occur, these stimuli elicited anxiety. . . . Since [heartbeat] counting is a highly preoccupying kind of response, no other thoughts could enter her mind during this time. While counting, the sexy thoughts which excited fear dropped out. Mrs. A. "felt better" immediately when she started count-

ing, and the counting habit was reinforced by the drop in anxiety. (1950, p. 21)

Neurotic symptoms are learned because they reduce fear or anxiety. Such symptoms do not solve the basic problem any more than repression does, but they make life temporarily more bearable.

> The symptoms do not solve the basic conflict in which the neurotic person is plunged, but they mitigate it. They are responses which tend to reduce the conflict, and in part they succeed. When a successful symptom occurs it is reinforced because it reduces neurotic misery. *The symptom is thus learned as a habit.* One very common function of symptoms is to keep the neurotic person away from those stimuli which would activate and intensify his neurotic conflict. Thus, the combat pilot with a harrowing military disaster behind him may walk away from the sight of any airplane. As he walks towards the plane his anxiety goes up; as he walks away it goes down. Walking away is thus reinforced. It is this phobic walking away which constitutes his symptom. If the whole situation is not understood, such behavior seems bizarre to the casual witness. (Dollard & Miller 1950, pp. 15–16, italics added)

We have seen that neurotics are miserable and stupid about the nature of their problem and therefore are unable to help themselves. In the next section we will see how the professional therapist attempts to help neurotics using Freudian notions as interpreted by Dollard and Miller.

PSYCHOTHERAPY

The major assumption that Dollard and Miller make about neurosis is that it is learned, and if it is learned, it can be unlearned. Psychotherapy provides a situation in which neurosis can be unlearned.

> If neurotic behavior is learned, it should be unlearned by some combination of the same principles by which it was taught. We believe this to be the case. Psychotherapy establishes a set of conditions by which neurotic habits may be unlearned and nonneurotic habits learned. Therefore, we view the therapist as a kind of teacher and the patient as a learner. In the same way and by the same principles that bad tennis habits can be corrected by a good coach, so bad mental and emotional habits can be corrected by a psychotherapist. There is this difference, however. Whereas only a few people want to play tennis, all the world wants a clear, free, efficient mind. (Dollard & Miller 1950, pp. 7–8)

As we have seen, the only way for a learned response to be extinguished is for it to occur and not be followed by reinforcement. For unrealistic fears to be extinguished they must occur and then not be followed by the kind of events that produced the fears in the first place. However, as previously mentioned, the individual has learned to repress such fears, thus preventing their expression and therefore their subsequent extinction. Psychotherapy can be regarded as a situation in which the expression of repressed thoughts is encouraged. If the patient can be made to express these painful thoughts, the therapist is extremely careful to be encouraging, positive, and not punitive. The therapist tries to help the patient understand these prohibited thoughts and how they developed.

To persuade a patient to express a repressed thought is no easy matter, and typically a procedure similar to successive approximations is used. Let us imagine that a patient, for whatever reason, has learned to fear his mother to the point at which he cannot talk about her or about anything directly related to her. The therapist using Dollard's and Miller's theory would not confront the patient directly with a conversation about his mother. Rather, the therapist would begin the discussion with events only indirectly related to the patient's mother. How indirect this needs to be depends on the magnitude of the avoidance the patient has toward his mother. As the therapist and patient discuss events only remotely related to the mother *in a nonthreatening environment*, a small amount of the avoidance of the mother is extinguished, or there occurs what Freud called catharsis. With the avoidance response somewhat reduced, the therapist can steer the conversation a bit closer to the mother but still stay a safe distance away. When doing so, the avoidance response is further reduced, and the therapist can move still closer to the ultimate target, the mother. Gradually, usually over several sessions, the therapist moves closer and closer to a discussion of the mother and then, when the avoidance response is sufficiently reduced, to a discussion of the mother herself. Now with most of the avoidance gone, the patient can talk about his mother phobia openly and logically.

We see then that psychotherapy, as seen by Dollard and Miller (and also Freud) is a process of gradual extinction (catharsis) which depends on generalization, since the events discussed must be related in some way to the object, person, or event of ultimate concern. It also can be said that avoidance is displaced onto objects similar to the one that is avoided the most, so not only will the patient avoid his mother, he will also avoid people looking like her (primary generalization) or all mothers (secondary generalization); he may even be mildly apprehensive of women in general. Thus, conflict, extinction, generalization, and displacement all are part of the therapeutic process.

Psychotherapy usually does not stop when repressions have been released. Since the patient has spent such a large amount of his or her life with repressed thoughts and since it is impossible to deal effectively with repressed material, there will be important gaps in the person's life even after successful therapy. For example, a person who is suddenly able to ponder her sex drive at the age of thirty-five will need to be given some guidance as to how best to adjust to the relative absence of inhibition. Such guidance also is considered by Dollard and Miller to be essential to the therapeutic process.

THE MURRAY AND BERKUN EXPERIMENT

We saw earlier in this chapter that Dollard and Miller and their followers see nothing wrong with using rat research to learn about humans or to verify hunches about principles that have come from observing humans. The experiment by Murray and Berkun (1955) clearly demonstrated this philosophy. Essentially, Murray and Berkun created a situation analogous to psychotherapy, only they used rats as patients. First, they created an approach-avoidance conflict in the rats by first feeding the animals in a goal box and then shocking the animals in the same goal box. Thus the animals had a strong approach tendency to the goal box because they had been fed there and a strong avoidance tendency because they had been shocked in the same goal box.

Training took place in the apparatus shown in Figure 10–6. Some of the animals received their approach-avoidance training in the white

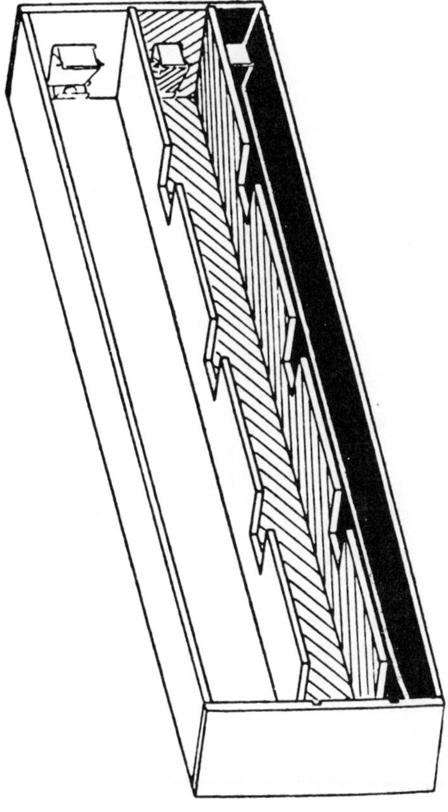

Figure 10–6 The apparatus used by Murray and Berkun to train their rats. (From Murray & Berkun 1955, p. 50.)

runway, and others received their training in the black runway. As can be seen in Figure 10–6, there are escape doors all along the three runways. One runway was white, one was medium gray, and one was black. After the initial approach-avoidance training, no further shocks were given.

The purpose of the experiment was to test how conflict, generalization, displacement, and extinction operate in a situation roughly analogous to psychotherapy. Based on conflict theory, one would predict that the animal experiencing an approach-avoidance conflict would approach the goal until it reached the point at which the avoidance gradient became stronger than the approach gradient (see Figure 10–1). At that point the animal should displace to a similar but less threatening object if one were available. In this case, one would expect the animal to leave the runway in which it had been shocked and enter the gray runway. However, since the gray runway is not the same color runway in which the animal was shocked, one would expect the animal to go farther toward the goal box in the gray runway than in the runway in which it was shocked. Even in the gray runway, however, the animal should eventually experience enough fear to cause it to displace to the black runway (if it were trained on the white runway). Since the black runway is so dissimilar to the one in which the animal was originally shocked, it probably will go all the way to the goal box. However, since the black runway has some similarities to the white runway and since the animal was not shocked when it made a goal response in the black runway, one might expect some of the fear of the white runway to be extinguished.

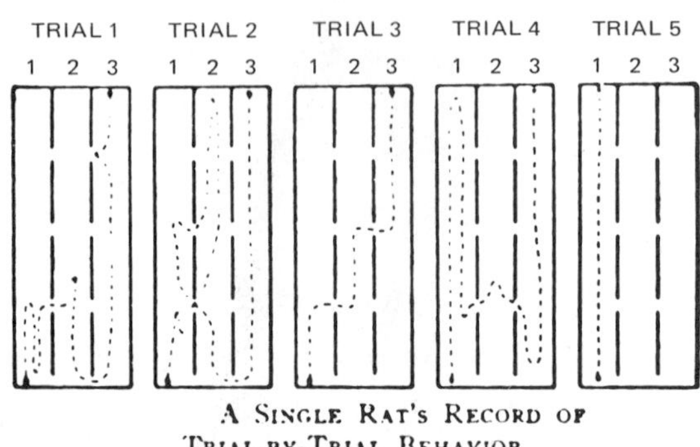

Figure 10–7 The behavior of a rat in the Murray and Berkun experiment showing the "therapeutic effect" of displaced responses. Original training took place in alley 1; alleys 2 and 3 are the alleys of diminishing similarity. The goals are at the top of the diagram. Each trial was begun by placing the rat at the starting point, shown here by the open circle. The rat was removed when he made a response at a goal, shown by the solid circle (from Murray & Berkun 1955, p. 51).

The situation is not unlike the one described in the last section in which some of the patient's fear of his mother was reduced when he talked about events related to his mother without being punished for doing so.

The behavior of one rat across five trials is shown in Figure 10–7. Notice that because of the animal's nonshocked goal responses in runway 3, it was eventually able to make a goal response in the runway in which it was originally shocked. Murray and Berkun concluded: "*Goal responding in displaced situations will have a therapeutic effect on the original conflict*. This is shown simply by the fact that 10 of the 10 animals who made goal responses in the gray or farthest alleys eventually made goal responses in the alley of original training" (1955, p. 53).

Murray and Berkun then related their findings to human psychotherapy and gave an example of what they had found using rats in a verbatim account of a therapeutic process. Their experiment bolstered Dollard's and Miller's contention that most effective psychotherapy utilizes conflict, generalization, displacement, and extinction. We might add that a form of Skinner's notion of shaping seems also to be included.

THE FOUR CRITICAL TRAINING PERIODS OF CHILDHOOD

As we have seen throughout this chapter, Dollard and Miller agreed with Freud that most neuroses have their origin in early childhood. This is an especially vulnerable time because children have no verbal labels for their feelings and experiences and are not aware of time; for example, they do not know that "in a little while" their hunger, thirst, or pain will be reduced. Their lives vacillate from extreme discomfort to bliss and back again. Also, infants, because of their helplessness, are completely at the mercy of their parents for the satisfaction of their needs and how the parents go about satisfying their infants' needs will make the difference between a normal healthy adult and a neurotic. Dollard and Miller (1950, pp. 132–156) describe four critical training situations that they feel have a profound influence on adult personality.

1. The Feeding Situation The conditions under which the hunger drive is satisfied will be learned and generalized into personality attributes. If, for example, children are fed when active, they may become active people; if they are fed while quiet and passive, they may become passive or apathic individuals. If their hunger drives are satisfied in an unpredictable manner, they may grow up believing the world is an unpredictable place. If children are left alone for long periods when they are hungry, they may develop a fear of being alone. If the mother is harsh and punitive during the feeding situation, the child may grow up disliking other people and avoid them at all costs. If, however, the mother is kind, warm, and positive during the feeding situation, the child may grow up with a positive attitude toward other people and seek them out as friends. All of this is very similar to what Freud, Horney, and Erikson said about early childhood experiences and their influence on subsequent personality development.

2. Cleanliness Training Dollard and Miller, like Freud, believe the events surrounding toilet training to be extremely important to personality development. If the parents respond negatively to children's inability to control their bladder or bowels, the children may not be able to distinguish between parental disapproval of what they have done and disapproval of themselves.

> . . . the child may not be able to discriminate between parental loathing for its excreta and loathing for the whole child himself. If the child learns to adopt these reactions, feelings of unworthiness, insignificance, and hopeless sinfulness will be created—feelings which sometimes so mysteriously reappear in the psychotic manifestations of guilt. (Dollard & Miller 1950, p. 140)

Although it is necessary to toilet train a child, how it is done may have a profound influence on the child's emerging personality.

3. Early Sex Training The first sex training a child normally receives in our culture is related to the child's early efforts to masturbate. Typically, such behavior elicits physical punishment and/or such terms as "nasty" and "dirty." So it is with most sexually oriented activities in which the child engages. There are probably more taboos in our culture related to sexual matters than there are for any other kind of activity, and these taboos are all part of our child-rearing practices. No wonder that sexual conflict is such a common theme in the analyst's office. The sex drive is innate, but the fear of sexual thoughts and activities is learned in childhood.

4. Anger-Anxiety Conflicts Frustration is inevitable in childhood (and at any other age), and as we learned above, the most common reaction to frustration is aggression. However, aggressive behavior on the part of the children in our culture is usually met with parental disapproval and/or punishment. Children are placed in still another approach-avoidance conflict; that is, they want to be aggressive but inhibit this impulse because of the fear of punishment. This may result in being too passive to compete successfully in modern society.

> . . . After this learning has occurred, the first cues produced by angry emotions may set off anxiety responses which "outcompete" the angry emotional responses themselves. The person can thus be made helpless to use his anger even in those situations where culture does permit it. He is viewed as abnormally meek or long-suffering. Robbing a person of his anger completely may be a dangerous thing since some capacity

for anger seeems to be needed in the affirmative personality. (Dollard & Miller 1950, p. 149)

The importance of child rearing to personality development has been a common theme throughout this book, and Dollard's and Miller's theory is no exception. According to them, how needs surrounding hunger, elimination, sex, and anger are treated by parents will make the difference between a normal, mentally healthy, creative adult on the one hand or a miserable neurotic on the other.

EVALUATION

Dollard and Miller have been criticized for their use of rats to learn about humans, their overemphasis on primary drives in determining behavior, their failure to recognize the concept of the self in their theory, and their overemphasis on conditioning and environmental stimuli in human behavior. They have been characterized as rigid determinists who emphasize past experiences, deny free choice, picture humans as continuous with other animals, and minimize striving for future goals.

On the positive side, Dollard and Miller took two great theoretical positions and combined them into one, thus creating a theory more powerful than the other two were by themselves. They objectified Freud's concepts making them much more amenable to experimental testing than they were previously. They analyzed in detail the variables in the development of neuroses and also in the therapeutic process necessary to remove neurotic conflict that is usually caused in childhood. What has become known as behavior therapy has been given a tremendous boost by their work.

Perhaps most importantly, Dollard and Miller have described the kinds of childhood experiences that lead to adult neuroses. Their message is clear: *Change these childhood conditions and neuroses can be eliminated.*

> . . . As a learning theorist sees it, the existence of neuroses is an automatic criticism of our culture of child rearing. Misery-producing, neurotic habits which the therapist must painfully unteach have been as painfully taught in the confused situation of childhood. A system of child training built on the laws of learning might have the same powerful effect on the neurotic misery of our time as Pasteur's work had on infectious diseases. (Dollard & Miller 1950, p. 8)

Dollard and Miller have provided information that is certainly helpful in treating neuroses and that information may also someday be responsible for a reduction in their frequency of occurrence. If this is true, one can forgive them for favoring animal research and for having a deterministic model of human nature. Every theory must be judged by its ultimate effectiveness, not by its origins or by its assumptions. We agree with Marx and Hillix who stated:

> . . . Dollard and Miller deserve a tremendous amount of credit for indicating the character, the scope, and the feasibility of synthesizing laboratory-derived and clinic-derived concepts in a theory of personality. *Personality and Psychotherapy* was a milestone, as yet perhaps too little appreciated, in the history of psychology. (1973, p. 375)

SUMMARY

Dollard's and Miller's goal was to combine learning theory, mainly Hullian, with Freud's theory. Hull's theory of learning equated reinforcement with drive reduction and defined a habit as a strong association of a stimulus (cue) and a response. Hull, unlike Skinner, was willing to speculate on the nature of reinforcement and on the nature of mediational processes such as thinking and reasoning. Skinner was content to make a functional analysis between environmental events and behavior. Central to Dollard's and Miller's theory are the concepts of drive, cue, response, and reinforcement. Drive impels an organism to action, cue directs its behavior, response is what the organism does either overtly or internally, and reinforcement occurs when the motivational drive is either reduced or terminated. In other words, in order to learn, the organism must want something, notice something, do something, and get something.

Every cue elicits a number of responses arranged in accordance with their probability of occurrence. This set of responses is called the habit family hierarchy. Shortly after birth, before learning has taken place, this is called the innate hierarchy of responses. The hierarchy that exists before new learning occurs is called the initial hierarchy of responses. The hierarchy that exists after learning has taken place is called the resultant hierarchy of reponses. The most likely response to any situation is called the dominant response. The learning dilemma refers to the fact that old learned responses or innate responses must fail to solve a problem before learning can take place. Thus, all learning depends on failure.

Dollard and Miller demonstrated that events associated with the experience of pain themselves will become feared, and an organism will learn responses that will allow it to escape from those fear-producing cues. Stimulus generalization refers to the fact that a learned response will be elicited not only by the cue in the actual learning, but by a variety of similar stimuli as well. The more similar a cue is to the one actually used in training, the greater the probability is that it will elicit the same response. Primary generalization is determined by the physical properties of stimuli. Secondary generalization is caused by using the same verbal label to describe things. For example, one responds to all things labeled "dangerous" in a similar fashion. Discrimination is the opposite of generalization.

Dollard and Miller studied four kinds of conflict; approach-approach conflicts, in which the organism is attracted to two things at the same time; avoidance-avoidance conflicts, in which the organism is repelled by two things at the same time; approach-avoidance conflicts, in which the organism is attracted and repelled by the same object; and double approach-avoidance conflicts, in which the organism is both attracted and repelled by two objects at the same time. Dollard and Miller did most of their research on the approach-avoidance conflict and found that at great distances from the goal the approach tendency is strongest, but as one approaches the goal, the avoidance tendency becomes stronger. This causes vacillation in which the two tendencies have about equal strength.

If the goal object of choice is not available, the organism will choose a substitute goal object; this is called displacement. If one cannot aggress toward the object, event, or person that caused frustration, one will aggress toward a substitute object; this is called displaced aggression. If one is very fearful of aggressing toward an object, event, or person causing frustration, displacement will be toward dissimilar objects, events, or people. If there is little fear, displacement will be to more similar things.

The frustration-aggression hypothesis originally stated that aggression followed from frustration and that frustration always resulted in aggression. This was later modified, however, to state that aggression was just one result of frustration, instead of the only one.

Language is very important to Dollard and Miller's theory. Thinking is essentially talking to oneself. Thinking allows for cognitive trial and error to replace behavioral trial and error. Dollard and Miller call images, perceptions, and words cue-producing responses because they determine what the next response in a series will be. Thinking consists of a series of cue-producing responses. Two important kinds of thinking are reasoning, which is directed at solving a current problem, and planning, which is directed at solving a future problem.

The unconscious mind, according to Dollard and Miller, consists of experiences that were never verbalized and experiences that have been repressed. Repression is considered "a response of not thinking" which is reinforced because it prevents an anxiety-provoking thought from becoming conscious. Suppression is the act of driving an anxiety-provoking thought out of consciousness. Repressed thoughts are practically immune to extinction because they are not experienced consciously long enough for the person to realize that they are no longer followed by reinforcement.

Most neurotic conflicts are learned in childhood and therefore are not verbally labeled. Neurotics are miserable and stupid about matters related to their repressions. Neurotics often develop symptoms which stem from their repressed conflict. Symptoms such as phobias, compulsions, or physical disorders temporarily relieve neurotics' distress because they act as a barrier between them and anxiety-provoking situations. For example, by becoming obese a person can decrease the likelihood of confronting sexual situations. Thus, for the person with a repressed sexual conflict being obese is reinforcing. However, the desire for sex does not go away, so the conflict continues to manifest itself in strange ways. Both repressions and neurotic symptoms are learned for the same reason; they reduce or prevent anxiety.

Psychotherapy is a situation in which patients are encouraged to label their conflicts verbally and to confront them gradually. The therapist is encouraging and nonthreatening so that if and when repressed material emerges, it will extinguish. Therapy usually starts by discussing objects, people, or events that are only indirectly related to those causing strong anxiety. As distant, but related, events are discussed, a certain amount of anxiety is extinguished and gradually the person can talk directly about events that previously were too anxiety provoking. Psychotherapy, as Dollard and Miller see it, treats conflict, repression, generalization, displacement, and extinction.

Dollard and Miller believe that neurotic conflicts are learned in childhood. The difference between a mentally healthy normal adult and a neurotic adult is thought to be fairly well determined by how parents handle the four critical training periods of childhood: namely, the feeding situation, cleanliness training, sex training, and anger-anxiety training.

Discussion Questions

1. Dollard and Miller's theory is often called a blending of Hullian learning theory and Freudian psychoanalytic theory. Expain why their theory is called this. Give several examples of such a blend.
2. Compare and contrast Dollard's and Miller's theory of personality with Skinner's.
3. Discuss the concepts of drive, cue, response, and reinforcement. Give both the formal definition and a concrete example of each.
4. Discuss the concept of habit family hierarchy. Include in your answer definitions of innate, initial, and resultant hierarchies.
5. What did Dollard and Miller mean by the term "learning dilemma"? Discuss the implications of this concept for education and child rearing.
6. Outline the procedures that Miller used to demonstrate that fear was an acquired drive.
7. Discuss the topic of stimulus generalization. Include in your answer a discussion of both primary and secondary generalization.
8. Compare discrimination to generalization, and explain why both processes are important when adjusting to the world.
9. Give the formal definitions and then examples of each of the

following kinds of conflict: approach-approach, avoidance-avoidance, approach-avoidance, and double approach-avoidance.

10. List as many characteristics of an approach-avoidance conflict as you can.
11. What effect do you think the ingestion of alcohol would have on an approach-avoidance conflict? For example, do you feel it would raise or lower the avoidance gradient? Explain why you feel the way you do.
12. Define displacement and then discuss it in relation to generalization. Describe several variables influencing displacement.
13. Outline the procedures Miller followed in order to demonstrate displaced aggression.
14. What is the frustration-aggression hypothesis? How was it first stated by Dollard and Miller and how was it later revised?
15. Discuss the status of language in Dollard and Miller's theory. Include in your answer the terms cue-producing responses, reasoning, and planning.
16. Of what, according to Dollard and Miller, does the unconscious mind consist? Give examples.
17. Describe what Dollard and Miller meant when they referred to repression as the conditioned avoidance response of not-thinking.
18. Differentiate between suppression and repression.
19. Explain how, according to Dollard and Miller, neuroses typically develop.
20. Explain what Dollard and Miller mean when they say neurotic symptoms have drive-reducing properties.
21. Give a specific example of how early childhood experiences can produce neurotic conflict.
22. Explain what is meant when the kind of psychotherapy that is prescribed by Dollard and Miller is said to involve conflict, generalization, displacement, and extinction. Describe a theoretical therapeutic situation in which each of these concepts is involved.
23. Summarize the Murray and Berkun experiment.
24. Summarize the four critical training periods of childhood as described by Dollard and Miller. Explain why what a child experiences during each of these periods is so important.
25. Compare what Dollard and Miller say about the importance of early childhood experiences with what Horney and Erikson say. On which points do the three theories agree and on which do they differ?

Glossary

Acquired Drive. A drive that is learned and not innate. Fear is an example of an acquired drive.

Anger-Anxiety Conflicts. One of the four training situations in childhood which, if not handled properly, could result in neurotic conflict.

Approach-Approach Conflict. The situation that exists when a person must choose between two equally attractive goals.

Approach-Avoidance Conflict. The situation that exists when a person is both attracted to and repelled by the same goal.

Avoidance-Avoidance Conflict. The situation that exists when a person must choose between two equally aversive goals.

Cleanliness Training. One of the four critical training situations in childhood which, if not handled properly, could lead to neurotic conflict.

Conditioned Fear Reaction. Learning to fear something that was not previously feared.

Conflict. The situation in which two or more incompatible response tendencies exist simultaneously.

Cue. A stimulus that indicates the appropriate direction that an activity should take.

Cue-producing Responses. Images, perceptions, and words the main functions of which are to determine subsequent behavior. Thinking is an example of cue-producing responses.

Discrimination. The opposite of generalization. That is, stimuli similar to the stimulus in the learning process do *not* elicit a learned response.

Displaced Aggression. Aggressing toward a substitute person or object when the actual object of aggression is either not available or is feared.

Displacement. The act of substituting one goal for another when the primary goal is not available.

Dominant Response. That response in a habit family hierarchy that has the greatest probability of occurrence.

Double Approach-Avoidance Conflict. The situation that exists when a person has both positive and negative feelings about two goals.

Drive. Any strong stimulus that impels an organism to action and whose elimination or reduction is reinforcing.

Drive Reduction. Constitutes reinforcement in Hull's theory of learning.

Early Sex Training. One of the four critical training situations in childhood, which, if not handled properly, could result in neurotic conflict.

Feeding Situation. One of the four critical training situations in childhood which, if not handled properly, could result in neurotic conflict.

First Signal System. The term used by Pavlov to describe the conditioned responses that we develop to physical objects.

Frustration-Aggression Hypothesis. Originally the contention that frustration always leads to aggression and aggression results only from frustration. Later modified to state that aggression is only one of several possible reactions to frustration.

Functional Analysis. Skinner's approach to research which notes the relationship between certain environmental events and behavior.

Habit. An association of a stimulus and a response.

Habit Family Hierarchy. The group of responses elicited by a single stimulus that are arranged in accordance with their probability of occurrence.

Hull's Theory of Learning. The theory of learning that Dollard and Miller synthesized with Freud's theory. Hull's theory equates reinforcement with drive reduction. In other words, in order for learning to take place, the organism must engage in an activity that leads to the elimination or reduction of a need.

Initial Hierarchy of Responses. The hierarchy of responses elicited by a cue prior to learning.

Innate Hierarchy of Responses. A habit family hierarchy that is genetically determined

Learning Dilemma. The contention that in order for learning to occur, both innate responses and previously learned responses must be ineffective in solving a problem. Therefore, learning is said to depend on failure.

Neurosis. A condition which causes a person to function at less than maximal efficiency, which typically results from unconscious conflict which originated in early childhood.

Planning. The utilization of cue-producing responses (thinking) in attempting to solve some future problem.

Primary Generalization. Generalization that is determined by the physical properties of stimuli.

Psychotherapy. For Dollard and Miller, a situation in which repressed conflicts can be unlearned, that is, extinguished.

Reasoning. The attempted solution of an immediate problem through the use of cue-producing responses (thinking) rather than of overt trial and error.

Reinforcement. In Hull's theory of learning, drive reduction constitutes reinforcement.

Reinforcement Theory. Any theory of learning that states that reinforcement must occur before learning can take place.

Reinforcer. A stimulus capable of reducing a drive.

Repression. The learned response of "not thinking" an anxiety-provoking thought. The reinforcement for this response comes from the avoidance of anxiety.

Response. Any overt or internal action elicited by a stimulus.

Resultant Hierarchy of Responses. The hierarchy of responses elicited by a cue after learning has taken place.

Second Signal System. The term used by Pavlov to describe the conditioned responses we develop to words and other symbols.

Secondary Generalization. Generalization that is based on verbal labels (words) and not on the physical similarity among stimuli.

Stimulus Generalization. The tendency for stimuli other than the stimulus actually in the learning process to elicit a learned response. The more similar these stimuli are to the one actually in the learning process, the greater the probability is that they will elicit a learned response.

Suppression. Actively putting an anxiety-provoking thought "out of one's mind." Suppression is reinforced by the escape from anxiety.

Symptom Formation. The neurotic's tendency to develop such things as phobias, compulsions, or physical disorders because they reduce anxiety temporarily.

PART SIX

EXISTENTIAL-HUMANISTIC PARADIGM

chapter 11

george kelly

George Alexander Kelly was born on a farm near Perth, Kansas on April 28, 1905. He was an only child. Kelly's father had been trained as a Presbyterian minister but, because of poor health, gave up the ministry and turned to farming. In 1909, Kelly's father converted a lumber wagon into a covered wagon and used it to move his family to Colorado where they staked a claim to a plot of land offered free to settlers. They moved back to their farm in Kansas, however, when they were unable to find water on their claim. Kelly never seemed to lose the pioneer spirit derived from his early experiences. He remained a very practical person throughout his life; his overriding concern with an idea or a device was whether it worked or not; if it did not, he had no time for it. Furthermore, Kelly was strongly influenced by his parents' deep religious convictions and remained an active member of the church.

Kelly's early education consisted of attending a one-room school house and being tutored by his parents. When he was thirteen he was sent to Wichita where he eventually attended four different high schools. After the age of thirteen, Kelly seldom lived at home again. Upon graduation from high school, he enrolled in the Friends University in Wichita, a Quaker school. After three years he moved to Park College where he earned his B.A. degree in physics and mathematics in 1926.

Kelly had originally planned on a career as an engineer but decided such a career would not allow him to deal with social problems, with which he was becoming increasingly interested. As a result, he enrolled in the M.A. program at the University of Kansas with a major in educational sociology and a minor in labor relations. For his master's thesis, he studied how workers in Kansas City spent their leisure time. He was awarded an M.A. degree in 1928.

The next year was a busy one for Kelly. He taught part-time in a labor college in Minneapolis, taught speech classes for the American Bankers Association, and taught an Americanization class to immigrants wishing to become citizens. Finally, in the winter of 1928, he joined the faculty at a junior college in Sheldon, Iowa, where he met his future wife, Gladys Thompson. Among his other duties he coached dramatics which, as we shall see, may have influenced Kelly's later theorizing.

In 1929, Kelly was awarded an exchange scholarship which enabled him to spend a year at the University of Edinburgh in Scotland where he worked closely with Sir Godfrey Thomson. Sir Godfrey was largely responsible for Kelly developing an interest in psychology. In 1930, Kelly earned a degree in education from the Univerity of Edinburgh. His thesis, under the supervision of Sir Godfrey, was on predicting teaching success.

Upon returning to the United States in 1930, he enrolled in psychology at Iowa State University where he earned his Ph.D. in 1931. His dissertation was on the common factors in speech and reading disabilities. Two days after graduation he married Gladys Thompson and they had two children.

Kelly's academic career began at Fort Hays Kansas State College in the midst of the Great Depression. He learned very soon that his interest in physiological psychology, which he pursued at Iowa State University, would do him little good under his present circumstances. He noted that the people with whom he had contact simply did not

George Kelly. Courtesy Brandeis University.

know what to do with their lives—they were confused. Kelly, therefore, switched his interests to clinical psychology, for which there was a great need. It turns out that Kelly had a great advantage at this point in that *he was not formally trained in any particular clinical technique.* This, along with his practical nature, gave him great latitude in trying a variety of approaches in treating emotional problems. What worked was salvaged, what did not work was discarded. Kelly had heard of Freud, of course, and did try some of his ideas but found them basically ineffective and boring.

During his thirteen-year (1931 to 1943) stay at Fort Hays, Kelly developed traveling clinics which serviced the state's public school system. This service allowed Kelly and his students to experience a wide range of psychological problems and to experiment with ways of treating them. It was during this time that Kelly made two observations that were to have a profound influence on his later theory. First, Kelly found that even if he made up a radical explanation for a client's problem, the client would accept it and usually improve. In other words, Kelly noted that anything that would cause clients to look at themselves or their problems differently caused improvement in the situation. Logic, or "correctness," seemed to have little to do with it. Kelly described his experiment with psychotherapy as follows:

> . . . I began fabricating "insights." I deliberately offered "preposterous interpretations" to my clients. Some of them were about as un-Freudian as I could make them—first proposed somewhat cautiously, of course, and then, as I began to see what was happening, more boldly. My only criteria were that the explanation account for the crucial facts as the client saw them, and that it carry implications for approaching the future in a different way. (1969, p. 52)

Second, Kelly noted that a teacher's complaint about a student often said more about the teacher than it did about the student. It was the way the teacher was *seeing things* that was the problem, rather than some objective event that everyone could experience. It was observations like these that stimulated Kelly to develop perhaps one of the boldest theories of personality since Freud's theory.

At the beginning of World War II, Kelly was in charge of a local civilian pilot-training program. Eventually he joined the navy as a psychologist in the Bureau of Medicine and Surgery and was stationed in Washington, D.C. While in the service, he did much to improve the quality and effectiveness of clinical psychology in the armed forces. Kelly remained active in a number of government programs related to clinical psychology until his death.

In 1945, when the war ended, Kelly was appointed associate professor at the University of Maryland where he remained for one year. In 1946 he became professor of psychology and director of clinical psychology at Ohio State University. Although the department was extremely small, Kelly, along with Julian B. Rotter, himself destined to become a leading psychologist, developed a clinical psychology program that many considered to be the best in the country. It was during his nineteen years at Ohio State that Kelly refined and tested his theory of personality.

During the year of 1960 to 1961, Kelly and his wife received a grant from the Human Ecology Fund that allowed them to travel around the world lecturing on the relationship between Kelly's theory and various international problems. Their journey carried them to Madrid, London, Oslo, Louvain, Copenhagen, Prague, Warsaw, Moscow, the Caribbean area, and South America. It was quite an adventure for someone who claimed never to have gotten all the Kansas mud off his shoes.

In 1965 Kelly left Ohio State to accept an appointment to an endowed chair at Brandeis University. Kelly died on March 6, 1967 at the young age of sixty-two.

Compared to the other theorists covered in this book, Kelly wrote relatively little. The major presentation of his theory is found in his two-volume work entitled *The Psychology of Personal Constructs* (1955).

This chapter is based primarily on these two volumes. Currently, the two major proponents of Kelly's theory are the British psychologist Donald Bannister and one of Kelly's former students, Lee Sechrest.

A CATEGORIZATION OF KELLY'S THEORY

As already mentioned, Kelly started as a clinical psychologist without any formal clinical training. In other words, he was not indoctrinated in any particular school of thought. Kelly was confronted by people with problems and, since he had no clinical skills, had to improvise his own

Donald Bannister. *APA Monitor.*

techniques. He had no mentor to guide him; he came from no department with a particular philosophical leaning; and he was not surrounded by a group of colleagues that steered him in a certain direction. He therefore "played it by ear." Thus, if Kelly's theory resembles anyone else's, it is not Kelly's fault; it is a coincidence. As we shall see, Kelly believed that a person's present personality need not be tied to his or her past. He believed the same to be true of personality theories; that is, in order to be valid, a theory need not grow out of those theories already in existence. Kelly's theory of personality is probably as independent of other theoretical positions as a theory can be. The similarities between his and other theories have been noted mainly by other people; Kelly did not care much about them.

Kelly's theory, however, can be classified in certain ways. First, Kelly was a *phenomenologist*. Phenomenologists believe that intact conscious experience should be psychology's focus of attention. It should not matter where such experiences originate; the important thing to study, the phenomenologists believe, is a person's own individual conscious experiences without breaking them down into component parts or attempting to determine their origin.

Kelly's theory also can be labeled *cognitive* since it emphasizes mental events. It is clearly not a behavioral theory since the emphasis is not on behavior and its causal relationship to the environment; it is not a psychoanalytic theory since it does not stress unconscious mechanisms or early experience in the determination of adult personality; and it is not a trait theory since it does not attempt to categorize individuals in terms of their traits. It is a cognitive theory because it stresses how individuals *view* and *think about* reality.

Kelly's theory also can be considered *existential* since it emphasizes the future rather than the past and since it assumes that humans are free to choose their own destinies. In general, existentialism assumes that humans are free and future-oriented, that their subjective feelings and personal experience are extremely important and that they are concerned with the meaning of life. The existentialists also believe that, since humans are free, they also are responsible for their own destinies. Generally, existentialists examine the problems of human existence. The statement, man "is what he wills to be" by the famous existential philosopher, Jean-Paul Sartre (1956, p. 291), fairly well summarizes both Kelly's and the existentialist's position.

Last, Kelly's theory can be considered *humanistic* since it emphasizes people's creative power and de-emphasizes the importance of heredity and environment to determining personality. The humanists typically are optimistic about human beings, stressing their power to solve the problems that were caused by humans in the first place. There is a strong kinship between existentialism and humanism with much overlap between the two philosophies. Both believe that animal research is a nonsensical means of investigating the human being.

Kelly's theory, then, can be labeled phenomenological because it focuses on *intact* subjective experience, cognitive because it emphasizes the study of mental events, existential because it stresses the future and humans' ability to choose their own destinies, and humanistic because it is optimistic about humans in that it emphasizes humans' creative abilities which can be directed at solving individual and/or sociological problems.

THE BASIC POSTULATE—PEOPLE AS SCIENTISTS

Kelly took the scientist as the model for describing all humans. He noted that scientists are constantly seeking clarity and understanding in their lives by developing theories that will allow them to predict future events; in other words, *the scientist's main goal is to reduce uncertainty*. Kelly believed that, like scientists, all humans are attempting to clarify their lives by reducing uncertainty, and therefore the distinction between the scientist and the nonscientist is not a valid one.

> It is as though the psychologist were saying to himself, "I, being a *psychologist,* and therefore a *scientist,* am performing this experiment in order to improve the prediction and control of certain human phenomena; but my subject, being merely a human organism, is obviously propelled by inexorable drives welling up within him, or else he is in gluttonous pursuit of sustenance and shelter." (Kelly 1955, p. 5)

According to Kelly, all humans are like scientists in that they are interested in the future and use the present only to test a theory's ability to anticipate events. "Anticipation is not merely carried on for its own sake; it is carried on so that future reality may be better represented. It is the future which tantalizes man, not the past. Always he reaches out to the future through the window of the present" (Kelly 1955, p. 49).

The major tool a person uses in anticipating events is the *personal construct.* Personal constructs are used by individuals to *construe* or interpret, explain, give meaning to, or predict experiences. A construct is an idea or thought that a person uses when attempting to interpret his or her own personal experiences. A construct is like a mini-scientific theory in that it makes predictions about reality. If the predictions generated by a construct are confirmed by experience, it is useful; if the predictions are not confirmed, the construct must be revised or abandoned. "Man looks at his world through transparent patterns or templets which he creates and then attempts to fit over the realities of which the world is composed. . . . Let us give the name *constructs* to these patterns that are tried on for size. They are ways of construing the world" (Kelly 1955, pp. 8–9).

We will have much more to say about constructs in the next section, but it is important to note that they are usually verbal labels that a person applies to environmental events and then tests with subsequent experience with those events. For example, upon meeting a person for the first time, one might construe that person with the construct "friendly." If the person's subsequent behavior is in accordance with the construct of friendly, then the construct will be useful in anticipating that person's behavior. If the new acquaintance acts in an unfriendly manner, he or she will need to be construed either with different constructs or by using the other pole (see below) of the friendly-unfriendly construct. The major point is that constructs are used to anticipate the future so they must fit reality. Arriving at a construct system that corresponds fairly closely to reality is largely a matter of trial and error.

Kelly emphasized the fact that each person *creates his or her own constructs* for dealing with the world. Kelly believed that, although all people have the goal of reducing future uncertainty, they are free to construe reality any way they wish. He called this belief *constructive alternativism* which he described as follows: "We take the stand that there are always some alternative constructions available to choose among in dealing with the world. No one needs to paint himself into a corner; no one needs to be completely hemmed in by circumstances; no one needs to be the victim of his biography" (1955, p. 15).

Although it is true that no one *needs* to "paint himself into a corner," it does not mean that people do not do so. Here we have an interesting distinction between freedom and determinism. Although Kelly believed that individuals are free to create thir own construct systems, he also believed that they were controlled by them after they were created. In other words, a person's life is strongly influenced by the way he or she construes experiences, and some ways of construing things are better than others. According to Kelly, some individuals arrive at inflexible convictions about the world and become slaves to them. The lives of such individuals are dominated by rules and regulations, and they live within a narrow range of highly predictable events. Others have a broader perspective. Their lives are lived in accordance with flexible principles rather than with rigid rules. Such individuals live a richer life because of their openness to experience.

According to Kelly, whether one lives an open, creative life or a restrictive one is largely a matter of personal choice. Likewise, some individuals can look at a situation positively, and others can look at the same situation negatively. Again, it is a matter of personal choice. Kelly's position on this matter is nicely summarized by the old saying, "Two men looked out from prison bars, one saw mud and the other saw stars." This brings us to the fundamental postulate in Kelly's theory: "*A person's processes are psychologically channelized by the ways in which he anticipates events*" (Kelly 1955, p. 46). In other words, an individual's activities (behavior and thoughts) are guided in certain directions by the personal constructs used to predict future events. We will explore several of Kelly's elaborations of this postulate.

ELABORATIONS—THE ELEVEN COROLLARIES

Kelly embellished his basic postulate by adding eleven corollaries.

*1. **Construction Corollary*** "A person anticipates events by construing their replications" (Kelly 1955, p. 50).

Events in one's life occur with some regularity; for example, a friendly person will tend to remain friendly; day follows night; it tends to be cold in the winter; and the physical objects in one's environment will tend to remain in place, for instance, the refrigerator probably will still be in the kitchen tomorrow. Although no two events are ever the same ("No man ever steps into the same river twice"), there are, nonetheless, themes running through events which bind them together. It is on the basis of these themes that constructs are formed and that predictions about the future are made. In other words, if the events in our lives did not occur with some regularity, it would be impossible to form constructs which represent them.

*2. **Individuality Corollary*** "Persons differ from each other in their construction of events" (Kelly 1955, p. 55).

This corollary cannot be stressed too much; it is the essence of Kelly's theory. According to Kelly, not only is beauty in the eye of the beholder, so is everything else. Reality is what we perceive it to be. This, of course, is a restatement of Kelly's notion of constructive alternativism, which says that we are free to construe events as we wish. This freedom is thought not only to apply to our interpretation of external reality but to ourselves as well.

> . . . on occasion I may say of myself . . . "I am an introvert." "I," the subject, "am an introvert," the predicate. The language form of the statement clearly places the onus of being an introvert on the subject—me. What I actually am, the words say, is an introvert.
>
> . . . the proper interpretation of my statement is that *I construe* myself to be an introvert, or, if I am merely being coy or devious, I am inveigling *my listener into construing me* in terms of introversion. The point that gets lost in the shuffle of words is the psychological fact that I have identified myself in terms of a personal construct—"introversion." (Kelly 1958, p. 38)

This corollary has implications for Kelly's version of psychotherapy which we will cover later in the chapter.

*3. **Organization Corollary*** "Each person characteristically evolves, for his convenience in anticipating events, a construction system embracing ordinal relationships between constructs" (Kelly 1955, p. 56).

Not only do individuals differ in the constructs they use to construe events, but they also differ in how they organize their constructs.

According to Kelly, personal constructs are arranged in a hierarchy, some being more comprehensive than others. For example, the construct extrovert-introvert subsumes such constructs as likes people-dislikes people and likes parties-dislikes parties. A construct that subsumes other constructs within it is called a *superordinate construct,* and the constructs that are subsumed under it are called *subordinate constructs.*

Kelly believed that without this hierarchical arrangement of constructs one would experience contradictions and would make inaccurate predictions of events. Since this is undesirable, a person organizes constructs in a way that reduces contradictions and increases predictive efficiency.

4. Dichotomy Corollary "A person's construction system is composed of a finite number of dichotomous constructs" (Kelly 1955, p. 59).

According to Kelly, all constructs are bipolar or dichotomous. He believed that in order for a construct to be significant, it must indicate at least two elements that are similar to each other and a third element that is different from those two. For example, the notion of tall is meaningless without the notion of short, as is the concept of beautiful without the concept of ugly. One must be able to say that those two people are beautiful because they possess certain attributes and that this person is ugly because he or she lacks those attributes. Likewise, the notion of masculinity is meaningless without the notion of femininity. For Kelly, then, a construct is a way of construing certain things as being alike and yet different from other things.

5. Choice Corollary "A person chooses for himself that alternative in a dichotomized construct through which he anticipates the greater possibility for extension and definition of his system" (Kelly 1955, p. 64).

Here the person can either be safe or take a risk. If a person applies constructs to a new situation which has been accurate in the past when applied to similar situations, one is merely seeking further validation of one's construct system. Kelly referred to this relatively safe path as *definition,* since such experiences further define or validate a construct system. On the other hand, the person can use the occasion to try new constructs which, if validated, would further expand the person's construct system, thereby making it better able to assimilate experiences that before were foreign to it. Kelly refers to this as *extension.* The danger in extension, as opposed to definition, is the possibility of failure. When choosing a construct, the person is torn between "security" and "adventure." One can make safe predictions or one can attempt to expand one's construct system, thereby making an ever increasing number of experiences understandable. For example, on the one hand, one can choose to live under stable conditions for many years; that is, same house, neighborhood, schools and friends, and thereby build a construct system which generates almost absolute certainty; or, on the other hand, one can choose to place oneself in situations which are constantly changing and for which one has no constructs. In other words, a person may have too much certainty if definition of one's construct system is emphasized and too much uncertainty if extension is emphasized. *Clearly, a middle ground seems best.*

6. Range Corollary "A construct is convenient for the anticipation of a finite range of events only" (Kelly 1955, p. 68).

Obviously a construct such as hot versus cold cannot be applied to a situation that requires a good versus bad judgment. Each construct has a *range of convenience* which includes all of the events to which the construct is relevant.

> Suppose, for example, A and B are men, C is a woman, and O is the time of day. We abstract an aspect of A, B, and C which we may call *sex*. Sex, then is our *z*. Sex is not applicable to O, the time of day; at least most of us would not so abstract it. The time of day, O, does not fall within the range of convenience of sex, *z*. Now, with respect to sex, z, the two men, A and B, are alike and in contrast to the woman, C. (Kelly 1955, p. 60)

The events within the range of convenience for which a construct is maximally pertinent define the construct's *focus of convenience*. For example, if one sees a wild animal rapidly approaching, the construct of danger-safe may be a useful one to employ in construing the situation. Certainly the event of being charged by a wild animal would fall within the range of convenience of the danger-safe construct. Furthermore, the notion of very dangerous would seem especially appropriate within that construct. In this situation, the construct of danger-safe would be employed, and the notion of very dangerous would be the focus of convenience within that construct's range of convenience. Constructs such as nice weather-bad weather or politically liberal-politically conservative would seem irrelevant to the situation. In other words, the range of convenience of the latter constructs would not include the situation at hand.

7. Experience Corollary "A person's construction system varies as he successively construes the replications of events" (Kelly 1955, p. 72).

Experience alone was unimportant to Kelly; what was important was the construing of experience. Every construct system was compared to a scientific theory and every construct to an hypothesis. As in science, if an hypothesis is not confirmed by experience, it must be revised or replaced. Life, according to Kelly, requires the constant testing of various constructs in order to find those that are the most reliable predictors of experience. Those constructs found to be reliable in predicting events are useful and are retained, and those that are not validated by experience are either revised or abandoned. A "good" construct system has the same characteristics as a "good" scientific theory.

> A good psychological theory has an appropriate focus and range of convenience. . . . It should be fertile in producing new ideas, in generating hypotheses, in provoking experimentation, in encouraging inventions. The hypotheses which are deduced from it should be brittle enough to be testable, though the theory itself may be cast in more resilient terms. The more frequently its hypotheses turn out to be valid, the more valuable the theory. (Kelly 1955, p. 44)

A theory (construct system) provides the basis for an active search for meaning in life, and what Kelly meant by meaning was the ability to predict accurately the events in one's life.

8. Modulation Corollary "The variation in a person's construction system is limited by the permeability of the constructs within whose range of convenience the variants lie" (Kelly 1955, p. 77).

Some constructs are more *permeable,* that is, open to experience, than are others. "A construct is permeable if it will admit to its range of convenience new elements which are not yet construed within its framework" (Kelly 1955, p. 79).

For example, an individual's construct nice people-awful people might be defined in terms of certain individuals, nice people consisting of a circle of close friends and awful people consisting of everyone else. Such an individual is not open to experience, since one pole of the construct nice people-awful people is not permeable. Thus, even if the individual encountered a person with several admirable characteristics, that person could not be assimilated into the individual's construct system because of its lack of permeability.

Obviously, a person who has a number of permeable constructs will be in a better position to extend his or her construct system than a person who has an abundance of impermeable constructs will. The former individual can be characterized as "open-minded" and the latter individual as "closed-minded."

9. Fragmentation Corollary "A person may successively employ a variety of construction subsystems which are inferentially incompatible with each other" (Kelly 1955, p. 83).

Kelly said that a person's construction system is in a state of continual flux. Different constructs are constantly being tested, and new elements are constantly entering into one's more permeable constructs. Likewise, one is constantly reorganizing one's construct system so that the most reliable predictions are made. This experimentation with one's construct system creates the possibility for inconsistent behavior. One may not respond in a consistent way to the same event each time that it is encountered. For example, the interaction with one's boss on the job and in a local bar may be totally different. One may act differently because the situation has changed, one's constructs have changed, or the organization of one's constructs has changed. Kelly felt that a certain number of inconsistencies were inevitable since construct systems "are in flux," but he felt that even with minor inconsistencies, the overall outcome was still consistent. " . . . We can say that while a person's bets on the turn of minor events may not appear to add up, his wagers on the outcome of life do tend to add up" (Kelly 1955, p. 88).

10. Commonality Corollary "To the extent that one person employs a construction of experience which is similar to that employed by another, his psychological processes are similar to those of the other person" (Kelly 1955, p. 90).

With this corollary Kelly emphasized the point that it is not common *experiences* that make people similar, but the fact that they construe their experiences in a similar way. Two people can have the same physical experiences but construe them differently. Likewise, it is conceivable that two similar construct systems can result from distinctly different sets of physical experiences.

> It is important to make clear that we have not said that if one person has experienced the same events as another he will duplicate the other's psychological processes. . . . One of the advantages of this position is that it does not require us to assume that it would take identical events in the lives of two people to make them act alike. Two people can act alike even if they have each been exposed to quite different phenomenal stimuli. It is in the similarity in the construction of events that we find the basis for similar action, not in the identity of the events themselves. (Kelly 1955, pp. 90–91)

11. Sociality Corollary "To the extent that one person construes the construction processes of another, he may play a role in a social process involving the other person" (Kelly 1955, p. 95).

The concept of *role* is very important to Kelly's theory, but he does not use the concept in the traditional way. Kelly defined role as "an ongoing pattern of behavior that follows from a person's understanding of how the others who are associated with him in his task think" (1955, pp. 97–98).

In other words, playing a role is acting in accordance with the expectations of others. In order to play a role one must understand at least one other person's construct system. For example, if a man wants to play the role of "husband" to his wife, he must first understand her expectations for the construct "husband" and then act accordingly. Kelly called our understanding of another person's outlook and expectations a *role construct;* how we act in light of this understanding is called a *role.* "A *role* is a psychological process based upon the role player's construction of aspects of the construction systems of those with whom he attempts to join in a social enterprise" (Kelly 1955, p. 97).

This corollary is Kelly's major statement on social behavior. He is saying that if we want to engage in constructive interactions with other people, we must first determine how other people see things and then take their perceptions into consideration when dealing with them. The deepest kind of social interaction occurs when this role playing is reciprocal.

THE CPC CYCLE

According to Kelly, the CPC cycle characterizes the actions of a person confronted with a novel situation. The initials CPC symbolize the three phases of the cycle: circumspection, preemption, and control.

The Circumspection Phase In this phase, the person tries a number of *propositional constructs,* which are nothing more than possible interpretations of the situation. This phase involves "if-then" thinking or thinking that might be labeled cognitive trial and error.

The Preemption Phase In this phase, the person chooses from all the constructs pondered in the preceding phase those constructs that seem especially relevant to the situation. In other words, one cannot go on pondering the situation forever; one must choose a strategy for dealing with one's experience.

The Control Phase In this phase, the choice is actually made and a course of action is established. Those constructs are chosen which we believe will best define and/or extend our construct system. We choose those constructs that we feel will best allow us to anticipate the outcome of the novel situation that we have encountered. If we choose the correct constructs, our "theory" will be confirmed and strengthened; if we choose incorrect constructs, or incorrect poles of constructs, our "theory" will not be confirmed and will need to be revised.

It is important to remember that, in Kelly's theory, individuals do not seek reinforcement or the avoidance of pain. *Individuals seek validation of their construct systems.* If an individual predicts that something unpleasant is going to occur and it does, his or her construct system will have been validated even though the experience was a negative one. According to Kelly, the primary goal in one's life is to reduce uncertainty.

MOTIVATION

We again can use the example of our being attacked by a wild animal to demonstrate the CPC cycle. Upon seeing the animal approaching, the person being attacked enters the circumspection phase of the CPC cycle by pondering a number of constructs that seem to be pertinent to the situation, for example, stand still-run, fight-not fight, or hide-not hide. In the preemption phase the person chooses from the constructs pondered in the preceding phase. Let us say the person decides on the construct stand still-run. In the control phase he or she will choose that pole of the chosen construct which seems most useful under the circumstances and will then act upon it. Let us say the person chooses to run. Because the whole idea was to predict personal safety, if the individual's course of action had got him or her out of trouble, the construct stand still-run would be validated and would thus tend to dominate that person's thinking if again attacked by a wild animal.

KELLY'S INTERPRETATION OF TRADITIONAL PSYCHOLOGICAL CONCEPTS

In the preface of volume one of his 1955 book, Kelly warned the reader that he has ignored many traditional concepts, has redefined others, and has invented a number of new ones. In this section we will review a sample of the traditional psychological concepts that Kelly redefined in accordance with his personal construct theory.

Motivation Kelly strongly disagreed with most of the traditional views of motivation. He felt that they looked upon humans as naturally inert and therefore needed to be set in motion by something. In other words, traditional theories of motivation claimed that humans needed a drive, a need, a goal, or a stimulus to set them in motion. Kelly felt that this was nonsense. He believed that humans are born motivated and nothing more needs to be said. Every person, according to Kelly, is motivated "for no other reason than that he is alive" (1958, p. 49).

> Motivational theories can be divided into two types, push theories and pull theories. Under push theories we find such terms as drive, motive, or even stimulus. Pull theories use such contructs as purpose, value, or need. In terms of a well-known metaphor, these are the pitchfork theories on the one hand and the carrot theories on the other. But our theory is neither of these. Since we prefer to look to the nature of the animal himself, ours is probably best called a jackass theory. (Kelly 1958, p. 50)

Examples of what Kelly called push theories would include those of Freud, Skinner, and Dollard and Miller. Examples of what Kelly called pull theories would include those of Jung and Adler. Other "jackass theories" would include those of Rogers and Maslow to which we turn in the next two chapters.

Anxiety Kelly defined anxiety as "the recognition that the events with which one is confronted lie outside the range of convenience of one's construct system" (1955, p. 495).

As we have seen, the ability to predict the future accurately is everyone's goal. The extent to which our predictions are invalid is the extent to which we experience anxiety.

> We become anxious when we can only partially construe the events which we encounter and too many of their implications are obscure. Sex for the chaste, adulthood for the adolescent, books for the illiterate, power for the humble and death for nearly all of us tend to provoke anxiety. It is the *unknown* aspects of things that go bump in the night that give them their potency. (Bannister & Fransella 1971, p. 35)

In the extreme, life can become so unpredictable that the only certain thing that one can imagine is death. For some this may stimulate suicide. "For the man of constricted outlook whose world begins to crumble, death may appear to provide the only immediate certainty which he can lay his hands on" (Kelly 1955, p. 64). Anxiety is caused by the uncertainty that results when one's construct system does not permit the accurate construing of life's experiences. In some extreme cases the certainty of death may be preferred to the uncertainty of the future.

Hostility Kelly defined hostility as the *"continued effort to extort validational evidence in favor of a type of social prediction which has already proven itself a failure"* (1955, p. 510).

Hostility is related to anxiety. Anxiety is experienced when one's predictions are incorrect. According to Kelly, anxiety is to be avoided. When it is clear that one's construct system has failed to construe the situation properly (that is, when anxiety is inevitable), one may refuse to accept this fact and attempt to demand validation from the environment. Such demands characterize hostility. Bannister and Fransella (1971) say:

> There are times when, if his construct system is to be preserved, a person simply cannot afford to be wrong. If he acknowledges that some of his expectations are ill-founded, this might involve the modification or abandonment of the constructions on which those expectations were based. If, in turn, these constructions are central to the whole of his system, he might well be faced with chaos, having no alternative way of viewing his situation. In such a position the person is likely to become *hostile,* to extort evidence, to bully people into behaving in ways which confirm his predictions, to cook the books, to refuse to recognize the ultimate significance of what is happening [p. 35].

Aggression Kelly (1955) defines aggressiveness as ". . . the active elaboration of one's perceptual field [p. 508]." Thus, according to Kelly, the aggressive individual opts to extend his construct system rather than define it (see the choice corollary). He seeks adventure rather than security. He seeks to expand his construct system so that it includes an increasing range of events. Aggression, then, in Kelly's theory, is the opposite of hostility. Bannister and Fransella (1971) put it as follows:

> It is interesting to note that Kelly is here attempting to define aggression (and similarly attempts to define hostility) in terms of what is

> going on *within the individual* rather than in terms of other people's reaction to him. Thus, a person is being aggressive when he actively experiments to check the validity of his construing; when he extends the range of his constructions (and thereby his activities) in new directions; when he is exploring. Obviously from the point of view of the people around and about such a person, this can be a very uncomfortable process and they may well see it as an attack upon them and handle it as such. But in terms of the aggressive person's construction system it is essentially an extending and elaborating process and thereby the opposite of hostility. (Bannister & Fransella, pp. 37–38)

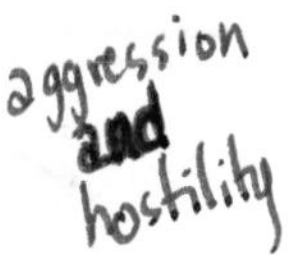

To Kelly, hostility is the unwillingness to give up an ineffective system, and aggression is an attempt to expand one's construct system to an ever increasing range of events.

Guilt Kelly defined guilt as the *"perception of one's apparent dislodgment from his core role structure"* (1955, p. 502).

The term *core role structure* refers to the constructs we use to predict our own behavior. The phrase comes close to what other theorists call the self or what Erikson called one's identity. Guilt, according to Kelly, is the feeling we have when we act contrary to the predictions of our own behavior.

> . . . If you find yourself doing, in important respects, those things you would not have expected to do if you are the kind of person you always thought you were, then you suffer from guilt. . . . To live in a world where you cannot understand and predict others can be terrifying—how much more terrifying is it to find that one cannot understand or predict oneself. (Bannister & Fransella 1971, p. 36)

There is some similarity between Kelly's concept of guilt and Freud's concept of moral anxiety. According to Kelly, we experience guilt when there is a discrepancy between how we think we will act in a situation and how we actually act. According to Freud, we internalize values which act as a guide in determining what is right and what is wrong in our lives. When we act contrary to one or more of these internalized values, we experience moral anxiety. For both Kelly and Freud, when we depart from the behavior that is expected from us, we experience discomfort; guilt for Kelly, moral anxiety for Freud.

Threat Kelly defined threat as the *"awareness of imminent comprehensive change in one's core structures"* (1955, p. 489).

Just as we have a core role structure for understanding ourselves, we have other constructs for predicting external events on which we rely heavily. These *core structures* are used to make sense out of life. They become the heart of what others may call our "belief system." When these basic core constructs suddenly seem no longer to be validated by experience, we feel threatened. To challenge our core constructs is to challenge our very existence and that could be dangerous.

> . . . We are threatened when our major beliefs about the nature of our personal, social and practical situation are invalidated and the world around us appears about to become chaotic. Threat is an extremely important construct for anyone engaged in attempts to help other people. For example, the psychotherapist in his enthusiasm to change what he considers to be the restrictive and poorly developed ideas of his client may plunge the client into over-hasty experimentation and thereby threaten him. The client may then either become hostile and resist all change or may plunge into the kind of chaos that earns him the title of psychotic. By threatening, in the construct theory sense of the term, we do psychological violence to a person. (Bannister & Fransella 1971, p. 37)

For Kelly, guilt is experienced when the constructs we use to predict our own behavior are not validated, and we feel threatened when previously validated constructs for dealing with external events lose their validity. For example, an individual who spent most of his life avoiding alcohol would feel guilty if he accepted a drink at a party; and if a person looked out her window in the middle of summer and saw snow, she would feel threatened.

Fear Fear, according to Kelly, is similar to threat but less severe. Fear results when a peripheral element of one's construct system is invalidated rather than one's core constructs. *"Fear is like threat, except that, in this case, it is a new incidental construct, rather than a comprehensive construct, that seems about to take over"* (Kelly 1955, p. 494). A person may experience fear if a previously friendly dog growls at him. The change this experience necessitates in one's construct system is a minor one; for instance, a friendly dog now becomes a friendly dog that sometimes growls.

The Unconscious Kelly felt that constructs could be described in terms of their "cognitive awareness." Constructs with low cognitive awareness could be considered more or less as unconscious. According to Kelly, there are three kinds of constructs with low cognitive awareness: preverbal, submerged, and suspended.

Kelly defined a preverbal construct as *"one which continues to be used even though it has no consistent word symbol"* (1955, p. 459). Preverbal constructs typically are formed early in life before language is available. Even though words are not available to infants, they still describe and anticipate events in terms of nebulous, nonverbal constructs such as feelings of warmth and security. Since verbally labeling a construct makes it much easier to use, preverbal constructs are less definite and more cumbersome than those that are verbally labeled.

As we saw earlier, every construct has two poles. However, sometimes an individual will act as if only one of the two poles exists; for example, to believe that "all people are good" or "everything is living." Emphasizing one pole of a construct and ignoring the other pole is what

Kelly called *submergence.* "There is the *likeness* and the *contrast* end. Sometimes one of these two ends is less available than the other. When this is markedly true we may refer to the less available end as the *submerged* end" (Kelly 1955, p. 467). An anxious person may choose not to entertain one pole of a construct because doing so would challenge his or her construct system. Kelly's notion of submergence is similar to Freud's notion of repression.

Another way by which an element of experience can have low cognitive awareness is through *suspension.* An element of experience is suspended when it cannot be used constructively in one's construct system. It is as if an experience is kept in a holding pattern until a construct system that can assimilate it is created.

> . . . Our theory does not place the emphasis upon remembering what is pleasant or forgetting what is unpleasant; rather, it emphasizes that one remembers what is structured and forgets what is unstructured. In contrast with some notions of repression, suspension implies that the idea or element of experience is forgotten simply because the person can, at the moment, tolerate no structure within which the idea would have meaning. Once he can entertain such a structure the idea may become available within it. (Kelly 1955, p. 473)

For Kelly, then, what others call the unconscious is explained in terms of preverbal constructs, submergence, and suspension.

Learning Learning, for Kelly, was the constant alteration of one's construct system with the goal of increasing its predictive efficiency. Any change in one's construct system exemplifies learning.

PSYCHOTHERAPY

According to Kelly, neurotic individuals are like bad scientists; they keep making the same predictions in the absence of validating experiences. In other words, a neurotic's construct system does not adequately predict future events, and therefore anxiety is inescapable. What the neurotic person needs is a more adequate construct system, and psychotherapy is a procedure designed to help that person develop one. For Kelly, psychotherapy provides an individual with an opportunity to examine and reformulate his or her construct system. In other words, psychotherapy trains people to be better scientists.

Since psychotherapy must deal with a client's constructs, the therapist must first discover what those constructs are. Kelly devised the *Role Construct Repertory Test* in order to identify the constructs a client uses to construe the relevant people in his or her life. This test has come to be called the *Rep Test.* A typical form used in administering the Rep

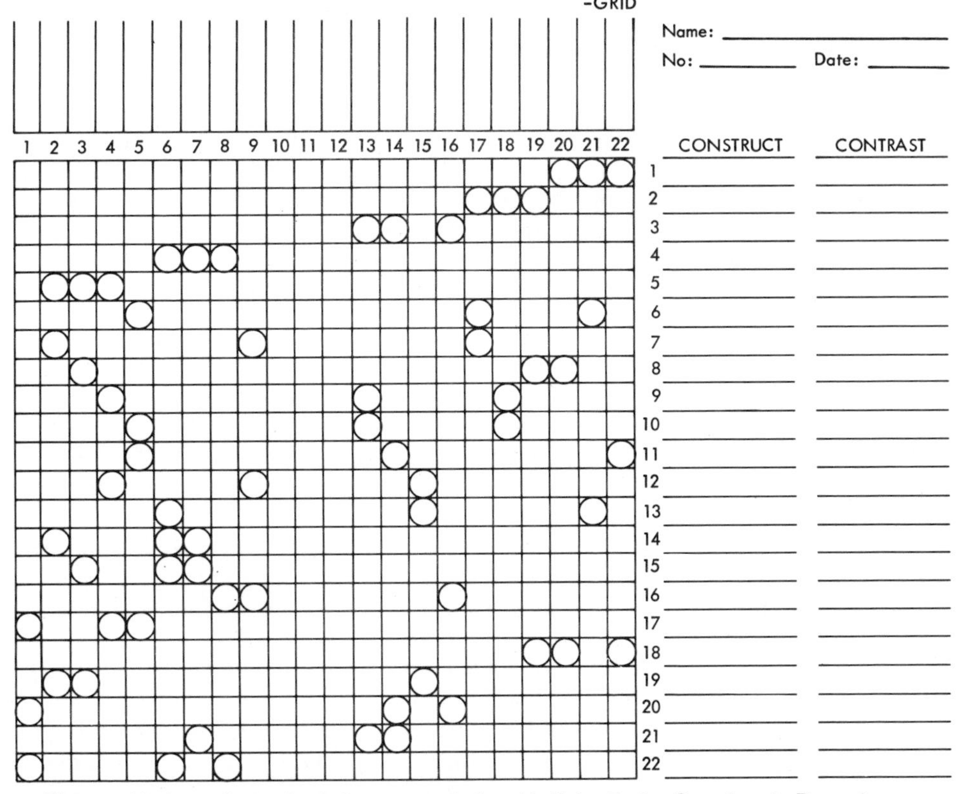
-GRID

Name:

No: Date:

1 2 3 4 5 6 7 8 9 10 11 12 13 14 15 16 17 18 19 20 21 22

CONSTRUCT CONTRAST

1 2 3 4 5 6 7 8 9 10 11 12 13 14 15 16 17 18 19 20 21 22

Figure 11–1 A typical form used for Kelly's Role Construct Repertory (REP) Test. (From Kelly 1955.)

Test is shown in Figure 11–1. The reader is encouraged to take the test himself or herself in order to gain information about his or her own construct system.

The first step in administering the Rep Test is to ask the client to fill in the grid portion of the form, numbered 1–22, with the names of twenty-two persons relevant to his or her life. The client taking the test usually is asked to place the names of the following individuals in the blanks above the numbers on the test sheet:

Blank Number

1. The name of the client taking the test
2. Mother's first name (or stepmother)
3. Father's first name (or stepfather)
4. Brother nearest to you in age, or if no brother, a boy near your age most like a brother.
5. Sister nearest to you in age, or if no sister, a girl near your age most like a sister.

6. Your wife or husband, or if not married, your closest friend of the opposite sex.
7. Closest friend of the opposite sex after the person listed in item 6.
8. Closest friend of your own sex.
9. A person who was once a close friend but no longer is.
10. A religious leader, for example, a minister, priest, or rabbi to whom you would be willing to discuss your feelings about religion.
11. Your medical doctor.
12. The neighbor you know best.
13. A person you now know who dislikes you.
14. A person for whom you feel sorry and would like to help.
15. The person with whom you feel most uncomfortable.
16. A recent acquaintance whom you would like to know better.
17. Your most influential teacher when you were in your teens.
18. The teacher with whom you disagreed the most.
19. An employer or supervisor under whom you worked while you were experiencing stress.
20. The most successful person whom you know personally.
21. The happiest person whom you know personally.
22. The most ethical person whom you know personally.

When the names have been furnished, the client is asked to compare them in groups of three. The three names that are to be compared are indicated by circles on the test sheet. For example, the first comparison is of the individuals whose names appear in blanks 20, 21, and 22. The second comparison is of the individuals whose names appear in blanks 17, 18, and 19, and so on. For each triad the client is asked to choose a word or phrase that describes how two of the three individuals are alike and a word or phrase that describes how the third person is different from the other two. The way in which the two people are the same is listed under construct, and the way in which the third person is different is listed under contrast. An X is placed in the circles of the two people who are alike, and the circle of the person thought to be different is left blank. A partially completed Rep Test is shown in Figure 11–2.

It can be seen in Figure 11–2 that the client felt that individuals

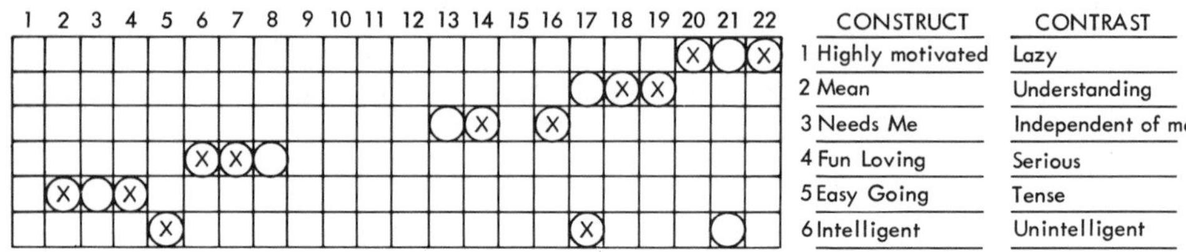

Figure 11–2 An example of a partially completed REP test. Typically the client is asked to make twenty-two comparisons instead of the six indicated in the figure.

20 and 22 were highly motivated but that individual 21 was lazy; individuals 18 and 19 were thought to be mean, whereas individual 17 was thought to be understanding, and the like.

By analyzing the client's performance on the Rep Test, the psychotherapist can answer a number of questions about a client's construct system. For example, which constructs are used? What aspects of people do they emphasize, for example, physical characteristics and social characteristics? Which people are seen as most like or different from the client? Does the client have a large number of constructs available or only a few?

How valid is the Rep Test? The answer depends on whom you ask. In a recent interview with Evans, Bannister, who is one of Kelly's disciples, describes his experience with the Rep Test as follows:

> I arrived at this brain-crunching chapter on the grid and set to work to do one on *me*. Then I scored it. It was a fairly murderous task, taking about three weeks to get through it all. Then when I looked at it it seemed ridiculous. I wasn't, I said to myself, the overemotional, bigoted bastard portrayed there, so I stuck it in a file and did other things. About two weeks later I took it out again and said "Yes, I *am* the overemotional, bigoted etcetera portrayed in the grid," It was a troubled time for me personally and the grid had picked it up. (Evans 1978, p. 7)

The Rep Test was only one tool that Kelly used to learn about his clients' construct system. Another tool was simply to ask the clients about themselves. Kelly adopted what he called a *credulous attitude* toward his clients. In other words, he felt that the information they furnished about themselves could be trusted. *"If you don't know what's wrong with a client, ask him; he may tell you"* (Kelly 1955, p. 201).

In keeping with his credulous attitude, Kelly often had his clients write a *self-characterization* of themselves.

> I want you to write a character sketch of Harry Brown (i.e., client's name), just as if he were the principal character in a play. Write it as it might be written by a friend who knew him very *intimately* and very *sympathetically,* perhaps better than anyone ever really could know him. Be sure to write it in the third person. For example, start out by saying, "Harry Brown is . . . " (Kelly 1955, p. 323)

Again, as with the Rep Test, the purpose of this sketch was to help the therapist see how clients construed themselves and their interactions with the world and with other people.

Fixed-role Therapy Kelly believed that one way to cause clients to explore different ways of construing things is to have them pretend they are different people. In fixed-role therapy the therapist presents the client with a personality sketch and asks the client to act it out, just as an actor would play a part in a play. To enhance the development of new constructs, the personality of the person the client is asked to play is markedly different from the client's own personality. Kelly asks the client to try on a new personality as one would try on a new suit of clothes. Under these circumstances the therapist becomes a supporting actor. Kelly said the therapist must "play in strong support of an actor—the client—who is continually fumbling his lines and contaminating his role" (1955, p. 399).

The client plays his role for about two weeks during which time he lives "as if" he were the person in the role he is playing. The therapist, during this time, responds to the client "as if" he were the person in the part and offers encouragement and validating experiences for the new constructs with which the client is experimenting. The therapist must give the client enough courage to overcome the threat involved in giving up his core constructs and develop new ones.

> What I am saying is that it is not so much what man is that counts as it is what he ventures to make of himself. To make the leap he must do more than disclose himself; he must risk a certain amount of confusion. Then, as soon as he does catch a glimpse of a different kind of life, he needs to find some way of overcoming the paralyzing moment of threat, for this is the instant when he wonders what he really is—whether he is what he just was or is what he is about to be. (Kelly 1964, p. 147)
>
> By providing validating data in the form of responses to a wide variety of constructions on the part of the client, some of them quite loose, fanciful, or naughty, the clinician gives the client an opportunity to validate constructs, an opportunity which is not normally available to him. (Kelly 1955, p. 165)

We see, then, that Kelly maintains his cognitive viewpoint even in psychotherapy. Emotional problems are *perceptual* problems. To resolve a perceptual problem, one must be made to *look at* things differently. Psychotherapy is a process by which a client is encouraged to look at things differently while the therapist attempts to minimize the anxiety in doing so.

Kelly is suggesting that neurotics have lost their ability to make believe, and the therapist tries to help them regain it. Healthy individuals make believe all the time. In fact, in Kelly's opinion, brilliant novelists and brilliant scientists do much the same thing, that is, they make believe.

> Both [the novelist and the scientist] employ . . . human tactics. The fact that the scientist is ashamed to admit his phantasy probably accomplishes little more than to make it appear that he fits a popular notion of the way scientists think. And the fact that a novelist does not continue his project to the point of collecting data in support of his portrayals and generalizations suggests only that he hopes that the experiences of man will, in the end, prove him right without anyone's resorting to formal proof.
>
> But the brilliant scientist and the brilliant writer are pretty likely to end up saying the same thing—given, of course, a lot of time to con-

> verge upon each other. The poor scientist and the poor writer, moreover, fail in much the same way—neither of them is able to transcend the obvious. Both fail in their make-believe. (Kelly 1964, p. 140)

CONSTRUCT SYSTEMS AND PARADIGMS

In many ways Kelly's view of personality is similar to Kuhn's view of science. Kelly maintains that the way in which an individual construes reality is only one of many possible ways, but for that particular individual his or her construct system *is* reality, and it is sometimes difficult for him or her to imagine other constructions. For Kuhn, as we saw in chapter 1, a paradigm is a way of looking at a subject matter, and scientists doing research while following a paradigm are said to be doing "normal science." Such scientists, according to Kuhn, are often blinded to other, perhaps more effective, ways of looking at a body of information.

It seems that the most important similarity between Kelly and Kuhn is that they both emphasize *perceptual mechanisms*. For Kelly, a construction system is a set of personal constructs which result in a person construing the world in a certain way. Likewise, Kuhn's paradigm is a perceptual habit shared by a number of scientists that causes them to *view* their subject matter in a similar way.

Both Kelly and Kuhn insist that there are many equally valid interpretations of reality, not just one. Whereas Kelly took this view of an individual's adjustment to the world and Kuhn took this view of science, we take the same view of personality theory. One of the main functions of this book is to offer the various personality theories, not as "truths" but as *ways of viewing* personality. In other words, we feel that, like reality in general, personality can be construed in a number of equally valid ways. It is hoped that the student's construct for personality is a highly permeable one which allows a variety of viewpoints to enter it.

We end our coverage of Kelly's theory with the following quotation which seems to summarize Kelly's philosophy of the individual, Kuhn's philosophy of science, and this book's approach to personality theory: "Whatever nature may be, or howsoever the quest for truth will turn out in the end, the events we face today are subject to as great a variety of constructions as our wits will enable us to contrive" (Kelly 1970, p. 1).

EVALUATION

Starting with practically no formal training in clinical psychology, Kelly ended up developing a unique theory of personality and psychotherapeutic procedures that were both innovative and effective. Kelly's belief that truth is mainly a way of looking at things both freed him from the dogma of the past and gave him latitude to experiment with his own theory. We agree with Pervin's eloquent evaluation of Kelly's theory:

> In George Kelly, then, we have a man who refused to accept things as black or white, right or wrong. We have a man who liked to test out new experiences; a man who dismissed truth in any absolute sense and, therefore, felt free to reconstrue phenomena; a man who challenged the concept of "objective" reality and felt free to play in the world of "make-believe"; a man who perceived events as occurring to individuals and, therefore, was interested in the interpretations of these events by individuals; a man who viewed his own theory as only a tentative formulation and who, consequently, was free to challenge views that others accepted as dogma; a man who experienced the frustration and challenge, the threat and joy, of exploring the unknown. (1975, p. 271)

Many prominent psychologists have praised Kelly's theory but by no means has his theory gone uncriticized. Common criticisms of Kelly's theory are that he ignores the realm of human emotions, that it is difficult to predict a person's behavior using his theory, that he was not concerned with the origins of personal constructs, that he does not explain why some individuals choose security and others adventure in their choice of constructs, that he does not explain why two people construe the same physical experience differently, and that his therapeutic techniques are applicable to only intelligent articulate adults experiencing only minor distress.

The criticisms of Kelly's theory should not disturb the reader who found it enlightening. No personality theory, indeed no theory of any kind, is without valid criticism. As Kelly would have said, every theory, like any construct, has a range of convenience and a focus of convenience, and that includes his own theory as well.

SUMMARY

Kelly was born in the Midwest and raised by educated, religious parents. From his early pioneering experiences with his parents came a practical, flexible outlook which characterized Kelly all of his life. Kelly's theory can be categorized as phenomenological because it studied intact, significant cognitive experiences; cognitive because it studied mental events; existential because it emphasized the future and people's freedom to choose their own destinies; and humanistic because he emphasized people's creative powers and was optimistic about people's ability to solve their problems.

Kelly's major premise was that all humans act like scientists in that they attempt to reduce uncertainty by developing theories (construct systems) which allow them to anticipate future events accurately. Individuals construe, that is, interpret, explain, or predict, the events in their lives by utilizing constructs. A construct is a category of thought that describes how events are similar to each other and yet different from other events. All individuals are free to create whatever constructs they choose in their attempts to give meaning to their experiences. This freedom to choose constructs is called constructive alternativism. People are free to choose constructs but are more or less bound to them once they have been selected.

Kelly elaborated his theory through eleven corollaries. The construction corollary states that constructs are formed on the basis of the common themes in our experiences. The individuality corollary states that all individuals construe their experiences in their own unique way. The organization corollary states that some constructs are subsumed under, or contained within, other constructs. The dichotomy corollary states that each construct must describe how certain events are similar and also how those events are contrasted with other events. The choice corollary states that those constructs are chosen which have the best chance of either defining (validating) or extending (generalizing) one's construct system. The range corollary states that each construct has a range of convenience consisting of the events to which the construct is relevant and a focus of convenience to which the construct is maximally relevant. The experience corollary states that it is not physical experience that is important but the active construing of physical experiences. It is construing that provides for the testing and revision of one's construct system. The modulation corollary states that some constructs are more permeable, that is, more open to experience, than other constructs. The fragmentation corollary states that while trying new constructs people may at times be inconsistent but if the larger picture is viewed, people tend to be consistent. The commonality corollary states that in order for two individuals to be considered similar they must construe their experiences in a similar manner. The sociality corollary states that in order to play a role, one must first determine what another person's expectations are and then act in accordance with those expectations.

When individuals are confronted with a novel situation, they apply the CPC cycle. In the circumspection phase of the cycle people ponder a number of constructs that they feel may be appropriate to the situation. In the preemption phase they choose those constructs that seem to be the most relevant. In the control phase they act on the basis of those constructs chosen in the preemption phase.

Kelly redefined a number of traditional psychological concepts in terms of his theory. The concept of motivation was thought unnecessary since humans are born motivated. Anxiety was defined as the feeling one gets when it is recognized that what is being experienced lies outside one's construct system. Hostility was defined as an attempt to force the validation of one's construct system when it is clear that it is generating inaccurate predictions. Aggression was defined as the attempt to expand one's construct system. The aggressive person, according to Kelly, is one who typically seeks new experiences. Guilt, according to Kelly, is experienced when one's core role structure is threatened, in other words, when one's identity is challenged. Threat was defined as the feeling one experiences when one's core structures are invalidated. Fear was defined as the feeling one has when constructs, other than core constructs, are invalidated. The unconscious, to Kelly, was explained in terms of perverbal constructs; submergence, in which one pole of a construct is emphasized; and suspension, in which certain elements of experience are ignored until they can be made to fit into one's construct system in a constructive way. Learning was defined as any change in one's construct system.

Kelly compared a neurotic individual to a bad scientist, since he or she keeps making inaccurate predictions in the absence of validating experiences. Psychotherapy, to Kelly, was a process in which a client could try out different, potentially more effective, construct systems. In order to discover what constructs a client used in dealing with experiences, Kelly devised the Role Construct Repertory Test, better known as the Rep Test. Kelly maintained a credulous attitude toward his clients, believing that they could provide a great deal of valid information about themselves. For example, he often had his clients write a self-characterization in which they described themselves in the third person. Kelly used fixed-role therapy in which he had clients act "as if" they were different people and in which the therapist was much like a supporting actor. Such a procedure allowed clients to test an alternative construct system while the therapist provided encouragement and validating experiences.

Kelly's theory was compared to Kuhn's notion of scientific paradigms in that both emphasize that reality can be viewed in a number of equally valid ways.

Discussion Questions

1. Describe as many categories as you can into which Kelly's theory fits.
2. Explain how Kelly used the model of the scientist to explain the psychological processes of all humans.
3. Define the term construct as Kelly used it. List as many characteristics of constructs as you can.
4. Explain how Kelly accounts for inconsistencies in a person's behavior.
5. According to Kelly, what is required before we can call two individuals similar?
6. Describe the CPC cycle.
7. Discuss each of the following terms from Kelly's point of view:

motivation, anxiety, hostility, aggression, guilt, threat, fear, and learning.

8. What, in Kelly's theory, corresponds to the concept of the unconscious in other theories?
9. Describe the procedures in administering the Rep Test.
10. What did Kelly mean when he said that he maintained a credulous attitude toward his clients?
11. Summarize the procedures of fixed-role therapy.
12. According to Kelly, what is the goal of psychotherapy?
13. Elaborate on Kelly's contention that playing a role requires that one's behavior be guided by the perception of another person's expectations.
14. How did Kelly differentiate between a healthy person and an emotionally disturbed person?
15. Answer the following question as if you were Kelly: "If playing different parts is so useful in calling different construct systems to the attention of a client, why is it that there seem to be so many emotionally disturbed actors and actresses? Are they not experimenting with different construct systems all the time?"
16. Describe those theories of motivation that Kelly labeled "pitchfork" theories and those that he labeled "carrot" theories. Why did Kelly refer to his own theory of motivation as a "jackass" theory?
17. In chapter 1 it was pointed out that all cognitive theories have the problem of explaining how something cognitive is translated into behavior. This is one manifestation of the mind-body problem. Discuss this problem as it relates to Kelly's theory.
18. Compare the terms motivation, anxiety, and aggression as they are used in Freudian theory with the way they are used in Kellian theory.
19. Assuming that anxiety is a basic ingredient of humor, what types of things, according to Kelly, should make us laugh? Does Kelly's suggestion coincide with your experience with humor? Explain.
20. Respond personally to the existentialist's belief, which is shared by Kelly, that "Humans are free to choose their own destiny."

Glossary

Aggression. The effort to expand one's construct system so that it is capable of assimilating a greater range of experiences.

Anxiety. The feeling one has when it is realized that an experience lies outside one's construct system.

Choice Corollary. States that people will choose a construct which will either further define or extend their construct system. See also definition and extension of a construct system.

Circumspection Phase. That phase of the CPC Cycle in which a person ponders a number of constructs that might be useful in construing a novel situation.

Cognitive Theory. Any theory that focuses on the study of mental events.

Commonality Corollary. States that people can be considered similar, not because of similar physical experiences, but because they construe their experiences in a similar fashion.

Construct. See personal construct.

Construction Corollary. States that constructs are formed on the basis of the recurring events in one's life.

Constructive Alternativism. A term that reflects Kelly's belief that there are numerous ways of construing one's experiences and therefore one is free to choose from a number of construct systems.

Construe. One's active effort to interpret, explain, and give meaning to experiences.

Control Phase. That phase of the CPC Cycle in which people act in accordance with the constructs they choose to construe a novel situation.

Core Role Structure. The constructs we use to predict our own behavior. Close to what others call the "self" or "identity."

Core Structures. Those constructs on which we rely most heavily when construing experience, that is, those that have been most consistently validated.

CPC Cycle. The series of activities engaged in by a person confronted with a novel situation. See also circumspection phase, preemption phase, and control phase.

Credulous Attitude. The assumption that the information provided by clients about themselves can be trusted as accurate and valid.

Definition of a Construct System. The choice of a construct in construing a situation which has already been successful in construing similar situations. Such a choice has the effect of further validating one's construct system.

Dichotomy Corollary. States that each construct has two poles, one pole which describes what characteristics the events to which the construct is relevant have in common, the other which describes events without those characteristics. For example, if one pole of a construct describes beautiful things, the other pole will describe things without beauty, or ugly things.

Existential Theory. Any theory that focuses on the nature of, and/or the problems related to, human existence.

Experience Corollary. States that mere passive experience is unimportant. It is the active construing of experience that ultimately results in a more effective construct system.

Extension of a Construct System. The choice of a construct in construing a situation which has never been tried before. Such a choice has the potential effect of extending one's construct system so that it is capable of assimilating a greater range of experience.

Fear. The feeling one has when a relatively unimportant construct is about to be invalidated, thus requiring a minor change in one's construct system.

Fixed-role Therapy. The clinical techniques which asks clients to act as if they were other people. Thus clients become actors, and the therapist becomes a supporting actor. The idea is to have the clients try different ways of construing their experiences in a nonthreatening situation as the therapist provides validating information about the new construct system.

Focus of Convenience. The events within the range of convenience of a construct to which that construct is maximally significant.

Fragmentation Corollary. States that as a construct system is being tested, revised, or extended certain inconsistencies in behavior may result.

Guilt. The feeling one has when one acts contrary to the predictions one has made of one's own behavior.

Hostility. The attempt to force the validation of a prediction that has already proved to be erroneous.

Humanistic Theory. Any theory that assumes that humans are basically good and rational and that their behavior is purposive.

Individuality Corollary. States that each individual is unique in his or her manner of construing experience.

Jackass Theory of Motivation. Kelly's description of his own theory, since it focused on the nature of the organism itself rather than on the events that either push or pull the organism.

Learning. Any change in one's construct system.

Man the Scientist. A statement reflecting Kelly's belief that all humans act like scientists in that they attempt to devise "theories" that allow them to predict future events, thereby reducing uncertainty in their lives.

Modulation Corollary. States that a construct system is more likely to change if the constructs contained in it are permeable. See also permeable construct.

Motivation. For Kelly, a synonym for life.

Organization Corollary. States that constructs are arranged in a hierarchy from most general to most specific. See also superordinate and subordinate constructs.

Permeable Construct. A construct that easily assimilates new experiences.

Personal Construct. An idea or thought that a person uses when construing personal experience. Sometimes simply called a construct.

Phenomenologist. One who studies intact, subjective, conscious, and personal experience.

Phenomenology. The study of intact, subjective, conscious, and personal experience.

Preemption Phase. That phase of the CPC Cycle in which people decide which constructs they are going to use to construe a novel situation.

Propositional Construct. A construct that is cognitively tested as one that might be useful in construing a novel situation.

Psychotherapy. Since Kelly equated people suffering emotional problems with bad scientists, therapy was regarded as a setting in which the client could learn to be a better scientist, that is, learn to develop a more effective construct system.

Pull Theories of Motivation. Those theories that emphasize terms such as purpose, value, or need. Kelly also called these carrot theories.

Push Theories of Motivation. Those theories that emphasize terms such as drive, motive, and stimulus. Kelly also called these pitchfork theories.

Range Corollary. States that a construct is relevant to only a finite range of events. See also range of convenience and focus of convenience.

Range of Convenience. The finite range of events to which a particular construct is relevant.

Role. For Kelly, a role is acting in accordance with another person's expectations of how one will act.

Role Construct Repertory Test (REP Test). A test developed by Kelly to identify the constructs clients use to construe the relevant people in their lives.

Self-characterization. The sketch that Kelly sometimes had his clients write about themselves (in the third person) in order to learn what constructs they used to construe themselves and other people.

Sociality Corollary. States that in order to engage in constructive social interaction with another person, one must first understand how that person construes his or her experiences. Only then can one play a role in that person's life. See also role.

Submergence. The situation in which one pole of a construct is utilized, but the other pole tends not to be. The unused pole is said to be submerged or unconscious.

Subordinate Construct. A construct that is subsumed under a more general construct.

Superordinate Construct. A general construct that subsumes other constructs.

Suspension. The situation in which an experience has low cognitive awareness because it is incompatible with one's current construct system. If one's construct system is changed so that it can assimilate the experience, it (the experience) will enter full awareness, that is, it will no longer be suspended.

Threat. The awareness that one or more of the constructs depended on most in construing experience is going to be invalidated, thus requiring a major change in one's construct system. See also core structures.

Unconscious. Constructs with low cognitive awareness. See also submergence and suspension.

Validation. Results when a construct or a construct system is successful in anticipating an experience.

chapter 12

carl rogers

Carl Ranson Rogers was born on January 8, 1902 in Oak Park (a Chicago suburb), Illinois and was the fourth of six children. Because his father was a successful civil engineer and contractor, there were no economic problems in Rogers's early life. Rogers described himself as "the middle child in a large, close knit family, where hard work and a highly conservative (almost fundamentalist) Protestant Christianity were about equally revered" (1959, p. 186). Rogers's parents discouraged the development of friendships outside their home because, it was argued, nonfamily members engaged in questionable activities. Rogers commented:

> I think the attitudes toward persons outside our large family can be summed up schematically in this way: Other persons behave in dubious ways which we do not approve in our family. Many of them play cards, go to movies, smoke, drink, and engage in other activities—some unmentionable. So the best thing to do is to be tolerant of them, since they may not know better, and to keep away from any close communication with them and live your life within the family. (1973a, p. 3)

As a result of the attitude toward "outsiders" decribed above, Rogers spent a great deal of time by himself reading everything he could get his hands on, including encyclopedias and a dictionary.

When he was twelve years old Rogers and his family moved to a farm about thirty miles from Chicago. It was here that Rogers first developed an interest in science. Because his father insisted that the farm be run scientifically, Rogers read about many agricultural experiments. He also developed an interest in a species of moth about which he read and captured, raised, and bred. This interest in science is something that has never left Rogers, although he has worked in one of the more subjective areas of psychology all of his professional life.

Rogers's tendency toward solitude lasted all through high school, during which time he had only two dates. He was an excellent student and obtained almost straight *A*'s. His main interests were English and science.

In 1919 Rogers enrolled at the University of Wisconsin, which both his parents, two brothers, and a sister had attended, and chose to study agriculture. Rogers was very active in church work through his early years in college. In 1922 he was one of ten college students selected to attend the World Student Christian Federation Conference in Peking, China. This six-month trip had a profound effect on Rogers. Having experienced, firsthand, people of different cultures with different religions, he wrote to his parents declaring his independence from their conservative religious viewpoint. Upon returning to the University of Wisconsin, he changed his major from agriculture to history. Rogers received his B.A. degree in 1924.

After graduation, Rogers married (with strong parental disapproval) his childhood sweetheart, Helen Elliott, and they had two children. Also in 1924, Rogers enrolled in the liberal Union Theological Seminary in New York. Although by now Rogers was very interested in helping individuals with problems, he was increasingly doubtful that the best vehicle for help was to be found in religious doctrine. After two years at the seminary, Rogers transferred to Columbia University to study clinical and educational psychology. He received his M.A. in 1928 and his Ph.D. in 1931. His dissertation was on the measurement of personality adjustment in children.

Upon receiving his Ph.D., Rogers accepted a position as psycholo-

Carl Rogers. The Bettmann Archive, Inc.

gist in the Child Study Department of the Society for the Prevention of Cruelty to Children in Rochester, New York where he had worked as an intern while pursuing his Ph.D. It was here that Rogers had a number of experiences that greatly influenced his later theory of personality and his approach to psychotherapy. First, he learned that the psychoanalytic approach to therapy, which dominated the department, was often ineffective. Second, because of both the vastly different approaches to therapy he had studied at Columbia and the child study department he learned that so-called authorities could not agree on what constituted the best treatment for a troubled person. Third, he learned that looking for an "insight" into a problem is often met with frustration. Rogers described one situation in which he felt that a mother's rejection of her son was the cause of his delinquent behavior. He tried his best to share this "insight" with the mother but failed.

> Finally I gave up. I hold her that it seemed we had both tried, but we had failed. . . . She agreed. So we concluded the interview, shook hands, and she walked to the door of the office. Then she turned and asked, "Do you ever take adults for counseling here?" When I replied in the affirmative, she said, "Well then, I would like some help." She came to the chair she had left, and began to pour out her despair about her marriage, her troubled relationship with her husband, her sense of failure and confusion, all very different from the sterile "case history" she had given before. Real therapy began then. . . .
>
> This incident was one of a number which helped me to experience that fact—only fully realized later—that it is the *client* who knows what hurts, what directions to go, what problems are crucial, what experiences have been deeply buried. It began to occur to me that unless I had a need to demonstrate my own cleverness and learning, I would do better to rely upon the client for the direction of movement in the process. (Rogers 1961, pp. 11–12)

Rogers wrote his first book while at the Child Study Department; it was entitled *The Clinical Treatment of the Problem Child* (1939). In 1940, Rogers moved from a clinical setting to an academic setting by accepting a faculty position in clinical psychology at Ohio State University. It was here that Rogers began to formulate and test his own approach to psychotherapy.

> I found that the emerging principles of therapy, which I had experienced largely on an implicit basis, were by no means clear to well-trained, critically minded graduate students. I began to sense that what I was doing and thinking in the clinical field was perhaps more of a new pathway than I had recognized. The paper I presented to the Minnesota Chapter of Psi Chi in December, 1940, (Later Chapter 2 of *Counseling and Psychotherapy*) was the first conscious attempt to develop a relatively new line of thought. Up to that time, I had felt that my writings were essentially attempts to distill out more clearly the principles which "all clinicians" were using. (Rogers 1959, p. 187)

In 1942, Rogers published his now famous book *Counseling and Psychotherapy: Newer Concepts in Practice,* which many thought described the first major alternative to psychoanalysis. The publisher was very reluctant to publish this book, feeling that it would not sell two thousand copies, the number necessary to break even. By 1961 it had sold over seventy thousand copies and is still going strong.

In 1945, Rogers left Ohio State to become professor of psychology and director of counseling at the University of Chicago. It was during his stay at the University of Chicago that Rogers published what many considered to be his major work, *Client-centered Therapy: Its Current Practice, Implications and Theory* (1951).

In 1957, Rogers left the University of Chicago to return to the University of Wisconsin where he held the dual position of professor of psychology and professor of psychiatry. In 1963, he resigned his positions at the University of Wisconsin to become a member of the Western Behavioral Sciences Institute (WBSI) in La Jolla, California. In 1968, Rogers, and several of the more humanistically oriented members of WBSI, left that organization to form the Center for the Studies of the Person, in La Jolla, California. It is at this center that Rogers is currently working.

Many of Rogers's moves were coupled with a shift in his interests, techniques, or philosophy. His last move stressed his current interest in the individual as he experiences the world. In a recent publication Rogers explained: "We are deeply interested in persons but are rather 'turned-off' by the older methods of studying them as 'objects' for research" (1972, p. 67). Currently Rogers is working with encounter groups and is teaching sensitivity training. He is mainly interested in discovering the conditions under which a person can fully develop his or her potentialities. According to Rogers, the most important resource that individuals have within themselves is the actualizing tendency, and it is to a discussion of that tendency to which we turn next.

THE ACTUALIZING TENDENCY

Rogers postulates one master motive which he calls the *actualizing tendency.*

> The organism has one basic tendency and striving—to actualize, maintain, and enhance the experiencing organism. (Rogers 1951, p. 487)

> . . . there is one central source of energy in the human organism; that it is a function of the whole organism rather than some portion of it; and that it is perhaps best conceptualized as a tendency toward fulfillment, toward actualization, toward the maintenance and enhancement of the organism. (Rogers 1963, p. 6)

According to Rogers, all humans, as well as all other living organisms, have an innate need to survive, grow, and enhance themselves.

All biological drives are subsumed under the actualizing tendency, because they must be satisfied if the organism is to continue its positive development. This "forward thrust of life" continues in spite of many obstacles. For example, children first learning to walk stumble again and again, but, despite the pain, press on with their attempts to walk. There are numerous examples of humans who, while living under dire circumstances, not only survive but continue to enhance their lives.

One might ask toward what is the actualizing tendency moving? Rogers's answer to this question specifies a view of human nature which is essentially the opposite of the view suggested by Freud. Freud viewed humans as having the same needs, drives, and motives as any other animal has. Therefore, humans' tendencies toward uninhibited sex and aggression must be controlled by society. Rogers believes that humans are basically good and therefore need no controlling. In fact, he believes that it is the attempt to control humans that makes them "act" bad. Rogers's view of human nature clearly places him in the humanistic camp.

> I have little sympathy with the rather prevalent concept that man is basically irrational, and that his impulses, if not controlled, will lead to the destruction of others and self. Man's behavior is exquisitely rational, moving with subtle and ordered complexity toward the goals his organism is endeavoring to achieve. (Rogers 1961, pp. 194–195)

Rogers, of course, is aware that individuals sometimes act in unfortunate ways. But, he claims, such actions are not in accordance with human nature. Such actions result from fear and defensiveness.

> I do not have a Pollyanna view of human nature. I am quite aware that out of defensiveness and inner fear individuals can and do behave in ways which are incredibly cruel, horribly destructive, immature, regressive, anti-social, and hurtful. Yet one of the most refreshing and invigorating parts of my experience is to work with such individuals and to discover the strongly positive directional tendencies which exist in them, as in all of us, at the deepest levels. (Rogers 1961, p. 27)

The actualizing tendency, which is the driving force in everyone's life, causes the individual to become more differentiated (complex), more independent, and more socially responsible. We will say more about the goals of the actualizing tendency when we describe the fully functioning individual in a later section of this chapter.

All of an organism's experiences are evaluated using the actualizing tendency as a frame of reference. Rogers calls this method of evaluation of one's experiences the *organismic valuing process.* Those experiences that are in accordance with the actualizing tendency are satisfying and therefore are approached and maintained. Those experiences that are contrary to the actualizing tendency are unsatisfying and therefore are avoided or terminated. The organismic valuing process, therefore, creates a feedback system which allows the organism to coordinate its experiences with its tendency toward self-actualization.

THE PHENOMENOLOGICAL FIELD

According to Rogers, all people live in their own subjective world which can be known, in any complete sense, only to themselves. It is this *phenomenological reality,* rather than the physical world, that determines people's behavior. In other words, how people see things is, for them, the only reality. This private reality will correspond in varying degrees to physical reality, depending on the individual. It is this subjective, phenomenological reality that the therapist, according to Rogers, must attempt to understand. There is a great deal of similarity on this point between Rogers's theory and Kelly's. They both stress the individual's singular subjective interpretation of experience, and that is why they both are labeled phenomenologists. The major difference between Rogers and Kelly is in the actualizing tendency. Kelly's major point was that individuals keep trying out new constructs in order to find the set which best anticipates the future. There was, for Kelly, no innately determined condition toward which all humans were evolving. Rather, each individual, in a sense, invented his or her personality rather than having its major features genetically determined.

Rogers differentiates between *experience* and *awareness.* Experience is all that is going on within the organism's environment at any given moment which is potentially available to awareness. When these potential experiences become *symbolized,* they enter awareness and become part of the person's phenomenological field. The symbols that act as vehicles for experiences to enter awareness are usually words, but they need not be. Rogers felt that symbols also could be visual and auditory images. The distinction between experience and awareness is important to Rogers since, as we shall see, there are certain conditions that cause the individual to deny or distort certain experiences, thereby preventing them from entering his or her awareness.

Rogers (1959, p. 222) summarizes these points by describing the characteristics that he feels the human infant possesses.

1. What infants perceive *is* their reality and therefore they are the only ones that can be aware of their reality since no one else can assume their internal frame of reference.
2. All infants are born with a self-actualizing tendency.
3. Infants attempt to satisfy their need for self-actualization and therefore their behavior is goal-directed.
4. In their interactions with the environment, infants behave as an organized whole. That is, everything they do is interrelated.
5. Infants use their own organismic valuing process as a frame of

reference in evaluating their experiences. Those experiences which are perceived as being in accordance with their actualizing tendency are valued positively. Those experiences which are perceived as contrary to that tendency are valued negatively.

6. Infants seek and maintain experiences which are conducive to self-actualization and avoid those experiences which are not.

THE EMERGENCE OF THE SELF

Rogers confesses to having resisted using the concept of self because he felt it was not scientific. It was the fact that his clients used the term so much that gradually changed his mind.

> Speaking personally, I began my work with the settled notion that the "self" was a vague, ambiguous, scientifically meaningless term which had gone out of the psychologist's vocabulary with the departure of the introspectionists. Consequently I was slow in recognizing that when clients were given the opportunity to express their problems and their attitudes in their own terms, without any guidance or interpretation, they tended to talk in terms of the self. Characteristic expressions were attitudes such as these: "I feel I'm not being my real self." "I wonder who I am, really." "I wouldn't want anyone to know the real me." "I never had a chance to be myself." "It feels good to let myself go and just *be* myself here." "I think if I chip off the plaster facade I've got a pretty solid self—a good substantial brick building, underneath." It seemed clear from such expressions that the self was an important element in the experience of the client, and that in some odd sense his goal was to become his "real self." (Rogers 1959, pp. 200–201)

Since this early reluctance, however, the concept of self has become the cornerstone of Rogers's theory. In fact, his theory of personality is often labeled a "self theory."

At first, infants do not distinguish between events in their phenomenological field; they all are blended together in a single configuration. Gradually, however, through experiences with verbal labels such as "me" and "I," a portion of their phenomenological field becomes differentiated as the *self*. At this point individuals can reflect on their self as a distinct object of which they are aware.

The development of the self is a major manifestation of the actualizing tendency which, as stated above, inclines the organism toward greater differentiation or complexity. The actualizing tendency which, prior to the development of the self, characterized the organism as a whole, now characterizes the self as well. In other words, those experiences seen as enhancing one's self-concept are positively valued; those seen as detrimental to the self-concept are negatively valued.

THE NEED FOR POSITIVE REGARD

With the emergence of the self comes *the need for positive regard* which Rogers felt was universal, although not necessarily innate (whether it was learned or innate was unimportant to Rogers). Positive regard is receiving such things as warmth, love, sympathy, care, respect, and acceptance from the relevant people in one's life. In other words, it is the feeling of being "prized" by those individuals who are most important to us.

As a typical part of the socialization process, children learn there are things they can do and things they cannot do. Most often parents will make positive regard contingent on desirable behavior on the part of their children. That is, if the children do certain things, they will experience positive regard, if they do other things, they will not. This creates what Rogers calls *conditions of worth*, which specify the circumstances under which children will experience positive regard. Through repeated experiences with these conditions of worth, children internalize them, making them part of their self-structure. Once internalized, they become a "conscience" or "superego" which guides the children's behavior even when the parents are not around. For example, if the children consistently received negative responses when they wrote on the walls with crayons, they gradually would feel bad when they wrote on walls, or even thought about writing on walls, even in the absence of an authority figure.

From the need for positive regard comes *the need for self-regard*. That is, children develop the need to view themselves positively. In other words, children first want others to feel good about them and then they want to feel good about themselves. The conditions that make relevant people in their lives regard them positively are "introjected" into their self-structure and thereafter they must act in accordance with those conditions in order to regard themselves positively. The children are now said to have acquired conditions of worth. Unfortunately, when conditions of worth have been established, the only way children can view themselves positively is by acting in accordance with someone else's values which they have internalized. Now children's behavior is no longer guided by their organismic valuing process but by the conditions in their environment which are related to positive regard. Rogers stated that the infant:

> . . . comes to be guided in his behavior not by the degree to which an experience maintains or enhances the organism, but by the likelihood of receiving maternal love. (Rogers 1959, p. 225)
>
> In order to hold the love of a parent, the child introjects as his own values and perceptions which he does not actually experience. He then denies to awareness the organismic experiencings that contradict these introjections. Thus, his self-concept contains false elements that are not based on what he is, in his experiencing. (Rogers 1966, p. 192)

Whenever there are conditions of worth in children's lives, they may be forced to deny their own evaluations of their experiences in favor of someone else's evaluation, and this causes an alienation between people's experiences and their self. This alienation creates a condition of incongruence which we will discuss in the next section.

Even when people turn to others for positive regard, they will not experience it consistently. For example, parents may not be consistent in what they reward and punish. In order to increase the likelihood of experiencing more consistent positive regard, people may affiliate themselves with a group in which the conditions of worth are relatively stable, for example, a fundamentalistic religion, the American Legion, the Elks, the Lions, the League of Women Voters, or a small group of predictable acquaintances. In so doing, people do not come any closer to their own organismic valuing process, they just have specified more clearly the conditions of worth which allow them to experience positive regard. For Rogers, each person's ultimate goal is to be true to his or her own feelings, not someone else's.

The only way not to interfere with children's actualizing tendencies is to give them *unconditional positive regard* which allows them to experience positive regard no matter what they do.

> If an individual should *experience* only *unconditional positive regard,* then no *conditions of worth* would develop, *self-regard* would be unconditional, the needs for *positive regard* and *self-regard* would never be at variance with *organismic evaluation,* and the individual would continue to be *psychologically adjusted,* and would be fully functioning. (Rogers 1959, p. 224)

This does not mean that Rogers believes that children should be allowed to do whatever they please. He believes that a rational, democratic approach to dealing with behavior problems is best. Since, according to Rogers, it is conditions of worth that are at the heart of all human adjustment problems, they should be avoided at all costs. Rogers suggested the following strategy for dealing with a misbehaving child:

> If the infant always felt prized, if his own feelings were always accepted even though some behaviors were inhibited, then no conditions of worth would develop. This could at least theoretically be achieved if the parental attitude was genuinely of this sort: "I can understand how satisfying it feels to you to hit your baby brother (or to defecate when and where you please or to destroy things) and I love you and am quite willing for you to have those feelings. But I am quite willing for me to have my feelings, too, and I feel very distressed when your brother is hurt, . . . and so I do not let you hit him. Both your feelings and my feelings are important, and each of us can freely have his own. (1959, p. 225)

In other words, Rogers felt that the following message should be conveyed to the child: "We love you deeply as you are but what you are doing is upsetting and therefore we would be happier if you would stop." The child should always be loved but some of his or her behaviors may not be.

THE INCONGRUENT PERSON

Incongruency exists when individuals are no longer using their organismic valuing process as a means of determining whether or not their experiences are in accordance with their actualizing tendency. If people do not use their own valuing process for evaluating their experiences, then they must be using someone's introjected values in doing so. That is, conditions of worth have replaced their organismic valuing process as the frame of reference for evaluating their experiences. This results in an alienation between the self and experience since, under these circumstances, what may truly be satisfying to the person may be denied awareness because it is not in accordance with the person's introjected conditions of worth. Rogers (1959, p. 226) summarizes the development of incongruence between the self and experience as follows:

1. Once conditions of worth develop, people respond to their experiences selectively. Those experiences that are in accordance with their conditions of worth are perceived and are symbolized accurately in awareness. Those experiences that are not in accordance with their conditions of worth are distorted or are denied awareness.
2. After conditions of worth develop, people must edit out of their awareness those experiences which are contrary to those conditions. Thus, the self is denied experiences which may be beneficial to it.
3. Selective perception creates an incongruence between the self and experience because certain experiences that may be conducive to positive growth may be distorted or denied. Once this incongruence between self and experience exists, people are vulnerable, and psychological maladjustment may result.

Rogers looks upon incongruence as the cause of all human adjustment problems. It follows then, that eliminating incongruence will solve those problems.

> This, as we see it, is the basic estrangement in man. He has not been true to himself, to his own natural organismic valuing of experience, but for the sake of preserving the positive regard of others has now come to falsify some of the values he experiences and to perceive them only in terms based upon their value to others. Yet this has not been a conscious choice, but a natural—and tragic—development in infancy. The path of development toward psychological maturity . . . is the undoing of this estrangement in man's functioning . . . the achievement of a self which is congruent with experience, and the restoration of unified organismic valuing process as the regulator of behavior. (Rogers 1959, pp. 226–227)

When an incongruency exists between self and experience the person is, by definition, maladjusted and is vulnerable to anxiety and threat and therefore is defensive.

Anxiety results when people "subceive" an experience as being incompatible with their self-structure and its introjected conditions of worth. In other words, anxiety is experienced when an event is encountered which *threatens* the existing self-structure. Note that Rogers says that the event is *subceived* rather than *perceived*. Subception is the detection of an experience before it enters full awareness. This way a potentially threatening event can be denied or distorted before it causes anxiety. According to Rogers, the process of *defense* consists of editing experiences, via the mechanisms of denial and distortion, to keep them in accordance with the self-structure. It is important to note that an experience, according to Rogers, is not denied symbolization, because it is "sinful" or "naughty" or contrary to cultural mores, as Freud would say. It is denied symbolization because it is contrary to the self-structure. For example, if a person's introjected conditions of worth include being a poor student, then receiving a good grade on a test would be threatening, and the experience would tend to be distorted or denied. The person may say, for example, that he or she was just lucky or that the teacher made a mistake.

According to Rogers, almost all individuals experience incongruency and therefore defend against certain experiences being symbolized in awareness. It is only when the incongruency is severe that adjustment problems occur.

We see that any given experience can have any one of three fates: (1) It can be symbolized accurately in awareness; (2) it can be distorted so that it no longer threatens the self-structure; or (3) it can be denied symbolization. If either 2 or 3 occurs, incongruency will result, and if the incongruency is pronounced enough, psychological maladjustment will result.

Next we turn to the procedures that Rogers recommends for eliminating or reducing incongruency.

PSYCHOTHERAPY

Like Freud's and Kelly's, Rogers's notions of personality came from his therapeutic practice. It has been therapy that has always been most important to Rogers; his personality theory developed only as he tried to become more effective as a therapist and as he tried to comprehend the principles that were operative during the therapeutic process.

Through the years, Rogers's description of the therapeutic process has changed. First, he referred to his approach to therapy as *nondirective*, which emphasized clients' ability to solve their own problems if they were given the proper atmosphere for doing so. Next, Rogers labeled his technique *client-centered therapy.* Now therapy was regarded as a joint venture deeply involving both client and therapist. Instead of simply providing an atmosphere in which clients could gradually see more clearly the nature of their problems, as was the case in the earlier stage, the therapist's job now was to attempt *actively* to understand the clients' phenomenological field or *internal frame of reference.* The next stage was called the *experiential stage.* It was during this stage in the evolution of Rogers's thinking that the therapist became as free as the client. Now the deep personal feelings of both therapist and client were equally important, and the therapeutic process was regarded as a struggle to put these feelings into words.

The current stage in Rogers's thinking has been labeled the *person-centered stage.* During this stage, Rogers's theory has been extended to many areas beyond the therapeutic process. A sample of the areas to which his theory has been applied includes education, marriage and the family, encounter groups, problems of minority groups, and international relationships. However, Rogers feels that it is not the greater applicability which is most important to this stage of development, rather it is the emphasis on the *total person* rather than looking at a person as merely a client or as a student.

> The shift in emphasis to person-centered points out more than the widespread applicability of the theory. It attempts to emphasize that it is as *person,* as *I am,* as *being,* and not just in terms of some role identity as client, student, teacher, or therapist that the individual is the unit of all interactions. The name change conveys the full complexity of each person; it indicates that each individual is more than the sum of the parts that make the person. (Holdstock & Rogers 1977, p. 129)

Throughout all the changes in Rogers's thinking through the years, however, certain basic components of his theory have remained unchanged. These are the importance of the actualizing tendency, the importance of the organismic valuing process as a frame of reference in living one's life, and the importance of unconditional positive regard in allowing a person to live a rich, full life.

Rogers (1959, p. 213) summarizes the conditions he feels are necessary for effective therapy.

1. The client and the therapist must be in psychological contact; that is, they both must make a difference in the phenomenological field of the other.
2. The client must be in a state of incongruence and therefore vulnerable or anxious.
3. The therapist must give the client unconditional positive regard.
4. The therapist must seek an empathic understanding of the client's internal frame of reference.
5. The client must perceive the fact the therapist is giving him or her

unconditional positive regard and is attempting to understand empathetically his or her internal frame of reference.

If the conditions necessary for effective therapy have been met, then, according to Rogers (1959, p. 216), the following changes in the client should be observed:

Results of effective

1. Clients will express their feelings about their life with increased freedom.
2. Clients become more accurate in their description of their experiences and of the events around them.
3. Clients will begin to detect the incongruity between their concept of self and certain experiences.
4. Clients will feel threatened as incongruity is experienced, but the unconditional positive regard of the therapist allows them to go on experiencing incongruent experiences without the necessity of distorting or denying them.
5. Clients eventually will be able to symbolize accurately, and thus be aware of, feelings which in the past had been denied or distorted.
6. Clients' concepts of self become reorganized and thus are able to include those experiences which had previously been denied awareness.
7. As therapy continues, clients' concepts of self become increasingly congruent with their experience; that is, they now include many experiences which were previously threatening. As clients feel less threatend by experience, they become less defensive.
8. As therapy continues, clients experience themselves more and more as the locus of evaluation in their life.
9. Therapy is successful if, in the end, clients' experiences are evaluated in terms of their organismic valuing process and not in terms of conditions of worth.
10. All of this is made possible by clients' perceptions of the therapist's unconditional positive regard toward them and the therapist's efforts to understand how they see things.

The process of therapy, as Rogers sees it, brings clients ever closer to using their own organismic valuing process in living their lives. Rogers describes what he hopes will happen to a client as the result of therapy: "He will *be,* in more unified fashion, what he organismically *is,* and this seems to be the essence of therapy" (1955, p. 269.) In psychotherapy the client "begins to drop the false fronts, or the masks, or the roles, with which he has faced life. He appears to be trying to discover something more basic, something more truly himself" (1961, p. 109).

Rogers reaffirms his belief in the innate goodness of people by the following description of what occurs as the result of psychotherapy:

> In therapy the individual has actually *become* a human organism, with all the richness which that implies. He is realistically able to control himself, and he is incorrigibly socialized in his desires. There is no

beast in man. There is only man in man, and this we have been able to release. (1953, p. 67)

Therapy, then, is designed to eliminate incongruity between experience and the self. When the person is living in accordance with his organismic valuing process, rather than conditions of worth, the defenses of denial and distortion are no longer needed and the individual is referred to as a *fully functioning person.*

THE FULLY FUNCTIONING PERSON

In many ways the fully functioning person is like a young infant because he or she is living in accordance with his or her own organismic valuing process rather than conditions of worth. It is this "being true to oneself" that describes the good life to Rogers. Happiness is not the tranquility that comes when all of one's biological needs are satisfied or when one attains a sought-after goal such as a house, a large amount of money, or a college degree. Happiness comes from the active participation in the actualizing tendency, which is a continuous process. It is important to note that Rogers stresses the *actualizing tendency* and not the *state* of self-actualization.

We have seen that in order to use one's organismic valuing process as a guide for living one's life, it is necessary to exist in an unconditional environment. Clearly, Rogers feels that unconditional positive regard is an essential ingredient of psychotherapy, but one need not undergo psychotherapy in order to experience unconditional positive regard. A few lucky individuals experience it in their home, in their marriage, or with their close friends. Such individuals are free to act in accordance with their own feelings and sensations. Such individuals will be fully functioning and, according to Rogers (1959, pp. 234–235), they will have at least the following characteristics:

1. They will be open to experience; that is, they will exhibit no defensiveness. Therefore, all their experiences will be accurately symbolized and thus available to awareness.
2. Their self-structures will be congruent with their experiences and will be capable of changing so as to assimilate new experiences.
3. They will see themselves as the locus of evaluation of their experiences. In other words, their organismic valuing process is used to evaluate their experiences instead of conditions of worth.
4. They will experience unconditional self-regard.
5. They will live in maximum harmony with others because of their willingness to give them unconditional positive regard.

Rogers believes that a "new person" is currently emerging who has many of these characteristics. Such a person is humanistically oriented rather than technologically oriented. It is because of the emergence of such an individual that Rogers is optimistic about the future.

> In all candor I must say that I believe that the humanistic view will in the long run take precedence. I believe that we are, as a people, beginning to refuse to allow technology to dominate our lives. Our culture, increasingly based on the conquest of nature and the control of man, is in decline. Emerging through the ruins is the new person, highly aware, self-directing, an explorer of inner, perhaps more than outer space, scornful of the conformity of institutions and the dogma of authority. He does not believe in being behaviorally shaped, or in shaping the behavior of others. He is most assuredly humanistic rather than technological. In my judgment he has a high probability of survival. (Rogers 1974, p. 119)

THE Q-SORT TECHNIQUE

One of the many interesting things about Rogers is that he stresses the importance of the completely subjective phenomenological field of the individual, on the one hand, and the importance of scientific methodology, on the other.

> . . . Therapy is the experience in which I can let myself go subjectively. Research is the experience in which I can stand off and try to view this rich subjective experience with objectivity, applying all the elegant methods of science to determine whether I have been deceiving myself. The conviction grows in me that we shall discover laws of personality and behavior which are as significant for human progress or human understanding as the law of gravity or the laws of thermodynamics. (Rogers 1961, p. 14)

It is not the emphasis on scientific method which differentiates Rogers's theory from theories like those of Skinner and Dollard and Miller. Rather, it is Rogers's insistence that research be directed to phenomenological experience rather than to overt behavior.

As a therapist with an inclination toward science, Rogers could not accept on faith the changes that were *supposed* to occur during therapy, or the changes that *appeared* to take place. Like any good scientist, Rogers had to find a way to *quantify* the extent to which a client changed as a function of therapy. The technique that Rogers found most useful was one developed by William Stephenson, a colleague of Rogers at the University of Chicago. The method was called the *Q-sort technique*.

The Q-sort technique can be administered in a number of different ways, but all of them use the same basic concepts and assumptions. First, it is assumed that the client can describe himself or herself accurately, and this is called the *real self*. Second, it is assumed that a person can describe those attributes that he or she would like to possess but currently does not; this is called the *ideal self*. Typically, when therapy begins, there is a great discrepancy between a person's real self (what he or she is) and the ideal self (what he or she would like to be).

The procedures used in administering the Q-sort are as follows:

1. The client is given one hundred cards, each containing a statement such as the following:

I have a warm emotional relationship with others
I put on a false front
I am intelligent
I have a feeling of hopelessness
I despise myself
I have a positive attitude toward myself
I often feel humiliated
I can usually make up my mind and stick to it
I express my emotions freely
I am afraid of sex

2. The client is asked to choose those statements which best describe the way he or she is. This creates the *self-sort*. To facilitate the statistical analysis of the results of the various Q-sorts, the client is asked to select cards in a manner that creates a normal distribution. This is done by asking the client to place the cards in nine piles. The piles are arranged to reflect those statements which are most like the client, on one extreme, to the statements least like the client, on the other. Statements placed in the middle pile are those for which the client cannot decide whether the trait listed is like him or her or not, that is, they are neutral. The number of piles and the number of cards the client is asked to place in each pile are shown in Figure 12–1.

3. Next, the client is asked to sort the cards again, only this time he or she is to sort them so that they describe the person he or she would most like to be. This creates the *ideal-sort*.

These procedures allow the therapist to examine a number of features of the therapeutic process. Most importantly, he can examine the relationship between the person's real self and his or her ideal self at the beginning, during, and at the end of therapy. The most common way of quantifying these changes is by using the correlation coefficient. When two sets of scores are perfectly correlated in a positive direction, the correlation coefficient is + 1.00. When there is a perfect negative or inverse relationship, the correlation coefficient is − 1.00. When there

	Least Like Me				*Undecided*				*Most Like Me*
Pile No.	0	1	2	3	4	5	6	7	8
No. of Cards (Total: 100)	1	4	11	21	26	21	11	4	1

Figure 12–1 A typical Q-sort arrangement.

is no relationship, the correlation coefficient is .00. The stronger the tendency is for two sets of measures to be positively related, the higher the positive correlation coefficients will be. For example, +.95, +.89, and +.75 all represent high positive correlations. The stronger the tendency is for two sets of measures to be inversely related, the higher the negative correlation coefficient will be. For example, −.97, −.85, and −.78 all represent high negative correlations.

Rogers (1954) reported the following correlation coefficients between a self-sort for a client before therapy and a self-sort for that client at the following points during the therapeutic process:

After seventh session	.50
After twenty-fifth session	.42
After therapy	.39
Twelve months after therapy	.30

The above correlation coefficients indicate that the self-concept of the client became increasingly *unlike* the self-concept the client had when she started therapy. Rogers also correlated the ideal-sort *after therapy* with the self-sort at various stages of therapy and obtained the following coefficients:

Before therapy	.36
After seventh session	.39
After twenty-fifth session	.41
After therapy	.67
Twelve months after therapy	.79

The above correlation coefficients clearly indicate that the self-concept became increasingly like the ideal self-concept as therapy progressed, with the tendency continuing even after therapy had terminated. In other words, the client was becoming more like the person she had described as ideal. It seems clear that in this case, based on the above data, therapy was accomplishing exactly what Rogers had hoped it would.

Several other researchers have used the Q-sort to evaluate the effectiveness of therapy. For example, Butler and Haigh (1954) found that for twenty-five clients the average correlation coefficient between the self-sort and the ideal-sort prior to therapy was −.01. Following therapy, the average correlation coefficient between the self-sort and the ideal-sort was +.31. This indicates a statistically significant change in the real self in the direction of ideal-self.

In addition to being the first therapist actually to measure the effectiveness (or ineffectiveness) of therapy, Rogers was also the first to record and film therapy sessions. He did this, with the client's permission, so that one would not need to rely on the therapist's memory (perhaps selective) of what happened in order to evaluate the session. In addition, recording and filming allowed the careful analysis of things like speech mannerisms and physical gestures as possible indicators of the extent to which the client was experiencing stress or anxiety.

It is somewhat paradoxical that the theorist who insists that the only way to know a person is to attempt to understand his private, unique, subjective world, is also the theorist who has done the most to stimulate the scientific evaluation of the therapeutic process.

THE ROGERS–SKINNER DEBATE

On September 4, 1955, members of the American Psychological Association held their breath as two of the world's most influential psychologists climbed on stage at the association's annual meeting in Chicago to engage in debate. What psychologist could ask for more? In one corner was Carl Rogers representing the phenomenological, subjective approach to understanding humans, who claimed the master motive behind human action is the actualizing tendency. Rogers also represented the belief in the innate goodness of the individual whose freedom comes from within. In the other corner was B. F. Skinner representing the behavioristic, objective approach to understanding humans. Skinner also represented the belief that what a person becomes is explained in terms of environmental reinforcement contingencies, not of a built-in actualizing tendency. The stage was set for a massive philosophical confrontation. What actually happened was less than a battle; in fact, there was about as much agreement between the two men as there was disagreement.

Both Rogers and Skinner agreed that humans always have attempted to understand, predict, and control human behavior. Both agreed that the behavioral sciences have made vast progress in developing the ability to predict and control human behavior. Both stated their commitment to the further development of the behavioral sciences.

The most important difference between Rogers and Skinner was over the idea of cultural engineering. Skinner felt that behavioral principles should be used in designing a culture that was more efficient in satisfying human needs. To Rogers that notion raised the following important questions: "Who will be controlled? Who will exercise control? What type of control will be exercised? Most important of all, toward what end or what purpose, or in the pursuit of what value, will control be exercised?" (1956b, p. 1060).

Rogers proposed a model of humans which emphasizes the actualizing tendency and creative powers. Rather than controlling human behavior from the outside, Rogers suggested that principles developed in the behavioral sciences be applied to the creation of conditions which would release and facilitate humans' inner strengths.

> It is quite clear that the point of view I am expressing is in sharp contrast to the usual conception of the relationship of the behavioral sciences to the control of human behavior. . . .
>
> 1) It is possible for us to choose to value man as a self-actualizing process of becoming; to value creativity, and the process by which knowledge becomes self-transcending.
> 2) We can proceed, by the methods of science, to discover the conditions which necessarily precede these processes and, through continuing experimentation, to discover better means of achieving these purposes.
> 3) It is possible for individuals or groups to set these conditions, with a minimum of power to control. According to present knowledge, the only authority necessary is the authority to establish certain qualities of interpersonal relationship.
> 4) Exposed to these conditions, present knowledge suggests that individuals become more self-responsible, making progress in self-actualization, become more flexible, and become more creatively adaptive.
> 5) Thus such an initial choice would inaugurate the beginnings of a social system or subsystem in which values, knowledge, adaptive skills, and even the concept of science would be continually changing and self-transcending. The emphasis would be upon man as a process of becoming. (Rogers 1956b, pp. 1063–1064)

Another major difference between Rogers and Skinner was over the issue of whether human behavior is free or determined. Skinner maintained that human behavior is determined by the reinforcement contingencies in the environment. Rogers, however, maintained that the existence of choice cannot be denied. He agreed that science must assume determinism, but this in no way should conflict with the existence of responsible choice on the individual level.

> Behavior, when it is examined scientifically, is surely best understood as determined by prior causation. This is one great fact of science. But responsible personal choice, which is the most essential element in being a person, which is the core experience in psychotherapy, which exists prior to any scientific endeavor, is an equally prominent fact in our lives. To deny the experience of responsible choice is, to me, as restricted a view as to deny the possibility of a behavioral science. That these two important elements of our experience appear to be in contradiction has perhaps the same significance as the contradiction between the wave theory and the corpuscular theory of light, both of which can be shown to be true, even though incompatible. We cannot profitably deny our subjective life, any more than we can deny the objective description of that life. (Rogers 1956b, p. 1064)
>
> My experience in therapy and in groups makes it impossible for me to deny the reality and significance of human choice. To me it is not an illusion that man is to some degree the architect of himself . . . for me the humanistic approach is the only possible one. It is for each person, however, to follow the pathway—behavioristic or humanistic—that he finds most congenial. (Rogers 1974, p. 119)

Skinner maintained that his major argument with Rogers was over method, since they both want to see approximately the same kind of person in the future.

> The whole thing is a question of method. That's the crux of my argument with Carl Rogers; I'd like people to be approximately as Rogers wants them to be. I want independent people, and by that I mean people who don't have to be told when to act or who don't do things just because they've been told they're the right things to do. . . . We agree on our goals; we each want people to be free of the control exercised by others—free of the education they have had, so that they profit by it but are not bound by it, and so on. (Evans 1968, pp. 67–68)

As already mentioned, Rogers agreed with Skinner that the behavioral sciences are, and should be, advancing, but to have such knowledge is not necessarily to know how to use it. It was Rogers's contention that, depending on how this information is used, we will experience great positive growth or destruction.

> So I conclude that knowledge in the science of psychology will in the near future be used and exploited as fully as knowledge in the physical sciences is used today. The challenge for educators is unreal only if we are looking a year or two ahead. From the long view I know of no problem holding greater potentiality of growth and of destruction than the question of how to live with the increasing power the behavioral sciences will place in our hands and the hands of our children. (Rogers 1956c, p. 322)

One change that Rogers would like to see in our society is the development of a better educational system. He would like to see a system that gives students the "freedom to learn," rather than having information imposed on them by an authority figure in a highly structured learning environment. Different kinds of learning environments create different kinds of individuals, so in choosing how to teach we are deciding what kind of person we find desirable.

> We know how to influence and mold behavior and personality in a great many significant ways. We also have available the choice of whether to set the conditions which develop a suggestible, submissive, unsure individual who can be easily influenced to behave in any way that "we" think wise, or the conditions which will develop an open, adaptive, independent, free-thinking, self-respecting individual. It is this latter person who will perhaps be able to use with intelligence and sensitivity to human values the enormous powers which the physical and behavioral sciences are putting at his disposal. The issue of what choice to make in this regard constitutes, I believe, the challenge of tomorrow both for education and for our whole culture. (Rogers 1956c, p. 322)

FREEDOM TO LEARN

Rogers has been highly critical of the American educational system and suspects that the worst will happen unless our educational system is changed radically. He feels strongly that education in our country is based on faulty assumptions about the learner. For example, it is widely believed that students must have information given to them and digested for them while they remain passive in the process. Instead of basing education on these, or other faulty assumptions, Rogers believes that education would be vastly improved if it took into consideration the following facts about the learning process (Rogers 1969, pp. 157–163):

1. Humans have a natural potential for learning.
2. Learning is best when the student sees relevance in what is being learned.
3. Some learning may require a change in the learner's self-structure, and such learning may be resisted.
4. Learning which necessitates a change in the learner's self-structure occurs more easily in a situation in which external threats are at a minimum.
5. When threats to the learner's self-concept are small, experience can be perceived in great detail, and learning will be optimal.
6. Much learning takes place by doing.
7. Learning proceeds best when the student participates responsibly in the learning process.
8. Self-initiated learning which involves the whole person, that is, both intellect and feelings, is the most long-lasting learning.
9. Independence and creativity are facilitated when self-criticism and self-evaluation are of primary importance, and evaluation by others is of secondary importance.
10. The most useful kind of learning is the learning to learn, which results in a continuing openness to experiences and a tolerance of change.

Rogers feels the term "teacher" is unfortunate, since it suggests a person who dispenses information to students. Instead, Rogers suggests the term "facilitator" to emphasize the fact that the person is there to create an atmosphere conducive to learning. A *facilitator of education* acts upon the principles of learning listed above and thereby treats each student as a unique person with feelings of his or her own, rather than as an object to be taught something.

We see that Rogers's approach to education is not unlike his approach to psychotherapy. In both cases, he insists that it must be recognized that each person is unique, each person has feelings, and each person has an actualizing tendency that functions best when experiencing unconditional positive regard and freedom. The reader will no doubt note a discrepancy between the educational conditions that Rogers considers optimal and those that generally now exist.

EVALUATION

No one, since Freud, has had more influence on psychotherapy than Rogers has had. His positive, humanistic approach to counseling and therapy has had widespread application to education, the church, and business. There seem to be three reasons for its popularity: (1) It is effective; (2) the approach does not require the long tedious training that psychoanalysis does; and (3) it is positive and optimistic about human nature.

Also among Rogers's accomplishments is the fact that he, more than any other therapist, exposed the psychotherapeutic process to scientific examination. Using techniques such as the Q-sort, Rogers and his colleagues were able to examine a client's tendency to congruency as a function of therapy. This was a major feat.

As with any theory, however, Rogers's theory has not gone uncriticized. Each of the following has been listed as a flaw in Rogers's theory: He ignores the unconscious mind after psychoanalytic theory has demonstrated its importance; he refuses to use diagnostic categories such as neurotic, psychotic, or manic depressive, in his therapeutic practice; his view of human nature is overly religious and simplistic in that it ignores the importance and forcefulness of sexual and aggressive drives; he cannot explain why some people seem to be "fully functioning," apparently without experiencing unconditional positive regard; he ignores dreams; he relies too heavily on self-reports which are known to be highly unreliable; and he ignores the fact that it is possible for a person to change verbally but not behaviorally, that is, a person's Q-sort may change but the behavior problem may not.

Even granting the validity of some of these criticisms, most would agree that Rogers has helped to illuminate a facet of human nature that was previously obscure. He has contributed to the development of a "third force" in psychology which is rapidly becoming more influential than psychology's other two dominant forces, behaviorism and psychoanalysis. This third force within psychology has been named humanistic psychology because of its emphasis on the goodness of human nature and its concern with the developing conditions which allow humans to reach their full potential. Clearly, these concerns run through every aspect of Rogers's writings.

SUMMARY

Rogers was born into a financially successful, religious family. He spent his adolescent years on a farm where he first became interested in science. A trip to the Far East while in college was very influential in that it introduced Rogers to several different cultures with their different religion and philosophies.

The main premise of Rogers's theory is that all individuals are born with an actualizing tendency which causes them to seek those experiences that will maintain and enhance their lives. This tendency drives individuals toward greater complexity, independence, creativity, and social responsibility. Ideally all individuals evaluate their experiences using the organismic valuing process which indicates whether or not experiences are in tune with the actualizing tendency. Those experiences that cause satisfaction are sought; those that are not are unsatisfying and avoided.

All people live in their own subjective reality called their phenomenological field. It is according to this field that people act, rather than with objective reality, that is, the physical environment. Experience was defined as all of those events happening around people of which they could be aware. However, only a small portion of those events is symbolized, thus entering awareness. Gradually, a portion of the phenomenological field becomes differentiated as the self. The self-concept emerges as a result of repeated experiences involving such terms as "I," "me," and "mine."

With the emergence of the self comes the need for positive regard, which is receiving such things as warmth, love, sympathy, and respect from the relevant people in one's life. The need for positive regard expands into the need for self-regard. Which means that now, in addition to children needing relevant individuals to respond to them positively, they also need to respond positively to themselves. Typically, adults do not give positive regard to children regardless of what they do. Rather, they respond selectively according to what children are doing. In other words, children experience positive regard after certain behaviors but not after other behaviors. This sets up conditions of worth which specify how children must behave or feel in order to be positively regarded. These conditions of worth are introjected into children's self-concept and thereby control their self-regard. Now, even in the absence of adults, children must act in accordance with those conditions of worth in order to feel good about themselves. The only way to escape imposing conditions of worth on children is to give them unconditional positive regard.

Conditions of worth create an incongruent person because they force the person to live in accordance with introjected values rather than his or her own organismic valuing process. The incongruent person is vulnerable since he or she must constantly watch out for experiences or feelings that violate his or her conditions of worth. Such experiences threaten the self-structure and therefore cause anxiety. When an experience is subceived as threatening, it is either distorted or denied symbolization. Thus, the incongruent person, because he or she is not living in accordance with his or her true feelings is more likely to experience anxiety and to perceive experiences selectively.

According to Rogers, the goal of psychotherapy is to make the incongruent person congruent again. His approach to therapy which was originally called nondirective, then client-centered, then experiential, and now person-centered, emphasizes unconditional positive regard which presumably will reduce threat, eliminate conditions of worth, and bring the person back in tune with his or her own organismic valuing process, thereby becoming a fully functioning person who is open to experience, not defensive, and is capable of living with others in maximum harmony.

Rogers has had two major interests in his professional life; one has been to encourage the phenomenological approach in psychology, and the other has been to study scientifically the changes that occur in a person as a function of therapy. His most frequently used method for accomplishing the latter goal has been the Q-sort technique. Using this technique, the client is asked to sort one hundred cards containing trait descriptions into nine piles. Into which pile a card goes depends on the extent to which the trait on the card is thought, by the client, to be like or unlike him or her. First, the client is asked to sort the cards in a way that describes how he or she is at the moment; this creates a self-sort. Next, the client is asked to sort the cards so that they describe what he or she thinks is an ideal person; this creates an ideal-sort. These two sorts allow the therapist to make many comparisons; for example, real self-concept before therapy versus real self-concept after therapy, or real self-concept after therapy versus ideal self-concept after therapy. Many other comparisons are possible. Research has indicated that Rogerian therapy is effective in changing a client's self-concept in a positive direction.

In 1955, Rogers debated with B. F. Skinner, the world's leading behaviorist. Both men agreed that the behavioral sciences had been growing exponentially, and both agreed that that was a good thing. However, the two parted company when they discussed how the principles generated by the behavioral sciences should be used. Skinner maintained they should be used as a guide in creating an environment that would encourage desirable behavior and satisfy human needs. His approach emphasized control of behavior from the outside. Rogers maintained that the principles should be used to avoid control from the outside; rather, they should be used to create an environment that gives humans as much freedom as possible so that their actualizing tendencies can function without interference. Skinner suggested that both he and Rogers wanted to see the same kind of people but differed in the methods they would employ in producing them.

Rogers feels that, generally speaking, our educational system is in poor shape. It treats the student as an object to be taught and the teacher as an authority figure who dispenses information in a highly structured environment. Rogers feels such an educational system is based on faulty assumptions about human nature. He feels that it would be more constructive if we assumed that each human wants to learn and that each human will learn if placed in a nonthreatening learning environment characterized by unconditional positive regard. Also, learning will occur much faster and will be retained better if the material to be learned has personal relevance to the learner. Rogers opposes the term "teacher" and feels that the term "facilitator of learning" is better.

Discussion Questions

1. Give as many examples as you can of how Rogers's early experiences may have influenced his later theorizing.
2. First define "the actualizing tendency" and then discuss its importance to Rogers's theory. Include in your answer a discussion of the "organismic valuing process."
3. Explain why Rogers's theory is labeled humanistic and existential. Could it also be labeled cognitive? Explain.
4. What did Rogers mean by the term "phenomenological field"? Include in your answer a discussion of the terms experience, awareness, and symbolization.
5. Explain how the self becomes differentiated within the phenomenological field.
6. First describe the need for positive regard, the need for self-regard, and conditions of worth, and then explain how the three are interrelated.
7. Under what circumstances is a person incongruent?
8. Discuss the terms vulnerability, threat, anxiety, defense, distortion, and denial as they apply to the incongruent person.
9. Discuss psychotherapy as Rogers views it. What is its goal and what procedures are followed to attain that goal?
10. Describe the fully functional person.
11. Describe the usual procedures in using the Q-sort technique. List a few of the more important comparisons that can be made using this technique.
12. Summarize the Rogers-Skinner debate.
13. Indicate why Rogers is so critical of the American educational system and what he proposes to improve the situation.
14. Describe what would characterize the self-actualized person if Freud's view of human nature were correct and Rogers's were wrong. In your opinion which view of human nature is correct? Defend your answer.
15. Assume there are two neighbors, one who felt loud music was in accordance with his actualizing tendency and the other who felt that silence was in accordance with his. Both wanted to give the other positive regard but did not want to violate their own organismic valuing process. In other words, one could not pretend to like loud music and the other could not pretend to like silence. Explain how, in your opinion, a Rogerian would solve the problem.
16. Rogers's theory is sometimes called the mirror image of Skinner's theory. Explain why you feel this is either true or not.
17. How does Rogers suggest that discipline problems with a child be handled?
18. Do you feel that you either experience or give unconditional positive regard? Without naming names, explain why you answered as you did.
19. Give an overall evaluation of Rogers's theory. Be as objective as you can.

20. How would Rogers explain that some humans engage in criminal activities? What, in your opinion, would Rogers recommend as the most effective way of dealing with criminals? In other words, what would most likely reduce the probability of them again committing a criminal act?

Glossary

Actualizing Tendency. The innate tendency in all humans to maintain and enhance themselves.

Anxiety. Results when a person subceives an experience as being incompatible with his or her self-structure and its introjected conditions of worth.

Awareness. Characterizes the events in one's experience that have been symbolized and therefore have entered consciousness.

Client-centered Therapy. Description of Rogers's second approach to therapy in which the therapist makes an active effort to understand the client's subjective reality.

Conditions of Worth. The conditions under which a person will experience positive regard.

Defense. The effort to change a threatening experience through distortion or denial.

Denial. The refusal to allow threatening experiences to enter awareness.

Distortion. The modification of a threatening experience so that it is no longer threatening.

Experience. All the events of which a person *could* be aware at any given moment.

Experiential Stage. The third stage in the evolution of Rogers's approach to therapy in which the feelings of the therapist became as important as the feelings of the client.

Facilitator of Education. A term that Rogers feels is better than teacher, since it suggests someone who is helpful and uncritical and who will provide the freedom that is necessary for learning to take place.

Fully Functioning Person. A person whose locus of evaluation is his or her own organismic valuing process rather than internalized conditions of worth.

Ideal Self. A client's description of how he or she would like to be.

Ideal-sort. The statements chosen by a client as best describing the person he or she would most like to be. Part of the Q-sort technique.

Incongruency Exists when a person is no longer using the organismic valuing process as a means of evaluating experiences. The person, under these conditions, is no longer acting honestly toward his or her own self-experiences.

Internal Frame of Reference. The subjective reality, or phenomenological field, according to which a person lives his or her life.

Introjected Values. The conditions of worth that are internalized and become the basis for one's self-regard.

Need for Positive Regard. The need to receive such things as warmth, sympathy, care, respect, and acceptance from the relevant people in one's life.

Need for Self-regard. The need a person develops to feel positively about himself or herself.

Nondirective Therapy. Description of Rogers's first approach to therapy in which the emphasis was on the client's ability to solve his or her own problem.

Openness to Experience. One of the chief characteristics of a fully functioning person.

Organismic Valuing Process. The frame of reference that allows an individual to know whether or not his or her experiences are in accordance with his or her actualizing tendency. Those experiences which maintain or enhance the person are in accordance with this process; other experiences are not.

Person-centered Stage. The current stage in Rogers's thinking in which the emphasis is on the understanding of the *total person* and not on understanding the person merely as a client.

Phenomenological Field. That portion of experience of which an individual is aware. It is this subjective reality, rather than physical reality, that directs a person's behavior.

Psychological Maladjustment. Results from severe incongruence.

Psychotherapy. To Rogers, an experience designed to help an incongruent person become congruent again.

Q-sort Technique. The method Rogers used to determine how a client's self-image changed as a function of therapy. See also Self-sort and Ideal-sort.

Real Self. A client's description of how he or she currently sees himself or herself.

Rogers-Skinner Debate. A debate held in 1955 between Rogers and Skinner over how best to utilize the principles discovered by the behavioral sciences.

Self. That portion of the phenomenological field which becomes differentiated because of experiences involving terms such as "I," "me" and "mine."

Self-sort. The statements chosen by a client as best describing how he or she sees himself or herself. Part of the Q-sort technique.

Subception. The detection of an experience before it enters full awareness.

Symbolization. The process by which an event enters the individual's awareness.

Teacher. A term that Rogers feels is unfortunate since it connotes an authoritarian figure who dispenses information to passive students.

Threat. Anything that is thought to be incompatible with one's self-structure.

Unconditional Positive Regard. The experience of positive regard without conditions of worth. In other words, positive regard is not contingent on certain acts or thoughts.

Vulnerability. The increased likelihood of experiencing anxiety because a person is incongruent.

chapter 13

abraham maslow

Abraham Harold Maslow was born on April 1, 1908 in Brooklyn, New York. His parents were Jewish immigrants from Russia. Being the only Jewish boy in his neighborhood, he was alone and unhappy much of the time. Like Rogers, Maslow took refuge in books. Maslow described his childhood as follows: "With my childhood, it's a wonder I'm not psychotic. I was a little Jewish boy in the non-Jewish neighborhood. It was a little like being the first Negro enrolled in the all-white school. I was isolated and unhappy. I grew up in libraries and among books, without friends" (1968, p. 37).

Due to parental pressure, Maslow began college by studying law, but after only two weeks he decided that his interests were elsewhere. He left home to study a variety of things, first at Cornell University, and, after two years, he transferred to the University of Wisconsin where he received his B.A. in 1930, his M.A. in 1931, and his Ph.D. in 1934.

It was shortly before he moved to the University of Wisconsin that he married his childhood sweetheart, Bertha Goodman, and they had two children. Maslow claimed that his life really did not start until he married and moved to Wisconsin. He was twenty years old at the time and Bertha was nineteen.

As strange as it now seems, Maslow decided to study psychology when he discovered the behaviorism of J. B. Watson. He described his excitement over his discovery:

> I had discovered J. B. Watson and I was sold on behaviorism. It was an explosion of excitement for me. . . . Bertha came to pick me up and I was dancing down Fifth Avenue with exuberance; I embarrassed her, but I was so excited about

> Watson's program. It was beautiful. I was confident that here was a real road to travel, solving one puzzle after another and changing the world. (1968, p. 37)

This infatuation with behaviorism ended when Maslow and his wife had their first child.

> Our first baby changed me as a psychologist. It made the behaviorism I had been so enthusiastic about look so foolish I could not stomach it anymore. That was the thunderclap that settled things. . . . I was stunned by the mystery and by the sense of not really being in control. I felt small and weak and feeble before all this. I'd say anyone who had a baby couldn't be a behaviorist. (Maslow 1968, p. 55)

While at the University of Wisconsin, Maslow worked under the supervision of Harry Harlow, the now famous experimental psychologist, who was just in the process of developing a primate laboratory to study the behavior of monkeys. Maslow's dissertation was on the establishment of dominance in a colony of monkeys. He noted that dominance seemed to result from a kind of "inner confidence" or "dominance-feeling" rather than through physical aggression.

After receiving his Ph.D. in 1934, Maslow returned to New York, first to Columbia University as a Carnegie Fellow and then to Brooklyn College where he stayed until 1951. During many of these years, besides being the plant manager of his family's barrel factory from 1947 to 1949,

Abraham H. Maslow. Courtesy Bertha G. Maslow.

he extended his research on dominance to the human level. He found that high-dominance individuals tended to be unconventional, less religious, and extroverted. Also, they tended *not* to be anxious, jealous, or neurotic.

Maslow found that high-dominance females were attracted to high-dominance males who were described as "highly masculine, self-confident, fairly aggressive, sure of what he wants and able to get it, generally superior in most things" (1942, p. 126). Low-dominance females, on the other hand, were attracted to males who were kind, friendly, gentle, faithful, and showed a love for children.

We see that in Maslow's early work, he was concerned with the healthy, exceptional, dominant specimen. It was but a minor step from these early interests to a concern for the most outstanding human beings. This step in the evolution of Maslow's concerns was stimulated by the tragedy of the Second World War. Maslow was in New York in the late 1930s and early 1940s when the best minds in Europe were arriving in this country in their effort to escape Nazi Germany. Among those individuals whom Maslow sought out and learned from were Alfred Adler, Max Wertheimer, Karen Horney, and Erich Fromm.

Also among those having a strong influence on Maslow at this time was the American anthropologist Ruth Benedict. In fact, it was Maslow's deep admiration for Max Wertheimer and Ruth Benedict that finally stimulated his interest in self-actualized individuals. Maslow described how his efforts to understand these two individuals evolved into what became his life's work:

> My investigations on self-actualization were not planned to be research and did not start out as research. They started out as the effort of a young intellectual to try to understand two of his teachers whom he loved, adored, and admired, and who were very, very wonderful people. It was a kind of high-IQ devotion. I could not be content simply to adore, but sought to understand why these two people were so different from the run-of-the-mill people in the world. These two people were Ruth Benedict . . . and Max Wertheimer. They were my teachers after I came with a Ph.D. from the West to New York City, and they were most remarkable human beings. My training in psychology equipped me not at all for understanding them. It was as if they were not quite people but something more than people. My own investigation began as a prescientific or nonscientific activity. I made descriptions and notes on Max Wertheimer, and I made notes on Ruth Benedict. When I tried to understand them, think about them, and write about them in my journal and my notes, I realized in one wonderful moment that their two patterns could be generalized. I was talking about a kind of person, not about two noncomparable individuals. There was wonderful excitement in that. I tried to see whether this pattern could be found elsewhere, and I did find it elsewhere, in one person after another.
>
> By ordinary standards of laboratory research, that is of rigorous and controlled research, this simply was not research at all. (1971, pp. 41–42)

By 1951, when Maslow went to Brandeis University, he was completely dedicated to the study of the most psychologically healthy individuals he could find. It was during these years that Maslow emerged as the leader of the humanistic movement in American psychology. He stayed at Brandeis until 1969, at which time he became resident fellow of the Laughlin Charitable Foundation in California. His job there was to explore the implications of humanistic psychology for a philosophy of politics, economics, and ethics. During this time, Maslow also became interested in sensitivity groups and was one of the founders of the Esalen Institute of California. Maslow died on June 8, 1970, of a heart attack.

Although it is clear that a number of personality theorists fall into the humanistic camp (for instance, Allport, Kelly, and Rogers), it is Maslow who emerged as spokesman for humanistic psychology. It was Maslow who took the development of humanistic psychology on as a cause, and he did so with a religious fervor.

THIRD FORCE PSYCHOLOGY

As noted above, Maslow felt that his training in psychology did not equip him to understand the positive qualities of people whom he considered remarkable. By viewing humans as victims of animal instincts and of the conflicts caused by culture, the psychoanalytic camp told only part of the story. Likewise the behaviorists who viewed humans as creatures whose behavior is molded by the environment, shed only limited light on the mysteries of human existence. In fact, Maslow believed that all of psychology had concentrated on the dark, negative, sick, and animalistic aspects of humans. By emphasizing the study of psychologically crippled individuals, we have created a "crippled" psychology. "It becomes more and more clear that the study of crippled, stunted, immature, and unhealthy specimens can yield only a cripple psychology and a cripple philosophy" (Maslow 1970, p. 180).

It was hoped, by Maslow, that humanistic psychology would attend to humans' positive aspects and thus provide information that could be used in formulating a complete theory of human motivation, a theory that would include both the positive and negative aspects of human nature. "Health is not simply the absence of disease or even the opposite of it. Any theory of motivation that is worthy of attention must deal with the highest capacities of the healthy and strong man as well as with the defensive maneuvers of crippled spirits" (Maslow 1970, p. 33).

Maslow felt that the typical *reductive-analytic* approach to science, which reduces human beings to a collection of habits or conflicts, overlooks the essence of human nature. The *holistic-analytic* approach which studies the person as a thinking, feeling totality is more likely to yield valid results. If, said Maslow, the standard scientific techniques cannot be applied to the study of the whole person, throw them out and develop techniques that can be used. It is the understanding of humans that is important, and if traditional scientific procedures do not aid in gaining that understanding, so much the worse for them. Maslow even suggested that some scientists are preoccupied with the reductive-analytic approach because it serves as a defense against knowing their own nature. In other words, some scientists in the name of "scientific rigor" cut themselves off from the poetic, romantic, tender, and spiritual aspects of themselves and other people. Maslow said that such scientists *desacralize* people by making them less marvelous, beautiful, and awesome than they really are.

> Briefly put, it appears to me that science and everything scientific can be and often is used as a tool in the service of a distorted, narrowed, humorless, de-eroticized, de-emotionalized, desacralized, and de-sanctified *Weltanschauung* [world view]. This desacralization can be used as a defense against being flooded by emotion, especially the emotions of humility, reverence, mystery, wonder and awe. (Maslow 1966, p. 139)

Maslow's goal, then, was to round out psychology by making it focus on a subject that it had ignored through the years, that is, the healthy, fully functioning human being. This effort was to become psychology's *third force,* with psychoanalysis and behaviorism constituting the other two forces.

In 1962, Maslow, along with several other humanistically oriented psychologists (including Carl Rogers), established the American Association of Humanistic Psychology, which operated in accordance with the following principles:

1. The primary study of psychology should be the experiencing person.
2. Choice, creativity, and self-realization, rather than mechanistic reductionism, are the concern of the humanistic psychologist.
3. Only personally and socially significant problems should be studied —significance, not objectivity, is the watchword.
4. The major concern of psychology should be the dignity and enhancement of people.

A humanistic science of psychology would consider these principles, and the result would be *less* external prediction and control of human behavior, but greater self-knowledge.

> If humanistic science may be said to have any goals beyond sheer fascination with the human mystery and enjoyment of it, these would be to release the person from external controls and to make him *less* predictable to the observer (to make him freer, more creative, more innerdetermined) even though perhaps more predictable to himself. (Maslow 1966, p. 40)

THE HIERARCHY OF NEEDS

The backbone of Maslow's position is his theory of motivation. He contends that humans have a number of needs which are *instinctoid*, that is, innate. Maslow chose the term instinctoid instead of instinctive to demonstrate the difference between our biological heritage and that of lower animals.

> This inner core, even though it is biologically based and "instinctoid," is weak in certain senses rather than strong. It is easily overcome, suppressed or repressed. It may even be killed off permanently. Humans no longer have instincts in the animal sense, powerful, unmistakable inner voices which tell them unequivocally what to do, when, where, how and with whom. All that we have left are instinct-remnants. And furthermore, these are weak, subtle and delicate, very easily drowned out by learning, by cultural expectations, by fear, by disapproval, etc. (Maslow 1968, p. 191)

Maslow also assumed that our needs are arranged in a hierarchy in terms of their potency. Although all needs are instinctoid, some are more powerful than others. The lower the need is in the hierarchy the more powerful it is, the higher the need is in the hierarchy the weaker it is and the more distinctly human it is. The lower or basic needs in the hierarchy are similar to those possessed by other "lower" animals, but no other animal, except humans, possesses the higher needs.

Maslow (1970, pp. 98–100) summarized the differences between the higher and lower needs:

1. The higher the need, the later it emerges in the evolutionary process.
2. Higher needs occur relatively late in an individual's development. Typically, some of the higher needs will not occur until middle age, if at all.
3. The higher needs are less directly related to survival than the lower needs are, thus there is less urgency associated with their satisfaction.
4. Even though the higher needs are not directly related to survival, their satisfaction is more desirable than the satisfaction of a lower need is. Satisfaction of the higher needs produces deep happiness, peace of mind, and a richer inner life.
5. The higher needs require more preconditions for their emergence and satisfaction than do the lower needs. They also require better environmental conditions for their functioning.

As one climbs the hierarchy of needs, one becomes less animallike and more human. A person progresses from one need level to the next by first satisfying the cluster of needs characteristic of one level in the hierarchy. This point will become clearer as we discuss the five levels of needs in the hierarchy.

1. Physiological Needs These are the needs directly related to survival, which we share with other animals. Included here are the needs for food, water, sex, elimination, and sleep. If one of the physiological needs is not met, it will completely dominate the individual's life.

> For our chronically and extremely hungry man, Utopia can be defined simply as a place where there is plenty of food. He tends to think that, if only he is guaranteed food for the rest of his life, he will be perfectly happy and will never want anything more. Life itself tends to be defined in terms of eating. Anything else will be defined as unimportant. Freedom, love, community feeling, respect, philosophy, may all be waved aside as fripperies that are useless, since they fail to fill the stomach. Such a man may fairly be said to live by bread alone. (Maslow 1970, p. 37)

Obviously such needs are extremely important and should be heeded. But, according to Maslow, psychology has overemphasized the importance of such needs to determining the behavior of humans in a modern society. For most humans, these needs are easily satisfied. The real question, to Maslow, was what happens *after* the physiological needs are satisfied. "It is quite true that man lives by bread alone—when there is no bread. But what happens to man's desires when there is bread and when his belly is chronically filled?" (Maslow 1970, p. 38). Maslow's answer was that the individual is then dominated by the next level or cluster of needs. It is important to note that Maslow did not feel that one set of needs had to be completely satisfied before the individual was released to deal with the next level. Rather, he felt that one set of needs had to be consistently and substantially satisfied. In other words, a person can be periodically hungry or thirsty and still be able to deal with higher needs, but the person's life cannot be *dominated* by hunger or thirst.

2. Safety Needs When the physiological needs are satisfactorily met, the safety needs emerge as dominant motives. Included here are the needs for structure, order, security, and predictability. The person operating at this level is very Kellian in that the primary goal is to reduce uncertainty in his or her life. These needs are most clearly seen operating in children who typically show great fear when confronted with novel (unpredictable) events. The satisfaction of the safety needs assures the individual that he or she is living in an environment that is free from danger.

3. Belongingness and Love Needs With the physiological and safety needs essentially satisfied, the individual now is driven by the need for affiliation. Humans need to love and to be loved. If this need is not met, the person will feel alone and empty. Maslow believed that the failure to satisfy needs at this level is a major problem in America today and explains why so many people are seeking psychotherapy and joining sensitivity or encounter groups. Maslow described the typical person joining such a group as:

> . . . motivated by this unsatisfied hunger for contact, for intimacy, for belongingness and by the need to overcome the widespread feelings of alienation, aloneness, strangeness, and loneliness, which have been worsened by our mobility, by the breakdown of traditional groupings, the scattering of families, the generation gap, the steady urbanization and disappearance of village face-to-faceness, and the resulting shallowness of American friendship. (1970, p. 44)

4. Esteem Needs If one has been fortunate enough to satisfy one's physiological, safety, and belongingness and love needs, the need for esteem will begin to dominate one's life. This group of needs requires both recognition from other people, which results in feelings of prestige, acceptance, status, and self-esteem, which results in feelings of adequacy, competence, and confidence. Both kinds of feelings usually result from engaging in activities considered to be socially useful. Lack of satisfaction of the esteem needs results in discouragement and feelings of inferiority.

5. Self-actualization If all the lower needs have been adequately satisfied, the person is in a position to become one of the rare individuals who is self-actualized.

> So far as motivational status is concerned, healthy people have sufficiently gratified their basic needs for safety, belongingness, love, respect and self-esteem so that they are motivated primarily by trends to self-actualization [defined as ongoing actualization of potentials, capacities and talents, as fulfillment of mission (or call, fate, destiny, or vocation), as a fuller knowledge of, and acceptance of, the person's own intrinsic nature, as an unceasing trend toward unity, integration or synergy within the person]. (Maslow 1968, p. 25)
>
> A musician must make music, an artist must paint, a poet must write if he is ultimately to be at peace with himself. What a man *can* be he *must* be. This need we may call self-actualization. (Maslow 1954, p. 91)

We will have much more to say about the characteristics of self-actualized people later in this chapter. Maslow's hierarchy of needs is diagrammed in Figure 13–1.

It should be noted that Maslow believed that as groups of needs were satisfied, one progressed up the hierarchy, but no matter how far one has progressed, if a lower need is frustrated for a considerable length of time, the person will regress to the level of the hierarchy corresponding to that need and will remain there until that need is satisfied. Thus, no matter what one has accomplished in life, if the need for food is suddenly unsatisfied, that need will once again dominate one's life.

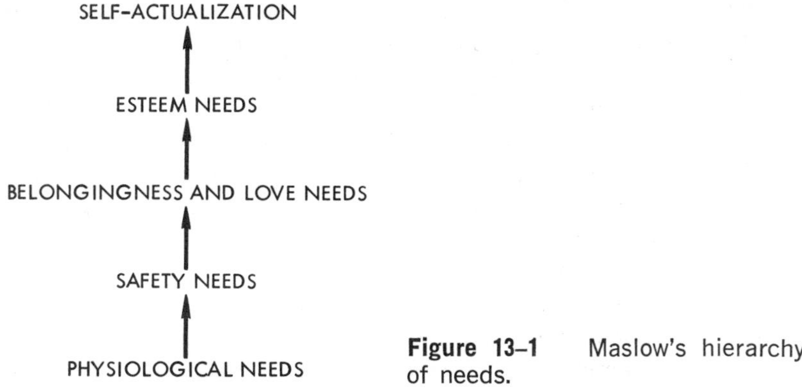

Figure 13–1 Maslow's hierarchy of needs.

The Desire to Know and Understand Maslow felt that the desire to know and understand was related to the satisfaction of the basic needs. In other words, knowing and understanding were thought to be tools used in solving problems and overcoming obstacles, thereby allowing the satisfaction of the basic needs.

> If we remember that the cognitive capacities (perceptual, intellectual, learning) are a set of adjustive tools, which have, among other functions, that of satisfaction of our basic needs, then it is clear that any danger to them, any deprivation or blocking of their free use, must also be indirectly threatening to the basic needs themselves. Such a statement is a partial solution of the general problems of curiosity, the search for knowledge, truth, and wisdom, and the everpersistent urge to solve the cosmic mysteries. Secrecy, censorship, dishonesty, blocking or communication threaten *all* the basic needs. (Maslow 1970, p. 47)

The Aesthetic Needs These are the needs for such things as order, symmetry, closure, structure, and for completion of the act, which are seen in some adults and almost universally in children. Maslow felt there is evidence for such needs in every culture as far back as the cavepeople.

Although the physiological safety, love and belongingness, and esteem needs and the need for self-actualization form a hierarchy, and the needs to know and understand are functionally related to their satisfaction, it is not clear how the aesthetic needs relate to the other needs. Two things are clear, however. First, Maslow believed that the aesthetic needs are instinctoid, and second, that they are given their fullest expression in self-actualizing individuals.

BEING MOTIVATION

What happens to an individual when all of the basic needs have been met to a satisfactory degree, and he or she enters the realm of self-actualization? Maslow's answer was that, in a sense, the person becomes qualitatively different from those who are still attempting to meet their basic needs. The self-actualizing person's life is governed by *being values* (B-values), which Maslow also labeled *metamotives.* "Self-actualizing people are not primarily motivated (i.e., by basic needs); they are primarily metamotivated (i.e., by metaneeds = B-values)" (Maslow 1971, p. 311). Because being motivation affects personal inner growth, it is also called *growth motivation.* Examples of B-values are beauty, truth, and justice.

The lives of nonactualizing people are governed by deficiency motives (D-motives); in other words, they are influenced by the absence of things that they need, like food, love, or esteem. The perception of a nonactualizing person is also influenced by his or her deficiencies and is therefore called *need-directed perception* (also called D-perception or D-cognition). "Need-directed perception is a highly focused searchlight darting here and there, seeking the objects which will satisfy needs, ignoring everything irrelevant to the need" (Jourard 1974, p. 68).

Being cognition (B-cognition), on the other hand, is qualitatively different from need-directed perception. "Being-cognition . . . refers to a more passive mode of perceiving. It involves letting oneself be reached, touched, or affected by what is there so that the perception is richer" (Jourard 1974, p. 68).

As an example of the difference between D-motivation and B-motivation, Maslow used the concept of love. He differentiated between D-love and B-love. D-love is motivated by the lack of fulfillment of the need for love and belongingness. A person in such a need-state craves love as a hungry person craves food. Such love is said to be selfish because, when obtained, it satisfies a personal deficiency. In contrast to D-love, Maslow (1968, pp. 42–43) lists some of the characteristics of B-love:

1. B-love is non-possessive.
2. B-love is insatiable, it can be enjoyed without end. It usually grows stronger rather than disappearing. D-love, however, can be satiated.
3. The B-love experience is often described as having the same effect as an aesthetic or mystic experience has.
4. B-love has a profound and widespread therapeutic effect.
5. B-love is a richer, higher, and more valuable experience than D-love is.
6. There is a minimum of anxiety and hostility in B-love.
7. B-lovers are more independent of each other, less jealous, less needful, more interested, and more autonomous than D-lovers are. Also, they are more eager to help the other toward self-actualization and are more proud of the other's triumphs.
8. B-love makes the truest, most penetrating perception of the other possible.
9. B-love, in a sense, creates the partner. It offers self-acceptance and a feeling of love-worthiness, both of which permit the partner to grow. Perhaps full human development cannot occur without the experience of B-love.

The list of fifteen B-values that Maslow felt dominated the lives of self-actualizing people is shown in Figure 13–2. The condition that results if the value is not given expression is shown under the column labeled "pathogenic deprivation."

The B-values are not arranged in a hierarchy and thus are given

B-Values and Specific Metapathologies

B-Values	*Pathogenic Deprivation*	*Specific Metapathologies*
1. Truth	Dishonesty	Disbelief; mistrust; cynicism; skepticism; suspicion.
2. Goodness	Evil	Utter selfishness. Hatred; repulsion; disgust. Reliance only upon self and for self. Nihilism. Cynicism.
3. Beauty	Ugliness	Vulgarity. Specific unhappiness, restlessness, loss of taste, tension, fatigue. Philistinism. Bleakness.
4. Unity; Wholeness	Chaos, Atomism, loss of connectedness.	Disintegration; "the world is falling apart." Arbitrariness.
4A. Dichotomy-Transcendence	Black and white dichotomies. Loss of gradations, of degree. Forced polarization. Forced choices.	Black-white thinking, either/or thinking. Seeing everything as a duel or a war, or a conflict. Low synergy. Simplistic view of life.
5. Aliveness; Process	Deadness. Mechanizing of life.	Deadness. Robotizing. Feeling oneself to be totally determined. Loss of emotion. Boredom (?); loss of zest in life. Experiential emptiness.
6. Uniqueness	Sameness; uniformity; interchangeability.	Loss of feeling of self and of individuality. Feeling oneself to be interchangeable, anonymous, not really needed.
7. Perfection	Imperfection; sloppiness; poor workmanship, shoddiness.	Discouragement (?); hopelessness; nothing to work for.
7A. Necessity	Accident; occasionalism; inconsistency.	Chaos; unpredictability. Loss of safety. Vigilance.

B-Values and Specific Metapathologies

B-Values	*Pathogenic Deprivation*	*Specific Metapathologies*
8. Comple-tion; Finality	Incompleteness	Feelings of incompleteness with perseveration. Hope-lessness. Cessation of striving and coping. No use trying.
9. Justice	Injustice	Insecurity; anger; cynicism; mistrust; lawlessness; jungle world-view; total selfishness.
9A. Order	Lawlessness. Chaos Breakdown of authority.	Insecurity. Wariness. Loss of safety, of predictability. Necessity for vigilance, alertness, tension, being on guard.
10. Simplicity	Confusing complexity. Disconnected-ness. Disintegra-tion.	Overcomplexity; confusion; bewilderment, conflict, loss of orientation.
11. Richness; Totality; Comprehen-siveness	Poverty. Coarctation.	Depression; uneasiness; loss of interest in world.
12. Effortless-ness	Effortfulness	Fatigue, strain, striving, clumsiness, awkwardness, gracelessness, stiffness.
13. Playfulness	Humorlessness	Grimness; depression; para-noid humorlessness; loss of zest in life. Cheerless-ness. Loss of ability to enjoy.
14. Self-sufficiency	Contingency; accident; occasionalism.	Dependence upon (?) the perceiver (?). It becomes his responsibility.
15. Meaning-fulness	Meaninglessness	Meaninglessness. Despair. Senselessness of life.

Figure 13–2 The figure shows the B-values, the condition that exists if a B-value is not satisfied (pathogenic deprivation), and the effect that not satisfying a B-value has in one's life (specific metapathologies). (From Maslow 1971, pp. 318–319.)

equal values, but Maslow felt that all the B-values influenced each other. In other words, to be truly self-actualized, a person would need to give expression to all the B-values.

It is my (uncertain) impression that any B-Value is fully and adequately defined by the total of the other B-Values. That is, truth, to be fully and completely defined, must be beautiful, good, perfect, just, simple, orderly, lawful, alive, comprehensive, unitary, dichotomy-transcending, effortless, and amusing. . . . It is as if all the B-Values have some kind of unity, with each single value being something like a facet of this whole. (Maslow 1971, p. 324)

Even though B-values are metaneeds, they are still needs and, as such, they must be satisfied if a person is to experience full psychological health. Failure to satisfy a metaneed (B-value) causes what Maslow called a *metapathology*. A description of the metapathologies caused by the failure to satisfy the various B-values is shown in Figure 13–2.

Moments of intense B-cognition cause feelings of ecstasy or rapture. Maslow called these mystic or oceanic feelings *peak experiences,* and we will have more to say about them in the next section as we consider the characteristics of self-actualizing people.

CHARACTERISTICS OF SELF-ACTUALIZING PEOPLE

As noted earlier, Maslow's interest in self-actualizing people began with his great admiration for Ruth Benedict and Max Wertheimer. After discovering that these two individuals had much in common, he began to search for others with the same qualities. He searched for individuals who seemed to be operating at full capacity, that is, doing the best that they were capable of doing. Such individuals were found among his students, his personal acquaintances and historical figures. The group that he finally isolated for more detailed study consisted of forty-eight persons: twelve "probable" actualizers, ten "partial" actualizers, and twenty-six "potential or possible" actualizers. Among the public and historical figures included in his study were the following:

Jane Addams
Ludwig van Beethoven
Albert Einstein
George Washington Carver
Eugene V. Debs
Thomas Eakins
Sigmund Freud
Albert Schweitzer
Baruch Spinoza
Johann Wolfgang von Goethe
William James
Thomas Jefferson
Abraham Lincoln
Fritz Kreisler
Eleanor Roosevelt
Franklin D. Roosevelt
Henry Thoreau
Walt Whitman

The reader may be interested to know that Maslow listed the following public or historical figures as probably self-actualized: Einstein, Eleanor Roosevelt, Jane Addams, William James, Schweitzer, Aldous Huxley, Spinoza, Lincoln, and Jefferson.

Maslow realized full well that his "research" on self-actualizers was not "scientific" and could be criticized on several levels, but he was so startled by what he found that he felt obliged to share his observations with others.

> [This] study . . . is unusual in various ways. It was not planned as an ordinary research; it was not a social venture but a private one, motivated by my own curiosity and pointed toward the solution of various personal moral, ethical, and scientific problems. I sought only to convince and to teach myself rather than to prove or to demonstrate to others.
>
> Quite unexpectedly, however, these studies have proved to be so enlightening to me, and so laden with exciting implications, that it seems fair that some sort of report should be made to others in spite of its methodological shortcomings. (Maslow 1970, p. 149)

Maslow compared his method of gathering data on his self-actualizing individuals to the gradual development of a global impression of a friend or acquaintance. In other words, the impression came from a large number of informal observations under a wide variety of circumstances, rather than from controlled observations under laboratory conditions. This, along with the fact that his conclusions were based on such a small sample, has stimulated much criticism of Maslow's work.

From his informal research, Maslow concluded that self-actualizing people exhibit the following characteristics:

1. They perceive reality accurately and fully Their perceptions are not colored by specific needs or defenses. In other words, their perception of the world is characterized by B-cognition rather than by D-cognition.

2. They demonstrate a greater acceptance of themselves, others, and/or nature in general Because self-actualizers have accepted both the good and the bad in everything, there is no need to deny the negative aspects of anyone or anything. They are therefore more tolerant of things as they are.

3. They exhibit spontaneity, simplicity, and naturalness Self-actualizers tend to be true to their feelings; what they really feel they tend to say and/or experience. They do not hide behind a mask and do not act in accordance with social roles. They are true to themselves.

4. They tend to be concerned with problems rather than with themselves Self-actualizers are typically committed to some task, cause, or mission toward which they can direct most of their energies. This is contrasted with the preoccupation with oneself often found in non-actualizers.

5. They have a quality of detachment and a need for privacy Because self-actualizing individuals depend on their own values and feelings to guide their lives, they do not need to be in constant contact with other people.

> It is often possible for them to remain above the battle, to remain unruffled, undisturbed by that which produces turmoil in others. They find it easy to be aloof, reserved, and also calm and serene; thus it becomes possible for them to take personal misfortunes without reacting violently as the ordinary person does. They seem to be able to retain their dignity even in undignified surroundings and situations. Perhaps this comes in part from their tendency to stick by their own interpretation of a situation rather than to rely upon what other people feel or think about the matter. This reserve may shade over into austerity and remoteness. (Maslow 1970, p. 160)

6. They are autonomous and therefore tend to be independent of their environment and culture Because self-actualizers are B-motivated rather than D-motivated, they are more dependent on their own inner world than on the outer world.

> Deficiency-motivated people *must* have other people available, since most of their main need gratifications (love, safety, respect, prestige, belongingness) can come only from other human beings. But growth-motivated [B-motivated] people may actually be *hampered* by others. The determinants of satisfaction and of the good life are for them now inner-individual and *not* social. They have become strong enough to be independent of the good opinion of other people, or even of their affection. The honors, the status, the rewards, the popularity, the prestige, and the love they can bestow must have become less important than self-development and inner growth. (Maslow 1970, p. 162)

7. They exhibit a continued freshness of appreciation Self-actualizers continue to experience the events in their lives with awe, wonder, and pleasure. Every baby or sunset is as beautiful and exciting as the first they had seen. Marriage is as exciting after forty years as it was in the beginning. Generally such individuals derive great inspiration and ecstasy from the basic experiences of everyday life.

8. They have periodic mystic or peak experiences Maslow believed that all humans had the potential for peak experiences, but only self-actualizers could have them full-blown, since such individuals were not threatened by them and therefore would not inhibit or defend them in any way. Generally, peak experiences are the embracing of B-values.

peak experience

> . . . Feelings of limitless horizons opening up to the vision, the feeling of being simultaneously more powerful and also more helpless than one ever was before, the feeling of great ecstasy and wonder and awe, the loss of placing in time and space with, finally, the conviction that something extremely important and valuable had happened, so that the subject is to some extent transformed and strengthened even in his daily life by such experiences. (Maslow 1970, p. 164)

Maslow concluded that some self-actualizers peak more often than others. The *nonpeakers* (low frequency of peak experiences) tend to be practical, effective people. *Peakers* (relatively high frequency of peak experiences) tend to be more poetic, aesthetically oriented, transcendent, and mystical.

9. They tend to identify with all of mankind The concerns that self-actualizers have for other people do not extend only to their friends and family but to all people in all cultures throughout the world. This feeling of brotherhood extends also to individuals who are aggressive, inconsiderate, or otherwise foolish. Self-actualizers have a genuine desire to help the human race.

10. They develop deep interpersonal relations with only a few individuals Self-actualizers tend to seek out other self-actualizers as their close friends. Such friendships are few in number but are deep and rich.

11. They tend to accept democratic values Self-actualizers do not respond to individuals on the basis of race, status, or religion. "They can be and are friendly with anyone of suitable character regardless of class, education, political belief, race, or color. As a matter of fact it often seems as if they are not even aware of these differences, which are for the average person so obvious and so important" (Maslow 1970, p. 167).

12. They have a strong ethical sense Although their notions of right and wrong are often unconventional, self-actualizers, nonetheless, almost always know the ethical implications of their own actions.

13. They have a well-developed, unhostile sense of humor Self-actualizers tend not to find humor in things that injure or degrade other humans. Rather, they are more likely to laugh at themselves or at human beings in general.

14. They are creative Maslow found this trait in all of the self-actualizers.

> This is a universal characteristic of all the people studied or observed. There is no exception. . . .
>
> This creativeness appears in some of our subjects not in the usual forms of writing books, composing music or producing artistic objects, but rather may be much more humble. It is as if this special type of creativeness, being an expression of healthy personality, is projected out upon the world or touches whatever activity the person is engaged in. In this sense there can be creative shoemakers or carpenters or clerks. (Maslow 1970, pp. 170–171)

This creativity comes from the fact that self-actualizers are more open to experience and more spontaneous in their feelings. It is directly related to B-motivation.

15. They resist enculturation Self-actualizers tend to be nonconformists since they are inner-directed people. If a cultural norm is contrary to their personal values, they simply will not adhere to it.

Negative Characteristics of Self-actualizing People Most people would list these fifteen characteristics as positive, but Maslow wanted to make it clear that self-actualizing individuals were far from perfect.

> Our subjects show many of the lesser human failings. They too are equipped with silly, wasteful, or thoughtless habits. They can be boring, stubborn, irritating. They are by no means free from a rather superficial vanity, pride, partiality to their own productions, family, friends, and children. Temper outbursts are not rare.
>
> Our subjects are occasionally capable of an extraordinary and unexpected ruthlessness. It must be remembered that they are very strong people. This makes it possible for them to display a surgical coldness when this is called for, beyond the power of the average man. The man who found that a long-trusted acquaintance was dishonest cut himself off from this friendship sharply and abruptly and without any observable pangs whatsoever. Another woman who was married to someone she did not love, when she decided on divorce, did it with a decisiveness that looked almost like ruthlessness. Some of them recover so quickly from the death of people close to them as to seem heartless. (Maslow 1970, p. 175)

Maslow concluded that as healthy, creative, democratic, and spontaneous as his self-actualizers were, *"there are no perfect human beings!"* (Maslow 1970, p. 176).

WHY SELF-ACTUALIZATION IS NOT UNIVERSAL

Why, if the tendency toward self-actualization is innate, is not every mature adult self-actualized instead of Maslow's estimate that only 1 percent of them are? Maslow felt that there were four basic explanations for this fact.

1. Since self-actualization is at the top of the hierarchy, it is the weakest of all the needs and therefore easily impeded.

"This inner nature is not strong and overpowering and unmistakable like the instincts of animals. It is weak and delicate and subtle and easily overcome by habit, cultural pressure, and wrong attitudes toward it" (Maslow 1968, p. 4).

2. Most people fear the kind of knowledge about themselves that self-actualization requires. Such knowledge requires giving up the known and entering a state of uncertainty.

> More than any other kind of knowledge we fear knowledge of ourselves, knowledge that might transform our self-esteem and our self-image. . . . While human beings love knowledge and seek it—they are curious—they also fear it. The closer to the personal it is, the more they fear it. (Maslow 1966, p. 16)

Maslow referred to this fear and doubt of one's own abilities and potentialities as the *Jonah complex*. To become self-actualized requires enough courage to sacrifice safety for personal growth.

3. The cultural environment can stifle one's tendency toward actualization by imposing certain norms on segments of the population. For example, defining "manly" in the way that our culture does tends to prevent the male child from developing such traits as sympathy, kindness, and tenderness, all of which characterize the self-actualized individual.
4. As indicated in item 2, in order to become self-actualized one must choose growth rather than safety. Maslow observed that children from warm, secure, friendly homes are more likely to choose experiences that lead to personal growth than are children from insecure homes. Thus, childhood conditions influence the probability of a person becoming self-actualized. Maslow characterized what he felt was the optimal set of circumstances for a child as *freedom within limits*. He felt that too much permissiveness was almost as harmful as too much control. What is needed, he felt, was a proper mixture of the two.

Conditions Necessary for Self-actualization In addition to satisfying the physiological needs, the safety needs, and the love and belongingness needs, an environment must have several other characteristics before self-actualization can occur. These characteristics, according to Maslow, include freedom of speech, freedom to do what one wants to do as long as it harms no one else, freedom of inquiry, freedom to defend oneself, order, justice, fairness, and honesty. Later Maslow added "challenge" (proper stimulation) as a characteristic of an environment conducive to self-actualization.

With these environmental prerequisites in mind, along with the four reasons why more people are not self-actualized cited earlier, it becomes easier to understand why only about 1 percent of the population becomes self-actualized. Most of the rest of us live out our days somewhere between the love and belongingness and self-esteem needs.

EUPSYCHIA

Because Maslow believed that all human needs, including the need for self-actualization, were instinctoid, it must be the environment (society, culture) that determines how far up the hierarchy of needs one will be able to climb. Maslow rejected the Freudian notion that humans and society had to be engaged in constant conflict. Rather, he believed that at best society could be designed so as to maximize the probability of self-actualization. Because Maslow believed that man's needs are good rather than bad (as the Freudians believed), their satisfaction should be encouraged rather than discouraged.

Maslow speculated on the kind of utopia that would be developed if one thousand healthy families moved to a deserted island where they could determine their own destiny. He called this potential utopia *Eupsychia* (pronounced Yew-sígh-key-a), which can be broken down as follows: Eu = good, psych = mind, and ia = country. In Eupsychia there would be complete *synergy,* a concept he borrowed from Ruth Benedict, syn = together and ergy = working. Thus, in Maslow's utopia there would be complete cooperation or working together.

What other features would characterize Eupsychia?

> What kind of education would they choose? Economic system? Sexuality? Religion?
>
> I am very uncertain of some things—economics in particular. But of other things I am *very* sure. One of them is that this would almost surely be a (philosophically) anarchistic group, a Taoistic [nature oriented] but loving culture, in which people (young people too) would have much more free choice than we are used to, and in which basic needs and metaneeds would be respected much more than they are in our society. People would not bother each other so much as we do, would be much less prone to press opinions or religions or philosophies or tastes in clothes or food or art or women on their neighbors. In a word, the inhabitants of Eupsychia would tend to be more Taoistic, nonintrusive, and basic need-gratifying (whenever possible), would frustrate only under certain conditions that I have not attempted to describe, would be more honest with each other than we are, and would permit people to make free choices wherever possible. They would be far less controlling, violent, contemptuous, or overbearing than we are. Under such conditions, the deepest layers of human nature could show themselves with greater ease. (Maslow 1970, pp. 277–278)

In 1962, Maslow went to Non-linear Systems, Inc. as a Visiting Fellow. His experiences at this voltmeter factory resulted in his book *Eupsychian Management* (1965). The basic message in the book was that if industrial management were more aware of human needs and what it takes to satisfy those needs, both the worker and the industry would be far healthier. "Eupsychian . . . conditions of work are often good not only for personal fulfillment, but also for the health and prosperity of the organization, as well as for the quantity and quality of the products or services turned out by the organization" (Maslow 1971, p. 237). Eupsychian management, then, is an attempt to create a working situation that is conducive to the satisfaction of human needs as Maslow describes them. It should be clear that Maslow believed that not only would industry run better if it became more humanistic, but so would our entire country.

ASHRAMS—PLACES FOR PERSONAL GROWTH

For hundreds of years India has had *ashrams* or retreats where individuals could escape the anxieties associated with everyday life. The pace of living in the ashram was radically slowed down so that individuals could meditate and reflect on the meaning of their lives. Each ashram was led by a *guru* (spiritual teacher) who acted as a guide for those seeking inner peace. People stayed in the ashram for a day, a week, months, or, in some cases, even years. Others, however, would use the ashram as a church is used in our country; that is, they would visit for a few hours, and then return to their regular, routine lives.

In 1963, Michael Murphy developed the first equivalent to the Indian ashram in this country, in Big Sur, California. The philosophy of the ashram was directly in accordance with Maslow's view that psychology should concentrate more on *healthy* individuals than on sick ones. Ashrams were places where nonneurotic individuals could go and search themselves and their own values and thus could become even more effective in their daily lives. Whereas psychotherapy is available to the emotionally disturbed, ashrams are places where the already healthy can become healthier.

It is not surprising, then, that Maslow was the first to conduct seminars at this newly founded ashram, which was named the Esalen Institute after the Esalen Indians who once inhabited the Big Sur region.

> Since Esalen Institute first came into being, the idea of a center devoted to personal growth has become widespread, and there are several hundred in existence around the Western world. Although growth centers are not identical with Indian ashrams, there is a similarity in that there is the commitment to self-exploration, to reinvention of one's life, and to radical honesty in one's relationships with others. The people who operate Esalen Institute bake the bread, cook the meals, conduct encounter groups and offer Rolfing sessions and massage. They live a kind of communal life and serve as exemplars of ways to be "in one's body," and ways to be with one another, which are believed to be most life-giving and conducive to personal growth. (Jourard 1974, p. 342)

The Western version of the Indian ashram has come to be called a *growth center.*

EVALUATION

There is no doubt that Maslow's contention that psychology had traditionally focused on the darker side of human nature was valid. Of course, there have been theorists whose works have been exceptions to this, for example, Adler, Allport, Rogers, and Kelly. In general, however, psychology has been preoccupied with either the importance of the physiological drives to determining behavior or the conditions under which neuroses and psychoses develop. Maslow did about as much as one person could have done to extend the domain of psychology to the study of healthy humans. His efforts, along with the efforts of other theorists such as Rogers, have indeed created a viable third force in psychology.

As with any theory, however, Maslow's has not gone uncriticized. He has been accused of being unscientific; that is, of using uncontrolled and unreliable research techniques, of basing his conclusions about self-actualizing people on a very small sample of people, of selecting subjects for his research in accordance with his own intuitive criteria as to what constitutes a self-actualizing person, and of using ambiguous terms such as metaneed and metapathology.

Maslow also has been accused of mixing ethical considerations with his logic. This mixture has led some critics to view Maslow as a social reformer instead of as an objective researcher. For example, Corsini commented: "It is evident that Maslow was a 'do-gooder' of the highest type, and he may essentially have been a religious reformer rather than an objective scientist . . . " (1977, p. 408).

Another criticism of Maslow's theory comes from the observation that some individuals seem to become highly productive and creative even though their basic needs do not seem to have been satisfied (e.g. see Maddi, 1972).

In spite of these criticisms, Maslow's theory is being found useful by large numbers of individuals in psychology, in education, and in the business world. Before Maslow died he said that his theory seemed to fit better in real life than it did in the laboratory. We agree, and of the two places, real life is the more useful place for it to fit.

It also is fitting that we conclude our coverage of personality theorists with Maslow who, in many ways, took a position opposite to Freud, the first personality theorist we considered. With Freud we pondered a view of humans as animals in conflict with a society which imposes restrictions on their animal impulses. With Maslow we pondered a view of humans as basically good, nonaggressive seekers of such things as truth, beauty, and perfection. For Freud, given complete freedom, humans would become sexually promiscuous and aggressive. For Maslow, given complete freedom, humans would create Eupsychia, a loving, harmonious, and nonaggressive society. The views of human nature held by Freud and Maslow are about as different as two views of human nature can be.

SUMMARY

Maslow's early research on dominance in monkeys led to research on dominance in humans and then finally to an interest in "the good specimen" or actualizing humans. His interest in the latter was stimulated by his efforts to understand two individuals whom he admired very much, Ruth Benedict and Max Wertheimer. He was distressed that his training in psychology had not equipped him to understand truly healthy, well-adjusted individuals. He concluded that the reason for this was that psychology had been preoccupied with either the study of lower animals, children, or maladjusted adults. Psychology also had borrowed the reductive-analytic approach from the natural sciences. This approach attempts to understand things by breaking them down in small elements. When applied to the study of humans, this technique is desacralizing since it denies or distorts many positive human qualities. Instead, Maslow suggested a holistic-analytic approach that studies the total person. Such an approach is humanistic because it emphasizes the positive qualities of humans. Humanistic psychology is also called "third force" psychology, since it is seen as an alternative to the psychoanalytic and behavioristic models of man. Maslow had no argument with the psychoanalysts or the behaviorists; he just felt that they did not tell the whole story. He felt that humans had a number of positive attributes which had been ignored by psychology.

Human nature, according to Maslow, consists of a number of instinctoidal (innate but weak) needs that are arranged in a hierarchy according to their potency. The nature of these needs is such that as one group of needs is satisfied, the next group in the hierarchy comes to dominate a person's life until they too are satisfied, at which time the next group becomes dominant, and so on. The needs from the most basic to the least basic are physiological needs, safety needs, belongingness and love needs, esteem needs, and the need for self-actualization.

Self-actualizing individuals are no longer motivated by deficiencies (D-motivation); they are motivated by being values (B-motivation). B-values include such things as truth, goodness, beauty, justice, and perfection. B-values are also called metamotives. D-motivated individuals search for specific need-related events in their environment; this is called D-perception (or D-cognition) because it is need motivated. B-motivated people perceive their environments more fully since they are not looking for anything in particular; this is called B-perception (or B-cognition). Failure to give expression to a B-value results in a metapathology.

Maslow attempted to correct the fact that psychology had concentrated too much on unhealthy humans by studying the characteristics of the healthiest individuals he could find. Some of these individuals were his friends, some were famous living individuals, and some were famous historical figures. He found that self-actualizing individuals tended to have in common the following characteristics: They perceive reality accurately; show great acceptance of themselves, others, and nature; are spontaneous; are problem-oriented rather than self-oriented; tend to be detached and private; are autonomous; exhibit continued freshness of appreciation; have peak experiences; identify with all of humanity;

have only a few deep friendships; accept democratic values; have a strong ethical sense; have a well-developed sense of humor which is not hostile; are creative; and tend to be nonconformists. In addition to these positive qualities, self-actualizers also show some negative qualities such as vanity, pride, partiality, silliness, temper outbursts, and a coldness toward death.

Although the tendency toward actualization was thought by Maslow to be innate, it is not universally experienced because the need is so weak that it is easily impeded, because it takes considerable courage to be self-actualized (this fear of self-development is called the Jonah complex), cultural norms are often incompatible with the self-actualizing process, and early childhood experiences must instill enough security in the child so that he or she is willing to grow rather than constantly to seek safety, but such childhood experiences are uncommon.

Maslow described a utopian society that he speculated a group of healthy people might design. He called this society Eupsychia. He felt that there would be complete synergy, or working together, in Eupsychia because all human needs would be recognized, respected, and gratified. When an industry attempts to consider human needs, as Maslow defines them, the process is known as Eupsychian management.

In his later years, Maslow contributed to the development of an ashram in California which came to be called the Esalen Institute. An ashram is a place where already healthy individuals can fully explore themselves and thus revitalize their lives. There are now several hundred of these centers for personal growth in the Western world.

Discussion Questions

1. Describe the evolution of Maslow's research from monkeys to self-actualizing humans.
2. What is "third force" psychology? Why did Maslow feel that this "third force" was needed? Include in your answer the difference between the reductive-analytic approach to science and the holistic-analytic approach. Also discuss the process of desacralization.
3. Discuss the hierarchy of needs. Which needs are included and how are they related to one another?
4. At what level in the hierarchy of needs do you feel you are currently operating? Justify your answer.
5. Differentiate between deficiency motivation (D-motivation) and being motivation (B-motivation).
6. What causes a metapathology? Give an example.
7. List the positive characteristics of self-actualizing individuals.
8. List the negative characteristics of self-actualizing individuals.
9. Discuss peak experiences. What are they, who has them, and what consequence do they have?

10. If the tendency toward self-actualization is innate, why is it that self-actualization is not universal?
11. Discuss Eupsychia and synergy.
12. Discuss Eupsychian management.
13. Discuss ashrams and Maslow's involvement in them.
14. Summarize the criticisms of Maslow's theory.
15. Compare Maslow's view of human nature with Freud's.
16. Give a few examples of how Maslow's theory might be utilized to improve our public school system.
17. Explain how Maslow's theory might be utilized as a guide to child rearing.
18. Why did Maslow refer to human needs as instinctoid?

Glossary

Acceptance of Democratic Values. Characterizes the self-actualizing person.

Acceptance of Self, Others, and Nature. Characterizes the self-actualizing person.

Accurate and Full Perception of Reality. Characterizes the self-actualizing person.

Aesthetic Needs. The innate need for such things as symmetry, closure, and order seen most clearly in children and in self-actualizing adults.

Ashrams. Retreats in India where ordinary citizens can go for various periods of time and search themselves and the meaning of their lives.

B-cognition. See Being Cognition.

Being Cognition. (also called B-perception or B-cognition). Thinking or perceiving that is governed by B-values rather than by D-motives. Such cognition is richer and fuller than D-cognition.

Being Motivation. Motivation that is governed by the pursuit of B-values instead of by the satisfaction of basic deficiencies. See also B-values. Also called growth motivation.

Being Values (B-values). Those higher aspects of life pursued by self-actualizing individuals. Included are such values as truth, goodness, beauty, justice, and perfection. Also called metamotives.

Belongingness and Love Needs. The third cluster of needs in the hierarchy of needs. Included are the needs for affiliation with others and for the feeling of being loved.

B-perception. See Being Cognition.

Continued Freshness of Appreciation. Characterizes the self-actualizing person.

Creativity. Characterizes the self-actualizing person.

D-cognition. See need-directed perception.

Deep Friendships with Only a Few Individuals. Characterizes the self-actualizing person.

Deficiency Motivation (D-motivation). Motivation that is governed by the basic needs. Characterizes the lives of individuals who are not self-actualizing.

Deficiency Motive (D-motive). Any need or deficiency that exists in the hierarchy of needs prior to the level of self-actualization.

Desacralization. Any process that distorts human nature and makes it less marvelous and dignified than it is.

Desire to Know and Understand. Innate curiosity that Maslow felt was functionally related to the ability to satisfy the basic needs.

Detachment and a Need for Privacy. Characterizes the self-actualizing person.

D-perception. See need-directed perception.

Esalen Institute. An institute in California modeled after the Indian ashram in that it is a place where nonneurotic, healthy individuals can go and further develop their inner resources.

Esteem Needs. The fourth cluster of needs in the hierarchy of needs. Included are the needs for status, prestige, competence, and confidence.

Eupsychia. Maslow's name for the utopia that he felt a community of healthy adults could create.

Eupsychian Management. Industrial or societal management which attempts to consider the basic human needs, as Maslow sees them.

Freedom within Limits. Maslow's description of what he considered the optimal psychological atmosphere for a child to experience.

Growth Center. The Western equivalent of the Indian ashram. A place where nonneurotic, healthy individuals can go to expand their potentialities. See also Esalen Institute.

Growth Motivation. See Being Motivation.

Guru. The spiritual leader of an ashram.

Hierarchy of Needs. The arrangement of the needs from lowest to highest in terms of their potency.

Holistic-Analytic Approach to Science. The strategy of studying an object of interest as a totality rather than attempting to reduce it into its component parts.

Humanistic Psychology. An approach to psychology that emphasizes the experiencing person, creativity, the study of socially and personally significant problems, and the dignity and enhancement of people.

Identification with All of Humanity. Characterizes the self-actualizing person.

Independence from the Environment and Culture. Characterizes the self-actualizing person.

Instinctoid. The term Maslow used to describe the nature of the human needs. An instinctoidal need is innate but weak and easily modified by environmental conditions.

Jonah Complex. The fear and doubt of one's own abilities and potentialities which results in a resistance to personal growth.

Metamotives. See B-values.

Metapathology. A psychological disorder that results when a being motive is not allowed proper expression.

Need-directed Perception. (also called D-perception or D-cognition). Perception that is motivated by a search for objects or events that will fulfill a basic need, for example, a hungry person looks for food.

Nonconformity. Characterizes the self-actualizing person.

Peak Experience. A mystical, oceanic experience that is accompanied by a feeling of ecstasy or rapture. Such experiences were thought by Maslow to reach their full magnitude as B-values are fully embraced.

Physiological Needs. The most basic cluster of needs in the hierarchy of needs. Included are the needs for water, food, oxygen, sleep, elimination, and sex.

Problem-oriented Rather than Self-oriented. Characterizes the self-actualizing person.

Reductive-Analytic Approach to Science. The strategy of reducing an object of interest into its component parts in order to study and understand it.

Safety Needs. The second cluster of needs in the hierarchy of needs. Included are the needs for order, security, and predictability.

Self-actualization. The highest level in the hierarchy of needs, which can be reached only if the preceding need levels have been adequately satisfied. The self-actualizing individual operates at full capacity and is B-motivated rather than D-motivated.

Sense of Humor Which Is Unhostile. Characterizes the self-actualizing person.

Spontaneity, Simplicity, and Naturalness. Characterizes the self-actualizing person.

Strong Ethical Sense. Characterizes the self-actualizing person.

Synergy. Working together. The individuals in a community characterized by synergy would work in harmony and would not be in conflict with their society.

Third Force Psychology. Humanistic psychology which was seen by Maslow and others as an alternative to psychoanalysis and behaviorism.

PART SEVEN

CONCLUSION

chapter 14

a final word

After our review of the major theories of personality in the preceding chapters, five conclusions can be drawn:

1. Much about personality remains unknown.
2. The best available explanation of personality comes from a composite of all the theories rather than from any single theory or paradigm.
3. Childhood experience is extremely important to the formation of adult personality characteristics.
4. If a psychological problem arises, it may be necessary to "shop around" for a therapist whose assumptions and techniques match both the problem and the person having the problem.
5. Each individual must judge for himself or herself what information from each theory is useful and what is not useful.

MUCH ABOUT PERSONALITY REMAINS UNKNOWN

One thing is certain, that the theories covered in this text, either individually or collectively, do not adequately account for personality. It is not that the theories are incorrect, rather that they are not correct enough. Personality remains much more complicated than the theories designed to account for it. In other words, although each theory illuminates part of what we call personality, much remains in darkness. Existing theories need to be extended, and new theories need to be developed before we will be able to say that we have a thorough understanding of personality. This conclusion remains valid even when it is realized that several important theories of personality were not mentioned in this text. For example, the theories of Sullivan,

Murray, Murphy, Levin, Fromm, and Sheldon were not covered, but even if they had been, the explanation of personality would still be incomplete.

To test how much you have learned about personality and how much remains unknown, just wander through one day attempting to account for your own actions and the actions of others by utilizing what you have learned in this text. Perhaps many events will be clear to you now. No doubt, you will encounter examples of repression (evidenced by such things as slips of the tongue, dreams, and humor) and other ego defense mechanisms such as projection, identification, and reaction formation. You will encounter various conflicts and may find symbols in art, music, and religion that may reflect our evolutionary experiences as a species. You will see parents instilling either basic anxiety or basic trust in their children. You will find evidence for the existence of traits and will see numerous examples in which reinforcement contingencies strongly influence behavior. You will see that much of life is a matter of interpretation or attitude. You will see different individuals struggling to satisfy different levels of needs, and perhaps you will see a person who appears to be self-actualizing.

At the end of the day many behaviors that were previously a mystery will have been explained, at least in part, but many mysteries will remain. Their solution will need the work and imagination of future personality theorists.

THE BEST EXPLANATION OF PERSONALITY COMES FROM A COMPOSITE OF ALL THE MAJOR THEORIES

The position we have taken throughout this text is that all the major personality theories add to our understanding of personality, and therefore it is not necessary to search for *the* correct theory or even the *most* correct theory. As mentioned in chapter 1, just as a carpenter would not attempt to build a house with only one tool, a person cannot hope to understand personality with only one theory. It is nonsensical to say that a screwdriver is any more correct or useful than a hammer. It is just that different tools have different functions, and it is the same way with personality theories. In other words, which personality theory is "best" depends on which aspect of personality one is attempting to explain. This position is *eclecticism*, which means taking the best from a number of different points of view. The eclectic is not bound to any single theory but chooses that theory which is most effective in dealing with a particular problem.

Is it not possible that society forces individuals to repress sexual and aggressive urges and that such repressed urges manifest themselves indirectly in an individual's life, as Freud and Dollard and Miller maintain? Is it not possible that we are born with tendencies to respond to the major categories of existence, such as birth, death, and members of the opposite sex, as Jung suggested? Is it not possible that we all strive for perfection or superiority and for the betterment of society as Adler suggested? Is there not evidence that some neurotics attempt to adjust to life by moving toward people, others by moving away from people, and still others by moving against people, as Horney suggested? Is there not evidence that life consists of various stages, each characterized by different needs and potential accomplishments, and that one of the most significant events in one's life is the development of an identity, as Erikson suggests? Does it not make sense to say that each individual is unique and that some adult motives are no longer tied to their earlier origins, as Allport proposed? Is it not possible that the many variables affecting human behavior, including constitutional, learning, and situational variables, can be stated in a single equation that can be utilized in predicting behavior, as Cattell suggests? Can anyone doubt the powerful influence of reward on behavior that Skinner describes? Does it not make sense to think of the various ego defense mechanisms and neurotic symptoms as learned because they temporarily reduce anxiety, as Dollard and Miller suggest? Who can doubt that the reduction of uncertainty is a major motive in human behavior, as Kelly suggested? Is there any doubt that much of our behavior is in accordance with our own subjective reality rather than with physical reality, as both Kelly and Rogers maintain? Can we not confirm Rogers's contention that because of our need for positive regard we develop conditions of worth which become our frame of reference for living rather than our own organismic valuing process? Last, can we not accept Maslow's contention that the motives of individuals with their basic needs satisfied are qualitatively different from the motives of individuals still struggling to satisfy their basic needs?

What the realm of personality theory needs is a grand synthesizer, a person who could coordinate the various terms and concepts from all the various theories. This person would look carefully at all the theories that discuss developmental stages, for example, Freud, Erikson, and Allport, and attempt to derive a more comprehensive picture of personality development. If our contention is true that all of the various theories add something different to our knowledge of personality, it would make sense for a person like Newton to come along and somehow put it all together.

CHILDHOOD EXPERIENCE IS EXTREMELY IMPORTANT TO DETERMINING ADULT PERSONALITY CHARACTERISTICS

Almost without exception, the personality theorists covered in this text link major adult personality characteristics to certain categories of childhood experience (there are exceptions to this contention, however, like

Allport and Kelly). The theories of Freud, Adler, Horney, Erikson, Skinner, Dollard and Miller, and Rogers all stress the importance of childhood experience to determining whether an adult will be healthy, neurotic, or at some point in between.

It seems reasonable to conclude that if childhood experiences are so important in molding various personality attributes, parents should know the basics of child rearing, but do they? It is ironic that the task judged by many to be one of the most complex that humans perform, that is, child rearing, requires no special training at all. Harriet Rheingold expresses her concern for this:

> The most difficult, the most important task in the world—the rearing of a child—at the present time is judged by our society to require no training at all. We behave as though the ability to conceive and bear a child, as though the acts of conception and birth, automatically confer on a mother, or a father, knowledge on how to rear that child. Fortunately, most children are born robust and with enough good sense that we do not end up with a population of incompetents—inexperienced and inept though their parents may be. (1973, p. 45)

Most inadequate child rearing appears to result from a lack of concern for the child. However, even when a serious effort is made to rear a child "properly," the effort often fails because child rearing is a tremendously complicated business. Few parents have the knowledge necessary for adequate child rearing, and sometimes the few that do possess such knowledge do not have the time and/or energy to apply it (see Hergenhahn 1972 for more on the complexities of child rearing).

Some parents feel that just being "nice" to their child is all that it takes to be an effective parent. However, overprotection and indiscriminate displays of affection may be as harmful as underprotection and too little affection. For example, Skinner remarked: "Children are our most valuable resources and they are now shamefully wasted. Wonderful things can be done in the first years of life, but we leave them to people whose mistakes range all the way from abuse to overprotection and the lavishing of affection on the wrong behavior" (1978, p. 62).

Since proper child rearing is so important, some have suggested that would-be parents be certified as to their competence just as nurses, teachers, and automobile drivers are certified.

> . . . parents must be taught how to rear their children. Although this cannot be done in a single generation, we can begin now with those who are parents. But we must also teach those who will be parents. We will teach children in grade school and high school how to be parents. We teach it in college. Parents-to-be must be certified as to their competence, and a practical examination is better than a paper one. We must take an examination to obtain a license to drive a car. The child deserves no less; the good of the country demands much more. (Rheingold 1973, pp. 45–46)

It seems that Rheingold's argument would receive at least indirect support from most of the theories covered in this text. Certification would not mean that all parents would need to rear their children in the same manner, any more than it means that all certified teachers teach in the same way or that all licensed drivers drive in the same way. Rather, it is a means of guaranteeing that all would-be parents be aware of the major influences on a child's life such as nutrition, types of discipline and their effects on the child, the effects of television and various toys and games on the child, and the kinds of experience that stimulate intellectual growth. With this and other kinds of information available, it is hoped that the parent would be in a better position to provide experiences for the child that would be conducive to positive, healthy growth.

HOW TO CHOOSE A THERAPIST

One of the most important lessons that can be learned from this text is that there are a number of different kinds of theories of personality, each making different assumptions about human nature. Theories in the psychoanalytic camp assume that the human has animal urges that are frustrated by society. Theories in the sociocultural camp assume the major influence on one's personality is interpersonal experience. Theories in the trait camp assume that personality can be described best in terms of traits that are either genetically or environmentally determined. Theories in the learning camp emphasize the importance of reinforcement contingencies to personality formation. Theories in the existential-humanistic camp emphasize the importance of subjective, phenomenological experience and the individual's freedom to choose alternative modes of existence.

We have seen throughout this text that there are practicing psychotherapists whose techniques reflect the assumptions of the various camps (paradigms) listed above. If one were to choose a therapist at random, it would be possible to find one whose assumptions and techniques were not optimally matched to the problem at hand. Therefore, the following facts should be considered when choosing a therapist:

a. There are vast differences between people. For example, some people are introverted, some are extroverted, some are gregarious, some are isolated, some are defensive, and some are open to experience.
b. People seek help for different reasons. Some people seek a therapist because they are mildly depressed over a bad habit (like smoking, drinking, or overeating); others seek help because they are extremely depressed over the apparent meaninglessness of their life and may even be suicidal.
c. Different therapists follow different theories. As we saw above,

therapists differ widely in the assumptions about human nature and therefore in their therapeutic techniques.

The best situation is if a therapist's assumptions and techniques are optimally matched with a client's personality and with the kind of problem that the client is experiencing. A mismatch can conceivably make things worse and can be costly. Since some therapists are more effective with certain kinds of people and with certain kinds of problems than other therapists are, it appears that "shopping around" is justifiable. This can be done by actually asking clinicians how they would label themselves (in other words, you are asking under what paradigm they would place themselves) and how they would treat the problem at hand. If two or three clinicians were asked these questions, the client would be in a better position to choose the therapeutic environment that would accomplish the most in the least amount of time. No therapist should be bothered by such questions; in fact, most would welcome them.

YOU ARE THE FINAL JUDGE

In the realm of personality theory, because one usually does not have rigorous laboratory experiments available to help decide what is valid and what is invalid, how does one know what information to accept and what information to reject? It seems that under existing circumstances, Buddha gave the best answer to this question:

> . . . Believe nothing on the faith of traditions, even though they have been held in honour for many generations, and in diverse places. Do not believe a thing because many speak of it. Do not believe on the faith of the sages of the past. Do not believe what you have imagined, persuading yourself that a god inspires you. Believe nothing on the sole authority of your masters or priests. After examination, believe what you yourself have tested and found to be reasonable, and conform your conduct thereto (Hawton 1949, p. 200).

SUMMARY

Five conclusions seem to be justified after our review of the major personality theories in the preceding chapters: (1) Much about personality remains unknown; (2) the best available explanation of personality comes from utilizing all the theories rather than attempting to use one or a few of them; (3) most of the major theorists conclude that childhood experience is an extremely important influence on adult personality; (4) if a psychological problem arises, it may be necessary to shop around for a therapist who will be maximally effective in treating it; and (5) each individual must judge for himself or herself what is useful in each theory and what is not useful.

Discussion Questions

1. Do you agree with Harriet Rheingold's proposal that would-be parents be certified as to their competence? Why or why not?
2. Explain why it might be important to shop around for a therapist who would be maximally effective in dealing with a particular psychological problem.
3. Do you find yourself leaning toward any particular theory or paradigm? Explain why you feel the way you do.
4. List some of your experiences or feelings that you believe are not adequately explained by the theories covered in this text.
5. Summarize the major assumptions about human nature made by each of the paradigms covered in this text.
6. How would you answer the question "What is personality?"
7. Suppose you were the "Grand Synthesizer" mentioned in this chapter; describe briefly how you might go about your job.
8. Give a few examples of what you learned from this text that could be used to improve child-rearing practices.
9. Give a few examples of what you have learned from this text that could be used to improve teaching practices.
10. Give a few examples of concepts that you learned in this text that have made your own life more understandable.

Discussion Questions

references

ADLER, A. *Study of organ inferiority and its physical compensation: A contribution to clinical medicine,* (S. E. Jeliffe, Trans.). New York: Nervous and Mental Disease Publication Co., 1917. (Originally published, 1907.)

ADLER, A. Individual psychology. In C. Murchison (Ed.), *Psychologies of 1930.* Worcester, Mass.: Clark University Press, 1930.

ADLER, A. *What life should mean to you.* New York: Putnam, 1931.

ADLER, A. The psychology of hermaphroditism in life and in neurosis. In H. L. Ansbacher & R. R. Ansbacher (Eds.), *The individual psychology of Alfred Adler.* New York: Basic Books, 1956. (Originally published, 1910.)

ADLER, A. The use of heredity and environment. In H. L. Ansbacher & R. R. Ansbacher (Eds.), *The individual psychology of Alfred Adler.* New York: Harper, 1956. (Originally published, 1935.)

ADLER, A. *The individual psychology of Alfred Adler: A systematic presentation of selections from his writings.* (H. L. Ansbacher & R. R. Ansbacher, Eds.), New York: Harper, 1956.

ADLER, A. *Problems of neurosis.* New York: Harper & Row, 1964. (Originally published, 1929.)

ADLER, A. *The science of living.* New York: Doubleday, 1969. (Originally published, 1929.)

ALLPORT, G. W. *Personality: A psychological interpretation.* New York: Henry Holt, 1937.

ALLPORT, G. W. *The individual and his religion.* New York: Macmillan, 1950.

ALLPORT, G. W. *The nature of prejudice.* Cambridge, Mass.: Addison-Wesley, 1954.

ALLPORT, G. W. *Becoming: Basic considerations for a psychology of personality.* New Haven, Conn.: Yale University Press, 1955.

ALLPORT, G. W. *Personality and social encounter: Selected essays.* Boston: Beacon Press, 1960.

ALLPORT, G. W. *Pattern and growth in personality.* New York: Holt, Rinehart & Winston, 1961.

ALLPORT, G. W. *Letters from Jenny.* New York: Harcourt, Brace and World, 1965.

ALLPORT, G. W. Autobiography. In E. G. Boring and G. Lindzey (Eds.), *A history of psychology in autobiography* (Vol. 5). New York: Appleton-Century-Crofts, 1967, 1–25.

Allport, G. W. *The person in psychology: Selected essays.* Boston: Beacon Press, 1968.

Allport, G. W., & Allport, F. H. Personality traits: Their classification and measurement. *Journal of Abnormal and Social Psychology,* 1921, *16,* 6–40.

Allport, G. W., & Cantril, H. Judging personality from voice. *Journal of Social Psychology,* 1934, *5,* 37–55.

Allport, G. W., & Odbert, H. S. Trait names: A psycho-lexical study. *Psychological Monographs,* 1936, *47*(211), 1–171.

Allport, G. W., & Postman, L. *The psychology of rumor.* New York: Holt, Rinehart & Winston, 1947.

Allport, G. W., & Vernon, P. E. *Studies in expressive movement.* New York: Macmillan, 1933.

Allport, G. W., Vernon, P., & Lindzey, G. *A study of values* (3rd ed.). Boston: Houghton Mifflin, 1960.

Ansbacher, H. L. Individual psychology. In R. J. Corsini, *Current personality theories.* Itasca, Ill.: Peacock Publishers, 1977.

Ansbacher, H. L., & Ansbacher, R. R. (Eds.). *The individual psychology of Alfred Adler.* New York: Basic Books, Inc., 1956.

Ansbacher, H. L., & Ansbacher, R. R. (Eds.). *Superiority and social interest by Alfred Adler.* Evanston, Ill.: Northwestern University Press, 1964.

Atthowe, J., & Krasner, L. Preliminary report on the application of contingent reinforcement procedures (token economy) on a "chronic" psychiatric ward. *Journal of Abnormal Psychology,* 1968, *73,* 37–43.

Ayllon, T., & Azrin, N. *The token economy: A motivational system for therapy and rehabilitation.* New York: Appleton-Century-Crofts, 1968.

Bannister, D., & Fransella, F. *Inquiring man: The theory of personal constructs.* Baltimore: Penguin Books, 1971.

Bischof, L. J. *Interpreting personality theories* (2nd ed.). New York: Harper & Row, 1970.

Boslough, J. Reformatory's incentive plan works. *Rocky Mountain News,* December 24, 1972. p. 13.

Bottome, P. *Alfred Adler: A portrait from life.* New York: Vanguard, 1957.

Breuer, J., & Freud, S. Studies on hysteria. In *The standard edition* (Vol. 2). London: Hogarth Press, 1955. (Originally published, 1895.)

Butler, J. M., & Haigh, G. V. Changes in the relation between self-concepts and ideal concepts consequent upon-client-centered counseling. In C. R. Rogers and R. F. Dymond (Eds.). *Psychotherapy and Personality Change; Co-Ordinated Studies in the Client-Centered Approach.* Chicago: Univ. of Chicago Press, 1954.

Cattell, R. B. *Personality: A systematic, theoretical and factual study.* New York: McGraw-Hill, 1950.

Cattell, R. B. *Personality and motivation structure and measurement.* Yonkers-on-Hudson, N.Y.: World Book Company, 1957.

Cattell, R. B. *The scientific analysis of personality.* Baltimore: Penguin Books, 1965.

Cattell, R. B., Breul, H., & Hartman, H. P. An attempt at more refined definition of the cultural dimensions of syntality in modern nations. *American Sociological Review,* 1952, *17,* 408–421.

Cattell, R. B., Saunders, D. R., & Stice, G. F. *The 16 personality factor questionnaire.* Champaign, Ill.: Institute of Personality and Ability Testing, 1950.

CATTELL, R. B., STICE, G. F. & KRISTY, N. F. A first approximation to nature-nurture ratios for eleven primary personality factors in objective tests. *Journal of Abnormal and Social Psychology,* 1957, *54,* 143–159.

CHOMSKY, N. A. A review of verbal behavior by B. F. Skinner. *Language,* 1959, *35,* 26–58.

CIACCIO, N. A test of Erikson's theory of ego epigenesis. *Developmental Psychology,* 1971, *4,* 306–311.

CORSINI, R. J. (Ed.). *Current personality theories.* Itasca, Ill.: Peacock Publishers, 1977.

DAVIS, A., & DOLLARD, J. *Children of bondage.* Washington, D.C.: American Council on Education, 1940.

DOLLARD, J. *Caste and class in a southern town.* New Haven, Conn.: Yale University Press, 1937.

DOLLARD, J. *Victory over fear.* New York: Reynal and Hitchcock, 1942.

DOLLARD, J. *Fear in battle.* New Haven, Conn.: Yale University Press, 1943.

DOLLARD, J., DOOB, L. W., MILLER, N. E., MOWRER, O. H., & SEARS, R. R. *Frustration and Aggression.* New Haven, Conn.: Yale University Press, 1939.

DOLLARD, J., & MILLER, N. E. *Social learning and imitation.* New Haven, Conn.: Yale University Press, 1941.

DOLLARD, J., & MILLER, N. E. *Personality and psychotherapy: An analysis in terms of learning, thinking and culture.* New York: McGraw-Hill, 1950.

DREIKURS, R. *Psychology in the classroom.* New York: Harper, 1957.

DREIKURS, R. (with VICKI SOLTZ). *Children: The challenge.* New York: Duell, Sloan and Pearce, 1964.

ELLIS, A. Tribute to Alfred Adler. *Journal of Individual Psychology,* 1970, *26,* 11–12.

ERIKSON, E. H. The dream specimen of psychoanalysis. In R. Knight and C. Friedman (Eds.), *Psychoanalytic psychiatry and psychology.* New York: International Universities Press, 1954.

ERIKSON, E. H. *Young man Luther: A study in psychoanalysis and history.* New York: Norton, 1958.

ERIKSON, E. H. *Identity and the life cycle. Selected papers.* New York: International Universities Press, 1959.

ERIKSON, E. H. *Childhood and society.* New York: Norton, 1963. (Originally published, 1950.)

ERIKSON, E. H. *Insight and responsibility.* New York: Norton, 1964.

ERIKSON, E. H. *Identity, youth, and crisis.* New York: Norton, 1968.

ERIKSON, E. H. *Ghandi's truth: on the origins of militant nonviolence.* New York: Norton, 1969.

ERIKSON, E. H. Once more the inner space. In E. H. Erikson, *Life history and the historical moment.* New York: Norton, 1975 (a).

ERIKSON, E. H. *Life history and the historical moment.* New York: Norton, 1975 (b).

EVANS, R. I. *B. F. Skinner: The man and his ideas.* New York: Dutton, 1968.

EVANS, R. I. Donald Bannister: On clinical psychology in Britain. *APA Monitor,* July 1978, *9*(7), 6–7.

FERSTER, C. B., & SKINNER, B. F. *Schedules of reinforcement.* Englewood Cliffs, N.J.: Prentice-Hall, 1957.

FRANKL, V. E. Tribute to Alfred Adler. *Journal of Individual Psychology,* 1970, *26,* 11–12.

FREUD, A. *The ego and the mechanisms of defense.* New York: International Universities Press, 1936.

FREUD, S. The interpretation of dreams. In *The standard edition* (Vols. 4 & 5). London: Hogarth Press, 1953. (Originally published, 1900.)

FREUD, S. Beyond the pleasure principle. In *The standard edition* (Vol. 18). London: Hogarth Press, 1955. (Originally published, 1920.)

FREUD, S. A note on the prehistory of the technique of analysis. In *The standard edition* (Vol. 18). London: Hogarth Press, 1955. (Originally published, 1920.)

FREUD, S. On the history of the psychoanalytic movement. In *The standard edition* (Vol. 14). London: Hogarth Press, 1957. (Originally published, 1914.)

FREUD, S. On beginning the treatment. In *The standard edition* (Vol. 12). London: Hogarth, 1958. (Originally published, 1913.)

FREUD, S. Psychopathology of everyday life. In *The standard edition* (Vol. 6). London: Hogarth, 1960. (Originally published, 1901.)

FREUD, S. Jokes and their relation to the unconscious. In *The standard edition* (Vol. 8). London: Hogarth, 1960. (Originally published, 1905.)

FREUD, S. Civilization and its discontents. In *The standard edition* (Vol. 21). London: Hogarth Press, 1961. (Originally published, 1930.)

GREENSPOON, J. The reinforcing effect of two spoken sounds on the frequency of two responses. *American Journal of Psychology,* 1955, *68,* 409–416.

HALL, C. S. *A primer of Freudian psychology.* Cleveland: World Publishing, 1954.

HALL, C. S., & LINDZEY, G. *Theories of personality* (2nd ed.). New York: Wiley, 1970.

HANNA, B. *Jung: His life and his work.* New York: Putnam's, 1976.

HAWTON, H. *Philosophy for pleasure.* London: Watts & Co., 1948.

HERGENHAHN, B. R. *Shaping your child's personality.* Englewood Cliffs, N.J.: Prentice-Hall, 1972.

HERGENHAHN, B. R. *A self-directing introduction to psychological experimentation* (2nd ed.). Monterey, Calif.: Brooks/Cole Publishing Co., 1974.

HERGENHAHN, B. R. *An introduction to theories of learning.* Englewood Cliffs, N.J.: Prentice-Hall, 1976.

HOLDSTOCK, T. L., & ROGERS, C. R. Person-centered theory. In R. J. Corsini (Ed.), *Current personality theories.* Itasca, Ill.: Peacock Publishers, 1977.

HORNEY, K. *The neurotic personality of our time.* New York: Norton, 1937.

HORNEY, K. *New ways in psychoanalysis.* New York: Norton, 1939.

HORNEY, K. *Self-analysis.* New York: Norton, 1942.

HORNEY, K. *Our inner conflicts.* New York: Norton, 1945.

HORNEY, K. *Neurosis and human growth.* New York: Norton, 1950.

HORNEY, K. *Feminine psychology.* New York: Norton, 1967.

HULL, C. L. *Principles of behavior.* New York: Appleton-Century-Crofts, 1943.

JONES, E. *The life and work of Sigmund Freud.* New York: Basic Books, Vol. 1, 1953; Vol. 2, 1955; Vol. 3, 1957.

JOURARD, S. M. *Healthy personality: An approach from the viewpoint of humanistic psychology.* New York: Macmillan, 1974.

JUNG, C. G. *Contributions to analytical psychology.* New York: Harcourt, Brace and World, 1928.

JUNG, C. G. The psychology of the unconscious. In *The collected works of C. G. Jung* (Vol. 7). Princeton, N.J.: Princeton University Press, 1953. (Originally published, 1912.)

JUNG, C. G. The relations between the ego and the unconscious. In *The collected works of C. G. Jung* (Vol. 7). Princeton, N.J.: Princeton University Press, 1953. (Originally published, 1945.)

JUNG, C. G. Two essays on analytical psychology. In *The collected works of C. G. Jung* (Vol. 7). Princeton, N.J.: Princeton University Press, 1953. (Originally published, 1917.)

JUNG, C. G. *Two essays on analytical psychology.* New York: Meridian Books, 1956.

JUNG, C. G. The psychology of dementia praecox. In *The collected works of C. G. Jung* (Vol. 3). Princeton, N.J.: Princeton Univesity Press, 1960. (Originally published, 1907.)

JUNG, C. G. *Memories, dreams, reflections.* New York: Random House, 1961.

JUNG, C. G. The theory of psychoanalysis. In *The collected works of C. G. Jung* (Vol. 4). Princeton, N.J.: Princeton University Press, 1961. (Originally published, 1913.)

JUNG, C. G. *Man and his symbols.* New York: Doubleday, 1964.

JUNG, C. G. *Analytical psychology: Its theory and practice.* (The Tavistock Lectures.) New York: Pantheon (Random House), 1968.

JUNG, C. G. Psychological types. In *The collected works of C. G. Jung* (Vol. 6). Princeton, N.J.: Princeton University Press, 1971. (Originally published, 1921.)

JUNG, C. G. On the doctrine of complexes. In *The collected works of C. G. Jung* (Vol. 2). Princeton, N.J.: Princeton University Press, 1973. (Originally published, 1913.)

JUNG, C. G. The psychological diagnosis of evidence. In *The collected works of C. G. Jung* (Vol. 2). Princeton, N.J.: Princeton University Press, 1973. (Originally published, 1909.)

KELLY, G. A. *The psychology of personal constructs: A theory of personality* (2 vols.). New York: Norton, 1955.

KELLY, G. A. Man's construction of his alternatives. In G. Lindzey (Ed.), *Assessment of human motives.* New York: Holt, Rinehart & Winston, 1958.

KELLY, G. A. The language of hypotheses: Man's psychological instrument. *Journal of Individual Psychology,* 1964, *20,* 137–152.

KELLY, G. A. The autobiography of a theory. In Brenden Maher (Ed.), *Clinical psychology and personality: Selected papers of George Kelly.* New York: Wiley, 1969.

KELLY, G. A. A brief introduction to personal construct theory. In D. Bannister (Ed.), *Perspectives in personal construct theory.* New York: Academic Press, 1970.

KINKADE, K. *A Walden Two experiment.* New York: William Morrow, 1973.

KUHN, T. S. *The structure of scientific revolutions* (3rd ed.). Chicago: University of Chicago Press, 1973.

LEWIN, K. *A dynamic theory of personality.* New York: McGraw-Hill, 1935.

MADDI, S. R. *Personality theories: A comparative analysis.* Homewood, Ill.: Dorsey, 1972.

MALOTT, R. W., RITTERBY, K., & WOLF, E. L. C. *An introduction to behavior modification.* Kalamazoo, Mich.: Behaviordelia, 1973.

MARX, M. H., & HILLIX, W. A. *Systems and theories in psychology* (2nd ed.). New York: McGraw-Hill, 1973.

MASLOW, A. H. Self-esteem (dominance-feeling) and sexuality in women. *Journal of Social Psychology,* 1942, *16,* 259–294.

MASLOW, A. H. *Motivation and Personality.* New York: Harper & Row, 1954.

MASLOW, A. H. *Eupsychian management: A journal.* Homewood, Ill.: Irwin-Dorsey, 1965.

MASLOW, A. H. *The psychology of science: A reconnaissance.* New York: Harper & Row, 1966.

MASLOW, A. H. *Toward a psychology of being* (2nd ed.). Princeton, N.J.: Van Nostrand, 1968.

MASLOW, A. H. *Motivation and personality* (2nd ed.). New York: Harper & Row, 1970.

MASLOW, A. H. *The farther reaches of human nature.* New York: Viking, 1971.

MASSERMAN, J. H. *Principles of dynamic psychiatry* (2nd ed.). Philadelphia: W. B. Saunders Co., 1961.

MCGUIRE, W. (Ed.). *The Freud/Jung letters.* Princeton, N.J.: Princeton University Press, 1974.

MILLER, G. A. Some preliminaries to psycholinguistics. *American Psychologist,* 1965, *20,* 15–20.

MILLER, N. E. Experimental studies of conflict. In J. M. Hunt (Ed.), *Personality and the behavior disorders* (Vol. 1). New York: Ronald Press, 1944.

MILLER, N. E. Studies of fear as an acquirable drive: I. Fear as motivation and fear reduction as reinforcement in the learning of new responses. *Journal of Experimental Psychology,* 1948 (a), *38,* 89–101.

MILLER, N. E. Theory and experiment relating psychoanalytic displacement to stimulus response generalization. *Journal of Abnormal and Social Psychology,* 1948, (b), *43,* 155–178.

MILLER, N. E. Liberalization of basic S-R concepts: Extensions to conflict behavior, motivation and social learning. In S. Koch (Ed.), *Psychology: A study of a science* (Vol. 2). New York: McGraw-Hill, 1959.

MILLER, N. E. Some implications of modern behavior theory for personality change and psychotherapy. In P. Worchel, and D. Bryne (Eds.), *Personality change.* New York: Wiley, 1964.

MILLER, N. E., & DOLLARD, J. *Social learning and imitation.* New Haven, Conn.: Yale University Press, 1941.

MONTE, C. F. *Beneath the mask: An introduction to theories of personality.* New York: Praeger, 1977.

MURRAY, E. J., & BERKUN, M. M. Displacement as a function of conflict. *Journal of Abnormal and Social Psychology,* 1955, *51,* 47–56.

ORGLER, H. *Alfred Adler: The man and his work.* New York: G. P. Putnam's Sons, 1963.

PAIGE, J. M. Letters from Jenny: An approach to the clinical analysis of personality structure by computer. In P. J. Stone, *et al. The general inquirer: A computer approach to content analysis.* Cambridge, Mass.: M.I.T. Press, 1966.

PERVIN, L. A. *Personality: Theory, assessment, and research* (2nd ed.). New York: Wiley, 1975.

PROGOFF, I. *Jung, synchronicity, and human destiny: Noncausal dimensions of human experience.* New York: Dell, 1973.

RHEINGOLD, HARRIET L. To rear a child. *American Psychologist,* 1973, *28,* 42–46.

ROAZEN, P. *Erik H. Erikson: The power and limits of a vision.* New York: Macmillan, 1976.

ROGERS, C. R. *The clinical treatment of the problem child.* Boston: Houghton Mifflin, 1939.

ROGERS, C. R. *Counseling and psychotherapy: Newer concepts in practice.* Boston: Houghton Mifflin, 1942.

ROGERS, C. R. *Client-centered therapy: Its current practice, implications, and theory.* Boston: Houghton Mifflin, 1951.

ROGERS, C. R. Some directions and end points in therapy. In O. H. Mowrer (Ed.), *Psychotherapy: Theory and research.* New York: Ronald Press, 1953.

ROGERS, C. R. The case of Mrs. Oak: A research analysis. In C. R. Rogers & R. F. Dymond, (Eds.), *Psychotherapy and personality change.* Chicago: University of Chicago Press, 1954.

ROGERS, C. R. Persons or science? A philosophical question. *American Psychologist,* 1955, *10,* 267–278.

ROGERS, C. R. Intellectualized psychotherapy. *Contemporary Psychology,* 1956 (a), *1,* 357–358.

ROGERS, C. R. Some issues concerning the control of human behavior (Symposium with B. F. Skinner). *Science,* 1956 (b), *124,* 1057–1066.

ROGERS, C. R. Implications of recent advances in prediction and control of behavior, Teachers College Record, LVII, (Feb., 1956c) 316–322.

ROGERS, C. R. Implications of recent advances in prediction and control of behavior. In E. L. Hartley & R. E. Hartley, (Eds.), *Outside readings in psychology* (2nd ed.). New York: Thomas Y. Crowell, 1957.

ROGERS, C. R. A theory of therapy, personality, and interpersonal relationships, as developed in the client-centered framework. In S. Koch (Ed.), *Psychology: A study of a science* (Vol. 3). New York: McGraw-Hill, 1959.

ROGERS, C. R. *On becoming a person: A therapist's view of psychotherapy.* Boston: Houghton Mifflin, 1961.

ROGERS, C. R. Actualizing tendency in relation to motives and to consciousness. In M. R. Jones (Ed.), *Nebraska Symposium on Motivation,* 1963. Lincoln: University of Nebraska Press, 1963.

ROGERS, C. R. Client-centered therapy. In S. Arieti (Ed.), *American handbook of psychiatry.* New York: Basic Books, 1966.

ROGERS, C. R. Autobiography. In E. G. Boring & G. Lindzey (Eds.), *A history of psychology in autobiography* (Vol. 5). New York: Naiburg Publishing, 1967.

ROGERS, C. R. *Freedom to learn.* Columbus, Ohio: Charles E. Merrill, 1969.

ROGERS, C. R. My personal growth. In A. Burton (Ed.), *Twelve therapists.* San Francisco: Jossey-Bass, 1972.

ROGERS, C. R. My philosophy of interpersonal relationships and how it grew. *Journal of Humanistic Psychology,* 1973 (a), *13,* 3–15.

SARTRE, J. P. Existentialism. In W. Kaufmann (Ed.), *Existentialism from Dostoevsky to Sartre.* New York: Meridian Books, 1956.

SCARF, M. The man who gave us "inferiority complex," "compensation," "aggressive drive" and "style of life." *New York Times Magazine,* February 28, 1971, pp. 10ff.

SCHUR, M. *Freud: Living and dying.* New York: International Universities Press, 1972.

SKINNER, B. F. *The behavior of organisms: An experimental analysis.* Englewood Cliffs, N.J.: Prentice-Hall, 1938.

SKINNER, B. F. *Walden two.* New York: Macmillan, 1948.

SKINNER, B. F. How to teach animals. *Scientific American,* 1951, *185,* 26–29.

SKINNER, B. F. *Science and human behavior.* New York: Macmillan, 1953.

SKINNER, B. F. *Verbal behavior.* Englewood Cliffs, N.J.: Prentice-Hall, 1957.

SKINNER, B. F. Distinguished scientific contribution award. *American Psychologist,* 1958, *13,* 735.

SKINNER, B. F. A case history in scientific method. In S. Koch, *Psychology: A study of a science* (Vol. 2). New York: McGraw-Hill, 1959.

SKINNER, B. F. Autobiography. In E. G. Boring & G. Lindzey (Eds.), *A history of psychology in autobiography* (Vol. 5). New York: Appleton-Century-Crofts, 1967, 387–413.

SKINNER, B. F. *Beyond freedom and dignity.* New York: Knopf, 1971.

SKINNER, B. F. Gold medal award. *American Psychologist,* 1972, *27,* 72.

SKINNER, B. F. *About behaviorism.* New York: Knopf, 1974.

SKINNER, B. F. *Particulars of my life.* New York: Knopf, 1976.

SKINNER, B. F. *Reflections on behaviorism and society.* Englewood Cliffs, N.J.: Prentice-Hall, 1978.

STERN, P. J. *C. G. Jung: The haunted prophet.* New York: Dell, 1976.

STEVENS, S. S. Psychology and the science of science. In M. H. Marx, *Psychological theory: Contemporary readings.* New York: Macmillan, 1951.

THOMPSON, G. G. George Alexander Kelly (1905–1967). *Journal of General Psychology,* 1968, *79,* 19–24.

VAIHINGER, H. *The philosophy of "as if".* New York: Harcourt, Brace and World, 1925. (Originally published, 1911.)

VERPLANCK, W. S. The operant, from rat to man: An introduction to some recent experiments on human behavior. *Transactions of The New York Academy of Science,* 1955, *17,* 594–601.

WEISSTEIN, N. Psychology constructs the female, or the fantasy life of the male psychologist (with some attention to the fantasies of his friends, the male biologist and the male anthropologist). In Ira Cohen (Ed.), *Perspectives on psychology.* New York: Praeger, 1975.

WATSON, J. B. Experimental studies on the growth of the emotions. In C. Murchison (Ed.), *Psychologies of 1925.* Worcester, Mass.: Clark University Press, 1926.

WIGGINS, J. S. Personality structure. In *Annual review of psychology* (Vol. 19). Palo Alto, Calif.: Annual Reviews, 1968.

ZIMBARDO, P., & RUCH, F. *Psychology and life* (9th ed.). Glenview, Ill.: Scott, Foresman, 1977.

Acknowledgments cont'd.

Assessment of Human Motives, edited by Gardner Lindzey. Copyright © 1958 by Gardner Lindzey. Reprinted by permission of Holt, Rinehart and Winston.

Allport, G. W., Autobiography. In E. G. Boring and G. Lindzey (eds.), *A History of Psychology in Autobiography,* Vol. V. New York: Appleton-Century-Crofts, 1967, 1–25. Reprinted by permission of Irvington Publishers, Inc.

Toward a Psychology of Being, 2nd ed., by Abraham H. Maslow, © 1968 by Litton Educational Publishing, Inc. Reprinted by permission of D. Van Nostrand Company.

Excerpts on pp. 76–77 from *The New York Times,* © 1971 by The New York Times Company. Reprinted by permission.

The Collected Works of C. G. Jung, trans. R. F. C. Hull, Bollingen Series XX, Vol. 2: *Experimental Researches,* copyright © 1973 by Princeton University Press; Vol. 7: Two Essays on Analytical Psychology, copyright 1953, © 1966 by Princeton University Press. Excerpts reprinted by permission.

The Freud/Jung Letters: The Correspondence between Sigmund Freud and C. G. Jung, ed. William McGuire, trans. Ralph Manheim and R. F. C. Hull. Bollingen Series XCIV. Copyright © 1974 by Sigmund Freud Copyrights Ltd. and Erbengemeinschaft Prof. Dr. C. G. Jung. Reprinted by permission.

Nebraska Symposium on Motivation, 1963, M. R. Jones, ed., by permission of the University of Nebraska Press. Copyright © by the University of Nebraska Press.

Alfred Adler: *A Portrait from Life* by Phyllis Bottome by permission of the publisher, Vanguard Press, Inc. Copyright © 1957 by Phyllis Bottome.

The Farthest Reaches of Human Nature by Abraham Maslow. Copyright © 1971 by Bertha G. Maslow. Reprinted by permission of Viking Penguin Inc.

Murray, E. J., & Berkun, M. M. Displacement as a function of conflict. *Journal of Abnormal and Social Psychology,* 1955, *51,* 47–56. Copyright 1955 by the American Psychological Association. Reprinted by permission.

Carl R. Rogers: On Becoming a Person. Copyright © 1961 by Carl R. Rogers. Reprinted by permission of Houghton Mifflin Company.

"Some Issues Concerning the Control of Human Behavior" by C. R. Rogers and B. F. Skinner in *Science,* Vol. 124, pp. 1057–66, Nov. 30, 1956. Reprinted by permission of *Science.*

Beneath the Mask by Christopher F. Monte. Copyright © 1977 by Christopher F. Monte. Reprinted by permission of Holt, Rinehart and Winston and Christopher F. Monte.

Pattern and Growth in Personality by Gordon W. Allport. Copyright 1937, © 1961 by Holt, Rinehart and Winston, Inc. Renewal © 1965 by Gordon W. Allport. Reprinted by permission of Holt, Rinehart and Winston.

Ansbacher, H. L., *Individual Psychology,* In R. J. Corsini, *Current Personality Theories* Itasca, Ill.: F. E. Peacock Publishers, Inc., © 1977. Used with permission.

Cattell, R. B. *The Scientific Analysis of Personality* from Personality and Motivation Structure and Measurement, Baltimore: Penguin, 1965. Reprinted by permission of author.

D. Bannister and Fay Fransella: Inquiring Man: The Theory of Personal Constructs (Penguin Education, 1971) pp. 35, 36, 37, 37–38 © D. Bannister and Fay Fransella, 1971.

Letters from Jenny, Gordon W. Allport, ed Copyright 1965 by Harcourt Brace Jovanovich, Inc.

Erik H. Erikson: The Power and Limits of a Vision by P. Roazen. © 1976 by Macmillan Publishing Co., Inc. Reprinted by permission.

Science and Human Behavior by B. F. Skinner. © 1953 by Macmillan Publishing Co., Inc. Reprinted by permission.

Healthy Personality: An Approach from the Viewpoint of Humanistic Psychology by Sidney M. Jourard. © 1974 by Macmillan Publishing Co., Inc. Reprinted by permission.

About Behaviorism by B. F. Skinner. © 1974 by Alfred A. Knopf, Inc. Reprinted by permission.

Beyond Freedom and Dignity by B. F. Skinner. © 1971 by Alfred A. Knopf, Inc. Reprinted by permission.

Analytical Psychology: Its Theory and Practice by C. G. Jung. © 1961 by Pantheon Books, a Division of Random House, Inc. Reprinted by permission.

Memories, Dreams, Reflections by C. G. Jung, edited by Aniela Jaffe, trans. by Clara and Richard Winston. © 1964 by Pantheon Books, a Division of Random House, Inc. Reprinted by permission.

Gordon W. Allport, *Personality and Social Encounter*. Published by Beacon Press. Reprinted by permission. Copyright © 1968.

Gordon W. Allport, *The Person in Psychology: Selected Essays*. Published by Beacon Press. Reprinted by permission. Copyright © 1960.

The Life and Work of Sigmund Freud, Vol. 2, by Ernest Jones, M.D., © 1955 by Ernest Jones, Basic Books, Inc., Publishers, New York.

The Interpretation of Dreams, by Sigmund Freud, translated from the German and edited by James Strachey, published in the United States by Basic Books, Inc., publishers, New York, by arrangement with George Allen and Unwin Ltd. and the Hogarth Press, London. Copyright 1953.

Excerpt on p. 170 reproduced with permission from the Annual Review of *Psychology,* Volume 19. © 1968 by Annual Reviews Inc. Reproduced with permission from author also.

Murray, E. J., & Berkun, M. M. *Displacement as a Function of Conflict. Journal of Abnormal and Social Psychology,* 1955, *51,* 47–56. Copyright 1955 by the American Psychological Association. Reprinted by permission.

Excerpts from *Motivation and Personality* (second edition) by Abraham H. Maslow. Copyright © 1970 by Abraham H. Maslow. Reprinted by permission of Harper & Row, Publishers, Inc.

indexes

NAME INDEX

SUBJECT INDEX